# Mastering TypeScript

*Second Edition*



Build enterprise-ready, industrial-strength web applications using TypeScript and leading JavaScript frameworks

**Nathan Rozentals**

Packt>

**BIRMINGHAM - MUMBAI**

# Mastering TypeScript

*Second Edition*



First published: April 2015

Second edition: February 2017

Production reference: 1210217

Published by Packt Publishing Ltd.
Livery Place
35 Livery Street
Birmingham
B3 2PB, UK.
ISBN 978-1-78646-871-0

www.packtpub.com

# Credits

**Author**

Nathan Rozentals

**Reviewers**

Guy Fergusson

Vilic Vane

**Commissioning Editor**

Kunal Parikh

**Acquisition Editor**

Nitin Dasan

**Content Development Editor**

Priyanka Mehta

**Technical Editor**

Abhishek Sharma

**Copy Editor**

Safis Editing

**Project Coordinator**

Izzat Contractor

**Proofreader**

Safis Editing

**Indexer**

Tejal Daruwale Soni

**Graphics**

Abhinash Sahu

**Production Coordinator**

Melwyn Dsa

# About the Author

**Nathan Rozentals** has been building commercial software for over 26 years and programming for a lot longer than that. Before the Internet even became a thing, he was building statistical analysis programs on mainframes. Like many programmers at that time, he helped save the world in the year 2000.

He has worked with and tried to master many object-oriented languages, starting by implementing object-oriented techniques in plain old C. Having spent many years working with C++, chasing obscure thread locking issues and recursive routines causing memory leakage, he decided to simplify his life by embracing automatic garbage collection in Java and then C#.

As the world moved from thick-client and n-tier to web technologies, his focus turned to modern web programming, and so to JavaScript. In TypeScript, he found a language in which he could bring all of the object-oriented design patterns he had learned over the years to JavaScript.

If it were not for extreme programming techniques, agile delivery, test-driven development, and continuous integration, he would have lost his mind many years ago.

When he is not programming, he is thinking about programming. To stop thinking about programming, he goes windsurfing, plays soccer, or simply watches the professionals play soccer. They are so much better at it than he is.

*I would like to thank my partner, Kathy, for her support and unconditional love over the past few years. Without you, I would not be in the great space that I am.*

*To Ayron and Dayna, it has been great seeing you guys grow up into mature young adults. You are always in my thoughts.*

*To Matt, thanks for keeping us all laughing - everyone needs to see the lighter side of life.*

*To Mum, Dad, Rach, Tash, and Tam, thanks for your unwavering and whole-hearted support – I truly appreciate all you have done for me.*

*Finally, to the great team at Vix, thanks for the many intense debates and discussions, and for making work such a rewarding experience.*

# About the Reviewers

**Guy Fergusson** is a passionate web developer, open source contributor, and gamer. He has built web applications for health, law enforcement, and the finance sector. He has worked with the author building Typescript applications and is now an advocate of Typescript, which he uses on a daily basis.

*I would like to thank my beautiful family, my little girl, Grace, and my amazing wife, Melisa.*

**Vilic Vane** is a JavaScript engineer with over 8 years of experience in web development. He started following the TypeScript project when it went public, and he is also a contributor to the project. He is now working on frameworks, libraries, and apps written in TypeScript. Vilic is the author of the book TypeScript Design Patterns.

# www.PacktPub.com

For support files and downloads related to your book, please visit www.PacktPub.com.

Did you know that Packt offers eBook versions of every book published, with PDF and ePub files available? You can upgrade to the eBook version at www.PacktPub.com and as a print book customer, you are entitled to a discount on the eBook copy. Get in touch with us at service@packtpub.com for more details.

At www.PacktPub.com, you can also read a collection of free technical articles, sign up for a range of free newsletters and receive exclusive discounts and offers on Packt books and eBooks.

Mapt

https://www.packtpub.com/mapt

Get the most in-demand software skills with Mapt. Mapt gives you full access to all Packt books and video courses, as well as industry-leading tools to help you plan your personal development and advance your career.

## Why subscribe?

- Fully searchable across every book published by Packt
- Copy and paste, print, and bookmark content
- On demand and accessible via a web browser

# Customer Feedback

Thanks for purchasing this Packt book. At Packt, quality is at the heart of our editorial process. To help us improve, please leave us an honest review on this book's Amazon page at https://www.amazon.com/dp/1786468719.

If you'd like to join our team of regular reviewers, you can e-mail us at customerreviews@packtpub.com. We award our regular reviewers with free eBooks and videos in exchange for their valuable feedback. Help us be relentless in improving our products!

# Table of Contents

# Preface

The TypeScript language and compiler has been a huge success story since its release in late 2012. It quickly carved out a solid footprint in the JavaScript development community and continues to go from strength to strength. Many large-scale JavaScript projects, including projects by Adobe, Mozilla, and Asana, have made the decision to switch their code base from JavaScript to TypeScript. Recently, the Microsoft and Google teams announced that Angular 2.0 will be developed with TypeScript, thereby merging the AtScript and TypeScript languages into one.

This large-scale industry adoption of TypeScript shows the value of the language, the flexibility of the compiler, and the productivity gains that can be realized with its rich development toolset. On top of this industry support, the ECMAScript 6 and ECMAScript 7 standards are getting closer and closer to publication, and TypeScript provides a way to use features of these standards in our applications today by generating compatible JavaScript.

Writing JavaScript single page applications in TypeScript has been made even more appealing with the large collection of declaration files that have been built by the TypeScript community. These declaration files seamlessly integrate a large range of existing JavaScript frameworks into the TypeScript development environment, bringing with it increased productivity, early error detection, and advanced IntelliSense features.

The JavaScript language is not confined to web browsers, however. We can now write server-side JavaScript, drive mobile phone applications using JavaScript, and even control micro devices designed for the Internet of Things with JavaScript.

This book is a guide for both experienced TypeScript developers, as well as those who are just beginning their TypeScript journey. With a focus on Test Driven Development, detailed information on integration with many popular JavaScript libraries, and an in-depth look at TypeScript's features, this book will help you with your exploration of the next step in JavaScript development.

## What this book covers

`Chapter 1`, *TypeScript - Tools and Framework Options*, sets the scene for beginning TypeScript development. It discusses the benefits of using TypeScript as a language and compiler, and then works through setting up a complete development environment using a number of popular IDEs.

`Chapter 2`, *Types, Variables, and Function Techniques*, introduces the reader to the TypeScript language, starting with basic types and type annotations, and then moves on to discuss variables, functions, and advanced language features.

`Chapter 3`, *Interfaces, Classes, and Inheritance*, builds on the work from the previous chapter, and introduces the object-oriented concepts and capabilities of interfaces, classes, and inheritance. It then shows these concepts at work through the Factory Design Pattern.

`Chapter 4`, *Decorators, Generics, and Asynchronous Features*, discusses the more advanced language features of decorators and generics, before working through the concepts of asynchronous programming. It shows how the TypeScript language supports these asynchronous features through promises and the use of async await constructs.

`Chapter 5`, *Writing and Using Declaration Files*, walks the reader through building a declaration file for an existing body of JavaScript code, and then lists some of the most common syntax used when writing declaration files. This syntax is designed to be a quick reference guide to the declaration file syntax, or a cheat sheet.

`Chapter 6`, *Third-Party Libraries*, shows the reader how to use declaration files from the DefinitelyTyped repository within the development environment. It then moves on to show how to write TypeScript code that is compatible with three popular JavaScript frameworks--Backbone, Angular 1, and ExtJs.

`Chapter 7`, *TypeScript Compatible Frameworks*, takes a look at popular frameworks that have full TypeScript language integration. It explores the MVC paradigm, and then compares how this design pattern is implemented in Backbone, Aurelia, Angular 2, and React.

`Chapter 8`, *Test Driven Development*, starts with a discussion on what Test Driven Development is, and then guides the reader through the process of creating various types of unit tests. Using the Jasmine library, it shows how to use data-driven tests, and how to test asynchronous logic. The chapter finishes with a discussion on test runners, test reporting, and using continuous integration build servers.

`Chapter 9`, *Testing TypeScript Compatible Frameworks*, shows how to unit test, integration test, and acceptance test a sample application built with each of the TypeScript compatible frameworks. It discusses the concept of testability, and shows how subtle changes in application design and implementation can provide far better application test coverage.

`Chapter 10`, *Modularization*, explores what modules are, how they can be used, and the two types of module generation that the TypeScript compiler supports--CommonJs and AMD. It then shows how modules can be used with module loaders, including Require and SystemJs. This chapter finishes with an in-depth look at using modules within Node, and builds a sample Express application.

`Chapter 11`, *Object-Oriented Programming*, discusses the concepts of object-oriented programming, and then shows how to arrange application components to conform to object-oriented principles. It then takes an in-depth look at implementing object-oriented best practices by showing how the State and Mediator design patterns can be used to manage complex UI interactions.

`Chapter 12`, *Dependency Injection*, discusses the concepts of Service Location and Dependency Injection, and how they can be used to solve common application design problems. It then shows how to implement a simple Dependency Injection framework using Decorators.

`Chapter 13`, *Building Applications*, explores the fundamental building blocks of web application development, including generating HTML pages from Node and Express, writing and consuming REST endpoints, and data binding. It shows how to integrate an Express server, REST endpoints, and data binding with Aurelia, Angular 2, and React.

`Chapter 14`, *Let's Get Our Hands Dirty*, builds a single-page application using Angular 2 and Express by combining all of the concepts and components built throughout the book into a single application. These concepts include Test Driven Development, the State and Mediator Pattern, using Express REST endpoints, object-oriented design principles, modularization, and custom CSS animations.

# What you need for this book

You will need the TypeScript compiler and an editor of some sort. The TypeScript compiler is available on Windows, MacOS, and Linux as a Node plugin. `Chapter 1`, *TypeScript - Tools and Framework Options*, describes the setup of a development environment.

# Who this book is for

Whether you are a JavaScript developer wanting to learn TypeScript, or an experienced TypeScript developer wanting to take your skills to the next level, this book is for you. From basic to advanced language constructs, Test Driven Development, and object-oriented techniques, you will learn how to get the most out of the TypeScript language and compiler. This book will show you how to incorporate strong typing, object-orientation, and design best practices into your JavaScript applications.

# Conventions

In this book, you will find a number of text styles that distinguish between different kinds of information. Here are some examples of these styles and an explanation of their meaning.

Code words in text, database table names, folder names, filenames, file extensions, pathnames, dummy URLs, user input, and Twitter handles are shown as follows: "We will define a new function named `MyClass`, and return this new function to the outer calling function. We then use the `prototype` keyword to inject a new function into the `MyClass` definition."

A block of code is set as follows:

```
class MyClass {
  add(x: number, y: number) {
    return x + y;
  }
}
```

Any command-line input or output is written as follows:

```
npm install @types/express
```

**New terms** and **important words** are shown in bold. Words that you see on the screen, for example, in menus or dialog boxes, appear in the text like this: "Click on **Run** | **Debug** and then edit configurations. Click on the plus (+) button, select the **JavaScript debug** option on the left, and give this configuration a name."

Warnings or important notes appear in a box like this.

Tips and tricks appear like this.

# Reader feedback

Feedback from our readers is always welcome. Let us know what you think about this book-what you liked or disliked. Reader feedback is important for us as it helps us develop titles that you will really get the most out of. To send us general feedback, simply e-mail `feedback@packtpub.com`, and mention the book's title in the subject of your message. If there is a topic that you have expertise in and you are interested in either writing or contributing to a book, see our author guide at `www.packtpub.com/authors`.

# Customer support

Now that you are the proud owner of a Packt book, we have a number of things to help you to get the most from your purchase.

## Downloading the example code

You can download the example code files for this book from your account at `http://www.packtpub.com`. If you purchased this book elsewhere, you can visit `http://www.packtpub.com/support`and register to have the files e-mailed directly to you.

You can download the code files by following these steps:

1. Log in or register to our website using your e-mail address and password.
2. Hover the mouse pointer on the **SUPPORT** tab at the top.
3. Click on **Code Downloads & Errata**.
4. Enter the name of the book in the **Search** box.
5. Select the book for which you're looking to download the code files.
6. Choose from the drop-down menu where you purchased this book from.
7. Click on **Code Download**.

Once the file is downloaded, please make sure that you unzip or extract the folder using the latest version of:

- WinRAR / 7-Zip for Windows
- Zipeg / iZip / UnRarX for Mac
- 7-Zip / PeaZip for Linux

The code bundle for the book is also hosted on GitHub at https://github.com/PacktPublishing/Mastering-TypeScript-Second-Edition. We also have other code bundles from our rich catalog of books and videos available at https://github.com/PacktPublishing/. Check them out!

# Downloading the color images of this book

We also provide you with a PDF file that has color images of the screenshots/diagrams used in this book. The color images will help you better understand the changes in the output. You can download this file from https://www.packtpub.com/sites/default/files/downloads/MasteringTypeScriptSecondEdition_ColorImages.pdf.

# Errata

Although we have taken every care to ensure the accuracy of our content, mistakes do happen. If you find a mistake in one of our books-maybe a mistake in the text or the code-we would be grateful if you could report this to us. By doing so, you can save other readers from frustration and help us improve subsequent versions of this book. If you find any errata, please report them by visiting http://www.packtpub.com/submit-errata, selecting your book, clicking on the **Errata Submission Form** link, and entering the details of your errata. Once your errata are verified, your submission will be accepted and the errata will be uploaded to our website or added to any list of existing errata under the Errata section of that title.

To view the previously submitted errata, go to https://www.packtpub.com/books/content/supportand enter the name of the book in the search field. The required information will appear under the **Errata** section.

# Piracy

Piracy of copyrighted material on the Internet is an ongoing problem across all media. At Packt, we take the protection of our copyright and licenses very seriously. If you come across any illegal copies of our works in any form on the Internet, please provide us with the location address or website name immediately so that we can pursue a remedy.

Please contact us at `copyright@packtpub.com` with a link to the suspected pirated material.

We appreciate your help in protecting our authors and our ability to bring you valuable content.

# Questions

If you have a problem with any aspect of this book, you can contact us at `questions@packtpub.com`, and we will do our best to address the problem.

# 1

# TypeScript - Tools and Framework Options

JavaScript is a truly ubiquitous language. Just about every website that you visit in the modern world is using JavaScript to make the site more responsive, more readable, or more attractive to use. Even traditional desktop applications are moving online. Where we once needed to download and install a program to generate a diagram, or write a document, we can now do all of this on the web, from within the confines of our humble browser.

This is the power of JavaScript. It enables us to rethink the way we use the web. But it also enables us to rethink the way we use web technologies. Node, for example, allows JavaScript to run server-side, rendering entire large scale web-sites, complete with session handling, load balancing, and database interaction. This shift in thinking about web technologies, however, is only the beginning.

**Apache Cordova** is a fully fledged web server that runs as a native mobile phone application. This means that we can build a mobile phone application using HTML, CSS, and JavaScript, and then interact with the phones accelerometer, geolocation services, or file storage. With Cordova, therefore, JavaScript and web technologies have moved into the realm of native mobile phone applications.

Likewise, projects such as *Kinoma* are using JavaScript to drive devices for the Internet Of Things, running on tiny microprocessors embedded in all sorts of devices. **Espruino** is a microcontroller chip purposefully designed to run JavaScript. Learning JavaScript, therefore, means that you have the ability to build websites, mobile phone applications, and even control microprocessors on embedded devices. JavaScript is becoming more and more popular, is being supported on more and more hardware, and is filtering through to nearly every corner of computing.

The JavaScript language is not a difficult language to learn, but it does present challenges when writing large, complex programs. One of these challenges is that JavaScript is an interpreted language and therefore has no compilation step. The only time you will know if you have made a simple syntax error is when you run the entire application through the run-time interpreter. Another challenge is that it is also not an object-oriented language, and it takes great care and discipline to build good, maintainable, and understandable JavaScript. For programmers that are moving from other object-oriented languages, such as Java, C#, or C++, JavaScript can seem like a completely foreign environment.

TypeScript bridges this gap. It is a strongly typed, object-oriented language that uses a compiler to generate JavaScript. It therefore allows us to use well known object-oriented techniques and design patterns to build JavaScript applications. Bear in mind that TypeScript-generated JavaScript is just plain JavaScript, and so will run wherever JavaScript can run – in the browser, on the server, on a mobile device, or on an embedded device.

This chapter is divided into two main sections. The first section is a quick overview of some of the benefits of using TypeScript, and the second section deals with setting up a TypeScript development environment.

If you are an experienced TypeScript programmer, and already have a development environment set up, then you might want to skip this chapter. If you have never worked with TypeScript before, and have picked up this book because you want to understand what TypeScript can do, then read on.

We will cover the following topics in this chapter:

- The benefits of TypeScript
    - Compilation
    - Strong typing
    - Integration with popular JavaScript libraries
    - Encapsulation
    - Private and public member variables
- Setting up a development environment
    - Visual Studio
    - WebStorm
    - Visual Studio Code
    - Other editors and grunt

# Introducing TypeScript

TypeScript is both a language and a set of tools to generate JavaScript. It was designed by Anders Hejlsberg at Microsoft (the designer of C#), and is an open source project to help developers write enterprise-scale JavaScript.

TypeScript generates JavaScript – it's as simple as that. Instead of requiring a completely new runtime environment, TypeScript-generated JavaScript can reuse all of the existing JavaScript tools, frameworks, and the wealth of libraries that are already available for JavaScript. The TypeScript language and compiler, however, bring the development of JavaScript closer to a more traditional object-oriented experience.

# The ECMAScript standard

JavaScript as a language has been around for a long time, and is governed by a language feature standard. The language defined in this standard is called ECMAScript, and each JavaScript interpreter must deliver functions and features that conform to this standard. The definition of this standard helped the growth of JavaScript and the web in general, and allowed websites to render correctly on many different browsers on many different operating systems. The ECMAScript standard was published in 1999 and is known as **ECMA-262**, third edition.

With the popularity of the language, and the explosive growth of Internet applications, the ECMAScript standard needed to be revised and updated. This revision process resulted in an updated draft specification for ECMAScript, called the fourth edition. Unfortunately, this draft also suggested a complete overhaul of the language, and therefore was not well received. Eventually, leaders from Yahoo, Google, and Microsoft tabled an alternate proposal, which they called **ECMAScript 3.1**. This proposal was numbered 3.1, as it was a smaller feature set of the third edition, and sat between edition three and four of the standard.

The proposal for a complete language overhaul was eventually adopted as the fifth edition of the standard, and was called ECMAScript 5. The ECMAScript fourth edition was never published, but it was decided to merge the best features of both the fourth edition and the 3.1 feature set into a sixth edition named **ECMAScript Harmony**.

The TypeScript compiler has a parameter that can switch between different versions of the ECMAScript standard. TypeScript currently supports ECMAScript 3, ECMAScript 5, ECMAScript 6, and even ECMAScript 7 (also known as ECMAScript 2016).

When the compiler runs over your TypeScript, it will generate compile errors if the code you are attempting to compile is not valid for that standard. The team at Microsoft has committed to following the ECMAScript standards in any new versions of the TypeScript compiler, so as new editions are adopted, the TypeScript language and compiler will follow suit.

An understanding of the finer details of what is included in each release of the ECMAScript standard is outside the scope of this book, but it is important to know that there are differences. Some browser versions do not support ES5 (IE8 is an example), but most do. When selecting a version of ECMAScript to target for your projects, you will need to consider which browser versions you will be supporting, or which standard your JavaScript runtime supports.

# The benefits of TypeScript

To give you a flavor of the benefits of TypeScript (and this is by no means the full list), let's take a very quick look at some of the things that TypeScript brings to the table:

- A compilation step
- Strong or static typing
- Type definitions for popular JavaScript libraries
- Encapsulation
- Private and public member variable decorators

## Compiling

One of the most frustrating things about JavaScript development is the lack of a compilation step. JavaScript is an interpreted language, and therefore needs to be run against an interpreter in order to test that it is valid. Every JavaScript developer has horror stories that they can recount of hours spent trying to find bugs in their code, only to find that they have missed a stray closing brace `{` , or a simple comma `,` - or even a double quote `"` where there should have been a single quote `'` . Even worse, the real headaches arrive when you misspell a property name, or unwittingly reassign a global variable.

TypeScript will compile your code, and generate compilation errors where it finds these sorts of syntax error. This is obviously very useful, and can help to highlight errors before the JavaScript is even run. In large projects, programmers will often need to do large code merges – and with today's tools doing automatic merges, it is surprising how often the compiler will pick up these types of errors.

While tools to do this sort of syntax checking like **JSLint** have been around for years, it is obviously beneficial to have these tools integrated into your development toolchain. Using the TypeScript compiler in a continuous integration environment will also fail a build completely when compilation errors are found, further protecting your code base against these types of bugs.

# Strong typing

JavaScript is not strongly typed. It is a language that is very dynamic, and therefore allows objects to change their properties and behavior on-the-fly. As an example of this, consider the following code:

```
var test = "this is a string";
test = 1;
test = function(a, b) {
    return a + b;
}
```

On the first line of this code snippet, the variable `test` is bound to a string. It is then assigned to a number, and finally is redefined completely to be a function that expects two parameters. This means that the type of the variable `test` has changed from being a string to being a number, and then to being a function. Traditional object-oriented languages, however, will not allow the type of a variable to change, hence they are called strongly typed languages.

While all of the preceding code is valid JavaScript, and therefore could be justified, it is quite easy to see how this could cause runtime errors during execution. Imagine that you were responsible for writing a library function to add two numbers, and then another developer inadvertently reassigned your function to subtract these numbers instead.

These sorts of error may be easy to spot in a few lines of code, but it becomes increasingly difficult to find and fix these as your code base and your development team grows.

Another feature of strong typing is that the IDE you are working in understands what type of variable you are working with, and can bring better autocomplete or Intellisense options to the fore.

## TypeScript's syntactic sugar

TypeScript introduces a very simple syntax to check the type of an object at compile time. This syntax has been referred to as "syntactic sugar", or more formally, type annotations. Consider the following TypeScript code:

```
var test: string = "this is a string";
test = 1;
test = function(a, b) { return a + b; }
```

Note that, on the first line of this code snippet, we have introduced a colon `:` and a `string` keyword between our variable and its assignment. This type annotation syntax means that we are setting the type of our variable `test` to be of type `string`, and that any code that does not treat the variable `test` as a `string` will generate a compile error. Running the preceding code through the TypeScript compiler will generate two errors:

```
hello.ts(3,1): error TS2322: Type 'number' is not assignable to type
'string'.
hello.ts(4,1): error TS2322: Type '(a: any, b: any) => any' is not
assignable
to type 'string'.
```

The first error is fairly obvious. We have specified that the variable `test` is a `string`, and therefore attempting to assign a number to it will generate a compile error. The second error is similar to the first, and is, in essence, saying that we cannot assign a function to a string.

In this way, the TypeScript compiler introduces strong or static typing to your JavaScript code, giving you all of the benefits of a strongly typed language. TypeScript is therefore described as a superset of JavaScript. We will explore this in more detail in the next chapter.

# JavaScript and TypeScript definitions

As we have seen, TypeScript has the ability to annotate JavaScript, and bring strong typing to the JavaScript development experience. But how do we strongly type existing JavaScript libraries? In other words, if we have an existing JavaScript library, how do we integrate this library for use within TypeScript? The answer is surprisingly simple–by creating a definition file. TypeScript uses files with a `.d.ts` extension as a sort of header file, similar to languages such as C++, to superimpose strongly typing on existing JavaScript libraries. These definition files hold information that describes each available function, and/or variables, along with their associated type annotations.

Let's take a quick look at what a definition would look like. As an example, consider the JavaScript `describe` function from the popular Jasmine unit testing framework, as follows:

```
var describe = function(description, specDefinitions) {
  return jasmine.getEnv().describe(description, specDefinitions);
};
```

Note that this function has two parameters–`description` and `specDefinitions`. Unfortunately JavaScript does not tell us what sort of variables these are. We would need to have a look at the Jasmine documentation to figure out how to call this function, and what variables are expected for both parameters. If we head over to `http://jasmine.github.io/2.0/introduction.html`, we will see an example of how to use this function:

```
describe("A suite", function () {
  it("contains spec with an expectation", function () {
    expect(true).toBe(true);
  });
});
```

From the documentation, then, we can easily see that the first parameter is a `string`, and the second parameter is a `function`. However, there is nothing in JavaScript that forces us to conform to this API definition. As mentioned before, we could easily call this function incorrectly, with two numbers for example, or by sending a function first and a string second. Making mistakes like these will obviously generate runtime errors. Using a simple TypeScript definition file, however, will generate compile-time errors before we even attempt to run this code.

Let's take a look at the corresponding TypeScript definition for this function, found in the `jasmine.d.ts` definition file:

```
declare function describe(
  description: string,
  specDefinitions: () => void
): void;
```

Here, we have the TypeScript definition for the Jasmine `describe` function. This definition looks very similar to the function itself, but gives us a little more information about the parameters.

Clearly, the `description` parameter is strongly typed to a `string`, and the `specDefinitions` parameter is strongly typed to be a `function` that returns `void`. TypeScript uses the double-brace `()` syntax to declare functions, and the arrow syntax `=>` to show the return type of the function. So `() => void` is a function that does not return anything. Finally, the describe function itself will also return `void`.

If our code were to try and pass in a function as the first parameter, and a string as the second parameter (clearly breaking the definition of this function), as follows:

```
describe(() => { /* function body */}, "description");
```

TypeScript would generate the following error:

```
hello.ts(11,11): error TS2345: Argument of type '() => void' is not
assignable to parameter of type 'string'.
```

This error is telling us that we are attempting to call the `describe` function with invalid parameters. We will take a look at definition files in more detail in later chapters, but this example clearly shows that the TypeScript compiler will generate errors if we attempt to use external JavaScript libraries incorrectly.

### DefinitelyTyped

Soon after TypeScript was released, Boris Yankov started a GitHub repository to house definition files, called DefinitelyTyped (`http://definitelytyped.org`). This repository has now become the first port of call for integrating external JavaScript libraries into TypeScript, and it currently holds definitions for over 1,600 JavaScript libraries.

## Encapsulation

One of the fundamental principles of object-oriented programming is encapsulation–the ability to define data, as well as a set of functions that can operate on that data, into a single component. Most programming languages have the concept of a class for this purpose, providing a way to define a template for data and related functions.

Let's first take a look at a simple TypeScript class definition, as follows:

```
class MyClass {
  add(x, y) {
    return x + y;
  }
}

var classInstance = new MyClass();
```

```
var result = classInstance.add(1,2);
console.log(`add(1,2) returns ${result}`);
```

This code is pretty simple to read and understand. We have created a class, named `MyClass`, with a simple `add` function. To use this class we simply create an instance of it, and call the `add` function with two arguments.

JavaScript, unfortunately, does not have a class statement, but instead uses functions to reproduce the functionality of classes. Encapsulation through classes is accomplished by either using the prototype pattern, or by using the closure pattern. Understanding prototypes and the closure pattern, and using them correctly, is considered a fundamental skill when writing enterprise-scale JavaScript.

A closure is essentially a function that refers to independent variables. This means that variables defined within a closure function remember the environment in which they were created. This provides JavaScript with a way to define local variables, and provide encapsulation. Writing the `MyClass` definition in the preceding code, using a closure in JavaScript, would look something like the following:

```
var MyClass = (function () {
  // the self-invoking function is the
  // environment that will be remembered
  // by the closure
  function MyClass() {
  // MyClass is the inner function,
  // the closure
  }
  MyClass.prototype.add = function (x, y) {
    return x + y;
  };
  return MyClass;
}());
var classInstance = new MyClass();
var result = classInstance.add(1, 2);
console.log("add(1,2) returns " + result);
```

We start with a variable called `MyClass`, and assign it to a function that is executed immediately–note the `})();` syntax near the bottom of the closure definition. This syntax is a common way to write JavaScript in order to avoid leaking variables into the global namespace. We then define a new function named `MyClass`, and return this function to the outer calling function. We then use the `prototype` keyword to inject another function into the `MyClass` definition. This function is named `add` and takes two parameters, returning their sum.

The last few lines of the code show how to use this closure in JavaScript. Create an instance of the closure type, and then execute the `add` function. Running this code will log `add(1,2)` returns `3` to the console, as expected.

Looking at the JavaScript code versus the TypeScript code, we can easily see how simple the TypeScript code looks compared to the equivalent JavaScript. Remember how we mentioned that JavaScript programmers can easily misplace a brace `{` or a bracket `(` ? Have a look at the last line in the closure definition–`})();`. Getting one of these brackets or braces wrong can take hours of debugging to find.

### TypeScript classes generate closures

The JavaScript, as shown above, is actually the output of the TypeScript class definition. So TypeScript actually generates closures for you.

> Adding the concept of classes to the JavaScript language has been talked about for years, and is currently a part of the ECMAScript sixth edition (Harmony) standard – but this is still a work in progress. Microsoft has committed to following the ECMAScript standard in the TypeScript compiler, as and when these standards are published.

## Public and private accessors

A further object oriented principle that is used in Encapsulation is the concept of data hiding–the ability to have public and private variables. Private variables are meant to be hidden from the user of a particular class, as these variables should only be used by the class itself. Inadvertently exposing these variables can easily cause runtime errors.

Unfortunately, JavaScript does not have a native way of declaring variables private. While this functionality can be emulated using closures, a lot of JavaScript programmers simply use the underscore character _ to denote a private variable. At runtime, though, if you know the name of a private variable, you can easily assign a value to it. Consider the following JavaScript code:

```
var MyClass = (function() {
    function MyClass() {
        this._count = 0;
    }
    MyClass.prototype.countUp = function() {
      this._count ++;
    }
    MyClass.prototype.getCountUp = function() {
      return this._count;
```

```
    }
    return MyClass;
}());

var test = new MyClass();
test._count = 17;
console.log("countUp : " + test.getCountUp());
```

The `MyClass` variable is actually a closure with a constructor function, a `countUp` function, and a `getCountUp` function. The variable `_count` is supposed to be a private member variable that is used only within the scope of the closure. Using the underscore naming convention gives the user of this class some indication that the variable is private, but JavaScript will still allow you to manipulate the variable `_count`. Take a look at the second last line of the code snippet. We are explicitly setting the value of `_count` to `17`,which is allowed by JavaScript, but not desired by the original creator of the class. The output of this code would be `countUp : 17`.

TypeScript, however, introduces `public` and `private` keywords (among others), which can be used on class member variables. Trying to access a class member variable that has been marked as `private` will generate a compile time error. As an example of this, the JavaScript code above can be written in TypeScript, as follows:

```
class CountClass {
  private _count: number;
    constructor() {
      this._count = 0;
    }
  countUp() {
    this._count ++;
  }
  getCount() {
    return this._count;
  }
}
var countInstance = new CountClass() ;
countInstance._count = 17;
```

On the second line of our code snippet, we have declared a `private` member variable named `_count`. Again, we have a constructor, a `countUp`, and a `getCount` function. If we compile this file, the compiler will generate an error:

```
hello.ts(39,15): error TS2341: Property '_count' is private and only
accessible within class 'CountClass'.
```

This error is generated because we are trying to access the private variable `_count` in the last line of the code.

The TypeScript compiler, therefore, is helping us to adhere to public and private accessors by generating a compile error when we inadvertently break this rule.

> TIP: Remember, though, that these accessors are a compile-time feature only, and will not affect the generated JavaScript. You will need to bear this in mind if you are writing JavaScript libraries that will be consumed by third parties. Note that by default, the TypeScript compiler will still generate the JavaScript output file, even if there are compile errors. This option can be modified, however, to force the TypeScript compiler not to generate JavaScript if there are compilation errors.

# TypeScript IDEs

The purpose of this section of the chapter is to get you up-and-running with a TypeScript environment so that you can edit, compile, run, and debug your TypeScript code. TypeScript has been released as open-source, and includes both a Windows variant, as well as a Node variant. This means that the compiler will run on Windows, Linux, OS X, and any other operating system that supports Node. On Windows environments, we can either install Visual Studio, which will register the `tsc.exe` (TypeScript compiler) in our `c:\Program Files` directory, or we can use Node. On Linux and OS X environments, we will need to use Node.

In this section, we will be looking at the following IDEs:

- Node-based compilation
- Visual Studio 2015
- WebStorm
- Visual Studio Code
- Using grunt

# Node-based compilation

The simplest and leanest TypeScript development environment consists of a simple text editor, and a Node-based TypeScript compiler. Head over to the Node website (`https://nodejs.org/`) and follow the instructions to install Node on your operating system of choice.

Once Node is installed, TypeScript can be installed by simply typing:

```
npm install -g typescript
```

This command invokes the Node Package Manager (`npm`) to install TypeScript as a global module (the `-g` option), which will make it available no matter what directory we are currently in. Once TypeScript has been installed, we can display the current version of the compiler by typing the following:

```
tsc -v
```

At the time of writing, the TypeScript compiler is at `version 2.1.5`, and therefore the output of this command is as follows:

```
Version 2.1.5
```

Let's now create a TypeScript file named `hello.ts`, with the following content:

```
console.log('hello TypeScript');
```

From the command line, we can use TypeScript to compile this file into a JavaScript file by issuing the command:

```
tsc hello.ts
```

Once the TypeScript compiler has completed, it will have generated a `hello.js` file in the current directory.

## Creating a tsconfig.json file

The TypeScript compiler uses a `tsconfig.json` file at the root of the project directory to specify any global TypeScript project settings and compiler options. This means that, instead of compiling our TypeScript files one by one (by specifying each file on the command line), we can simply type `tsc` from the project root directory, and TypeScript will recursively find and compile all TypeScript files within the root directory and all sub-directories. The `tsconfig.json` file that TypeScript needs in order to do this can be created from the command line by simply typing:

```
tsc --init
```

The result of this command is a basic `tsconfig.json` file as follows:

```
{
  "compilerOptions": {
    "module": "commonjs",
    "target": "es5",
    "noImplicitAny": false,
    "sourceMap": false
  }
}
```

This is a simple JSON format file, with a single JSON property named `compilerOptions`, which specifies compile options for the project. The `target` property indicates the preferred JavaScript output to generate, and can be either `es3`, `es5`, `es6`, `ES2016`, `ES2017`, or `ESNext`. The option named `sourceMap` is a flag indicating whether to generate source maps that are used for debugging. The `noImplicitAny` option is a flag indicating that we must attempt to strongly type all variables before use.

> TypeScript allows for multiple `tsconfig.json` files within a directory structure. This allows different sub directories to use different compiler options.

With our `tsconfig.json` file in place, we can compile our application by simply typing:

```
tsc
```

This command will invoke the TypeScript compiler, using the `tsconfig.json` file that we have created to generate a `hello.js` JavaScript file. In fact, any file TypeScript source file that has a file extension of `.ts` will generate a JavaScript file with an extension of `.js`. We can now run our application by typing:

```
node hello.js
```

As our application is simply logging some text to the command line, the output will be as follows:

```
λ node hello.js
hello TypeScript
```

We have successfully created a simple Node-based TypeScript development environment, with a simple text editor and access to the command line.

# Microsoft Visual Studio

Let's now look at Microsoft's Visual Studio. This is Microsoft's primary IDE, and comes in a variety of pricing combinations. At the time of writing, Microsoft had just released Visual Studio 2017 Release Candidate, as the successor to Visual Studio 2015. Microsoft has an Azure-based licensing model, starting at around $45 per month, all the way up to a professional license with an MSDN subscription at around $1,199. The good news is that Microsoft also has a Community edition, which can be used in non-enterprise environments for both free and non-paid products. The TypeScript compiler is included in all of these editions.

Visual Studio can be downloaded as either a web installer or an `.iso` CD image. Note that the web installer will require an Internet connection during installation, as it downloads the required packages during the installation step. Visual Studio will also require Internet Explorer 10 or later, but will prompt you during installation if you have not upgraded as yet. If you are using the `.iso` installer, just bear in mind that you may be required to download and install additional operating system patches if you have not updated your system in a while.

## Creating a Visual Studio project

Once Visual Studio 2017 is installed, fire it up and create a new project (**File** | **New Project**). There are many different options available for new project templates, depending on your choice of language. Under the **Templates** section on the left-hand side, you will see an **Other Languages** option, and under this a **TypeScript** option. The project templates that are available are slightly different in Visual Studio 2017 than they are in Visual Studio 2015, and are geared towards Node development.

Visual Studio 2015 has a template named **Html Application with TypeScript**, which will create a very simple, single-page Web application for you. Unfortunately, this option has been removed in Visual Studio 2017 as shown in the following screenshot:

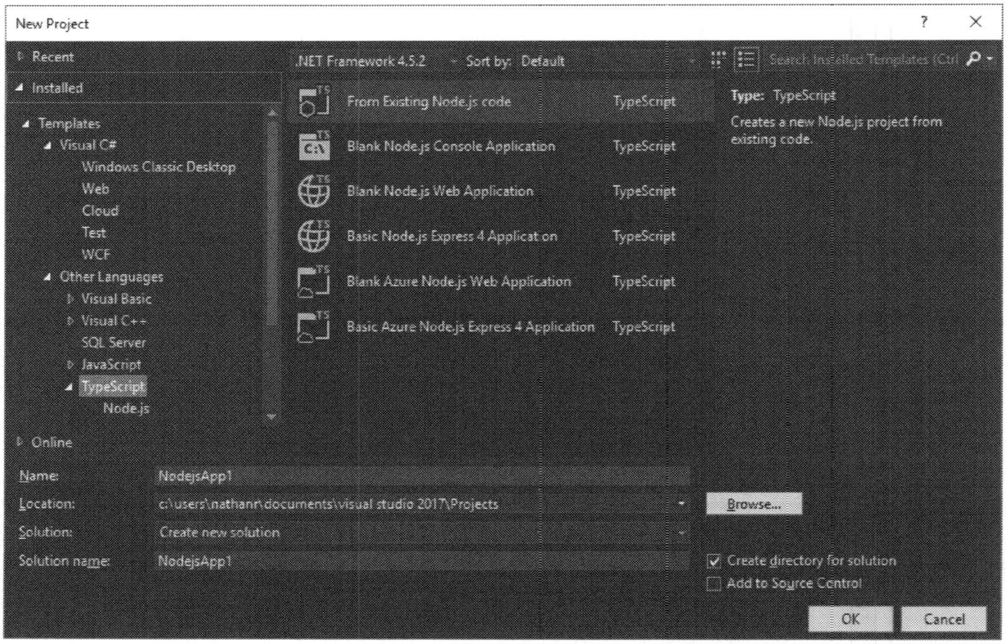


Visual Studio 2017 – TypeScript project templates

To create a simple TypeScript web application in Visual Studio 2017, we will need to create a blank web application first, and then we can add TypeScript files to this project as need be. From our **Templates** dialog, then, select the **Visual C#** template option, and then select the **Web** option. This will give us a project template named **ASP.NET Web Application**. Select a **Name** and a **Location** for the new project, and then click on **OK**, as shown in the following screenshot:

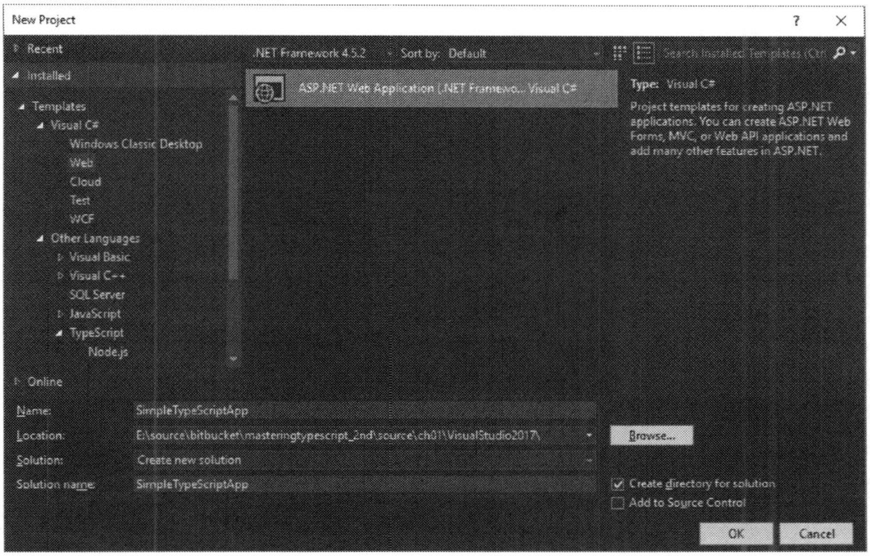

Visual Studio 2017 – creating an ASP.NET web application

Once we have selected the basic information for our new project, Visual Studio will generate a second dialog box asking what sort of ASP.NET project we would like to generate. Select the **Empty** template, and click on **OK**, as shown below:

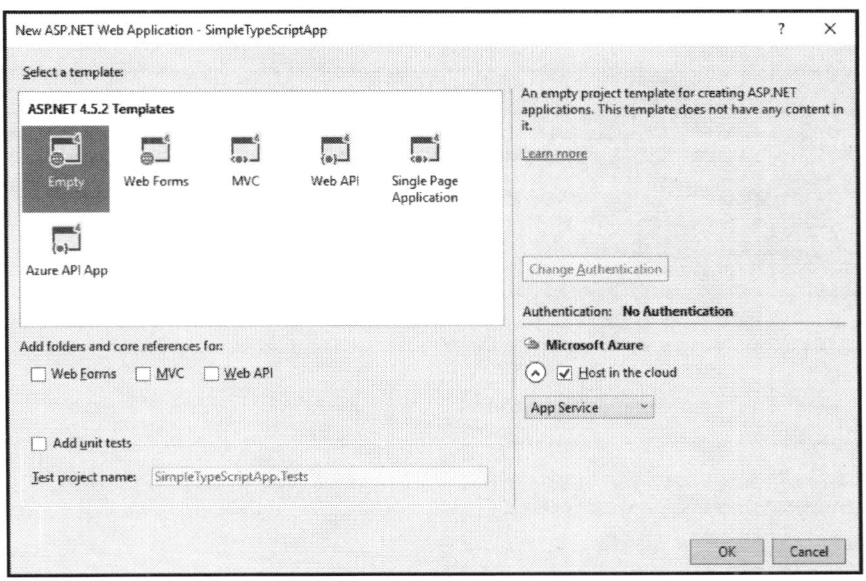

Visual Studio 2017 – options for creating an ASP.NET web application

Visual Studio 2017 will then pop up another dialog named **Create App Service**, which provides options for creating a host in Azure for your new web application. We will not be publishing our application to Azure, so we can click on **Skip** at this stage.

## Default project settings

Once a new Empty ASP.NET web application has been created, we can start adding files to the project by right-clicking on the project itself and selecting **Add** then **New Item**. There are two files that we are going to add to the project, namely an `index.html` file and an `app.ts` TypeScript file. For each of these files, select the corresponding Visual Studio template, as follows:

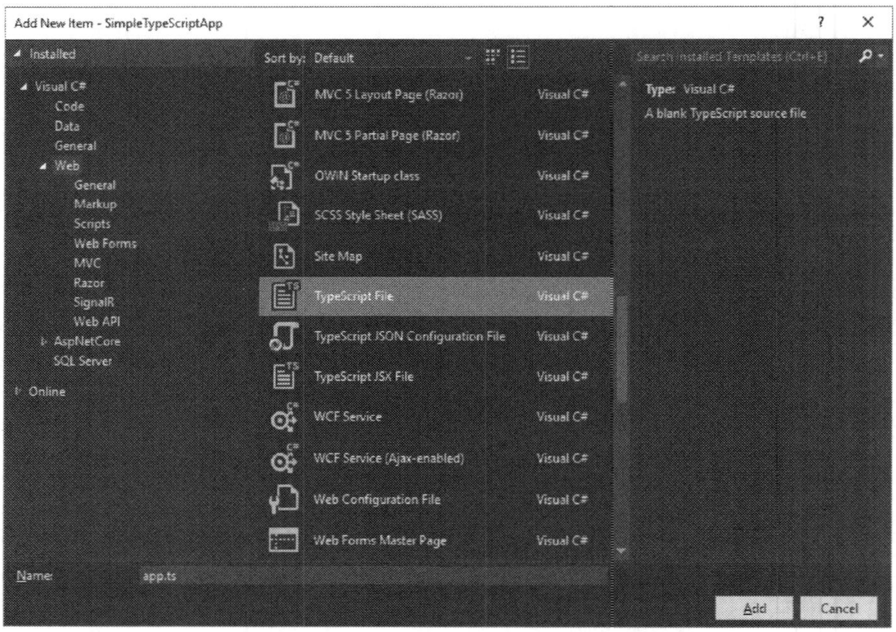


Visual Studio – adding a TypeScript file

We can now open up the `app.ts` file, and start typing the following code:

```
class MyClass {
  public render(divId: string, text: string) {
    var el: HTMLElement = document.getElementById(divId);
    el.innerText = text;
  }
}
```

```
window.onload = () => {
  var myClass = new MyClass();
  myClass.render("content", "Hello World");
};
```

Here, we have created a class named MyClass, that has a single render function. This function takes two parameters, named divId and text. The function finds an HTML DOM element that matches the divId argument, and then sets the innerText property to the value of the text argument. We then define a function to be called when the browser calls window.onload. This function creates a new instance of the MyClass class, and calls the render function.

> Do not be alarmed if this syntax and code is a little confusing. We will be covering all of the language elements and syntax in later chapters. The point of this exercise is simply to use Visual Studio as a development environment for editing TypeScript code.

You will notice that Visual Studio has very powerful Intellisense options, and will suggest code, function names, or variable names as and when you are typing your code. If they are not automatically appearing, then hitting *Ctrl–Space* will bring up the Intellisense options for the code you are currently typing.

With our app.ts file in place, we can compile it by hitting *Ctrl–Shift–B,* or *F6,* or by selecting the **Build** option from the toolbar. If there are any errors in the TypesScript code that we are compiling, Visual Studio will automatically pop up an **Error List** panel, showing current compilation errors. Double-clicking on any one of these errors will bring up the file in the editor panel, and automatically move the cursor to the offending code.

> The generated app.js file is not included in the Solution Explorer in Visual Studio. Only the app.ts TypeScript file is included. This is by design. If you wish to see the generated JavaScript file, simply click on the **Show All Files** button in the Solution Explorer toolbar.

To include our TypeScript file in the HTML page, we will need to edit the index.html file, and add a <script> tag to load app.js, as follows:

```
<!DOCTYPE html>
<html>
<head>
  <meta charset="utf-8" />
  <title></title>
  <script src="app.js"></script>
</head>
<body>
```

```
    <div id="content"></div>
  </body>
</html>
```

Here, we have added the `<script>` tag to load our `app.js` file, and have also created a `<div>` element with the `id` of `content`. This is the DOM element that our code will modify the `innerHtml` property of. We can now hit *F5* to run our application:

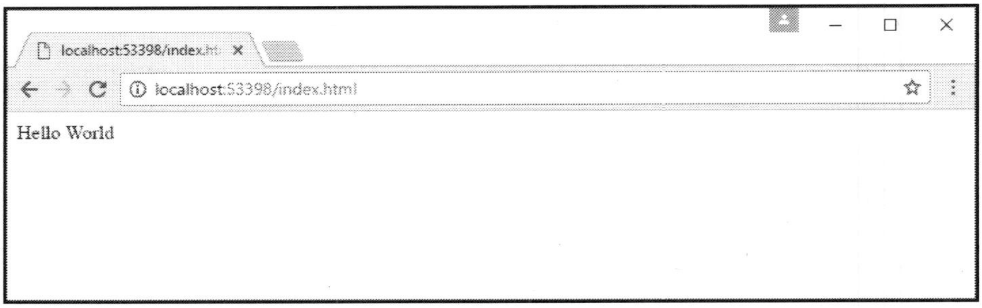


Visual Studio index.html running in Chrome

## Debugging in Visual Studio

One of the best features of Visual Studio is that it is truly an integrated environment. Debugging TypeScript in Visual Studio is exactly the same as debugging C# or any other language in Visual Studio, and includes the usual **Immediate**, **Locals**, **Watch**, and **Call stack** windows.

To debug TypeScript in Visual Studio, simply put a breakpoint on the line you wish to break on in your TypeScript file (move your mouse into the breakpoint area next to the source code line, and click). In the following screenshot, we have placed a breakpoint within the `window.onload` function. To start debugging, simply hit *F5:*

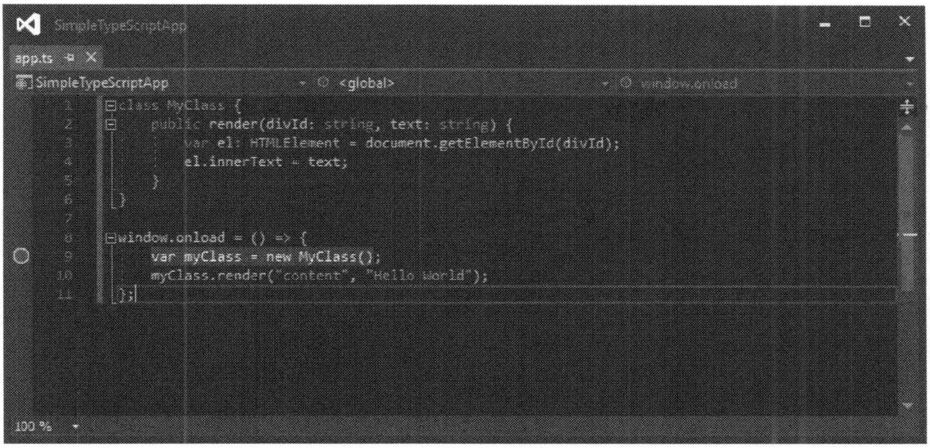


Visual Studio TypeScript editor with a breakpoint set in the code

When the source code line is highlighted in yellow, hover your mouse over any of the variables in your source, or use the **Immediate**, **Watch**, **Locals**, or **Call stack** windows.

> **TIP**
>
> Note that Visual Studio only supports debugging in Internet Explorer 11. If you have multiple browsers installed on your machine (including Microsoft Edge), make sure that you select **Internet Explorer** in your **Debug** toolbar, as shown in the following screenshot:

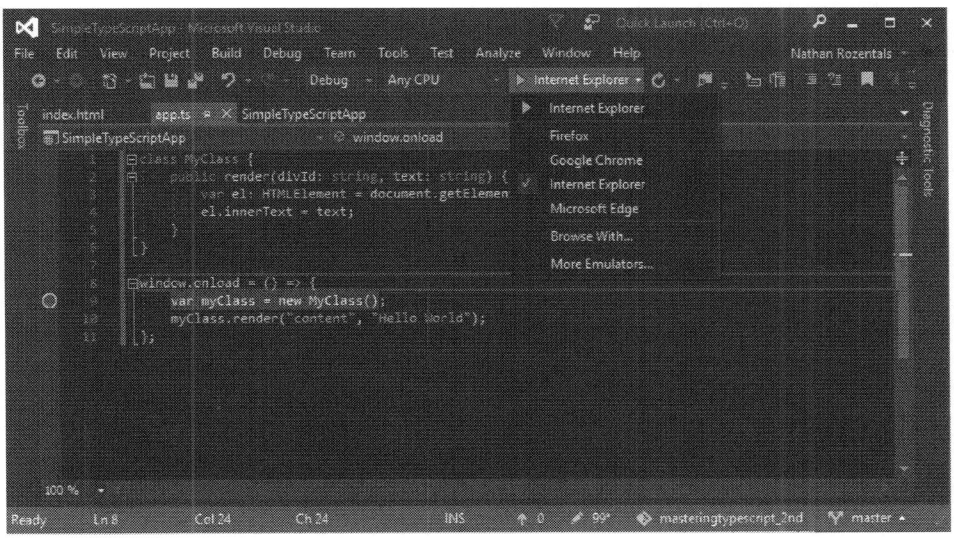


Visual Studio Debug toolbar showing browser options

# WebStorm

WebStorm is a popular IDE by JetBrains (`http://www.jetbrains.com/webstorm/`), and will run on Windows, Mac OS X, and Linux. Prices range from $59 per year for a single developer to $129 per year for a commercial license. JetBrains also offers a 30-day trial version.

WebStorm has a couple of great features, including live edit and code suggestions, or Intellisense. Live edit allows you to keep a browser open that will automatically update based on changes to CSS, HTML, and JavaScript as you type it. Code suggestions, which are also available with another popular JetBrains product, ReSharper, will highlight code that you have written and suggest better ways of implementing it. WebStorm also has a large number of project templates. These templates will automatically download and include the relevant JavaScript or CSS files, such as Twitter, Bootstrap, or HTML5 boilerplate.

On Windows systems, setting up WebStorm is as simple as downloading the package from the website, and running the installer. On Linux systems, Webstorm is provided as a tar ball. Once it's unpacked, install WebStorm by running the `webstorm.sh` script in the `bin` directory. Note that on Linux systems, a running version of Java must be installed before setup will continue.

## Creating a WebStorm project

To create a WebStorm project, fire up WebStorm and hit **File** | **New Project**. Select a name, location, and project type. For this project, we have selected **Twitter Bootstrap**:

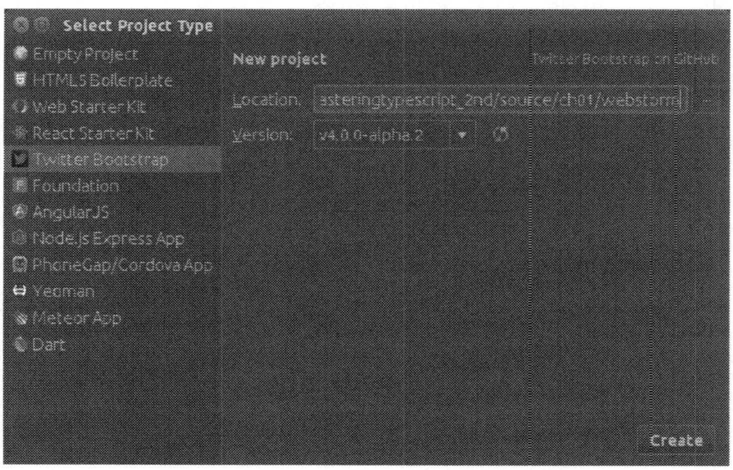


WebStorm new project dialog box

# Default files

WebStorm has conveniently created `css` and `js` directories as part of the new project and downloaded and included the relevant CSS and JavaScript files for us to start building a new Bootstrap-based site. Note that it has not created an `index.html` file for us, nor has it created any TypeScript files. So let's create an `index.html` file.

Simply click on **File** | **New**, select **HTML** file, enter `index` as a name, and click **OK**.

Next, let's create a TypeScript file in a similar manner. We will call this file `app` (or `app.ts`), in order to mirror the Visual Studio project. As we click inside the new `app.ts` file, WebStorm will pop up a message at the top of the file, with a suggestion reading **Compile TypeScript to JavaScript?** with three options–**OK**, **No**, and **Configure**, as shown in the following screenshot:

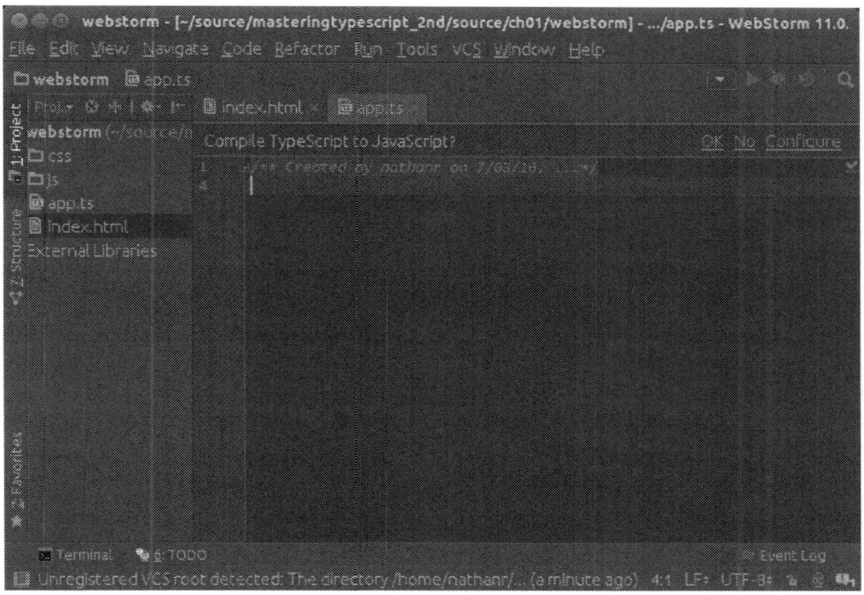


WebStorm editing a TypeScript file for the first time showing the file watcher bar

Clicking on **Configure** will bring up the **Settings** panel for TypeScript. Click on the **Enable TypeScript compiler** checkbox to enable modifications to the settings, then click on the **Use tsconfig.json** radio button, and click **OK**. WebStorm is now configured to use the `tsconfig.json` file in the projects root directory. As this file does not yet exist, a TypeScript error panel will open, indicating that the compiler cannot find `tsconfig.json` in the project. To fix this error, we will need to create a `tsconfig.json` file, so click on **File | New**, and type `tsconfig.json` as the filename. Switch back to the `app.ts` file, hit Ctrl-S to save, and the error message will disappear.

# Building a simple HTML application

Now that we have configured WebStorm to compile our Typescript files, let's create a simple TypeScript class and use it to modify the `innerText` property of an HTML `div`. While you are typing, you will notice WebStorm's auto-completion or Intellisense feature helping you with available keywords, parameters, naming conventions, and so on. This is one of the most powerful features of WebStorm, and is similar to the enhanced Intellisense seen in Visual Studio. Go ahead and type the following TypeScript code, during which you will get a good feeling for WebStorm's available auto-completion:

```
class MyClass {
  public render(divId: string, text: string) {
    var el: HTMLElement = document.getElementById(divId);
    el.innerText = text;
  }
}

window.onload = () => {
  var myClass = new MyClass();
  myClass.render("content", "Hello World");
}
```

This code is the same as we used in the Visual Studio example.

If you have any errors in your TypeScript file, these will automatically show up in the output window, giving you instant feedback while you type. With this TypeScript file created, we can now include it in our `index.html` file, and try some debugging.

Open the `index.html` file, and add a `script` tag to include the `app.js` JavaScript file, along with a `div` with an `id` of `"content"`. Just as we saw with TypeScript editing, you will find that WebStorm has powerful Intellisense features when editing HTML as well:

```
<!DOCTYPE html>
<html>
<head lang="en">
```

```
<meta charset="UTF-8">
<title></title>
<script src="app.js"></script>
</head>
<body>
  <div id="content"></div>
</body>
</html>
```

Again, this HTML is the same as we used earlier in the Visual Studio example.

## Running a web page in Chrome

When viewing or editing HTML files in WebStorm, you will notice a small set of browser icons popping up in the top-right corner of the editing window. Clicking on any one of the icons will launch your current HTML page using the selected browser:

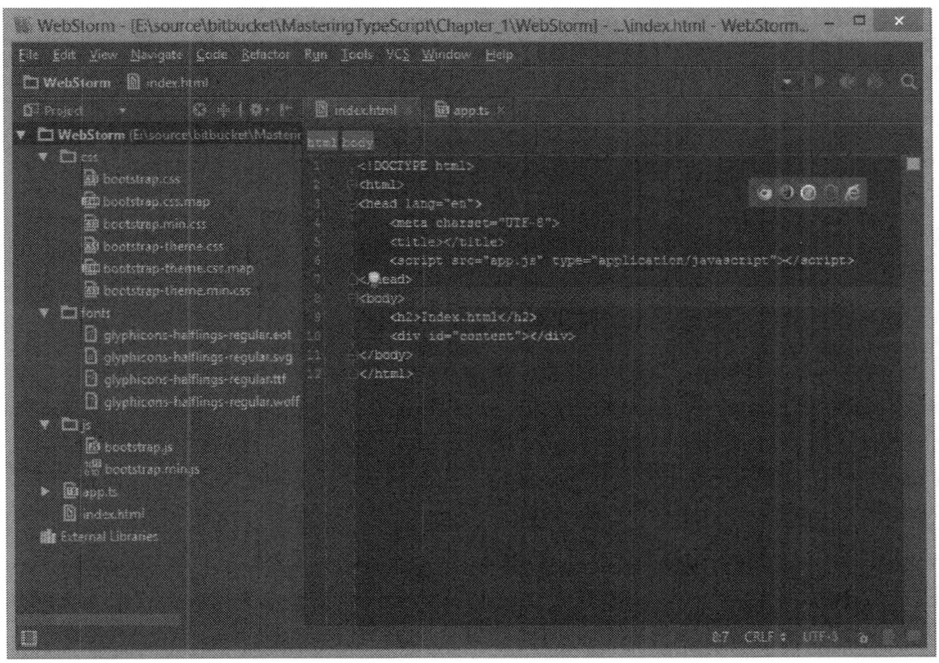

WebStorm editing an HTML file showing popup browser-launching icons

## Debugging in Chrome

To debug our web application in WebStorm, we will need to set up a debug configuration for the `index.html` file. Click on **Run** | **Debug** and then edit configurations. Click on the plus (+) button, select the **JavaScript debug** option on the left, and give this configuration a name. Note that WebStorm has already identified that `index.html` is the default page, but this can easily be modified. Next, click on **Debug** at the bottom of the screen, as shown in the following screenshot:

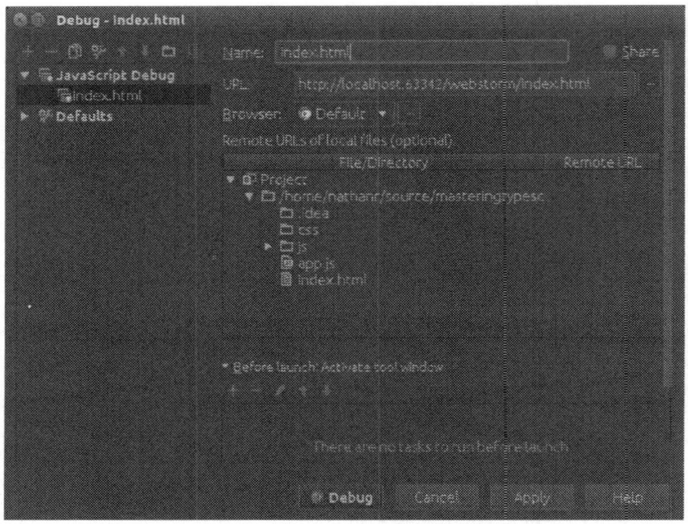


WebStorm debugging configuration for index.html

WebStorm uses a Chrome plugin to enable debugging in Chrome and will prompt you the first time you start debugging to download and enable the `JetBrains IDE Support` Chrome plugin. With this plugin enabled, WebStorm has a very powerful set of tools to inspect JavaScript code, add watchers, view the console, and many more, right inside the IDE.

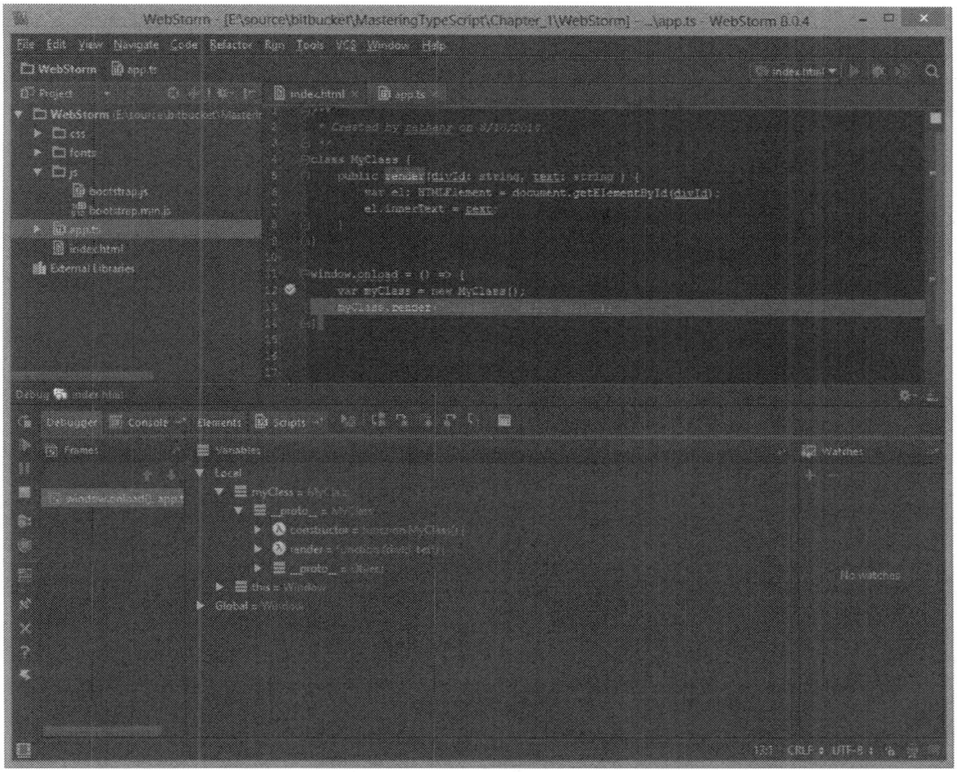

WebStorm debugging session showing debugger panels

# Visual Studio Code

Visual Studio Code is a lightweight development enviroment produced by Microsoft that runs on Windows, Linux, and Mac. It includes development features such as syntax highlighting, bracket matching, Intellisense, and also has support for many different languages. These languages include TypeScript, JavaScript, JSON, HTML, CSS, C#, C++ and many more – making it ideal for TypeScript development in either web pages or Node. Its main focus is currently ASP.NET development with C#, and Node development with TypeScript. It has also been built with strong git support out-of-the-box.

# Installing VSCode

VSCode can be installed on Windows by simply downloading and running the installer. On Linux systems, VSCode is provided as a `.deb` package, an `.rpm` package, or a binary tar file. Under Mac, download the `.zip` file, unzip it, and then copy the `Visual Studio Code.app` file to your applications folder.

# Exploring VSCode

Create a new directory to hold your source code and fire up VSCode. This can be done by navigating to the directory and executing `code .` from the command line. On Windows systems, fire up VSCode, and then Select **File** | **Open folder** from the menu bar. Hit *Ctrl–N* to create a new file, and type the following:

```
console.log("hello vscode");
```

Note that there is no syntax highlighting at this stage, as VSCode does not know what type of file it is working with. Hit *Ctrl–S* to save the file, and name it `hello.ts`. Now that VSCode understands this to be a TypeScript file, you will have full Intellisense and syntax highlighting available.

## Creating a tasks.json file

The keyboard shortcut to build a project in VSCode is *Ctrl–Shift–B*. If we try to build the project at this stage, VSCode will show a message–`No task runner configured`, and give us the option to **Configure Task Runner**. We can then select which sort of task runner we would like to configure, including Grunt, Gulp, and a number of other options. Selecting one of these options will automatically create a `tasks.json` file for us in the `.vscode` directory, and open it for editing.

As an example of this let's select the **TypeScript – tsconfig.json** option. We will make a single change to the generated `tsconfig.json` file, and set the value of the `"showOutput"` option to `"always"`, instead of `"silent"`. This will force VSCode to open an output window whenever it sees compilation issues.

Our `tasks.json` file now contains the following:

```
// A task runner that calls the Typescript compiler (tsc) and
// compiles based on a tsconfig.json file that is present in
// the root of the folder open in VSCode
{
  "version": "0.1.0",
  "command": "tsc",
  "isShellCommand": true,
  "showOutput": "always",
  "args": ["-p", "."],
  "problemMatcher": "$tsc"
}
```

## Building the project

Our sample project can now be built by hitting *Ctrl–Shift–B*. Note that in the base directory of our project, we now have a `hello.js` and a `hello.js.map` file as the result of the compilation step.

## Creating a launch.json file

VSCode includes an integrated debugger that can be used to debug TypeScript projects. If we switch to the **Debugger** panel, or simply hit *F5* to start debugging, VSCode will ask us to select a debugging environment. For the time being, select the **Node.js** option, which will create a `launch.json` file in the `.vscode` directory, and again open it for editing. Find the option named `"program"`, and modify it to read `"${workspaceRoot}/hello.js"`. Hit *F5* again, and VSCode will launch `hello.js` as a Node program and output the results to the debugging window:

```
node --debug-brk=34146 --nolazy hello.js
debugger listening on port 34146
hello vscode
```

## Setting breakpoints

Using breakpoints and debugging at this stage will only work on the generated `.js` JavaScript files. We will need to make another change to the `launch.json` file to enable debugging directly in our TypeScript files. Edit the `launch.json` file, and change the `"sourceMaps" : false` property to `true`. Now we can set breakpoints directly in our `.ts` files for use by the VSCode debugger:

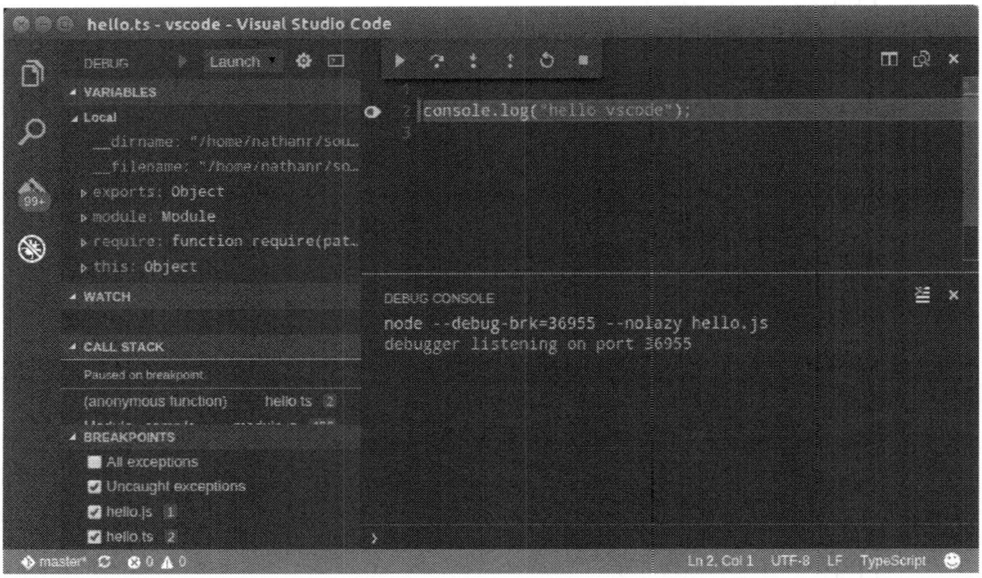


Debugging a Node application within Visual Studio Code

## Debugging web pages

Debugging TypeScript running within a web page in VSCode takes a little more setup. VSCode uses the Chrome debugger to attach to a running web page. To enable debugging web pages, we will firstly need to modify the `launch.json` file and add a new launch option, as follows:

```
"configurations": [
  {
    "name": "Launch",
    ...
  },
  {
    "name": "Attach 9222",
    "type": "chrome",
```

```
        "request": "attach",
        "port": 9222,
        "sourceMaps": true
      }
    ]
```

This launch option is named "Attach 9222", and will attach to a running instance of chrome using the debug port 9222. Save the launch.json file, and create an HTML page named index.html at the root directory of the project, as follows:

```
<html>
  <head>
  <script src="helloweb.js"></script>
  </head>
  <body>
    hello vscode
    <div id="content"></div>
  </body>
</html>
```

This is a very simple page that loads the helloweb.js file, and displays the text hello vscode. Our helloweb.ts file is as follows:

```
window.onload = () => {
  console.log("hello vscode");
};
```

This TypeScript code simply waits for the web page to load, and then logs "hello vscode" to the console.

The next step is to fire up Chrome using the debug port option. On Linux systems, this is done from the command prompt, as follows:

```
google-chrome --remote-debugging-port=9222
```

Note that you will need to ensure that there are no other instances of Chrome running in order to use it as a debugger with VSCode.

Next, load the index.html file in the browser by using the file://<full_path_to_file>/index.html syntax. You should see the HTML file rendering the "hello vscode" text.

Now we can go back to VSCode, click on the debugging icon, and select the **Attach 9222** option in the launcher drop-down. Hit F5, and the VSCode debugger should now be attached to the running instance of Chrome. We will then need to refresh the page in Chrome in order to start debugging:

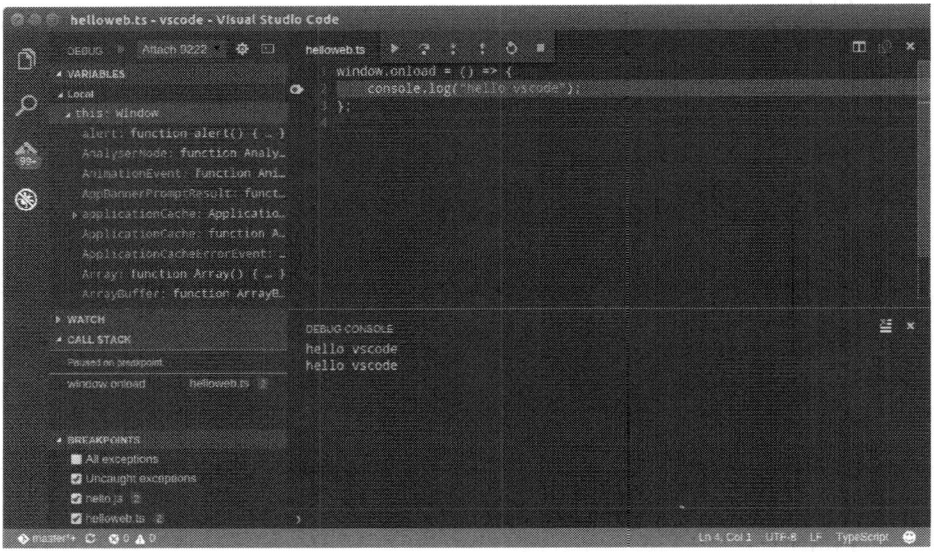


Debugging web pages in Visual Studio Code

With a slight tweak to our `launch.json`, we can combine these manual steps into a single launcher, as follows:

```
{
    "name": "Launch chrome",
    "type": "chrome",
    "request" : "launch",
    "url" : "file:/// ... insert full path here ... /index.html",
    "runtimeArgs": [
        "--new-window",
        "--remote-debugging-port=9222"
    ],
    "sourceMaps": true
}
```

In this launch configuration, we have changed the `request` property from `"attach"` to `"launch"`, which will launch a new instance of Chrome and automatically navigate to the file path specified in the `"url"` property. The `"runtimeArgs"` property now also specifies the remote debugging port of `9222`. With this launcher in place, we can simply hit F5 to launch Chrome, with the correct URL and debugging options for debugging of HTML applications.

# Other editors

There are a number of editors that include support for TypeScript, such as Atom, Brackets, and even the age-old Vim editor. Each of these editors has varying levels of TypeScript support, including syntax highlighting and Intellisense. Using these editors represents a bare-bones TypeScript development environment, relying on the command line to automate build tasks. They do not have built-in debugging tools, and therefore do not qualify as an **Integrated Development Environment** (**IDE**) per se, but can easily be used to build TypeScript applications. The basic workflow using these editors would be as follows:

- Create and modify files using the editor
- Invoke the TypeScript compiler from the command line
- Run or debug applications using existing debuggers

## Using Grunt

In a bare-bones environment, any change to a TypeScript file means that we need to re-issue the `tsc` command from the command line every time we wish to compile our project. Obviously, it is going to be very tedious to have to switch to the command prompt and manually compile our project every time we have made a change. This is where tools like Grunt come in handy. Grunt is an automated task runner (`http://gruntjs.com`) that can automate many tedious compile, build, and test tasks. In this section, we will use Grunt to watch our TypeScript files, and automatically invoke the `tsc` compiler when a file is saved.

Grunt runs in a Node environment, and therefore needs to be installed as an npm dependency of your project. It cannot be installed globally as most `npm` packages can. In order to do this, we will need to create a `packages.json` file in the root project. Open up a command prompt, and navigate to the root directory of your project. Then, simply type:

```
npm init
```

Then follow the prompts. You can pretty much leave all of the options at their defaults, and always go back to edit the `packages.json` file that is created from this step, should you need to tweak any changes.

Now we can install Grunt. Grunt has two components that need to be installed independently. Firstly, we need to install the Grunt command-line interface, which allows us to run Grunt from the command line. This can be accomplished as follows:

```
npm install -g grunt-cli
```

The second component is to install the grunt files within our project directory:

```
npm install grunt --save-dev
```

The `--save-dev` option will install a local version of Grunt in the project directory. This is done so that multiple projects on your machine can use different versions of Grunt. We will also need the `grunt-exec` package, as well as the `grunt-contrib-watch` package. These can be installed with the following commands:

```
npm install grunt-exec --save-dev
npm install grunt-contrib-watch --save-dev.
```

Lastly, we will need a `GruntFile.js`. Using an editor, create a new file, save it as `GruntFile.js`, and enter the following JavaScript. Note that we are creating a JavaScript file here, not a TypeScript file. You can find a copy of this file in the sample source code that accompanies this chapter:

```
module.exports = function (grunt) {
  grunt.loadNpmTasks('grunt-contrib-watch');
  grunt.loadNpmTasks('grunt-exec');
  grunt.initConfig( {
    pkg: grunt.file.readJSON('package.json'),
    watch : {
        files : ['**/*.ts'],
        tasks : ['exec:run_tsc']
    },
    exec: {
        run_tsc: { cmd : 'tsc'}
    }
  });
  grunt.registerTask('default', ['watch']);
};
```

This `GruntFile.js` contains a simple function to initialize the Grunt environment, and specify the commands to run. The first two lines of the function are loading `grunt-contrib-watch` and `grunt-exec` as `npm` tasks. We then call `initConfig` to configure the tasks to run. This configuration section has a `pkg` property, a `watch` property, and an `exec` property. The `pkg` property is used to load the `package.json` file that we created earlier as part of the `npm init` step.

The `watch` property has two sub-properties. The `files` property specifies what to watch for, in this case any `.ts` files in our source tree, and the `tasks` array specifies that we should kick off the `exec:run_tsc` command once a file has changed. Finally, we call `grunt.registerTask`, specifying that the default task is to watch for file changes.

We can now run `grunt` from the command line, as follows:

```
grunt
```

As can be seen from the command line output, Grunt is running the `watch` task, and is waiting for changes to any `.ts` files:

```
Running "watch" task
Waiting...
```

Open up any TypeScript file, make a small change (add a space or something), and then hit Ctrl-S to save the file. Now check back on the output from the Grunt command line. You should see something like the following:

```
>> File "hellogrunt.ts" changed.
Running "exec:run_tsc" (exec) task
Done, without errors.
Completed in 2.008s at Sat Mar 19 2016 20:27:17 GMT+0800
 (W. Australia Standard Time) - Waiting...
```

This command line output is a confirmation that the Grunt watch task has identified that the `hellogrunt.ts` file has changed, run the `exec:run_tsc` task, and is waiting for the next file to change. We should now also see a `hellogrunt.js` file in the same directory as our Typescript file.

# Summary

In this chapter, we have had a quick look at what TypeScript is and what benefits it can bring to the JavaScript development experience. We also looked at setting up a development environment using some popular IDEs, and had a look at what a bare-bones development environment would look like. Now that we have a development environment set up, we can start looking at the TypeScript language itself in a bit more detail. We will start with types, move on to variables, and then discuss functions in the next chapter.

# 2
# Types, Variables, and Function Techniques

TypeScript introduces strong typing to JavaScript through a simple syntax, referred to by Anders Hejlsberg as "syntactic sugar". This "sugar" is what assigns a type to a variable, a function parameter, or even the return type of a function itself. As we discussed in `Chapter 1`, *TypeScript – Tools and Framework Options*, the benefits of strong typing include better error checking, the ability for an IDE to provide more intelligent code suggestions, and the ability to introduce object-oriented techniques into the JavaScript coding experience. There are a number of basic types that the language uses, such as number, string and boolean, to name a few. There are also rules by which the TypeScript compiler identifies what the type of a variable is. Understanding these rules and applying them to your code is a fundamental skill when writing TypeScript code.

We will cover the following topics in this chapter:

- Basic types and type syntax – strings, numbers, and booleans
- Inferred typing and duck typing
- Template strings
- Arrays
- Using `for...in` and `for...of`
- The `any` type and explicit casting
- Enums
- Const enums and const values
- The `let` keyword
- Functions and anonymous functions
- Optional and default function parameters

- Argument arrays
- Function callbacks, function signatures, and function overloads
- Union types, type guards, and type aliases

> This chapter is an introduction to the syntax used in the TypeScript language to apply strong typing to JavaScript. It is intended for readers who have not used TypeScript before, and covers the transition from standard JavaScript to TypeScript. If you already have experience with TypeScript, and have a good understanding of the topics listed here, then by all means have a quick read through, or skip to the next chapter.

# Basic types

JavaScript variables can hold a number of data types, including numbers, strings, arrays, objects, functions, and more. The type of an object in JavaScript is determined by its assignment. This means that only at the point where we assign a value to a variable does the JavaScript runtime interpreter try to determine what the type of the particular variable is. While this may work in simple cases, the JavaScript runtime can also reassign the type of a variable depending on how it is being used, or on how it is interacting with other variables. It may assign a number to a string, for example, in certain cases. Let's take a look at an example of this dynamic typing in JavaScript, and what errors it can introduce, before exploring the strong typing that TypeScript uses, and its basic type system.

# JavaScript typing

As we saw in `Chapter 1`, *TypeScript – Tools and Framework Options*, JavaScript objects and variables can be changed or reassigned on-the-fly. As an example of this, consider the following JavaScript code:

```
function doCalculation(a,b,c) {
  return (a * b) + c;
}
var result = doCalculation(2,3,1);
console.log('doCalculation():' + result);
```

Here, we have a `doCalculation` function that is computing the product of the arguments `a` and `b`, and then adding the value of `c`. We are then calling the function with the arguments `2`, `3` and `1`, and logging the result to the console. The output of this sample would be:

```
doCalculation():7
```

This is the expected result, as 2 * 3 = 6, and 6 + 1 = 7. Now let's take a look at what happens if we inadvertently call the function with strings instead of numbers:

```
result = doCalculation("2","3","1");
console.log('doCalculation():' + result);
```

The output of this code sample is as follows:

```
doCalculation():61
```

The result of `61` is very different from our expected result of `7`. So what is going on here? If we take a closer look at the code in the `doCalculation` function, we start to understand what JavaScript is doing with our variables, and their types.

The product of two numbers, that is, `(a * b)`, returns a numeric value, so JavaScript is automatically converting the values `"2"` and `"3"` to numbers in order to compute the product, and correctly computing the value `6`. This is a particular rule that JavaScript applies in order to convert strings to numbers, when the result should be a number. But the addition symbol, that is, `+`, does not infer that both values are numeric. Because the argument `c` is a string, JavaScript is converting the value `6` into a string in order to add two strings. This results in the string `"6"` being added to the string `"1"`, which results in the value `"61"`. Obviously, these sorts of automatic type conversions can cause unwanted behavior in our code.

# TypeScript typing

TypeScript, on the other hand, is a strongly typed language. Once you have declared a variable to be of type `string`, you can only assign `string` values to it. All further code that uses this variable must treat it as though it has a type of `string`. This helps to ensure that code that we write will behave as expected.

JavaScript programmers have always relied heavily on documentation to understand how to call functions, and the order and type of the correct function parameters. But what if we could take all of this documentation and include it within the IDE? Then, as we write our code, our compiler could point out to us automatically that we were using variables in the wrong way. Surely this would make us more efficient, more productive programmers, allowing us to generate code with fewer errors?

TypeScript does exactly that. It introduces a very simple syntax to define the type of a variable to ensure that we are using it in the correct manner. If we break any of these rules, the TypeScript compiler will automatically generate errors, pointing us to the lines of code that are in error.

This is how TypeScript got its name. It is JavaScript with strong typing, hence TypeScript. Let's take a look at this very simple language syntax that enables the *Type* in TypeScript.

# Type syntax

The TypeScript syntax for declaring the type of a variable is to include a colon (`:`), after the variable name, and then indicate its type. Let's rewrite our problematic `doCalculation` function to only accept numbers. Consider the following TypeScript code:

```
function doCalculation(
  a : number,
  b : number,
  c : number) {
  return ( a * b ) + c;
}

var result = doCalculation(3,2,1);
console.log("doCalculation():" + result);
```

Here, we have specified that the `doCalculation` function needs to be invoked with three numbers. Again, the TypeScript syntax for declaring a type is to include a colon, and then the variable type, hence `: number` for the properties `a`, `b`, and `c`. If we now attempt to call this function with strings, as we did with the JavaScript sample, as follows:

```
var result = doCalculation("1", "2", "3");
console.log("doCalculation():" + result);
```

The TypeScript compiler will generate the following error:

```
error TS2345: Argument of type 'string' is not assignable
to parameter of type 'number'.
```

This error message clearly tells us that we cannot assign a string where a numeric value is expected.

To further illustrate this point, consider the following TypeScript code:

```
var myString : string;
var myNumber : number;
var myBoolean : boolean;
myString = "1";
myNumber = 1;
myBoolean = true;
```

Here, we are telling the compiler that the `myString` variable is of type `string`, even before the variable itself has been used. Similarly, the `myNumber` variable is of type `number`, and the `myBoolean` variable is of type `boolean`. TypeScript has introduced the `string`, `number`, and `boolean` keywords for each of these basic JavaScript types.

If we then attempt to assign a value to a variable that is not of the same type, the TypeScript compiler will generate a compile-time error. Given the variables declared in the preceding code, consider the following TypeScript code:

```
myString = myNumber;
myBoolean = myString;
myNumber = myBoolean;
```

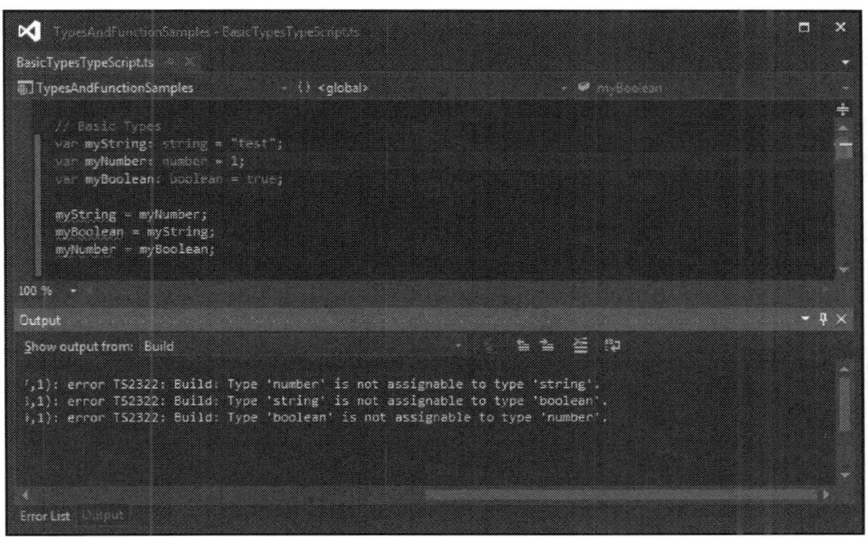


TypeScript build errors when assigning incorrect types

The TypeScript compiler is now generating compile errors because it has detected that we are attempting to mix these basic types. The first error is generated because we cannot assign a number value to a variable of type `string`. Similarly, the second compile error indicates that we cannot assign a `string` value to a variable of type `boolean`. Again, the third error is generated because we cannot assign a boolean value to a variable of type `number`.

The strong typing syntax that the TypeScript language introduces means that we need to ensure that the types on the left-hand side of an assignment operator (=) are the same as the types on the right-hand side of the assignment operator.

To fix the preceding TypeScript code, and remove the compile errors, we would need to do something similar to the following:

```
myString = myNumber.toString();
myBoolean = (myString === "test");
if (myBoolean) {
  myNumber = 1;
}
```

Our first line of code has been changed to call the `.toString()` function on the `myNumber` variable (which is of type `number`), in order to return a value that is of type `string`. This line of code, then, does not generate a compile error because both sides of the equal sign (or assignment operator) are strings.

Our second line of code has also been changed so that the right-hand side of the assignment operator returns the result of a comparison, `myString === "test"`, which will return a value of type `boolean`. The compiler will therefore allow this code, because both sides of the assignment resolve to a value of type `boolean`.

The last line of our code snippet has been changed to only assign the value `1` (which is of type `number`) to the `myNumber` variable, if the value of the `myBoolean` variable is `true`.

Anders Hejlsberg describes this feature as "syntactic sugar". In other words, with a little "sugar" on top of comparable JavaScript code, TypeScript has enabled our code to transform into a strongly typed language. Whenever you break these strong typing rules, the compiler will generate errors for your offending code.

# Inferred typing

TypeScript also uses a technique called inferred typing to determine the type of a variable. In other words, TypeScript will infer the type of a variable based on its first usage, and then assume the same type for this variable in the rest of your code block. As an example of this, consider the following TypeScript code:

```
var inferredString = "this is a string";
var inferredNumber = 1;
inferredString = inferredNumber;
```

We start by declaring a variable named `inferredString`, and assign a string value to it. TypeScript identifies that this variable has been assigned a value of type `string`, and will, therefore, infer any further usage of this variable to be of type `string`. Our second variable, named `inferredNumber`, has a number assigned to it. Again, TypeScript is inferring the type of this variable to be of type `number`. If we then attempt to assign the `inferredString` variable (of type `string`) to the `inferredNumber` variable (of type `number`) in the last line of code, TypeScript will generate a familiar error message:

```
error TS2011: Build: Cannot convert 'string' to 'number'
```

This error is generated because of TypeScript's inferred typing rules.

Remember that if we do not explicitly specify the type of a variable by using the colon ( : `type` ) syntax, then TypeScript will automatically infer the type of a variable based on its first assignment.

# Duck typing

TypeScript also uses a method called duck typing for more complex variable types. Duck typing means that if it looks like a duck, and quacks like a duck, then it probably is a duck. Consider the following TypeScript code:

```
var complexType = { name: "myName", id: 1 };
complexType = { id: 2, name: "anotherName" };
```

We start with a variable named `complexType` that has been assigned a simple JavaScript object with a `name` and an `id` property. On our second line of code, we are reassigning the value of this `complexType` variable to another object that also has an `id` and a `name` property. The compiler will use duck typing in this instance to figure out whether this assignment is valid. In other words, if an object has the same set of properties as another object, then they are considered to be of the same type.

To further illustrate this point, let's see how the compiler reacts if we attempt to assign an object to our `complexType` variable that does not conform to this duck typing:

```
var complexType = { name: "myName", id: 1 };
complexType = { id: 2 };
```

The first line of this code snippet defines our `complexType` variable, and assigns to it an object that contains both an `id` and a `name` property. From this point on, TypeScript will use this inferred type on any value we attempt to assign to the `complexType` variable. On our second line of code, we are attempting to reassign the `complexType` variable to a value that has an `id` property but not a `name` property. This line of code will generate the following compilation error:

```
error TS2322: Type '{ id: number; }' is not assignable to type
'{ name: string; id: number; }'.
 Property 'name' is missing in type '{ id: number; }'.
```

The error message is pretty self-explanatory. In this instance, TypeScript is using duck typing to ensure type safety. As the `complexType` variable has both an `id` and a `name` property, any value that is assigned to it must also have both an `id` and a `name` property.

Note that the following code will also generate an error message:

```
var complexType = { name: "myName", id: 1 };
complexType = { name : "extraproperty", id : 2, extraProp: true };
```

The error generated here is as follows:

```
error TS2322: Type '{ name: string; id: number;
extraProp: boolean; }' is not assignable to type '{ name: string; id:
number; }'.
Object literal may only specify known properties, and 'extraProp' does not
exist in type '{ name: string; id: number; }'.
```

As can be seen in this error message, the variable `complexType` does not have an `extraProp` property, and therefore the assignment fails.

Inferred typing and duck typing are powerful features of the TypeScript language, bringing strong typing to our code without the need to use explicit typing.

# Template strings

Before we continue our discussion on types, it is worth noting that TypeScript allows for ES6 template string syntax. This syntax provides a convenient method for injecting values into strings. Consider the following code:

```
var myVariable = "test";
console.log("myVariable=" + myVariable);
```

Here, we are simply assigning a value to a variable, and logging the result to the console, with a little bit of formatting to make the message readable. Note how we are concatenating the strings with the `"string" + variable` syntax. Let's now take a look at the equivalent TypeScript code:

```
var myVariable = "test";
console.log(`myVariable=${myVariable}`);
```

On the second line of this code snippet, we have introduced the ES6 template string syntax for easier manipulation of strings. There are two important things to note about this syntax. Firstly, we have switched the string definition from a double quote (`"`) to an apostrophe (`` ` ``). Using an apostrophe signals to the TypeScript compiler that it should look for template values within the string enclosed by the apostrophes, and replace them with actual values. Secondly, we have used a special `${ ... }` syntax within the string to denote a template. TypeScript will inject the value of any variable that is currently in scope into the string for us. This is a convenient method of dealing with strings.

> The TypeScript compiler will parse this ES6 style of string templates, and generate JavaScript code that uses standard string concatenation. In this way, the ES6 string template syntax can be used no matter what JavaScript version is being targeted.

In the remainder of this chapter, we will use this string template syntax.

# Arrays

Besides the base JavaScript types of string, number, and boolean, TypeScript has two other basic data types that we will now take a closer look at – arrays and enums. Let's look at the syntax for defining arrays.

An array is simply marked with the [] notation, similar to JavaScript, and each array can be strongly typed to hold a specific type, as seen in the code below:

```
var arrayOfNumbers: number [] = [1,2,3];
arrayOfNumbers = [3,4,5,6,7,8,9];
console.log(`arrayOfNumbers: ${arrayOfNumbers}`);
arrayOfNumbers = ["1", "2", "3"];
```

Here, we start by defining an array named `arrayOfNumbers`, and further specifying that each element of this array must be of type `number`. We then reassign this array to hold some different numerical values. Note that we can assign any number of elements to an array. We then use a simple template string to print the array to the console.

The last line of this snippet, however, will generate the following error message:

```
hello_ch02.ts(51,1): error TS2322: Type 'string[]' is not assignable to
type 'number[]'.
Type 'string' is not assignable to type 'number'.
```

This error message is warning us that the variable `arrayOfNumbers` is strongly typed to only accept values of type `number`. As our code is trying to assign an array of strings to this array of numbers, an error is generated. The output of this code snippet is as follows:

```
arrayOfNumbers: 3,4,5,6,7,8,9
```

# for...in and for...of

When working with arrays, it is common practice to loop through array items in order to perform some task. This is generally accomplished within a `for` loop by manipulating an array index, as shown in the following code:

```
var arrayOfStrings : string[] = ["first", "second", "third"];

for( var i = 0; i < arrayOfStrings.length; i++ ) {
  console.log(`arrayOfStrings[${i}] = ${arrayOfStrings[i]}`);
}
```

Here, we have an array named `arrayOfStrings`, and a standard `for` loop that is using the variable `i` as an index into our array. We access the array item using the syntax `arrayOfStrings[i]`. The output of this code is as follows:

```
arrayOfStrings[0] = first
arrayOfStrings[1] = second
arrayOfStrings[2] = third
```

TypeScript introduces the `for...in` syntax to simplify looping through arrays. Here is an example of the above `for` loop expressed using this new syntax:

```
for( var itemKey in arrayOfStrings) {
  var itemValue = arrayOfStrings[itemKey];
  console.log(`arrayOfStrings[${itemKey}] = ${itemValue}`);
}
```

Here, we have simplified the `for` loop by using the `itemKey in arrayOfStrings` syntax. Note that the value of the variable `itemKey` will iterate through the keys of the array, and not the array elements themselves. Within the `for` loop, we are first de-referencing the array to extract the array value for this `itemKey`, and then logging both the `itemKey` and the `itemValue` to the console. The output of this code is as follows:

```
arrayOfStrings[0] = first
arrayOfStrings[1] = second
arrayOfStrings[2] = third
```

If we do not necessarily need to know the keys of the array, and are simply interested in the values held within the array, we can further simplify looping through arrays using the `for...of` syntax. Consider the following code:

```
for( var arrayItem of arrayOfStrings ) {
  console.log(`arrayItem = ${arrayItem} `);
}
```

Here, we are using the `for...of` syntax to iterate over each value of the `arrayOfStrings` array. Each time that the for loop is executed, the `arrayItem` variable will hold the next element in the array. The output of this code is as follows:

```
arrayItem = first
arrayItem = second
arrayItem = third
```

# The any type

All this type checking is well and good, but JavaScript is flexible enough to allow variables to be mixed and matched. The following code snippet is actually valid JavaScript code:

```
var item1 = { id: 1, name: "item 1" };
item1 = { id: 2 };
```

Here, we assign an object with an id property and a name property to the variable item1. We then reassign this variable to an object that has an id property but not a name property. Unfortunately, as we have seen previously, this is not valid TypeScript code, and will generate the following error:

```
hello_ch02.ts(130,1): error TS2322: Type '{ id: number; }' is not
assignable to type '{ id: number; name: string; }'.
Property 'name' is missing in type '{ id: number; }'.
```

TypeScript introduces the any type for such occasions. Specifying that an object has a type of any, in essence, relaxes the compiler's strict type checking. The following code shows how to use the any type:

```
var item1 : any = { id: 1, name: "item 1" };
item1 = { id: 2 };
```

Note how our first line of code has changed. We specify the type of the variable item1 to be of type : any. This special TypeScript keyword then allows a variable to follow JavaScript's loosely defined type rules, so that anything can be assigned to anything. Without the type specifier of : any, the second line of code would normally generate an error.

# Explicit casting

As with any strongly typed language, there comes a time where you need to explicitly specify the type of an object. This concept will be expanded upon more thoroughly in the next chapter, but it is worthwhile to make a quick note of explicit casting here. An object can be cast to the type of another by using the < > syntax.

> This is not a cast in the strictest sense of the word; it is more of an assertion that is used at runtime by the TypeScript compiler. Any explicit casting that you use will be compiled away in the resultant JavaScript and will not affect the code at runtime.

Let's take a look at an example that uses explicit casting, as follows:

```
var item1 = <any>{ id: 1, name: "item 1" };
item1 = { id: 2 };
```

Here, have now replaced the : any type specifier on the left-hand side of the assignment, with an explicit cast of <any> on the right-hand side. This tells the compiler to explicitly treat the { id: 1, name: "item 1" } object on the right-hand side of the assignment operator as a type of any. So the item1 variable on the left-hand side of the assignment, therefore, also has the type of any (due to TypeScript's inferred typing rules).

This then allows us to assign an object with only the `{ id: 2 }` property to the variable `item1` on the second line of code. This technique of using the `< >` syntax on the right-hand side of an assignment is called explicit casting.

While the `any` type is a necessary feature of the TypeScript language and is used for backward compatibility with JavaScript, its usage should really be limited as much as possible. As we have seen with untyped JavaScript, over-use of the `any` type will quickly lead to coding errors that will be difficult to find.

Rather than using the type `any`, try to figure out the correct type of the object you are using, and then use this type instead. We use an acronym within our programming teams–**Simply Find an Interface for the Any Type** (**S.F.I.A.T**) pronounced as sviat or sveat. While this may sound silly, it brings home the point that the `any` type should always be replaced with an interface, so simply find it. An interface is a way of defining custom types in TypeScript, which we will cover in the next chapter. Just remember that, by actively trying to define what an object's type should be, we are building strongly typed code, and therefore, protecting ourselves from future coding errors and bugs.

# Enums

Enums are a special type borrowed from other languages such as C#, C++, and Java, and provides a solution to the problem of special numbers. An enum associates a human-readable name for a specific number. Consider the following code:

```
enum DoorState {
  Open,
  Closed,
  Ajar
}
```

Here, we have defined an enum called `DoorState` to represent the state of a door. Valid values for this door state are `Open`, `Closed`, or `Ajar`. Under the hood (in the generated JavaScript), TypeScript will assign a numeric value to each of these human-readable enum values. In this example, the `DoorState.Open` enum value will equate to a numeric value of `0`. Likewise, the enum value `DoorState.Closed` will equate to the numeric value of `1`, and the `DoorState.Ajar` enum value will equate to `2`. Let's take a quick look at how we would use these enum values:

```
var openDoor = DoorState.Open;
console.log(`openDoor is: ${openDoor}`);
```

The first line of this snippet creates a variable named `openDoor`, and sets its value to `DoorState.Open`. The second line simply logs the value of `openDoor` to the console. The output of this would be:

```
openDoor is: 0
```

This clearly shows that the TypeScript compiler has replaced the enum value of `DoorState.Open` with the numeric value `0`. Now let's use this enum in a slightly different way:

```
var closedDoor = DoorState["Closed"];
console.log(`closedDoor is : ${closedDoor}`);
```

This code snippet uses a string value of `"Closed"` to lookup the `enum` type, and assigns the resulting enum value to the `closedDoor` variable. The output of this code would be:

```
closedDoor is : 1
```

This sample clearly shows that the enum value of `DoorState.Closed` is the same as the enum value of `DoorState["Closed"]`, because both variants resolve to the numeric value of `1`. Finally, let's take a look at what happens when we reference an enum using an array type syntax:

```
var ajarDoor = DoorState[2];
console.log(`ajarDoor is : ${ajarDoor}`);
```

Here, we assign the variable `ajarDoor` to an enum value based on the second index value of the `DoorState` enum. The output of this code, though, is surprising:

```
ajarDoor is : Ajar
```

You may have been expecting the output to be simply `2`, but here we are getting the string `"Ajar"`, which is a string representation of our original enum name. This is actually a neat little trick allowing us to access a string representation of our enum value. The reason that this is possible is down to the JavaScript that has been generated by the TypeScript compiler. Let's take a look, then, at the closure that the TypeScript compiler has generated:

```
var DoorState;
(function (DoorState) {
  DoorState[DoorState["Open"] = 0] = "Open";
  DoorState[DoorState["Closed"] = 1] = "Closed";
  DoorState[DoorState["Ajar"] = 2] = "Ajar";
})(DoorState || (DoorState = {}));
```

This strange-looking syntax is building an object that has a specific internal structure. It is this internal structure that allows us to use this enum in the various ways that we have just explored. If we interrogate this structure while debugging our JavaScript, we will see that the internal structure of the `DoorState` object is as follows:

```
DoorState
{...}
[prototype]: {...}
[0]: "Open"
[1]: "Closed"
[2]: "Ajar"
[prototype]: []
Ajar: 2
Closed: 1
Open: 0
```

The `DoorState` object has a property called `"0"`, which has a string value of `"Open"`. Unfortunately, in JavaScript the number `0` is not a valid property name, so we cannot access this property by simply using `DoorState.0`. Instead, we must access this property using either `DoorState[0]` or `DoorState["0"]`. The `DoorState` object also has a property named `Open`, which is set to the numeric value `0`. The word `Open` is a valid property name in JavaScript, so we can access this property using `DoorState["Open"]`, or simply `DoorState.Open`, which equates to the same property in JavaScript.

While the underlying JavaScript can be a little confusing, all we need to remember about enums is that they are a handy way of defining an easily remembered, human-readable name to a special number. Using human-readable enums, instead of just scattering various special numbers around in our code, makes the intent of the code clearer. Using an application-wide value named `DoorState.Open` or `DoorState.Closed` is far simpler than remembering to set a value to `0` for `Open`, `1` for `Closed`, and `3` for `Ajar`. As well as making our code more readable and more maintainable, using enums also protects our code base whenever these special numeric values change because they are all defined in one place.

One last note on enums, is that we can set the numeric value manually, if required:

```
enum DoorState {
  Open = 3,
  Closed = 7,
  Ajar = 10
}
```

Here, we have overridden the default values of the enum to set `DoorState.Open` to `3`, `DoorState.Closed` to `7`, and `DoorState.Ajar` to `10`.

# Const enums

A slight variant of the enum type is the `const` enum, which simply adds the keyword `const` before the enum definition, as follows:

```
const enum DoorStateConst {
  Open,
  Closed,
  Ajar
}
var constDoorOpen = DoorStateConst.Open;
console.log(`constDoorOpen is : ${constDoorOpen}`);
```

`const` enums have been introduced largely for performance reasons, and the resultant JavaScript will not contain the full closure definition for the `DoorStateConst` enum as we saw previously. Let's take a quick look at the JavaScript that is generated from this `DoorStateConst` enum:

```
var constDoorOpen = 0 /* Open */;
```

Note how we do not have a full JavaScript closure for the `DoorStateConst` at all. The compiler has simply resolved the `DoorStateConst.Open` enum to its internal value of `0`, and removed the `const enum` definition entirely.

With `const` enums, we therefore cannot reference the internal string value of an enum, as we did in our previous code sample. If we try to reference a `const` enum using the array syntax, as follows:

```
console.log(`${DoorStateConst[0]}`);
```

We get the following error message:

```
error TS2476: A const enum member can only be accessed using a string
literal.
```

We can, however, still use the string property accessor on a `const` enum, as follows:

```
console.log(`${DoorStateConst["Open"]}`);
```

When using `const` enums, just keep in mind that the compiler will strip away all enum definitions and simply substitute the numeric value of the enum directly into our JavaScript code.

# Const values

The TypeScript language also allows us to define a variable as a constant, by using the `const` keyword. If a variable has been marked as `const`, then its value can only be set when the variable is defined, and cannot be changed afterwards. Consider the following code:

```
const constValue = "test";
constValue = "updated";
```

Here, we have defined a variable named `constValue`, and indicated that it cannot be changed by using the `const` keyword. Attempting to compile this code will result in the following compile error:

```
error TS2450: Left-hand side of assignment expression cannot be a
constant or a read-only property.
```

# The let keyword

Variables in JavaScript are defined by using the keyword `var`. The JavaScript runtime is very lenient, however, when it comes to variable definitions. If the JavaScript runtime comes across a variable that has not been previously defined or given a value, then the value for this variable will be `undefined`. Consider the following code snippet:

```
console.log(`anyValue = ${anyValue}`);
var anyValue = 2;
console.log(`anyValue = ${anyValue}`);
```

Here, we start by logging the value of a variable named `anyValue` to the console. Note, however, that the variable `anyValue` is only defined on the second line of this code snippet. In other words, we can use a variable in JavaScript before it is defined. The output of this code is as follows:

```
anyValue = undefined
anyValue = 2
```

The semantics of using the `var` keyword presents us with a small problem. Using the `var` keyword does not check to see whether the variable itself has been defined before we actually use it. This could obviously lead to unwanted behavior, as the value of an undefined or unallocated variable is always `undefined`.

TypeScript introduces the `let` keyword, which can be used in the place of the `var` keyword when defining variables. One of the advantages of using the `let` keyword is that we cannot use a variable name before it has been defined. Consider the following code:

```
console.log(`letValue = ${lValue}`);
let lValue = 2;
```

Here, we are attempting to log the value of the variable `lValue` to the console even before it has been defined, similar to how we were using the `anyValue` variable earlier. However, when using the `let` keyword instead of the `var` keyword, this code will generate an error, as follows:

```
error TS2448: Block-scoped variable 'lValue' used before its declaration.
```

Here, the TypeScript compiler generates an error if we attempt to use a variable before it is defined. To fix this code, then, we need to define our variable `lValue` before it is first used, as follows:

```
let lValue = 2;
console.log(`lValue = ${lValue}`);
```

This code will compile correctly, and output the following to the console:

```
lValue = 2
```

Another side-effect of using the `let` keyword, is that variables defined with `let` are block-scoped. This means that their value and definition are limited to the block of code that they reside in. As an example of this, consider the following code:

```
let lValue = 2;
console.log(`lValue = ${lValue}`);

if (lValue == 2) {
  let lValue = 2001;
  console.log(`block scoped lValue : ${lValue} `);
}
console.log(`lValue = ${lValue}`);
```

Here, we define the `lValue` variable on the first line using the `let` keyword, and assign a value of `2` to it. We then log the value of `lValue` to the console. On the first line within the `if` statement, note how we are redefining a variable named `lValue` to hold the value `2001`. We are then logging the value of `lValue` to the console (within the `if` statement block).

The last line of this code snippet again logs the value of the `lValue` variable to the console, but this time `lValue` is outside the `if` statement block-scope. The output of this code is as follows:

```
lValue = 2
block scoped lValue : 2001
lValue = 2
```

What these results are showing us is that `let` variables are confined to the scope in which they are defined. In other words, the `let lValue = 2001;` statement defines a new variable that will only be visible inside the `if` statement block of code. As it is a new variable, it will also not influence the value of the `lValue` variable that is outside its scope. This is why the value of `lValue` is `2` both before and after the `if` statement block, and `2001` within it.

The `let` statement, therefore, provides us with a safer way of declaring variables, and limiting their validity to the current scope.

# Functions

So far, we have seen how to add type annotations to variables, and have also seen how this syntax is easily extended to function parameters. There are, however, a few more typing rules that TypeScript uses when it comes to functions.

## Function return types

Using the very simple "syntactic sugar" TypeScript syntax, we can also define the type of a variable that a function should return. In other words, when we call a function, and it returns a value, what type should the value be treated as ?

Consider the following TypeScript code:

```
function addNumbers(a: number, b: number) : string {
  return a + b;
}
var addResult = addNumbers(2,3);
console.log(`addNumbers returned : ${addResult}`);
```

Here, we have added a `:number` type to both of the parameters of the `addNumbers` function (`a` and `b`), and we have also added a `:string` type just after the `( )` braces. Placing a type annotation after the function definition means that we are defining the return type of the entire function. In our example, then, the return type of the function `addNumbers` must be of type `string`.

Unfortunately, this code will generate an error message as follows:

```
error TS2322: Type 'number' is not assignable to type 'string'.
```

What this error message is telling us is that the return type of the `addNumbers` function must be a string. Unfortunately, the function itself is returning a number, and not a string – hence the error. Taking a closer look at the code, we note that the offending code is, in fact, `return a + b`. As `a` and `b` are numbers, we are returning the result of adding two numbers, which is of type number. To fix this code, then, we need to ensure that the function returns a string, as follows:

```
function addNumbers(a: number, b: number) : string  {
  return (a + b).toString();
}
```

This code will now compile correctly, and will output:

```
addNumbers returned : 5
```

# Anonymous functions

The JavaScript language also has the concept of anonymous functions. These are functions that are defined on the fly and don't specify a function name. Consider the following JavaScript code:

```
var addVar = function(a,b) {
  return a + b;
}

var addVarResult = addVar(2,3);
console.log("addVarResult:" + addVarResult);
```

This code snippet defines a function that has no name and adds two values. Because the function does not have a name, it is known as an anonymous function. This anonymous function is then assigned to a variable named `addVar`. The `addVar` variable can then be invoked as a function with two parameters, and the return value will be the result of executing the anonymous function. The output of this code will be:

```
addVarResult:5
```

Let's now rewrite the preceding anonymous JavaScript function in TypeScript, as follows:

```
var addFunction = function(a:number, b:number) : number {
  return a + b;
}
var addFunctionResult = addFunction(2,3);
console.log(`addFunctionResult : ${addFunctionResult}`);
```

Here, we see that TypeScript allows anonymous functions in the same way that JavaScript does, but also allows standard type annotations. The output of this TypeScript code is as follows:

```
addFunctionResult : 5
```

# Optional parameters

When we call a JavaScript function that is expecting parameters, and we do not supply these parameters, then the value of the parameter within the function will be `undefined`. As an example of this, consider the following JavaScript code:

```
var concatStrings = function(a,b,c) {
  return a + b + c;
}
var concatAbc = concatStrings("a", "b", "c");
console.log("concatAbc :" + concatAbc);

var concatAb = concatStrings("a", "b");
console.log("concatAb :" + concatAb);
```

The output of this code is as follows:

```
concatAbc :abc
concatAb :abundefined
```

Here, we have defined a function called `concatStrings` that takes three parameters, `a`, `b`, and `c`, and simply returns the sum of these values. We are then calling this function with three arguments, and assigning the result to the variable `concatAbc`. As can be seen from the output, this returns the string `"abc"`. If, however, we only supply two arguments, as seen with the usage of the variable `concatAb`, the function returns the string `"abundefined"`. In JavaScript, if we call a function and do not supply a parameter, then the missing parameter will be `undefined`, which in this case is the parameter `c`.

TypeScript introduces the question mark `?` syntax to indicate optional parameters. This allows us to mimic the JavaScript calling syntax where we can call the same function with some missing arguments. As an example of this, consider the following TypeScript code:

```
function concatStrings( a: string, b: string, c?: string) {
  return a + b + c;
}
var concat3strings = concatStrings("a", "b", "c");
console.log(`concat3strings : ${concat3strings}`);
var concat2strings = concatStrings("a", "b");
console.log(`concat2strings : ${concat2strings}`);
var concat1string = concatStrings("a");
```

This is a strongly typed version of the original `concatStrings` JavaScript function that we were using previously. Note the addition of the `?` character in the syntax for the third parameter: `c?: string`. This indicates that the third parameter is optional, and therefore, all of the above code will compile cleanly, except for the last line. The last line will generate an error:

```
error TS2081: Build: Supplied parameters do not
match any signature of call target.
```

This error is generated because we are attempting to call the `concatStrings` function with only a single parameter. Our function definition, though, requires at least two parameters, with only the third parameter being optional.

Any optional parameters must be the last parameters defined in the function definition. You can have as many optional parameters as you want, as long as non-optional parameters precede the optional parameters.

# Default parameters

A subtle variant of the optional parameter syntax allows us to specify the default value of a parameter. If an optional parameter value is not supplied, we can specify what the default value of this optional parameter should be. Let's modify our preceding function definition to use an optional parameter with a default value, as follows:

```
function concatStringsDefault(
  a: string,
  b: string,
  c: string = "c") {
    return a + b + c;
}
var defaultConcat = concatStringsDefault("a", "b");
console.log(`defaultConcat : ${defaultConcat}`);
```

This function definition has now dropped the `?` optional parameter syntax, but instead has assigned a value of `"c"` to the last parameter: `c:string = "c"`. By using default parameters, if we do not supply a value for the final parameter named `c`, the `concatStringsDefault` function will substitute the default value of `"c"` instead. The argument `c`, therefore, will not be `undefined`. The output of this code will therefore be:

```
defaultConcat : abc
```

Note that using the default parameter syntax will automatically make the parameter that has a default value optional.

# Rest parameters

The JavaScript language also allows a function to be called with a variable number of arguments. Every JavaScript function has access to a special variable, named `arguments`, that can be used to retrieve all arguments that have been passed into the function. As an example of this, consider the following JavaScript code:

```
function testArguments() {
  if (arguments.length > 0) {
    for (var i = 0; i < arguments.length; i++ ) {
      console.log("argument[" + i + "] = " + arguments[i]);
    }
  }
}
testArguments(1,2,3);
```

```
testArguments("firstArg");
```

Here, we have defined a function, named `testArguments`, which does not have any named parameters. Note, though, that we can use the special variable, named `arguments`, to test whether the function was called with any arguments. In our sample, we simply loop through the `arguments` array, and log the value of each argument to the console, by using an array index – `arguments[i]`. The output of this code is as follows:

```
argument[0] = 1
argument[1] = 2
argument[2] = 3
argument[0] = firstArg
```

In order to express the equivalent function definition in TypeScript, we will need to use a syntax that is known as the rest parameter syntax. Rest parameters use the TypeScript syntax of three dots (`...`) in the function declaration to express a variable number of function parameters. Here is the equivalent `testArguments` function, expressed in TypeScript:

```
function testArguments(... argArray: number []) {
  if (argArray.length > 0) {
    for (var i = 0; i < argArray.length; i++) {
      console.log(`argArray[${i}] = ${argArray[i]}`);
      // use JavaScript arguments variable
      console.log(`arguments[${i}] = ${arguments[i]}`)
    }
  }
}

testArguments(9);
testArguments(1,2,3);
```

Note the use of the `...argArray: number[]` syntax for our `testArguments` function parameters. This syntax is telling the TypeScript compiler that the function can accept any number of arguments. We can therefore call this function, as seen in the last two lines of the preceding code, with any number of arguments. There are also two `console.log` statements in this `for` loop. The first uses `argArray[i]`, and the second uses the standard JavaScript arguments variable, `arguments[i]`.

The output of this code is as follows:

```
argArray[0] = 9
arguments[0] = 9
argArray[0] = 1
arguments[0] = 1
argArray[1] = 2
```

```
arguments[1] = 2
argArray[2] = 3
arguments[2] = 3
```

The subtle difference between using `argArray` and `arguments` is the inferred type of the argument. Since we have explicitly specified that `argArray` is of type `number`, TypeScript will treat any item of the `argArray` array as a number. However, the internal `arguments` array does not have an inferred type, and so will be treated as the `any` type.

We can also combine normal parameters along with rest parameters in a function definition, as long as the rest parameters are the last to be defined in the parameter list, as follows:

```
function testNormalAndRestArguments(
  arg1: string,
  arg2, number,
  ...argArray: number[]
) {
}
```

Here, we have two normal parameters named `arg1` and `arg2` and then an `argArray` rest parameter. Mistakenly placing the rest parameter at the beginning of the parameter list will generate a compile error.

# Function callbacks

One of the most powerful features of JavaScript – and in fact the technology that Node was built on – is the concept of callback functions. A callback function is a function that is passed into another function, and is then generally invoked inside the function. Remember that JavaScript is not strongly typed, so we can declare a variable to be either a value, or a function. Therefore, just as we can pass a value into a function, we can also pass a function into a function.

This is best illustrated by taking a look at some sample JavaScript code:

```
var callbackFunction = function(text) {
  console.log('inside callbackFunction ' + text);
}
function doSomethingWithACallback( initialText, callback ) {
  console.log('inside doSomethingWithCallback ' + initialText);
  callback(initialText);
}

doSomethingWithACallback('myText', callbackFunction);
```

Here, we start with a variable named `callbackFunction`, which is a function that takes a single parameter. This `callbackFunction` simply logs the `text` argument to the console. We then define a function named `doSomethingWithACallback` that takes two parameters – `initialText` and `callback`. The first line of this function simply logs `"inside doSomethingWithACallback"` to the console. The second line of the `doSomethingWithACallback` is the interesting bit. It assumes that the `callback` argument is in fact a `function`, and invokes it, passing in the `initialText` variable. If we run this code, we will get two messages logged to the console, as follows:

```
inside doSomethingWithCallback myText
inside callbackFunction myText
```

But what happens if we do not pass a function as a callback? There is nothing in the above code that signals to us that the second parameter of `doSomethingWithACallback` must be a function. If we inadvertently called the `doSomethingWithACallback` function with two strings, as shown below:

```
doSomethingWithACallback('myText', 'anotherText');
```

We would get a JavaScript runtime error:

```
TypeError: callback is not a function
```

Defensively minded programmers, however, would first check whether the `callback` parameter was in fact a function before invoking it, as follows:

```
function doSomethingWithACallback( initialText, callback ) {
  console.log('inside doSomethingWithCallback ' + initialText);
  if (typeof callback === "function") {
    callback(initialText);
  } else {
      console.log(initialText + ' is not a function !!')
    }
}
doSomethingWithACallback('myText', 'anotherText');
```

Note the third line of this code snippet, where we check the type of the `callback` variable before invoking it. If it is not a function, we then log a message to the console. The output of the code snippet would be:

```
inside doSomethingWithCallback myText
anotherText is not a function !!
```

JavaScript programmers, therefore, need to be careful when working with callbacks. Firstly, they need to code around the invalid use of callback functions, and secondly, they need to document and understand which parameters are, in fact, callbacks.

What if we could document our JavaScript callback functions in our code, and then warn users when they are not passing a function when one is expected?

# Function signatures

The TypeScript "syntactic sugar" that enforces strong typing on normal variables, can also be used with callback functions. In order to do this, TypeScript introduces a new syntax, named the fat arrow syntax, `() =>`. When the fat arrow syntax is used, it means that one of the parameters to a function needs to be another function. Let's take a closer look at what this means. We will rewrite our previous JavaScript callback sample in TypeScript, as follows:

```
function callbackFunction(text: string) {
  console.log(`inside callbackFunction ${text}`);
}
```

We start with the initial callback function, which takes a single text parameter and logs a message to the console when this function is called. We can then define the `doSomethingWithACallback` function, as follows:

```
function doSomethingWithACallback(
  initialText: string,
  callback : (initialText: string) => void
) {
  console.log(`inside doSomethingWithCallback ${initialText}`);
  callback(initialText);
}
```

Here, we have defined our `doSomethingWithACallback` function with two parameters. The first parameter is `initialText`, and is of type string. The second parameter is named `callback`, and now uses the fat arrow syntax. Let's take a look at this syntax in a little more detail:

```
callback: (initialText: string) => void
```

The `callback` argument used here is typed (by the : syntax) to be a function, by using the fat arrow syntax `() =>`. Additionally, this function takes a parameter named `initialText` that is of type `string`. To the right of the fat arrow syntax, we can see a new TypeScript basic type, called `void`. Void is a keyword to denote that a function does not return a value.

So, the `doSomethingWithACallback` function will only accept, as its second argument, a function that takes a single string parameter and returns void.

We can then use this function as follows:

```
doSomethingWithACallback("myText", callbackFunction);
```

This code snippet is the same as was used in our JavaScript sample earlier. TypeScript will check the type of the `callbackFunction` parameter that was passed in, and ensure that it is, in fact, a function that accepts a single string as an argument and does not return anything. If we try to invoke this `doSomethingWithACallback` incorrectly:

```
doSomethingWithACallback("myText", "this is not a function");
```

The compiler will generate the following message:

```
error TS2345: Argument of type 'string' is not assignable
to parameter of type '(initialText: string) => void'.
```

This error message is clearly stating that the second argument, that is, `"this is not a function"`, is of type string, where a parameter that is a function of type `(initialText: string) => void` is expected.

Given this function signature for the callback parameter, the following code would also generate compile-time errors:

```
function callbackFunctionWithNumber(arg1: number) {
  console.log(`inside callbackFunctionWithNumber ${arg1}`)
}
doSomethingWithACallback("myText", callbackFunctionWithNumber);
```

Here, we are defining a function named `callBackFunctionWithNumber`, which takes a number as its only parameter. When we attempt to compile this code, we will get an error message indicating that the `callback` parameter, which is now our `callBackFunctionWithNumber` function, also does not have the correct function signature, as follows:

```
error TS2345: Argument of type '(arg1: number) => void' is not
assignable to parameter of type '(initialText: string) => void'.
```

This error message is clearly stating that a parameter of type `(initialText: string) => void` is expected, but an argument of type `(arg1: number) => void` was used instead.

> In function signatures, the parameter name (`arg1` or `initialText`) does not need to be the same. Only the number of parameters, their types, and the return type of the function need to be the same.

This is a very powerful feature of TypeScript – defining in code what the signatures of functions should be, and warning users when they do not call a function with the correct parameters. As we saw in our introduction to TypeScript, this is most significant when we are working with third-party libraries. Before we are able to use third-party functions, classes, or objects in TypeScript, we need to define what their function signatures are. These function definitions are put into a special type of TypeScript file, called a declaration file, and saved with a `.d.ts` extension. We will take an in-depth look at declaration files in `Chapter 4`, *Decorators, Generics, and Asynchronous Features*.

# Function overloads

As JavaScript is a dynamic language, we can often call the same function with different argument types. Consider the following JavaScript code:

```
function add(x,y) {
  return x + y;
}

console.log('add(1,1)=' + add(1,1));
console.log('add("1","1")=' + add("1","1"));
```

Here, we are defining a simple `add` function that returns the sum of its two parameters, `x` and `y`. The last two lines of the preceding code snippet simply log the result of the `add` function with different types – two numbers and two strings. If we run the preceding code, we will see the following output:

```
add(1,1)=2
add("1","1")=11
```

In order to reproduce this ability to call the same function with different types, TypeScript introduces a specific syntax, called function overloads. If we were to replicate the above code in TypeScript, we would need to use this function overload syntax, as follows:

```
function add(a: string, b: string) : string;
function add(a: number, b:number) : number;
function add(a: any, b: any): any {
  return a + b;
}

console.log(`add(1,1)= ${add(1,1)}`);
console.log(`add("1","1")= ${add("1","1")}`);
```

Here, we specify a function overload signature for the `add` function that accepts two strings and returns a `string`. We then specify a second function overload that uses the same function name but uses numbers as parameters. These two function overloads are then followed by the actual body of the function. The last two lines of this snippet are calling the `add` function, firstly with two numbers, and then with two strings. The output of this code is as follows:

```
add(1,1)= 2
add("1","1")= 11
```

There are three points of interest in the previous code snippet. Firstly, none of the function signatures on the first two lines of the snippet actually have a function body. Secondly, the final function definition uses the type specifier of `any` and eventually includes the function body. To overload functions in this way, we must follow this convention, and the final function signature (that including the body of the function) must use the `any` type specifier, as anything else will generate compile-time errors.

The last point to note is that, even though the final function body uses the type of `any`, this signature is essentially hidden by using this convention. We are actually limiting the `add` function to only accepting either two strings, or two numbers. If we called the function with two `boolean` values, as follows:

```
console.log(`add(true,false)= ${add(true,false)}`);
```

TypeScript would generate compile errors:

```
error TS2345: Argument of type 'boolean' is not
assignable to parameter of type 'number'.
```

# Advanced types

TypeScript also has some advanced language features that can be used when working with basic types and objects. In this section of the chapter, we will take a quick look at these advanced type features, including:

- Union types
- Type guards
- Type aliases
- Null and undefined
- Object rest and spread

# Union types

TypeScript allows us to express a type as the combination of two or more other types. This technique is known as union types, and uses the pipe symbol (|). Consider the following TypeScript code:

```
var unionType : string | number;

unionType = 1;
console.log(`unionType : ${unionType}`);

unionType = "test";
console.log(`unionType : ${unionType}`);
```

Here, we have defined a variable named `unionType`, which uses the union type syntax to denote that it can hold either a `string` or a `number`. We are then assigning a number to this variable, and logging its value to the console. We then assign a string to this variable, and again log its value to the console. This code snippet will output the following:

```
unionType : 1
unionType : test
```

# Type guards

When working with union types, the compiler will still apply its strong typing rules to ensure that we are not mixing and matching our types. As an example of this, consider the following code:

```
function addWithUnion(
  arg1 : string | number,
  arg2 : string | number
) {
    return arg1 + arg2;
}
```

Here, we are defining a function named `addWithUnion`, which accepts two parameters, and returns their sum. The `arg1` and `arg2` arguments are union types, and can therefore be either a `string` or a `number`. Compiling this code, however, will generate the following error:

```
error TS2365: Operator '+' cannot be applied to
types 'string | number' and 'string | number'.
```

What the compiler is telling us here is that within the body of the function it cannot tell what type `arg1` is. Is it a string, or is it a number?

This is where type guards come in. A type guard is an expression that performs a check on our type, and then guarantees that type within its scope. Consider the following code:

```
function addWithTypeGuard(
  arg1 : string | number,
  arg2 : string | number
) : string | number {
  if( typeof arg1 ==="string") {
    // arg1 is treated as string within this code
    console.log('first argument is a string');
    return arg1 + arg2;
  }
  if (typeof arg1 === "number" && typeof arg2 === "number") {
    // arg1 and arg2 are treated as numbers within this code
    console.log('both arguments are numbers');
    return arg1 + arg2;
  }
  console.log('default return');
  return arg1.toString() + arg2.toString();
}
```

Here, we have a function named `addWithTypeGuard` that takes two arguments, and is using our union type syntax to indicate that `arg1` and `arg2` can be either a `string` or a `number`.

Within the body of the code, we have two `if` statements. The first `if` statement checks to see if the type of `arg1` is a string. If it is a string, then the type of `arg1` is treated as a string within the body of the `if` statement. The second `if` statement checks to see if both `arg1` and `arg2` are of type `number`. Within the body of this second `if` statement, both `arg1` and `arg2` are treated as numbers. These two `if` statements are our type guards.

Note that our final return statement is calling the `toString` function on `arg1` and `arg2`. All basic JavaScript types have a `toString` function by default, so we are, in effect, treating both arguments as strings, and returning the result. Let's take a look at what happens when we call this function with different combinations of types:

```
console.log(`addWithTypeGuard(1,2)= ${addWithTypeGuard(1,2)}`) ;
```

Here, we are calling the function with two numbers, and receive the following output:

```
both arguments are numbers
addWithTypeGuard(1,2)= 3
```

This shows that the code has satisfied our second `if` statement. If we call the function with two strings:

```
console.log(`addWithTypeGuard("1","2")= ${addWithTypeGuard("1","2")}`)
```

We can see here that the first `if` statement is being satisfied:

```
first argument is a string
addWithTypeGuard("1","2")= 12
```

Lastly, when we call the function with a number and a string:

```
console.log(`addWithTypeGuard(1,"2") =
  ${addWithTypeGuard(1,"2")}`) ;
```

In this case, both of our type guard statements return false, and so our default return code is being hit:

```
default return
addWithTypeGuard(1,"2")= 12
```

Type guards, therefore, allow you to check the type of a variable within your code, and then guarantee that the variable is of the type you expect within your block of code.

# Type aliases

Sometimes, when using union types, it can be difficult to remember what types are allowed. To cater for this, TypeScript introduces the concept of a type alias, where we can create a special named type for a type union. A type alias is, therefore, a convenient naming convention for union types. Type aliases can be used wherever normal types are used, and are denoted by the `type` keyword. We can, therefore, simplify our code as follows:

```
type StringOrNumber = string | number;

function addWithAlias(
  arg1 : StringOrNumber,
  arg2 : StringOrNumber
) {
    return arg1.toString() + arg2.toString();
}
```

Here, we have defined a type alias, named `StringOrNumber`, which is a union type that can be either a string or a number. We are then using this type alias in our function signature, to allow both `arg1` and `arg2` to be either a string or a number.

Type aliases can also be used for function signatures, as follows:

```
type CallbackWithString = (string) => void;

function usingCallbackWithString(
  callback: CallbackWithString) {
    callback("this is a string");
  }
```

Here, we have defined a type alias, named `CallbackWithString`, which is a function that takes a single `string` parameter and returns a `void`. Our `usingCallbackWithString` function accepts this type alias (which is a function signature) as its `callback` argument type.

When we need to use union types often within our code, type aliases provide an easier and more intuitive way of declaring named union types.

# Null and undefined

In JavaScript, if a variable has been declared, but not assigned a value, then querying its value will return `undefined`. JavaScript also includes the keyword `null`, in order to distinguish between cases where a variable is known, but has no value (`null`), and where it has not been defined in the current scope (`undefined`). Consider the following JavaScript code:

```
function testUndef(test) {
  console.log('test parameter :' + test);
}

testUndef();
testUndef(null);
```

Here, we have defined a function named `testUndef`, which takes a single argument named `test`. Within this function, we are simply logging the value to the console. We then call it in two different ways.

The first call to the `testUndef` function does not have any arguments. This is, in effect, calling the function without knowing, or without caring, what arguments it needs. JavaScript allows this sort of function-calling syntax. In this case, the value of the `test` argument within the `testUndef` function will be `undefined`, and the output will be:

```
test parameter :undefined
```

The second call to the `testUndef` function passes `null` as the first argument. This is basically saying that we are aware that the function needs an argument, but we choose to call it without a value. The output of this function call will be:

```
test parameter :null
```

TypeScript has included two keywords for these cases, named `null` and `undefined`. Let's re-write this function in TypeScript, as follows:

```
function testUndef(test : null | number) {
  console.log('test parameter :' + test);
}
```

Here, we have defined the `testUndef` function to allow for the function to be called with either a `number` value, or a null value. If we try to call this function in TypeScript without any arguments, as we did in JavaScript:

```
testUndef();
```

TypeScript will generate an error:

```
error TS2346: Supplied parameters do not
match any signature of call target.
```

Clearly, the TypeScript compiler is ensuring that we call the `testUndef` function with either a `number`, or `null`. It will not allow us to call it without any arguments.

This ability to specify that a function can be called with a `null` value allows us to ensure that the correct use of our function is known at compile time.

Similarly, we can define an object to allow `undefined` values, as follows:

```
let x : number | undefined;

x = 1;
x = undefined;
x = null;
```

Here, we have defined a variable named `x`, which is allowed to hold either a `number` or `undefined`. We then attempt to assign the values `1`, `undefined`, and `null` to this variable. Compiling this code will result in the following TypeScript error:

```
error TS2322: Type 'null' is not assignable to type 'number | undefined'.
```

The TypeScript compiler, therefore, is protecting our code, to make sure that the variable x can only hold either a number or undefined, but does not allow it to hold a null value.

# Object rest and spread

When working with basic JavaScript objects, we often need to copy the properties of one object to another, or do some mixing and matching of properties from various objects. In order to facilitate these requirements, TypeScript has adopted the ES7 proposal and language syntax, which is called object rest and spread. Consider the following TypeScript code:

```
let firstObj = { id: 1, name : "firstObj"};

let secondObj = { ...firstObj };
console.log(`secondObj.id : ${secondObj.id}`);
console.log(`secondObj.name : ${secondObj.name}`);
```

Here, we start by defining a simple JavaScript object named firstObj, that has an id and a name property. We then use the new ES7 syntax to copy all of the properties of firstObj into another object called secondObj, by specifying { ...firstObj }. To test that this has indeed copied all properties, we then log the values of secondObj.id and secondObj.name to the console. The output of this code is as follows:

```
secondObj.id : 1
secondObj.name : firstObj
```

Here, we can see that the values of the id and name properties have been copied from firstObj into secondObj, using the rest and spread ES7 syntax.

We can also use this syntax to combine multiple objects together, as follows:

```
let nameObj = { name : "nameObj"};
let idObj = { id : 2};

let obj3 = { ...nameObj, ...idObj };
console.log(`obj3.id : ${obj3.id}`);
console.log(`obj3.name : ${obj3.name}`);
```

Here, we have an object named `nameObj`, which defines a single property named `name`. We then define a second object named `idObj`, which also defines a single property named `id`. Note then how we create `obj3`, with the syntax `{ ...nameObj, ...idObj }`. This syntax means that we intend to copy all properties from `nameObj`, and all properties from `idObj`, into a new object named `obj3`. The result of this code is as follows:

```
obj3.id : 2
obj3.name : nameObj
```

This shows us that both object's properties have been merged into a single object.

> The rest and spread syntax to copy properties will apply these properties incrementally. In other words, if two objects both have a property with the same name, then the object property that was specified last will take precedence.

# Summary

In this chapter, we took a look at TypeScript's basic types, variables, and function techniques. We saw how TypeScript introduces "syntactic sugar" on top of normal JavaScript code, to ensure strongly typed variables and function signatures. We also saw how TypeScript uses duck typing and explicit casting, and finished up with a discussion on TypeScript functions, function signatures, and overloading. In the next chapter, we will build on this knowledge and see how TypeScript extends these strongly typed rules into object-oriented concepts such as interfaces, classes, and inheritance.

# 3

# Interfaces, Classes, and Inheritance

We have already seen how TypeScript uses basic types, inferred types, and function signatures to bring a strongly typed development experience to JavaScript. TypeScript also introduces object-oriented features that are similar to other languages, including interfaces, classes, and inheritance. These object-oriented language constructs are part of the ECMAScript 6 standard, and as such will be included in future versions of JavaScript. TypeScript allows us, therefore, to use these new object-oriented features from upcoming JavaScript versions in our code base. In this chapter, we will look at these object-oriented concepts, how they are used in TypeScript, and what benefits they bring to the JavaScript development experience.

Note that the TypeScript compiler will take care of generating compatible ECMAScript 3 or ECMAScript 5 JavaScript code when we use these language features. In this way, TypeScript programmers have the benefit of using these advanced object-oriented techniques in their code today.

This chapter is broken up into two main sections. The first section of this chapter is intended for readers using TypeScript for the first time, and covers interfaces, classes, and inheritance from the ground up. The second section of this chapter builds on this knowledge, and shows how to create and use classes, interfaces, and inheritance by building a sample **Factory Design Pattern**.

If you have experience with TypeScript, are actively using interfaces and classes, and understand inheritance, then you may be more interested in the later sections of the chapter, where we discuss the Factory Design Pattern, and abstract classes.

This chapter will cover the following topics:

- Interfaces
- Classes
- Class constructors
- Class modifiers
- Static functions and properties
- Inheritance
- Abstract classes
- JavaScript closures
- The Factory Design Pattern

# Interfaces

An interface provides us with a mechanism to define what properties and methods an object must implement, and is, therefore, a way of defining a custom type. We have already explored the TypeScript syntax for strongly typing a variable to one of the basic types, such as string or number. Using this syntax, we can also strongly type a variable to be of an interface type. This means that the variable must have the same properties as described in the interface. If an object adheres to an interface, it is said that the object implements the interface. Interfaces are defined by using the `interface` keyword.

Consider the following TypeScript code:

```
interface IComplexType {
  id: number;
  name: string;
}
```

We start with an interface named `IComplexType`, which has an `id` and a `name` property. The `id` property is strongly typed to be of type `number`, and the `name` property is of type `string`. This interface definition can then be applied to a variable, as follows:

```
let complexType : IComplexType;
complexType = { id: 1, name : "test" };
```

Here, we have defined a variable named `complexType`, and have strongly typed it to be of type `IComplexType`. We are then creating an object instance, and assigning values to the object's properties. Note that the `IComplexType` interface defines both an `id` and a `name` property, and as such, both must be present. If we attempt to create an instance of the object without both of these properties, as follows:

```
let incompleteType : IComplexType;
incompleteType = { id : 1};
```

TypeScript will generate the following error:

```
error TS2322: Type '{ id: number; }' is not assignable to type
'IComplexType'.
Property 'name' is missing in type '{ id: number; }'.
```

# Optional properties

Interface definitions may also include optional properties, similar to the way that functions may have optional properties. Consider the following interface definition:

```
interface IOptionalProp {
  id: number;
  name?: string;
}
```

Here, we have defined an interface named `IOptionalProp`, which has an `id` property of type number, and an optional property called `name` that is of type string. Note how the syntax for optional properties is similar to what we have seen for optional parameters in function definitions. In other words, the `?` character after the `name` property is used to specify that this property is optional. We can therefore use this interface definition, as follows:

```
let idOnly : IOptionalProp = { id: 1 };
let idAndName : IOptionalProp = { id: 2, name : "idAndName" };

idAndName = idOnly;
```

Here we have two variables, both of which are implementing the `IOptionalProp` interface. The first variable, named `idOnly` is just specifying the `id` property. This is valid TypeScript, as we have marked the `name` property of the `IOptionalProp` interface as optional. The second variable is called `idAndName`, and is specifying both the `id` and `name` properties.

Note the last line of this code snippet. Because both variables are implementing the `IOptionalProp` interface, we are able to assign them to each other. Without using an interface definition that has optional properties, this code would normally have caused an error.

If you are using an editor that has support for TypeScript, you should start to see some auto-complete, or Intellisense options popping up as you work with interfaces. This is because your editor is using TypeScript's language service to automatically pick up what type you are working with, and what properties and functions are available, as follows:

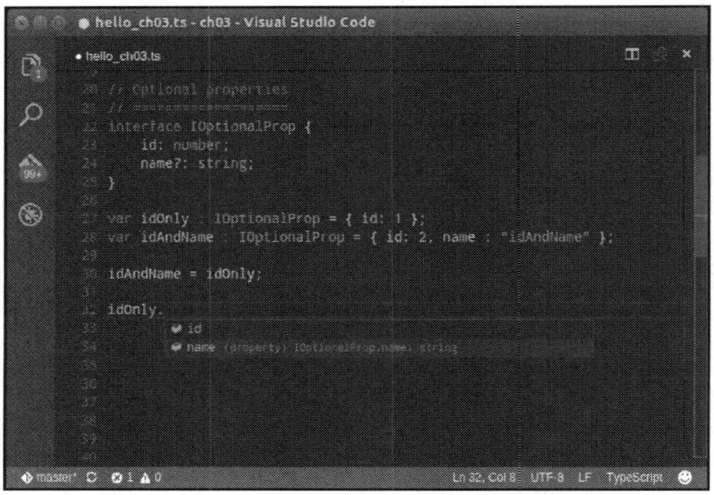


Visual Studio Code showing Intellisense options for an interface

# Interface compilation

Interfaces are a compile-time language feature of TypeScript, and the compiler does not generate any JavaScript code from interfaces that you include in your TypeScript projects. Interfaces are only used by the compiler for type checking during the compilation step.

> In this book, we will be sticking to a simple naming convention for interfaces, which is to prefix the interface name with the letter `I`. Using this naming scheme helps when dealing with large projects where code is spread across multiple files. Seeing anything prefixed with `I` in your code helps you distinguish it as an interface immediately. You can, however, call your interfaces anything.

# Classes

A class is a definition of an object, what data it holds, and what operations it can perform. Classes and interfaces form the cornerstone of the principles of object-oriented programming, and often work together in design patterns. A design pattern is a way of using classes and interfaces in a certain way to help tackle common programming problems. More on design patterns later.

Let's take a look at a simple class definition:

```
class SimpleClass {
  id: number;
  print() : void {
    console.log(`SimpleClass.print() called`);
  }
}
```

Here, we have used the `class` keyword to define a class named `SimpleClass`, and we have defined this class to have a property named `id`, and a `print` function. The `print` function simply logs a message to the console. We can then use this class, as follows:

```
let mySimpleClass = new SimpleClass();
mySimpleClass.print();
```

This code snippet shows how to create an instance of a class. We first define a variable to hold the class instance, and then create the class using the `new` keyword. This code snippet will output the following:

```
SimpleClass.print() called
```

# Class properties

In order to access the properties of a class from within a class itself, we need to use the `this` keyword. As an example of this, let's update our `SimpleClass` definition, and print out the value of the `id` property within the `print` function, as follows:

```
class SimpleClass {
  id: number;
  print() : void {
    console.log(`SimpleClass has id : ${this.id}`);
  }
}
```

Our `print` function is now referencing the `id` property of the class instance within the template string, `${ this.id }`. Whenever we are inside a class instance, we must use the `this` keyword in order to access any property or function available on the class definition. We can now set the `id` property of the class instance, and call the updated `print` function, as follows:

```
let mySimpleClass = new SimpleClass();
mySimpleClass.id = 1001;
mySimpleClass.print();
```

Here, we are creating our class instance as before, and are then setting the `id` property of the class instance to `1001`. The output of this code will be as follows:

```
SimpleClass has id : 1001
```

# Implementing interfaces

Before we continue, let's take a look at the relationship between classes and interfaces. A class is a definition of an object, including its properties and functions. An interface is the definition of a custom type, also including its properties and functions. The only real difference is that classes must implement functions and properties, whereas interfaces only describe them. This allows us to use interfaces to describe some common behaviors of a group of classes, and then write code that will work with any one of these classes. Consider the following class definitions:

```
class ClassA {
  print() {
    console.log('ClassA.print()')
  };
}

class ClassB {
  print() {
    console.log(`ClassB.print()`)
  };
}
```

Here we have class definitions for two classes, `ClassA` and `ClassB`. Both of these classes just have a `print` function. Suppose that we wanted to write some code that did not really care what type of class we used; all it cares about is whether the class has a `print` function. Instead of writing a complex class that needs to deal with instances of both `ClassA` and `ClassB`, we can easily create an interface describing the behavior we need, as follows:

```
interface IPrint {
  print();
}

function printClass( a : IPrint ) {
  a.print();
}
```

Here, we have created an interface named `IPrint` to describe the attributes of an object that we need within the `printClass` function. This interface has a single function named `print`. Therefore, any variable that is passed in as an argument to the `printClass` function must itself have a function named `print`.

We can now modify our class definitions to ensure that they can both be used by the `printClass` function, as follows:

```
class ClassA implements IPrint {
  print() { console.log('ClassA.print()') };
}

class ClassB implements IPrint {
  print() { console.log(`ClassB.print()`)};
}
```

Our class definitions now use the `implements` keyword to implement the `IPrint` interface. This allows us to use both classes within the `printClass` function, as follows:

```
let classA = new ClassA();
let classB = new ClassB();

printClass(classA);
printClass(classB);
```

Here, we are creating instances of `ClassA` and `ClassB`, and then calling the same `printClass` function with both instances. Because the `printClass` function is written to accept any object that implements the `IPrint` interface, it will work correctly with both class types.

Interfaces, therefore, are a way of describing class behavior. Interfaces can also be seen as a type of contract that classes must implement, if they are expected to provide certain behaviors.

# Class constructors

Classes can accept parameters during their initial construction. This allows us to combine the creation of a class and setting its parameters into a single line of code. Consider the following class definition:

```
class ClassWithConstructor {
  id: number;
  name: string;
  constructor(_id: number, _name: string) {
    this.id = _id;
    this.name = _name;
  }
}
```

Here, the `ClassWithConstructor` class has two properties, an `id` property of type number, and a `name` property of type string. It also has a `constructor` function that accepts two parameters. The constructor function is assigning the value of the `_id` argument to the class property of `id`, and the value of the `_name` argument to the class property `name`. We can then construct an instance of this class, as follows:

```
var classWithConstructor = new ClassWithConstructor(1, "name");

console.log(`classWithConstructor.id =
  ${classWithConstructor.id}`);
console.log(`classWithConstructor.name =
  ${classWithConstructor.name}`);
```

The first line of this code creates an instance of the `ClassWithConstructor` class, using the constructor function. We are then simply logging the `id` and `name` properties to the console. The output of this code is:

```
classWithConstructor.id = 1
classWithConstructor.name = name
```

# Class functions

All functions within a class adhere to the syntax and rules that we covered in the previous chapter on functions. As a refresher, all class functions can:

- Be strongly typed
- Use the `any` keyword to relax strong typing
- Have optional parameters

- Have default parameters
- Use argument arrays, or the rest parameter syntax
- Allow function callbacks and specify the function callback signature
- Allow function overloads

As an example of each of these rules, let's examine a class that has a number of different function signatures, and we will then discuss each one in detail, as follows:

```
class ComplexType implements IComplexType {
  id: number;
  name: string;
  constructor(idArg: number, nameArg: string);
  constructor(idArg: string, nameArg: string);
  constructor(idArg: any, nameArg: any) {
    this.id = idArg;
    this.name = nameArg;
  }
  print(): string {
    return "id:" + this.id + " name:" + this.name;
  }
  usingTheAnyKeyword(arg1: any): any {
    this.id = arg1;
  }
  usingOptionalParameters(optionalArg1?: number) {
    if (optionalArg1) {
      this.id = optionalArg1;
    }
  }
  usingDefaultParameters(defaultArg1: number = 0) {
    this.id = defaultArg1;
  }
  usingRestSyntax(...argArray: number []) {
    if (argArray.length > 0) {
      this.id = argArray[0];
    }
  }
  usingFunctionCallbacks( callback: (id: number) => string  ) {
    callback(this.id);
  }

}
```

The first thing to note is the `constructor` function. Our class definition is using function overloading for the `constructor` function, allowing the class to be constructed using either a number and a string, or two strings. The following code shows how we would use each of these constructor definitions:

```
let ct_1 = new ComplexType(1, "ct_1");
let ct_2 = new ComplexType("abc", "ct_2");
let ct_3 = new ComplexType(true, "test");
```

The `ct_1` variable uses the number, string variant of the constructor function, and the `ct_2` variable uses the string, string variant. The `ct_3` variable will generate a compile error, as we are not allowing a constructor to use a boolean, boolean variant. You may argue, however, that the last constructor function specifies an any, any variant and this should allow for our boolean, boolean usage. Just remember that constructor overloads follow the same rules as the function overloads we discussed in `Chapter 2`, *Types, Variables, and Function Techniques*.

We must be careful when using overloaded constructors, however. Let's take a closer look at what happens when we call the string, string variant of the constructor:

```
let ct_2 = new ComplexType("abc", "ct_2");
ct_2.print();
```

Within the constructor function, we are assigning the value of the `idArg` argument to the `id` property on the class, as follows:

```
class ComplexType implements IComplexType {
  id: number;
  name: string;
  constructor(idArg: number, nameArg: string);
  constructor(idArg: string, nameArg: string);
  constructor(idArg: any, nameArg: any) {
    this.id = idArg;
    // careful - assigning a string to a number type
    this.name = nameArg;
}
```

Even though we have defined the `id` property of the class to be of type number, when we call the constructor function with a string (because we have a constructor overload), then the `id` property will actually be `"abc"`, which is clearly not a number type. TypeScript will not generate an error in this case, and will not automatically try to convert the value `"abc"` to a number. In cases where this type of functionality is required, we would need to use type guards to ensure type safety, as follows:

```
constructor(idArg: any, nameArg: any) {
  if (typeof idArg === "number") {
    this.id = idArg;
  }
  // careful - assigning a string to a number type
  this.name = nameArg;
}
```

Here, we have introduced a type guard to ensure that the `id` property (which is of type number) is only assigned if the type of the `idArg` parameter is, in fact, a number.

Let's now take a look at the rest of the function definitions that we have defined for the class, starting with the `usingTheAnyKeyword` function:

```
ct_1.usingTheAnyKeyword(true);
ct_1.usingTheAnyKeyword({ id: 1, name: "string"});
```

The first call in this sample is using a boolean value to call the `usingTheAnyKeyword` function, and the second is using an arbitrary object. Both of these function calls are valid, as the parameter `arg1` is defined with the `any` type.

Next, the `usingOptionalParameters` function:

```
ct_1.usingOptionalParameters(1);
ct_1.usingOptionalParameters();
```

Here, we are calling the `usingOptionalParameters` function firstly with a single argument, and then without any arguments. Again, these calls are valid, as the `optionalArg1` argument is marked as optional.

Now for the `usingDefaultParameters` function:

```
ct_1.usingDefaultParameters(2);
ct_1.usingDefaultParameters();
```

Both of these calls to the `usingDefaultParameters` function are valid. The first call will override the default value of `0`, and the second call–without an argument–will use the default value of `0`.

Next up is the `usingRestSyntax` function:

```
ct_1.usingRestSyntax(1,2,3);
ct_2.usingRestSyntax(1,2,3,4,5);
```

Our rest function, `usingRestSyntax`, can be called with any number of arguments, as we are using the rest parameter syntax to hold these arguments in an array. Both of these calls are valid.

Finally, let's look at the `usingFunctionCallbacks` function:

```
function myCallbackFunction(id: number): string {
  return id.toString();
}
ct_1.usingFunctionCallbacks(myCallbackFunction);
```

This snippet shows the definition of a function named `myCallbackFunction`, which matches the callback signature required by the `usingFunctionCallbacks` function. This allows us to pass in the `myCallbackFunction` as a parameter to the `usingFunctionCallbacks` function.

Note that, if you have any difficulty understanding these various function signatures, then view the relevant sections in `Chapter 2`, *Types, Variables, and Function Techniques*, regarding functions, where each of these concepts is explained in detail.

# Interface function definitions

Interfaces, like classes, follow the same rules when dealing with functions. To update our `IComplexType` interface definition to match the `ComplexType` class definition, we need to write a function definition for each of the new functions, as follows:

```
interface IComplexType {
  id: number;
  name: string;
  print(): string;
  usingTheAnyKeyword(arg1: any): any;
  usingOptionalParameters(optionalArg1?: number);
  usingDefaultParameters(defaultArg1?: number);
  usingRestSyntax(...argArray: number []);
  usingFunctionCallbacks(callback: (id: number) => string);
}
```

This interface definition includes the `id` and `name` properties and a `print` function. We then have a function signature for the `usingTheAnyKeyword` function. It looks surprisingly like our actual class function, but does not have a function body. The `usingOptionalParameters` function definition shows how to use an optional parameter within an interface. The interface definition for the `usingDefaultParameters` function, however, is slightly different from our class definition. Remember that an interface defines the shape of our class or object, and therefore cannot contain variables or values. We have therefore defined the `defaultArg1` parameter as optional, and left the assignment of the default value up to the class implementation itself. The definition of the `usingRestSyntax` function contains the rest parameter syntax, and the definition of the `usingFunctionCallbacks` function, shows how to define a callback function signature. They are pretty much identical to the class function signatures.

The only thing missing from this interface is the signature for the `constructor` function. Interfaces cannot include signatures for a constructor function.

Let's take a look at why this causes errors in our compilation step. Suppose we were to include a definition for the `constructor` function in the `IComplexType` interface:

```
interface IComplexType {
  constructor(arg1: any, arg2: any);
}
```

The TypeScript compiler would then generate an error:

```
error TS2420: Class 'ComplexType' incorrectly implements
interface 'IComplexType'.
Types of property 'constructor' are incompatible.
```

This error shows us that when we use a `constructor` function, the return type of the constructor is implicitly typed by the TypeScript compiler. Therefore, the return type of the `IComplexType` constructor would be `IComplexType`, and the return type of the `ComplexType` constructor would be `ComplexType`. Even though the `ComplexType` function implements the `IComplexType` interface, they are actually two different types. Therefore, the `constructor` signatures will always be incompatible.

# Class modifiers

As we discussed briefly in the opening chapter, TypeScript introduces the `public` and `private` access modifiers to mark class variables and functions as either `public` or `private`. Additionally, we can also use the `protected` access modifier, which we will discuss later.

A public class property can be accessed by any calling code. Consider the following code:

```
class ClassWithPublicProperty {
  public id: number;
}

let publicAccess = new ClassWithPublicProperty();
publicAccess.id = 10;
```

Here, we define a class named `ClassWithPublicProperty`, which has a single property named `id`. We then create an instance of this class, named `publicAccess`, and assign the value of `10` to the `id` property of this instance. Let's now explore how marking a property `private` will affect the access to this property, as follows:

```
class ClassWithPrivateProperty {
  private id: number;
  constructor(_id : number) {
    this.id = _id;
  }
}

let privateAccess = new ClassWithPrivateProperty(10);
privateAccess.id = 20;
```

Here, we have defined a class named `ClassWithPrivateProperty`, that has a single property named `id`, which has now been marked as `private`. This class also has a `constructor` function that takes a single argument, named `_id`, and assigns the value of this argument to the `id` property. Note that we are using the `this.id` syntax in this assignment.

We then create an instance of this class, named `privateAccess`, and then attempt to assign the value `20` to the private `id` property. This code, however, will generate the following error:

```
error TS2341: Property 'id' is private and
only accessible within class 'ClassWithPrivateProperty'.
```

As we can see from the error message, TypeScript will not allow assignment to the `id` property of this class outside the class itself, as we have marked it as `private`. Note that we are able to assign a value to the `id` property from within the class, as we have done in the constructor function.

Class functions are `public` by default. Not specifying an access modifier of `private` for either properties or functions will cause their access level to default to `public`. Classes can also mark functions and properties as `protected`, but we will cover this keyword a little later when we discuss inheritance.

# Constructor access modifiers

TypeScript also introduces a shorthand version of the constructor function, allowing you to specify parameters with access modifiers directly in the constructor. Consider the following code:

```
class classWithAutomaticProperties {
  constructor(public id: number, private name: string){
  }
}

let myAutoClass = new classWithAutomaticProperties(
  1, "className");
console.log(`myAutoClass id: ${myAutoClass.id}`);
console.log(`myAutoClass.name: ${myAutoClass.name}`);
```

This code snippet defines a class named `ClassWithAutomaticProperties`. The `constructor` function uses two arguments–an `id` of type `number`, and a `name` of type string. Notice, however, the access modifiers of `public` for `id` and `private` for `name`. This shorthand automatically creates a public `id` property on the `ClassWithAutomaticProperties` class, and a private `name` property.

This shorthand syntax is available only within the `constructor` function.

We then create a variable named `myAutoClass` and assign a new instance of the `ClassWithAutomaticProperties` class to it. Once this class is instantiated, it automatically has two properties: an `id` property of type number, which is `public`, and a `name` property of type string, which is `private`. Compiling the previous code, however, will produce a TypeScript compile error:

```
Property 'name' is private and only accessible
within class 'classWithAutomaticProperties'.
```

This error is telling us that the automatic property `name` is declared as `private`, and it is therefore unavailable to code outside the class itself.

> While this shorthand technique of creating automatic member variables is available, it can make the code more difficult to read. In the author's opinion, it is generally better to use the more verbose class definitions that do not use this shorthand technique. By not using this technique, and instead listing all of the properties at the top of the class, it becomes immediately visible to someone reading the code what variables this class uses, and whether they are `public` or `private`. Using the constructor's automatic property syntax hides these parameters somewhat, forcing developers to sometimes reread the code to understand it. Whichever syntax you choose, however, try to make it a coding standard, and use the same syntax throughout your code base.

# Readonly properties

In addition to the public, private, and protected access modifiers, we can also mark a class property as `readonly`. This means that, once the value of the property has been set, it is not able to be modified, either by the class itself, or by any users of the class. There is only one place where a `readonly` property can be set, and this is within the constructor function itself. Consider the following code:

```
class ClassWithReadOnly {
  readonly name: string;
  constructor(_name : string) {
    this.name = _name;
  }
  setReadOnly(_name: string) {
    // generates a compile error
    this.name = _name;
  }
}
```

Here, we have defined a class named `ClassWithReadOnly` that has a `name` property of type string that has been marked with the `readonly` keyword. The constructor function is setting this value. We have then defined a second function named `setReadOnly`, where we are attempting to set this `readonly` property. This code will generate the following error:

```
error TS2540: Cannot assign to 'name' because it is
a constant or a read-only property.
```

This error message is telling us that the only place where a `readonly` property can be set is in the constructor function.

# Class property accessors

ECMAScript 5 introduces the concept of property accessors. An accessor is simply a function that is called when a user of our class either sets a property, or retrieves a property. This means that we can detect when users of our class are either getting or setting a property, and this can be used as a trigger mechanism for other logic. To use accessors, we create a pair of `get` and `set` functions (with the same function name) in order to access an internal property. This concept is best understood with some code samples:

```
class ClassWithAccessors {
  private _id : number;
  get id() {
    console.log(`inside get id()`);
    return this._id;
  }
  set id(value:number) {
    console.log(`inside set id()`);
    this._id = value;
  }
}
```

This class has a private `_id` property and two functions, both called `id`. The first of these functions is prefixed by the `get` keyword. This `get` function is called when a user of our class retrieves or reads the property. In our sample, the `get` function logs a debug message to the console, and then simply returns the value of the internal `_id` property.

The second of these functions is prefixed with the `set` keyword and accepts a `value` parameter. This `set` function will be called when a user of our class assigns a value, or sets the property. In our sample, we simply log a message to the console, and then set the internal `_id` property. Note that the internal `_id` property is private, and as such cannot be accessed outside the class itself.

We can now use this class, as follows:

```
var classWithAccessors = new ClassWithAccessors();
classWithAccessors.id = 2;
console.log(`id property is set to ${classWithAccessors.id}`);
```

Here, we have created an instance of this class, and named it `classWithAccessors`. Note how we are not using the two separate functions named `get` and `set`. We are simply using them as a single `id` property.

When we assign a value to this property, the ECMAScript 5 runtime will call the `set id(value)` function, and when we retrieve this property, the runtime will call the `get id()` function. The output of this code is as follows:

```
inside set id()
inside get id()
id property is set to 2
```

Using getter and setter functions allows us to hook in to class properties, and execute code when these class properties are accessed.

This feature is only available when using ECMAScript 5 and above. Be aware that some browsers do not support ECMAScript 5 (such as Internet Explorer 8), and will cause JavaScript runtime errors when attempting to use class accessors.

# Static functions

Static functions are functions that can be called on a class without having to create an instance of the class first. These functions are almost global in their nature, but must be called by prefixing the function name with the class name. Consider the following class definition:

```
class StaticClass {
  static printTwo() {
    console.log(`2`);
  }
}

StaticClass.printTwo();
```

This class definition includes a single function, named `printTwo`, which is marked as `static`. As we can see from the last line of the code, we can call this function without newing up an instance of the `StaticClass` class. We can just call the function directly, as long as we prefix it with the class name.

# Static properties

Similar to static functions, classes can also have static properties. If a property of a class is marked as static, then each instance of this class will have the same value for the property. In other words, all instances of the same class will share the static property. Consider the following code:

```
class StaticProperty {
  static count = 0;
  updateCount() {
    StaticProperty.count ++;
  }
}
```

This class definition uses the `static` keyword on the class property `count`. It has a single function named `updateCount`, which increments the static `count` property. Note the syntax within the `updateCount` function. Normally, we would use the `this` keyword to access properties of a class. Here, however, we need to reference the full name of the property, including the class name, that is, `StaticProperty.count`, to access this property. This is similar to what we have seen for static functions. We can then use this class, as follows:

```
let firstInstance = new StaticProperty();

console.log(`StaticProperty.count = ${StaticProperty.count}`);
firstInstance.updateCount();
console.log(`StaticProperty.count = ${StaticProperty.count}`);

let secondInstance = new StaticProperty();
secondInstance.updateCount();
console.log(`StaticProperty.count = ${StaticProperty.count}`);
```

This code snippet starts with a new instance of the `StaticProperty` class named `firstInstance`. We are then logging the value of `StaticProperty.count` to the console. We then call the `updateCount` function on this instance of the class, and again log the value of `StaticProperty.count` to the console. We then create another instance of this class, named `secondInstance`, call the `updateCount` function, and log the value of `StaticProperty.count` to the console. This code snippet will output the following:

```
StaticProperty.count = 0
StaticProperty.count = 1
StaticProperty.count = 2
```

What this output shows us is that the static property named `StaticCount.count` is indeed shared between two instances of the same class, that is, `firstInstance` and `secondInstance`. It starts out as `0`, and is incremented when `firstInstance.updateCount` is called. When we create a second instance of the class, it also retains its original value of `1` for this class instance. When `secondInstance` updates this count, it will then also be updated for `firstInstance`.

# Namespaces

When working with large projects, and particularly when working with external libraries, there may come a time when two classes or interfaces share the same name. This will obviously cause compilation errors. TypeScript uses the concept of namespaces to cater for these situations.

Let's take a look at the syntax used for namespaces, as follows:

```
namespace FirstNameSpace {
  class NotExported {
  }
  export class NameSpaceClass {
    id: number;
  }
}
```

Here, we are defining a namespace using the `namespace` keyword, and have called this namespace `FirstNameSpace`. A namespace declaration is similar to a class declaration, in that it is scoped by the opening and closing braces, that is, `{` starts the namespace, and `}` closes the namespace. This namespace has two classes defined within it. These classes are named `NotExported`, and `NameSpaceClass`.

When using namespaces, a class definition will not be visible outside of the namespace, unless we specifically allow this using the `export` keyword. To create classes that are defined within a namespace, we must reference the class using the full namespace name. Let's take a look at how we would create instances of these classes:

```
let firstNameSpace = new FirstNameSpace.NameSpaceClass();
let notExported = new FirstNameSpace.NotExported();
```

Here, we are creating an instance of the `NameSpaceClass`, and an instance of the `NotExported` class. Note how we need to use the full namespace name in order to correctly reference these classes, that is, `new FirstNameSpace.NameSpaceClass()`. As the class `NotExported` has not used the `export` keyword, the last line of this code will generate the following error:

```
error TS2339: Property 'NotExported' does not
exist on type 'typeof FirstNameSpace'.
```

We can now introduce a second namespace, as follows:

```
namespace SecondNameSpace {
  export class NameSpaceClass {
    name: string;
  }
}

let secondNameSpace = new SecondNameSpace.NameSpaceClass();
```

This namespace also exports a class named `NameSpaceClass`. On the last line of this code snippet, we are again creating an instance of this class using the full namespace name, that is, `new SecondNameSpace.NameSpaceClass();`. Using the same class name in this instance will not cause compilation errors, as each class (prefixed by the namespace name) is seen by the compiler as a separate class name.

# Inheritance

Inheritance is another paradigm that is one of the cornerstones of object-oriented programming. Inheritance means that an object uses another object as its base type, thereby inheriting all of the base object's characteristics. In other words, all of the base object's properties and functions. Both interfaces and classes can use inheritance. An interface or class that is inherited from is known as the base interface, or base class, and the interface or class that does the inheritance is known as the derived interface, or derived class. TypeScript implements inheritance using the `extends` keyword.

# Interface inheritance

As an example of interface inheritance, consider the following TypeScript code:

```
interface IBase {
  id: number;
}

interface IDerivedFromBase extends IBase {
  name: string;
}

class InterfaceInheritanceClass implements
  IDerivedFromBase {
    id: number;
    name: string;
}
```

We start with an interface called `IBase` that defines an `id` property, of type number. Our second interface definition, `IDerivedFromBase`, extends (or inherits) from `IBase`, and therefore automatically includes the `id` property. The `IDerivedFromBase` interface then defines a `name` property, of type string. As the `IDerivedFromBase` interface inherits from `IBase`, it therefore actually has two properties–`id` and `name`. We then have a class definition, named `InterfaceInheritanceClass` which implements this `IDerivedFromBase` interface. This class must, therefore, define both an `id` and a `name` property, in order to successfully implement all of the properties of the `IDerivedFromBase` interface. Although we have only shown properties in this example, the same rules apply for functions.

# Class inheritance

Classes can also use inheritance in the same manner as interfaces. Using our definitions of the `IBase` and `IDerivedFromBase` interfaces, the following code shows an example of class inheritance:

```
class BaseClass implements IBase {
  id: number;
}

class DerivedFromBaseClass extends BaseClass
  implements IDerivedFromBase {
    name: string;
}
```

The first class, named BaseClass, implements the IBase interface, and as such, is only required to define a property of id, of type number. The second class, DerivedFromBaseClass, inherits from the BaseClass class (using the extends keyword), but also implements the IDerivedFromBase interface. As BaseClass already defines the id property required in the IDerivedFromBase interface, the only other property that the DerivedFromBaseClass class needs to implement is the name property. Therefore, we only need to include the definition of the name property in the DerivedFromBaseClass class.

TypeScript does not support the concept of multiple inheritance. Multiple inheritance means that a single class can be derived from multiple base classes. TypeScript supports only single inheritance and therefore any class can only have a single base class. A class can, however, implement multiple interfaces, as follows:

```
interface IFirstInterface {
  id : number
}
interface ISecondInterface {
  name: string;
}
class MultipleInterfaces implements
  IFirstInterface, ISecondInterface {
    id: number;
    name: string;
}
```

Here, we have defined two interfaces named IFirstInterface and ISecondInterface. We then have a class named MultipleInterfaces that implements both IFirstInterface and ISecondInterface. This means that it must implement an id property to satisfy the IFirstInterface interface, and it must implement a name property to satisfy the ISecondInterface interface.

# The super keyword

When using inheritance, both a base class and a derived class may have the same function name. This is most often seen with class constructors. If a base class has a defined constructor, then the derived class may need to call through to the base class constructor and pass through some arguments. This technique is called constructor overloading. In other words, the constructor of a derived class overloads, or supersedes, the constructor of the base class.

TypeScript includes the `super` keyword to enable calling a base class's function with the same name. Consider the following classes:

```
class BaseClassWithConstructor {
  private id: number;
  constructor(_id: number) {
    this.id = _id;
  }
}


class DerivedClassWithConstructor extends
  BaseClassWithConstructor {
    private name: string;
    constructor(_id: number, _name: string) {
      super(_id);
      this.name = _name;
    }
}
```

In this code snippet, we define a class named `BaseClassWithConstructor`, which holds a private `id` property. This class has a `constructor` function that requires an `_id` argument. Our second class, named `DerivedClassWithConstructor`, extends (or inherits from) the `BaseClassWithConstructor` class. The constructor of `DerivedClassWithConstructor` takes an `_id` argument and a `_name` argument. However, it needs to pass the incoming `_id` argument through to the base class. This is where the `super` call comes in. The `super` keyword calls the function in the base class that has the same name as the function in the derived class. The first line of the constructor function for `DerivedClassWithConstructor` shows the call using the `super` keyword, passing the `id` argument it received through to the base class constructor.

# Function overloading

The constructor of a class is, however, just a function. In the same way that we can use the `super` keyword in a constructor, we can also use the `super` keyword when a base class and its derived class use the same function name. This technique is called function overloading. In other words, the derived class has a function name that is the same name as that of a base class function, and it overloads this function definition. Consider the following code snippet:

```
class BaseClassWithFunction {
  public id : number;
  getProperties() : string {
    return `id: ${this.id}`;
  }
}

class DerivedClassWithFunction extends
  BaseClassWithFunction {
    public name: string;
    getProperties() : string {
      return `${super.getProperties()}`
      + ` , name: ${this.name}`;
    }
}
```

Here, we have defined a class named `BaseClassWithFunction`, which has a public `id` property, and a function named `getProperties`, which just returns a string representation of the properties of the class. Our `DerivedClassWithFunction` class, however, also includes a function called `getProperties`. This function is a function overload of the `getProperties` base class function. In order to call through to the base class function, we need to use the `super` keyword, as shown in the call to `super.getProperties`.

Let's take a look at how we would use these classes:

```
var derivedClassWithFunction = new DerivedClassWithFunction();
derivedClassWithFunction.id = 1;
derivedClassWithFunction.name = "derivedName";
console.log(derivedClassWithFunction.getProperties());
```

This code creates a variable named `derivedClassWithFunction`, which is an instance of the `DerivedClassWithFunction` class. It then sets both the `id` and `name` properties, and then logs to the console the result of calling the `getProperties` function. This code snippet will result in the following:

```
id: 1 , name: derivedName
```

The results show that the `getProperties` function of the `derivedClassWithFunction` variable will call through to the base class `getProperties` function, as expected.

# Protected class members

When using inheritance, it is sometimes logical to mark certain functions and properties as accessible only within the class itself, or accessible to any class that is derived from it. Using the `private` keyword, however, will not work in this instance, as a private class member is hidden even from derived classes. TypeScript introduces the `protected` keyword for these situations. Consider the following two classes:

```
class ClassUsingProtected {
  protected id : number;
  public getId() {
    return this.id;
  }
}

class DerivedFromProtected extends
  ClassUsingProtected {
    constructor() {
      super();
      this.id = 0;
  }
}
```

We start with a class named `ClassWithProtected`, which has an `id` property that is marked as `protected`, and a public function named `getId`. Our next class, `DerivedFromProtected` inherits from `ClassUsingProtected`, and has a single constructor function. Note, within this constructor function, that we are calling `this.id = 0`, in order to set the protected `id` property to `0`. Again, a derived class has access to protected member variables. Now let's try to access this `id` property outside of the class, as follows:

```
var derivedFromProtected = new DerivedFromProtected();
derivedFromProtected.id = 1;
console.log(`getId returns: ${derivedFromProtected.getId()}`);
```

Here, we create an instance of the `DerivedFromProtected` class, and attempt to assign a value to its protected `id` property. The compiler will generate the following error message:

```
error TS2445: Property 'id' is protected and only accessible
within class 'ClassUsingProtected' and its subclasses.
```

So this `id` property is acting like a private property outside of the class `ClassUsingProtected`, but still allows access to it within the class, and any class derived from it.

# Abstract classes

Another fundamental principle of object-oriented design is the concept of abstract classes. An abstract class is a definition of a class that cannot be instantiated. In other words, it is a class that is designed to be derived from. The abstract classes, sometimes referred to as abstract base classes, are often used to provide a set of basic functionality or properties that are shared amongst a group of similar classes. They are similar to interfaces in that they cannot be instantiated but they can have function implementations, which interfaces cannot.

Abstract classes are a technique that allows for code reuse amongst groups of similar objects. Consider the following two classes:

```
class Employee {
  public id: number;
  public name: string;
  printDetails() {
    console.log(`id: ${this.id}`
     + `, name ${this.name}`);
  }
}

class Manager {
  public id: number;
  public name: string;
  public Employees: Employee[];
  printDetails() {
    console.log(`id: ${this.id} `
    + `, name ${this.name}, `
    + ` employeeCount ${this.Employees.length}`);
  }
}
```

We start with a class named `Employee` that has an `id` and `name` property, as well as a function called `printDetails`. The next class is named `Manager`, and is very similar to the `Employee` class. It also has an `id` and `name` property, but has an extra property named `Employees`, which is a list of employees that this manager oversees. There is a lot of code that is common to these two classes. Both have an `id` and `name` property, and both have a `printDetails` function. Using an abstract base class for both of these classes overcomes this problem with common properties and code. Let's rewrite these two classes, and introduce the concept of an abstract base class, as follows:

```
abstract class AbstractEmployee {
  public id: number;
  public name: string;
  abstract getDetails(): string;
```

```
  public printDetails() {
    console.log(this.getDetails());
  }
}

class NewEmployee extends AbstractEmployee {
  getDetails(): string {
    return `id : ${this.id}, name : ${this.name}`;
  }
}

class NewManager extends NewEmployee {
  public Employees: NewEmployee[];
  getDetails() : string {
    return super.getDetails()
    + `, employeeCount ${this.Employees.length}`;
  }
}
```

Here, we have defined an abstract class named `AbstractEmployee`, which includes an `id` and `name` property, common to both managers and employees. We then define what is known as an abstract function name `getDetails`. Using an abstract function means that any class that derives from this abstract class must implement this function. We then define a `printDetails` function to log details of this `AbstractEmployee` to the console. Note how we are calling the abstract function `getDetails` from within the abstract class. This means that our code in the `printDetails` function will call the actual implementation of the function in the derived class.

Our second class, named `NewEmployee`, extends the `AbstractEmployee` class. As such, it must implement the `getDetails` function that has been marked as `abstract` in the base class. This `getDetails` function returns a string representation of the `NewEmployee`'s `id` and `name` property.

Next, we have a class named `NewManager` that derives from `NewEmployee`. This `NewManager` class, therefore, also has an `id` and `name` property, but has an extra property named `Employees`. Because this class already derives from `NewEmployee`, it does not necessarily need to define the function `getDetails` again. It could simply use the version of the `getDetails` function that the `NewEmployee` class provides. Note, however, that we have actually defined this `getDetails` function within the `NewManager` class. This function calls the base class `getDetails` function, via the `super` keyword, and then adds some extra information about its `Employees` property. Let's take a look at what happens when we create and use these classes, as follows:

```
var employee = new NewEmployee();
employee.id = 1;
employee.name = "Employee Name";

employee.printDetails();
```

Here, we have created an instance of the `NewEmployee` class, named `employee`, set its `id` and `name` properties, and called the `printDetails` function from the abstract class. Recall that the abstract class will then call the implementation of the `getDetails` function that we provided in the `NewEmployee` class, and therefore output the following to the console:

```
id: 1, name : Employee Name
```

Now let's use our `NewManager` class in a similar way:

```
var manager = new NewManager();
manager.id = 2;
manager.name = "Manager Name";
manager.Employees = new Array();

manager.printDetails();
```

Here, we have created an instance of the `NewManager` class, named `manager`, and set its `id` and `name` properties as before. Because this class also has an array of `Employees`, we are setting the `Employees` property to a blank array. Notice what happens, however, when we call the abstract class `printDetails` function on the last line:

```
id: 2, name : Manager Name, employeeCount 0
```

The abstract class implementation of the `printDetails` function calls the `getDetails` function of the derived class. Because the `NewManager` class also defines a `getDetails` function, the abstract class will call this function on the `NewManager` instance. The `getDetails` function on the `NewManager` instance then calls through to the base class implementation, that is, the `NewEmployee` instance of the `getDetails` function, as seen in the code `super.getDetails()`. It then appends some information about its employee count.

Using abstract classes and inheritance allows us to write our code in a cleaner and more reusable way. Abstraction, inheritance, polymorphism, and encapsulation are the foundations of good object-oriented design principles. As we have seen, the TypeScript language gives us the ability to incorporate each of these principles to help write good, clean JavaScript code.

# JavaScript closures

Before we continue with this chapter, let's take a quick look at how TypeScript implements classes in generated JavaScript through a technique called closures. As we mentioned in Chapter 1, *TypeScript – Tools and Framework Options*, a closure is a function that refers to independent variables. These variables essentially remember the environment in which they were created. Consider the following JavaScript code:

```
function TestClosure(value) {
  this._value = value;
  function printValue() {
    console.log(this._value);
  }
  return printValue;
}

var myClosure = TestClosure(12);
myClosure;
```

Here, we have a function named TestClosure, which takes a single parameter named value. The body of the function first assigns the value argument to an internal property named this._value, and then defines an inner function named printValue. The printValue function simply logs the value of the this._value to the console. The interesting bit is the last line in the TestClosure function–we are returning the printValue function.

Now take a look at the last two lines of the code snippet. We create a variable named myClosure and assign to it the result of calling the TestClosure function. Note that, because we are returning the printValue function from inside the TestClosure function, this essentially also makes the myClosure variable a function. When we execute this function on the last line of the snippet, it will execute the inner printValue function, but remember the initial value of 12 that was used when creating the myClosure variable. The output of the last line of the code will log the value of 12 to the console.

This is the essential nature of closures. A closure is a special kind of JavaScript object that combines a function with the initial environment in which it was created. In our preceding sample, since we stored whatever was passed in via the value argument into a local variable named this._value, JavaScript remembers the environment in which the closure was created, in other words, whatever was assigned to the this._value property at the time of creation will be remembered, and can be reused later.

With this in mind, let's take a look at the JavaScript that is generated by the TypeScript compiler for the `BaseClassWithConstructor` class we were just working with:

```
var BaseClassWithConstructor = (function () {
  function BaseClassWithConstructor(_id) {
    this.id = _id;
  }
  return BaseClassWithConstructor;
})();
```

Our closure starts with `function () {` on the first line, and ends with `}` on the last line. This closure first defines a function to be used as a constructor: `BaseClassWithConstructor(_id)`.

This closure is surrounded with an opening bracket, `(`, on the first line, and a closing bracket, `)`, on the last line, defining what is known as a JavaScript function expression. This function expression is then immediately executed by the last two braces, `();`. This technique of immediately executing a function is known as an **Immediately Invoked Function Expression** (**IIFE**). Our earlier IIFE is then assigned to a variable named `BaseClassWithConstructor`, making it a first-class JavaScript object, and one that can be created with the `new` keyword. This is how TypeScript implements classes in JavaScript.

The implementation of the underlying JavaScript code that TypeScript uses for class definitions is actually a well-known JavaScript pattern known as the **module** pattern.

The good news is that an in-depth knowledge of closures, how to write them, and how to use the module pattern for defining classes will all be taken care of by the TypeScript compiler, allowing us to focus on object-oriented principles without having to write JavaScript closures using this sort of boilerplate code.

# Using interfaces, classes, and inheritance – the Factory Design Pattern

To illustrate how we can use interfaces and classes in a large TypeScript project, we will take a quick look at a very well-known object-oriented design pattern–the Factory Design Pattern.

# Business requirements

As an example, let's assume that our business analyst gives us the following requirements:

1. You are required to categorize people, given their date of birth, into three different age groups—Infants, Children, and Adults.
2. Indicate with a true or false flag whether they are of a legal age to sign a contract.
3. A person is deemed to be an infant if they are less than 2 years old.
4. Infants cannot sign contracts.
5. A person is deemed to be a child if they are less than 18 years old.
6. Children cannot sign contracts either.
7. A person is deemed to be an adult if they are more than 18 years of age.
8. Only adults can sign contracts.
9. For reporting purposes, each type of person must be able to print their details. This should include the following:
    - Date of birth
    - Category of person
    - Whether they can sign contracts or not

# What the Factory Design Pattern does

The Factory Design Pattern uses a Factory class to return an instance of one of several possible classes based on the information provided to it.

The essence of this pattern is placing the decision-making logic for what type of class to create in a separate class named the Factory class. The Factory class will then return one of several classes that are all subtle variations of each other, and will do slightly different things based on their specialty. As we do not know what type of class the Factory pattern will return, we need a way to work with any variation of the different types of class returned. Sounds like the perfect scenario for an interface.

To implement our required business functionality, we will create an `Infant` class, a `Child` class, and an `Adult` class. The `Infant` and `Child` classes will return `false` when asked whether they can sign contracts, and the `Adult` class will return `true`.

## The IPerson interface

According to our requirements, the class instance that is returned by the Factory must be able to do two things–print the category of the person in the required format, and tell us whether they can sign contracts or not. Let's start by defining an enum and an interface to satisfy this requirement:

```
enum PersonCategory {
  Infant,
  Child,
  Adult
}

interface IPerson {
  Category: PersonCategory;
  canSignContracts(): boolean;
  printDetails();
}
```

We start with an enum to hold the valid values for a `PersonCategory`, that is, `Infant`, `Child`, or `Adult`. We then define an interface named `IPerson`, which holds all of the functionality that is common to each type of person. This includes their `Category`, a function named `canSignContracts` that returns either `true` or `false`, and a function to print out their details, named `printDetails`.

## The Person class

To simplify our code, we will create an abstract base class to hold all code that is common to infants, children, and adults. Again, abstract classes can never be instantiated, and as such are designed to be derived from. We will call this class `Person`, as follows:

```
abstract class Person implements IPerson {
  Category: PersonCategory;
  private DateOfBirth: Date;

  constructor(dateOfBirth: Date) {
    this.DateOfBirth = dateOfBirth;
  }
  abstract canSignContracts(): boolean
  printDetails() : void {
    console.log(`Person : `);
    console.log(`Date of Birth : `
    + `${this.DateOfBirth.toDateString()}`);
    console.log(`Category : `
    + `${PersonCategory[this.Category]}`);
```

```
      console.log(`Can sign : `
      + `${this.canSignContracts()}`);
    }
  }
```

This abstract `Person` class implements the interface `IPerson`, and as such, will need three things–A `Category` property, a `canSignContracts` function, and a `printDetails` function. In order to print the person's date of birth, we also need a `DateOfBirth` property, which we will set in our constructor function.

There are a couple of interesting things to note about this `Person` class. Firstly, the `DateOfBirth` property has been declared `private`. This means that the only class that has access to the `DateOfBirth` property is the `Person` class itself. Our requirements do not mention using the date of birth outside of the printing function, so there is no need to access or modify the date of birth once it has been set.

Secondly, the `canSignContracts` function has been marked as `abstract`. This means that any class that derives from this class is forced to implement the `canSignContracts` function, which is exactly what we wanted.

Thirdly, the `printDetails` function has been fully implemented in this abstract class. This means that a single `print` function is automatically available for any class that derives from `Person`.

## Specialist classes

Now for the three types of specialist class, all derived from the `Person` base class:

```
class Infant extends Person  {
  constructor(dateOfBirth: Date) {
    super(dateOfBirth);
    this.Category = PersonCategory.Infant;
  }
  canSignContracts(): boolean { return false; }
}

class Child extends Person  {
  constructor(dateOfBirth: Date) {
    super(dateOfBirth);
    this.Category = PersonCategory.Child;
  }
  canSignContracts(): boolean { return false; }
}
```

```
class Adult extends Person  {
  constructor(dateOfBirth: Date) {
    super(dateOfBirth);
    this.Category = PersonCategory.Adult;
  }
  canSignContracts(): boolean { return true; }
}
```

Each of these classes uses inheritance to extend the `Person` class. As the `DateOfBirth` property has been declared as `private`, and is therefore only visible to the `Person` class itself, we must pass it down to the `Person` class in each of our constructors. Each constructor also sets the `Category` property based on the class type. Finally, each class implements the abstract function `canSignContracts`.

One of the benefits of using inheritance in this way is that the definitions of the actual classes become very simple. In essence, our classes are only doing two things–setting the `Category` property correctly, and defining whether or not they can sign contracts.

## The Factory class

Let's now move on to the Factory class itself. This class has a single, well defined responsibility. Given a date of birth, figure out whether it is less than two years ago, less than 18 years ago, or more than 18 years ago. Based on these decisions, return an instance of either an `Infant`, `Child`, or `Adult` class, as follows:

```
class PersonFactory {
  getPerson(dateOfBirth: Date) : IPerson {
    let dateNow = new Date(); // defaults to now.
    let currentMonth = dateNow.getMonth() + 1;
    let currentDate = dateNow.getDate();

    let dateTwoYearsAgo = new Date(
      dateNow.getFullYear() - 2,
      currentMonth, currentDate);

    let date18YearsAgo = new Date(
      dateNow.getFullYear() - 18,
      currentMonth, currentDate);
    if (dateOfBirth >= dateTwoYearsAgo) {
      return new Infant(dateOfBirth);
    }
    if (dateOfBirth >= date18YearsAgo) {
      return new Child(dateOfBirth);
    }
    return new Adult(dateOfBirth);
```

```
        }
    }
```

The `PersonFactory` class has only one function, `getPerson`, which returns an object of type `IPerson`. The function creates a variable named `dateNow`, which is set to the current date. We then find the current month and date from the `dateNow` variable. Note that the JavaScript function `getMonth` returns `0 - 11`, and not `1 - 12`, so we are correcting this by adding `1`. This `dateNow` variable is then used to calculate two more variables, `dateTwoYearsAgo`, and `date18YearsAgo`. The decision logic then takes over, comparing the incoming `dateOfBirth` variable against these dates, and returns a new instance of a new `Infant`, `Child`, or `Adult` class.

## Using the Factory class

To illustrate how simple it becomes to use this `PersonFactory` class, consider the following code:

```
let factory = new PersonFactory();
let p1 = factory.getPerson(new Date(2015, 0, 20));
p1.printDetails();
let p2 = factory.getPerson(new Date(2000, 0, 20));
p2.printDetails();
let p3 = factory.getPerson(new Date(1969, 0, 20));
p3.printDetails();
```

We start with the creation of a variable, `personFactory`, to hold a new instance of the `PersonFactory` class. We then create three variables, named `p1`, `p2`, and `p3`, by calling the `getPerson` function of the `PersonFactory` – passing in three different dates to the same function. The output of this code is as follows:

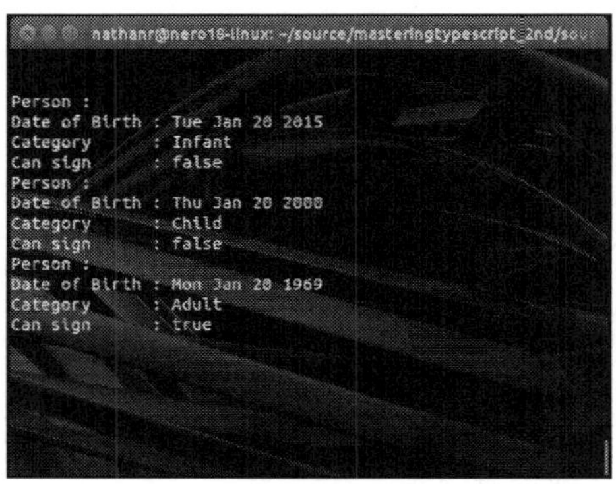


Output of the Factory Design Pattern

We have satisfied our business requirements and implemented a very common design pattern at the same time. If we look back at our code, we can see that we have a few well defined and simple classes. Our `Infant`, `Child`, and `Adult` classes are only concerned with logic relating to their classification, and whether they can sign contracts. Our `Person` abstract base class is only concerned with logic related to the `IPerson` interface, and our `PersonFactory` is only concerned with the logic surrounding the date of birth. This sample illustrates how object-oriented design patterns and the object-oriented features of the TypeScript language can help with writing good, extensible, and maintainable code.

# Summary

In this chapter, we explored the object-oriented concepts of interfaces, classes, and inheritance. We discussed both interface inheritance and class inheritance, and used our knowledge of interfaces, classes, and inheritance to create a Factory Design Pattern implementation in TypeScript. In the next chapter, we will look at advanced language features, including generics, decorators, and asynchronous programming techniques.

# 4
# Decorators, Generics, and Asynchronous Features

Above and beyond the concepts of classes, interfaces, and inheritance, the TypeScript language introduces a number of advanced language features in order to aid the development of robust object-oriented code. These features include decorators, generics, promises, and the use of the `async` and `await` keywords when working with asynchronous functions. Decorators allow for the injection and query of metadata when working with class definitions, as well as the ability to programmatically attach to the act of defining a class. Generics provide a technique for writing routines where the exact type of an object used is not known until runtime. Promises provide the ability to write asynchronous code in a fluent manner, and async await functions will pause execution until an asynchronous function has completed.

When writing large-scale JavaScript applications, these language features become part of the programmers' toolbox and allow for the application of many design patterns within JavaScript code.

This chapter is broken into three parts. The first part covers decorators, the second part covers generics, and the third part deals with asynchronous programming techniques using promises and async await. In earlier versions of TypeScript, promises and async await could only be used in ECMAScript 6 and above, but this functionality has now been extended to include ECMAScript 3 targets.

We will cover the following topics in this chapter:

- Decorators syntax
- Decorator factories
- Class, method, and parameter decorators
- Decorator metadata
- Generics syntax
- Using and constraining the type of T
- Generic interfaces
- Promises and promise syntax
- Using promises
- Async and await
- Handling await errors

# Decorators

Decorators in TypeScript provide a way of programmatically tapping into the process of defining a class. Remember that a class definition describes the shape of a class. In other words, a class definition describes what properties a class has, and what methods it defines. It is only when a class is instantiated, that is, when an instance of the class is created that these properties and methods become available.

Decorators; however, allow us to inject code into the actual definition of a class. Decorators can be used on class definitions, class properties, class functions, and even method parameters. The concept of decorators exists in other programming languages, and are called attributes in C#, or annotations in Java.

In this section, we will explore what decorators are, how they are defined, and how they can be used. We will look at class, property, function, and method decorators.

Decorators are an experimental feature of the TypeScript compiler, and have been proposed as part of the ECMAScript 7 standard. TypeScript, however, allows for the use of decorators in ES3 and above. In order to use decorators, a new compile option needs to be added to the `tsconfig.json` file in the root of your project directory. This option is named `experimentalDecorators`, and needs to be set to `true`, as follows:

```
{
    "compilerOptions": {
      "module": "commonjs",
      "target": "es3",
      "sourceMap": true,
      "experimentalDecorators": true
    },
    "exclude": [
      "node_modules"
    ]
}
```

# Decorator syntax

A decorator is simply a function which is called with a specific set of parameters. These parameters are automatically populated by the JavaScript runtime, and contain information about the class to which the decorator has been applied. The number of parameters and the types of these parameters determine where a decorator can be applied. To illustrate the syntax used for decorators, let's define a simple class decorator, as follows:

```
function simpleDecorator(constructor : Function) {
  console.log('simpleDecorator called.');
}
```

Here we have defined a function named `simpleDecorator` that takes a single parameter, named `constructor` of type `Function`. This `simpleDecorator` function simply logs a message to the console indicating that it has been called. This function is our decorator definition. In order to use it, we will need to apply it to a class definition, as follows:

```
@simpleDecorator
class ClassWithSimpleDecorator {
}
```

Here, we have applied the decorator to the class definition of `ClassWithSimpleDecorator` by using the at symbol (`@`), followed by the decorator name. Running this simple decorator code will produce the following output:

```
simpleDecorator called.
```

Note, however, that we have not created an instance of the class as yet. We have simply specified the class definition, added a decorator to it, and our decorator function has automatically been called. This indicates to us that the decorators are applied when a class is being defined, and not when it is being instantiated. As a further example of this, consider the following code:

```
let instance_1 = new ClassWithSimpleDecorator();
let instance_2 = new ClassWithSimpleDecorator();

console.log(`instance_1: ${instance_1}`);
console.log(`instance_2 : ${instance_2}`);
```

Here, we have created two instances of the `ClassWithSimpleDecorator` class, named `instance_1` and `instance_2`. We are then simply logging a message to the console. The output of this code snippet is as follows:

```
simpleDecorator called.
instance_1 : [object Object]
instance_2 : [object Object]
```

What this output shows us is that the decorator function has only been called once, no matter how many instances of the same class have been created or used. Decorators are only invoked as the class is being defined.

# Multiple decorators

Multiple decorators can be applied one after another to the same target. As an example of this, consider the following code:

```
function secondDecorator(constructor : Function) {
  console.log('secondDecorator called.')
}

@simpleDecorator
@secondDecorator
class ClassWithMultipleDecorators {
}
```

Here, we have created another decorator named `secondDecorator` which also simply logs a message to the console. We are then applying both the `simpleDecorator` (from our earlier code snippet) and the `secondDecorator` decorators to the class definition of the class named `ClassWithMultipleDecorators`. The output of this code is as follows:

```
secondDecorator called.
simpleDecorator called.
```

The output of this code shows us an interesting point about decorators. They are called in reverse order of their definition.

> Decorators are evaluated in the order they appear in the code, but are then called in reverse order.

# Decorator factories

In order to allow for decorators to accept parameters, we need to use what is known as a decorator factory. A decorator factory is simply a wrapper function that returns the decorator function itself. As an example of this, consider the following code:

```
function decoratorFactory(name: string) {
  return function (constructor : Function ) {
    console.log(`decorator function called with : ${name}`);
  }
}
```

Here, we have defined a function named `decoratorFactory` that accepts a single argument, named `name` of type string. This function simply returns an anonymous decorator function that takes a single argument named `constructor` of type `Function`. The anonymous function (our decorator function) logs the value of the `name` parameter to the console.

Note here how we have wrapped the decorator function within the `decoratorFactory` function. This wrapping of a decorator function is what produces a decorator factory. As long as the wrapping function returns a decorator function, this is a valid decorator factory.

We can now use our decorator factory, as follows:

```
@decoratorFactory('testName')
class ClassWithDecoratorFactory {
}
```

Note how we can now pass a parameter to the decorator factory, as shown in the usage of `@decoratorFactory('testName')`. The output of this code is as follows:

```
decorator function called with : testName
```

There are a few things to note about decorator factories. Firstly, the decorator function itself will still be called by the JavaScript runtime with automatically populated parameters. Secondly, the decorator factory must return a function definition. Lastly, the parameters defined for the decorator factory can be used within the decorator function itself.

# Class decorator parameters

The examples we have seen so far are all class decorators. Remember that a decorator function will automatically be called by the JavaScript runtime when the class is declared. Our decorator functions up until this point have all been defined to accept a single parameter named `constructor`, which is of type `Function`. The JavaScript runtime will populate this `constructor` parameter automatically for us. Let's delve into this parameter in a little more detail.

Class decorators will be invoked with the constructor function of the class that has been decorated. As an example of this, consider the following code:

```
function classConstructorDec(constructor: Function) {
  console.log(`constructor : ${constructor}`);
}

@classConstructorDec
class ClassWithConstructor {
}
```

Here, we start with a decorator function named `classConstructorDec` that accepts a single argument named `constructor` of type `Function`. The first line of this function then simply prints out the value of the `constructor` argument. We are then applying this decorator to a class named `ClassWithConstructor`. The output of this code is as follows:

```
constructor : function ClassWithConstructor() {
}
```

This output therefore shows us that our decorator function is being called with the `constructor` function of the class that it is decorating.

Let's then update this decorator, as follows:

```
function classConstructorDec(constructor: Function) {
  console.log(`constructor : ${constructor}`);
  console.log(`constructor.name : ${(<any>constructor).name}`);
  constructor.prototype.testProperty = "testProperty_value";
}
```

Here, we have updated our `classConstructorDec` decorator with two new lines of code. The first new line prints the `name` property of the `constructor` function to the console. Note how we have had to cast the `constructor` parameter to a type of `any` in order to successfully access the `name` property. This is necessary, as the `name` property of a function is only available from ECMAScript 6, and is only partially available in earlier browsers.

The last line of this decorator function is actually modifying the class prototype, and adding a property named `testProperty` ( with the value `"testProperty_value"` ) to the class definition itself. This is an example of how decorators can be used to modify a class definition. We can then access this class property, as follows:

```
let classConstrInstance = new ClassWithConstructor();
console.log(`classConstrInstance.testProperty : `
  + `${(<any>classConstrInstance).testProperty}`);
```

Here, we are creating an instance of the `ClassWithConstructor` class, named `classConstrInstance`. We are then logging the value of the `testProperty` property to the console. Note how we need to cast the type of the variable `classConstrInstance` to `any` in order to access the `testProperty` property. This is because we have not defined the `testProperty` property on the class definition itself, but are injecting this property via the decorator. The output of this code would be as follows:

```
constructor : function ClassWithConstructor() {
}
constructor.name : ClassWithConstructor
classConstrInstance.testProperty : testProperty_value
```

This output shows us that we can use the `name` property of the class constructor to find the name of the class itself. We can also inject a class property, named `testProperty`, into the class definition. As can be seen by the output, the value of this `testProperty` property is `"testProperty_value"`, which is being set within the decorator function.

# Property decorators

Property decorators are decorator functions that can be used on class properties. A property decorator is called with two parameters–the class prototype itself, and the property name. As an example of this, consider the following code:

```
function propertyDec(target: any, propertyKey : string) {
  console.log(`target : ${target}`);
  console.log(`target.constructor : ${target.constructor}`);
  console.log(`class name : `
    + `${target.constructor.name}`);
  console.log(`propertyKey : ${propertyKey}`);
}

class ClassWithPropertyDec {
  @propertyDec
  name: string;
}
```

Here, we have defined a property decorator named `propertyDec` that accepts two parameters–`target` and `propertyKey`. The `target` parameter is of type `any`, and the `propertyKey` parameter is of type `string`. Within this decorator, we are logging some values to the console. The first value we log to the console is the `target` argument itself. The second value logged to the console is the `constructor` property of the `target` object. The third value logged to the console is the name of the constructor function, and the fourth value is the `propertyKey` argument itself.

We are then defining a class named `ClassWithPropertyDec` that is now using this property decorator on the property named `name`. As in the case with class decorators, the syntax used to decorate a property is simply `@propertyDec` before the property to be decorated.

The output of this code is as follows:

```
target : [object Object]
target.constructor : function ClassWithPropertyDec() {
}
target.constructor.name : ClassWithPropertyDec
propertyKey : name
```

Here we can see the output of our various `console.log` calls. The `target` argument resolves to `[object Object]`, which simply indicates that it is an object prototype. The `constructor` property of the `target` argument resolves to a function named `ClassWithPropertyDec`, which is, in fact, our class constructor. The `name` property of this constructor function gives us the name of the class itself, and the `propertyKey` argument is the name of the property itself.

Property decorators, therefore, give us the ability to check whether a particular property has been declared on a class instance.

# Static property decorators

Property decorators can also be applied to static class properties. There is no difference in calling syntax in our code, they are the same as normal property decorators. However, the actual arguments that are passed in at runtime are slightly different. Given our earlier definition of the property decorator `propertyDec`, consider what happens when this decorator is applied to a static class property, as follows:

```
class StaticClassWithPropertyDec {
  @propertyDec
  static name: string;
}
```

The output of the various `console.log` functions in our decorator is as follows:

```
target : function StaticClassWithPropertyDec() {
}
target.constructor : function Function() { [native code] }
target.constructor.name : Function
propertyKey : name
```

Note here that the `target` argument (as printed in the first line of output) is not a class prototype (as seen before), but an actual constructor function. The definition of this `target.constructor` is then simply a function, named `Function`. The `propertyKey` remains the same, that is, `name`.

This means that we need to be a little careful about what is being passed in as the first argument to our property decorator. When the class property being decorated is marked as `static`, then the target argument will be the class constructor itself. When the class property is not static, the target argument will be the class prototype.

Let's modify our property decorator to correctly identify the name of the class in both of these cases, as follows:

```
function propertyDec(target: any, propertyKey : string) {
  if(typeof(target) === 'function') {
    console.log(`class name : ${target.name}`);
  } else {
      console.log(`class name : ${target.constructor.name}`);
    }
  console.log(`propertyKey : ${propertyKey}`);
}
```

Here, we start by checking the type of the `target` argument. If the `typeof(target)` call returns `'function'`, then we know that the target argument is the class constructor, and can then identify the class name through `target.name`. If the `typeof(target)` call does not return `'function'`, then we know that the `target` argument is an object prototype, and that you need to identify the class name via the `target.constructor.name` property. The output of this code is as follows:

```
class name : ClassWithPropertyDec
propertyKey : name
class name : StaticClassWithPropertyDec
propertyKey : name
```

Our property decorator is correctly identifying the name of the class, whether it is used on a normal class property, or a static class property.

# Method decorators

Method decorators are decorators that can be applied to a method on a class. Method decorators are invoked by the JavaScript runtime with three parameters. Remember that class decorators have only a single parameter (the class prototype) and property decorators have two parameters (the class prototype and the property name). Method decorators have three parameters–the class prototype, the method name, and (optionally) a method descriptor. The third parameter, the method descriptor is only populated if compiling for ES5 and above.

Let's take a look at a method decorator, as follows:

```
function methodDec (target: any,
  methodName: string,
  descriptor?: PropertyDescriptor) {
    console.log(`target: ${target}`);
    console.log(`methodName : ${methodName}`);
```

```
        console.log(`target[methodName] : ${target[methodName]}`);
    }
```

Here, we have defined a method decorator named `methodDec` that accepts our three parameters, `target`, `methodName`, and `descriptor`. Note that the `descriptor` property has been marked as optional. The first two lines inside the decorator simply log the values of `target` and `methodName` to the console. Note, however, the last line of this decorator. Here, we are logging the value of `target[methodName]` to the console. This will log the actual function definition to the console.

Now we can use this method decorator on a class, as follows:

```
class ClassWithMethodDec {
  @methodDec
  print(output: string) {
    console.log(`ClassWithMethodDec.print`
      + `(${output}) called.`);
  }
}
```

Here, we have defined a class named `ClassWithMethodDec`. This class has a single `print` function that accepts a single parameter named `output` of type string. Our `print` function is just logging a message to the console, including the value of the `output` argument. The `print` function has been decorated with the `methodDec` decorator. The output of this code is as follows:

```
target: [object Object]
methodName : print
target[methodName] : function (output) {
console.log(
"ClassWithMethodDec.print(" + output + ") called.");
}
```

As we can see by this output, the value of the target argument is the class prototype. The value of the `methodName` argument is, in fact, `print`. The output of the `target[methodName]` call is the actual definition of the `print` function.

# Using method decorators

Since we have the definition of a function available to us within a method decorator, we could use the decorator to inject new functionality into the class. Suppose that we wanted to create an audit trail of some sort, and log a message to the console every time a method was called. This is the perfect scenario for method decorators.

Consider the following method decorator:

```
function auditLogDec(target: any,
  methodName: string,
  descriptor?: PropertyDescriptor ) {
    let originalFunction = target[methodName];
    let auditFunction = function() {
      console.log(`auditLogDec : overide of `
        + ` ${methodName} called `);
      originalFunction.apply(this, arguments);
    }
  target[methodName] = auditFunction;
}
```

Here we have defined a method decorator named `auditLogDec`. Within this decorator, we are creating a variable named `originalFunction` to hold the definition of the method that we are decorating. Remember that `target[methodName]` returns the function definition itself. We then create a new function named `auditFunction`. The first line of this function logs a message to the console. Note, however, the last line of the `auditFunction` function. We are using the JavaScript `apply` function to call the original function, passing in the `this` parameter, and the `arguments` parameter.

The last line of the `auditLogDec` decorator function is assigning this new function to the original class function. In essence, this is wrapping the original function with a new function, and then calling through to the original class function. To show this in action, consider the following class declaration:

```
class ClassWithAuditDec {
  @auditLogDec
  print(output: string) {
    console.log(`ClassWithMethodDec.print`
      + `(${output}) called.`);
  }
}

let auditClass = new ClassWithAuditDec();
auditClass.print("test");
```

Here, we are creating a class named `ClassWithAuditDec`, and decorating the `print` function with our `auditLogDec` method decorator. The `print` function simply logs the value of the `output` argument to the console. The last two lines of this code snippet are an example of how this class would be used. Note, however, the output of this code:

```
auditLogDec : overide of print called
ClassWithMethodDec.print(test) called.
```

As can be seen in this output, our decorator audit function is being called before the actual implementation of the print function on the class. Using decorators in this way is a powerful method of injecting extra functionality non-intrusively into a class declaration. Any class we create can easily include the auditing functionality simply by decorating the relevant class methods.

# Parameter decorators

The final type of decorator that we will cover are parameter decorators. Parameter decorators are used to decorate the parameters of a particular method. As an example, consider the following code:

```
function parameterDec(target: any,
methodName : string,
parameterIndex: number) {
  console.log(`target: ${target}`);
  console.log(`methodName : ${methodName}`);
  console.log(`parameterIndex : ${parameterIndex}`);
}
```

Here, we have defined a function named parameterDec, with three arguments. The target argument will contain the class prototype as we have seen before. The methodName argument will contain the name of the method that contains the parameter, and the parameterIndex argument will contain the index of the parameter. We can use this parameter decorator function, as follows:

```
class ClassWithParamDec {
  print(@parameterDec  value: string) {
  }
}
```

Here, we have a class named ClassWithParamDec, that contains a single print function. This print function has a single argument named value which is of type string. We have decorated this value parameter with the parameterDec decorator. Note that the syntax for using a parameter decorator ( @parameterDec ) is the same as any other decorator. The output of this code is as follows:

```
target: [object Object]
methodName : print
parameterIndex : 0
```

As can be seen from the output, the parameter index for the value parameter is `0`, and it is a parameter on the method named `print`. Our target parameter is a class prototype.

Note that we are not given any information about the parameter that we are decorating. We are not told what type it is, or even what its name is. Parameter decorators, therefore, can only really be used to find out that a parameter has been declared on a method.

# Decorator metadata

The TypeScript compiler also includes experimental support for something called decorator metadata. Decorator metadata is metadata that is generated on class definitions in order to supplement the information that is passed into decorators. This option is called `emitDecoratorMetadata`, and can be added to the `tsconfig.json` file, as follows:

```
{
  "compilerOptions": {
     // other options
      "experimentalDecorators": true
      ,"emitDecoratorMetadata": true
  },
  "exclude": [
    "node_modules"
  ]
}
```

With this compile option in place, the TypeScript compiler will generate extra information relating to our class definitions. To see the results of this compile option, we will need to take a closer look at the generated JavaScript. Consider the following parameter decorator and class definition:

```
function metadataParameterDec(target: any,
  methodName : string,
  parameterIndex: number) {
  }

class ClassWithMetaData {
  print(
    @metadataParameterDec
    id: number,
    name: string) : number {
    return 1000;
    }
}
```

Here, we have a standard parameter decorator named metadataParameterDec, and a class definition named ClassWithMetaData. We are decorating the first parameter of the print function. If we are not using the emitDecoratorMetadata compile option, or if this option is set to false, our generated JavaScript would be defined as follows:

```
var ClassWithMetaData = (function () {
  function ClassWithMetaData() {
  }
  ClassWithMetaData.prototype.print = function (id, name) {
  };
  __decorate([
    __param(0, metadataParameterDec)
  ], ClassWithMetaData.prototype, "print");
  return ClassWithMetaData;
}());
```

This generated JavaScript defines a standard JavaScript closure for our ClassWithMetaData class. The code that we are interested in is near the bottom of the closure, where the TypeScript compiler has injected a method named __decorate. We will not concern ourselves with the full functionality of this __decorate method, other than to note that it contains information about the print function, and indicates that it is named "print", and that it has a single parameter at index 0.

When the emitDecoratorMetadata option is set to true, the generated JavaScript will contain some extra information about this print function, as follows:

```
var ClassWithMetaData = (function () {
  function ClassWithMetaData() {
  }
  ClassWithMetaData.prototype.print = function (id, name) {
  };
  __decorate([
    __param(0, metadataParameterDec),
    __metadata('design:type', Function),
    __metadata('design:paramtypes', [Number, String]),
    __metadata('design:returntype', Number)
  ], ClassWithMetaData.prototype, "print");
  return ClassWithMetaData;
}());
```

Note how the `__decorate` function now includes extra calls to a function named `__metadata`, which is called three times. The first call uses a special metadata key of `'design:type'`, the second uses the metadata key `'design:paramtypes'`, and the third call uses the metadata key `'design:returntype'`. These three function calls to the `__metadata` function are, in fact, registering extra information about the `print` function itself. The `'design:type'` key is used to register that the `print` function is of type `Function`. The `'design:paramtypes'` key is used to register that the `print` function has two parameters–the first a `Number`, and the second a `String`. The `'design:returntype'` key is used to register the return type of the print function which, in our case, is a number.

# Using decorator metadata

In order to use this extra information within a decorator, we will need to use a third-party library named `reflect-metadata`. We will discuss how to use third-party libraries in detail in future chapters, but for the time being, this library can be included in our project by typing the following from the command line:

```
npm install reflect-metadata --save-dev
```

Once this has been installed, we will need to reference it in our TypeScript file by including the following line at the top of the file:

```
import 'reflect-metadata';
```

Before we attempt to compile any code that is using the reflect-metadata library, we will need to install the declaration file for this library as follows:

```
npm install @types/reflect-metadata --save-dev
```

We will discuss declaration files in detail in the next chapter.

We can now start to use this class metadata by calling the `Reflect.getMetadata` function within our decorator. Consider the following update to our earlier parameter decorator:

```
function metadataParameterDec(target: any,
  methodName : string,
  parameterIndex: number) {

    let designType = Reflect.getMetadata(
      "design:type", target, methodName);
      console.log(`designType: ${designType}`)
    let designParamTypes = Reflect.getMetadata(
      "design:paramtypes", target, methodName);
    console.log(`paramtypes : ${designParamTypes}`);
```

```
        let designReturnType = Reflect.getMetadata(
          "design:returntype", target, methodName);
        console.log(`returntypes : ${designReturnType}`);
    }
```

Here, we have updated our parameter decorator, with three calls to the `Reflect.getMetadata` function. The first is using the `"design:type"` metadata key. This is the same metadata key that we saw earlier in the generated JavaScript, where the compiler generated calls to the `__metadata` function. We are then logging the result to the console. We then repeat this process for the `"design:paramtypes"` and `"design:returntype"` metadata keys. The output of this code is as follows:

```
designType: function Function() { [native code] }
paramtypes : function Number() { [native code] }
,function String() { [native code] }
returntypes : function Number() { [native code] }
```

We can see from this output, then, that the type of the `print` function (as recorded by the `"design:type"` metadata key) is a `Function`. We can also see that information returned by the `"design:paramtypes"` key is an array that includes a `Number` and a `String`. This array, therefore, indicates that the function has two parameters, the first of type `Number`, and the second of type `String`. Finally, our return type for this function is a `Number`.

Metadata that is generated automatically by the TypeScript compiler, and that can be read and interrogated at runtime can be extremely useful. In other languages, such as C#, this type of metadata information is called **reflection**, and is a fundamental principle when writing frameworks for dependency injection, or for generating code analysis tools.

# Generics

Generics are a way of writing code that will deal with any type of object but still maintain the object type integrity. So far, we have used interfaces, classes, and TypeScript's basic types to ensure strongly typed (and less error-prone) code in our samples. But what happens if a block of code needs to work with any type of object?

As an example, suppose we wanted to write some code that could iterate over an array of objects and return a concatenation of their values. So, given a list of numbers, say `[1,2,3]`, it should return the string `"1,2,3"`. Or, given a list of strings, say `["first","second","third"]`, return the string `"first,second,third"`. We could write some code that accepted values of type `any`, but this might introduce bugs in our code, remember S.F.I.A.T.? We want to ensure that all elements of the array are of the same type. This is where generics come in to play.

# Generic syntax

As an example of TypeScript generic syntax, let's write a class called `Concatenator` that will concatenate the values in an array. We will need to ensure that each element of the array is of the same type. This class should be able to handle arrays of strings, arrays of numbers, and in fact, arrays of any type. In order to do this, we need to rely on functionality that is common to each of these types. As all JavaScript objects have a `toString` function (which is called whenever a string is needed by the runtime) we can use this `toString` function to create a generic class that outputs all values held within an array.

A generic implementation of this `Concatenator` class is as follows:

```
class Concatenator< T > {
  concatenateArray(inputArray: Array< T >): string {
    let returnString = "";

    for (let i = 0; i < inputArray.length; i++) {
      if (i > 0)
        returnString += ",";
      returnString += inputArray[i].toString();
    }
    return returnString;
  }
}
```

The first thing we notice is the syntax of the class declaration, `Concatenator < T >`. This `< T >` syntax is the syntax used to indicate a generic type, and the name used for this generic type in the rest of our code is `T`. The `concatenateArray` function also uses this generic type syntax, `Array < T >`. This indicates that the `inputArray` argument must be an array of the type that was originally used to construct an instance of this class.

# Instantiating generic classes

To use an instance of this generic class, we need to construct the class and tell the compiler via the `< >` syntax what the actual type of `T` is. We can use any type for the type of `T` in this generic syntax, including base types, classes, or even interfaces. Let's create a few versions of this class, as follows:

```
var stringConcat = new Concatenator<string>();
var numberConcat = new Concatenator<number>();
```

Notice the syntax that we have used to instantiate the `Concatenator` class. On the first line of this sample, we create an instance of the `Concatenator` generic class, and specify that it should substitute the generic type, `T`, with the type `string` in every place where `T` is being used within the code. Similarly, the second line of this sample creates an instance of the `Concatenator` class, and specifies that the type `number` should be used wherever the code encounters the generic type `T`.

If we use this simple substitution principle, then for the `stringConcat` instance (which uses strings), the `inputArray` argument must be of type `Array<string>`. Similarly, the `numberConcat` instance of this generic class uses numbers, and so the `inputArray` argument must be an array of numbers. To test this theory, let's generate an array of strings and an array of numbers, and see what the compiler says if we try to break this rule:

```
var stringArray: string[] = ["first", "second", "third"];
var numberArray: number[] = [1, 2, 3];
var stringResult =
  stringConcat.concatenateArray(stringArray);
var numberResult =
  numberConcat.concatenateArray(numberArray);
var stringResult2 =
  stringConcat.concatenateArray(numberArray);
var numberResult2 =
  numberConcat.concatenateArray(stringArray);
```

Our first two lines define our `stringArray` and `numberArray` variables to hold the relevant arrays. We then pass in the `stringArray` variable to the `stringConcat` function–no problems there. On our next line, we pass the `numberArray` to the `numberConcat`–still okay.

Our problems, however, start when we attempt to pass an array of numbers to the `stringConcat` instance, which has been configured to only use strings. Again, if we attempt to pass an array of strings to the `numberConcat` instance, which has been configured to allow only numbers, TypeScript will generate errors as follows:

```
error TS2345: Argument of type 'number[]' is not assignable to parameter of
type 'string[]'.
Type 'number' is not assignable to type 'string'.
error TS2345: Argument of type 'string[]' is not assignable to parameter of
type 'number[]'.
Type 'string' is not assignable to type 'number'.
```

Clearly, we are attempting to pass an array of numbers where we should have used strings, and vice versa. Again, the compiler warns us that we are not using the code correctly, and forces us to resolve these issues before continuing.

> These constraints on generics are a compile-time-only feature of TypeScript. If we look at the generated JavaScript, we will not see reams of code jumping through hoops to ensure that these rules are carried through into the resultant JavaScript. All of these type constraints and generic syntax are actually compiled away. In the case of generics, the generated JavaScript is actually a very simplified version of our code, with no type in sight.

# Using the type T

When we use generics, it is important to note that all of the code within the definition of a generic class or a generic function must respect the properties of `T` as if it were any type of object. Let's take a closer look at the implementation of the `concatenateArray` function in this light:

```
class Concatenator< T > {
  concatenateArray(inputArray: Array< T >): string {
    let returnString = "";

    for (let i = 0; i < inputArray.length; i++) {
      if (i > 0)
        returnString += ",";
      returnString += inputArray[i].toString();
    }
    return returnString;
  }
}
```

The `concatenateArray` function strongly types the `inputArray` argument so that it should be of type `Array < T >`. This means that any code that uses the `inputArray` argument can use only those functions and properties that are common to all arrays, no matter what type the array holds. We have used `inputArray` in two places.

Firstly, within the declaration of the `for` loop, note where we have used the `inputArray.length` property. All arrays have a `length` property to indicate how many items the array has, so using `inputArray.length` will work on any array, no matter what type of object the array holds. Secondly, on the last line of the `for` loop, we referenced an object within the array when we used the `inputArray[i]` syntax.

This reference actually returns us a single object of type T. Remember that whenever we use T in our code, we must use only those functions and properties that are common to any object of type T. Luckily for us, we are only using the toString function, and all JavaScript objects, no matter what type they are, have a valid toString function. So this generic code block will compile cleanly.

Let's test this type T theory by creating a class of our own to pass into the Concatenator class:

```
class MyClass {
  private _name: string;
  constructor(arg1: number) {
    this._name = arg1 + "_MyClass";
  }
}
```

Here, we have a simple class definition, named MyClass, that has a constructor function accepting a number. This constructor function sets the internal variable _name to the value of the arg1 argument.

Let's now create an array of MyClass instances, as follows:

```
let myArray: MyClass[] = [
  new MyClass(1),
  new MyClass(2),
  new MyClass(3)];
```

We can now create an instance of our generic Concatenator class, as follows:

```
let myArrayConcatentator = new Concatenator<MyClass>();
let myArrayResult =
  myArrayConcatentator.concatenateArray(myArray);
console.log(myArrayResult);
```

We start with an instance of the Concatenator class, specifying that this generic instance will only work with objects that are of type MyClass. We then call the concatenateArray function and store the result in a variable named myArrayResult. Finally, we print the result on the console. Running this code will produce the following output:

```
[object Object],[object Object],[object Object]
```

Not quite what we were expecting. This output is due to the fact that the string representation of an object – that is not one of the basic JavaScript types – resolves to `[object type]`. Any custom object that you write needs to override the `toString` function to provide human-readable output. We can fix this code quite easily by providing an override of the `toString` function within our class, as follows:

```
class MyClass {
  private _name: string;
  constructor(arg1: number) {
    this._name = arg1 + "_MyClass";
  }
  toString(): string {
    return this._name;
  }
}
```

Here, we replaced the default `toString` function that all JavaScript objects inherit with our own implementation. Within this function, we simply returned the value of the `_name` private variable. Running this sample now produces the expected result:

```
1_MyClass,2_MyClass,3_MyClass
```

# Constraining the type of T

When using generics, it is sometimes desirable to constrain the type of `T` to be only a specific type, or subset of types. In these cases, we don't want our generic code to be available for any type of object, we only want it to be available for a specific subset of objects. TypeScript uses inheritance to accomplish this with generics.

As an example, let's define an interface for a football team, as follows:

```
enum ClubHomeCountry {
  England,
  Germany
}

interface IFootballClub {
  getName() : string;
  getHomeCountry(): ClubHomeCountry;
}
```

Here, we have defined an enum named ClubHomeCountry to indicate where the home country is for a football club. Our IFootballClub interface then defines two methods that any FootballClub class must implement–a getName function to return the name of the football club, and a getHomeCountry function to return the ClubHomeCountry enum value.

We will now define an abstract base class to implement this interface, as follows:

```
abstract class FootballClub implements IFootballClub {
  protected _name: string;
  protected _homeCountry: ClubHomeCountry;
  getName() { return this._name };
  getHomeCountry() { return this._homeCountry };
}
```

This class, named FootballClub implements the IFootballClub interface, by defining a getName and getHomeCountry function, which returns the values held in the protected variables named _name and _homeCountry respectively. As this is an abstract class, we will need to derive from it to create concrete classes, as follows:

```
class Liverpool extends FootballClub {
  constructor() {
    super();
    this._name = "Liverpool F.C.";
    this._homeCountry = ClubHomeCountry.England;
  }
}

class BorussiaDortmund extends FootballClub {
  constructor() {
    super();
    this._name = "Borussia Dortmund";
    this._homeCountry = ClubHomeCountry.Germany;
  }
}
```

Here, we have defined two classes, named Liverpool and BorussiaDortmund that derive from our abstract base class FootballClub. Both classes have a single constructor that sets the internal _name and _homeCountry properties.

We can now create a generic class that will work with any class implementing the `IFootballClub` interface, as follows:

```
class FootballClubPrinter< T extends IFootballClub >
  implements IFootballClubPrinter< T > {
    print(arg : T) {
      console.log(` ${arg.getName()} is ` +
        `${this.IsEnglishTeam(arg)}` +
        ` an English football team.`
      );
    }
  IsEnglishTeam(arg : T) : string {
    if ( arg.getHomeCountry() == ClubHomeCountry.England )
        return "";
    else
        return "NOT"
  }
}
```

Here, we have defined a class named `FootballClubPrinter` that uses the generic syntax. Note that the `T` generic type is now deriving from the `IFootballClub` interface, as indicated by the `extends` keyword in `< T extends IFootballClub >`. Using inheritance when defining a generic class constrains the type of class that can be used by this generic code. In other words, any usage of the type `T` within the generic code will substitute the interface `IFooballClub` instead. This means that the generic code will only allow functions or properties that are defined in the `IFootballClub` interface to be used wherever `T` is used.

These constraints can be seen within the `print` function, as well as within the `IsEnglishTeam` function. In the `print` function, the argument `arg` is of type `T`, and therefore, we are able to use `arg.getName`, which has been defined in the `IFootballClub` interface. In the `print` function, we are also calling the `IsEnglishTeam` function, and passing the argument `arg` to it. The `IsEnglishTeam` function is using the `getHomeCountry` function that is also defined in the `IFootballClub` interface.

To illustrate how this generic `FootballClubPrinter` class can be used, consider the following code:

```
let clubInfo = new FootballClubPrinter();
clubInfo.print(new Liverpool());
clubInfo.print(new BorussiaDortmund());
```

Here, we are creating an instance of the `FootballClubPrinter` class named `clubInfo`. Note how we do not need to specify the type (as we did with our earlier class `Concatenator`) when creating an instance of the class.

We are then calling the `print` function of the `clubInfo` generic class, passing in a new instance of the `Liverpool` class, and then passing in an instance of the `BorussiaDortmund` class. The output of this code is as follows:

```
Liverpool F.C. is an English football team.
Borussia Dortmund is NOT an English football team.
```

# Generic interfaces

We can also use interfaces with the generic type syntax. If we were to create an interface for our `FootballClubPrinter` generic class, the interface definition would be:

```
interface IFootballClubPrinter < T extends IFootballClub > {
  print(arg : T);
  IsEnglishTeam(arg : T);
}
```

This interface looks identical to our class definition, with the only difference being that the `print` and the `IsEnglishTeam` functions do not have an implementation. We have kept the generic type syntax using `< T >`, and further specified that the type `T` must implement the `IFootballClub` interface. To use this interface with the `FootballClubPrinter` class, we can modify the class definition, as follows:

```
class FootballClubPrinter< T extends IFootballClub >
  implements IFootballClubPrinter< T > {

}
```

This syntax seems pretty straightforward. As we have seen before, we use the `implements` keyword following the class definition, and then use the interface name. Note, however, that we pass the type `T` into the interface definition of `IFootballClubPrinter` as a generic type `IFootballClubPrinter<T>`. This satisfies the `IFootballClubPrinter` generic interface definition.

An interface that defines our generic classes further protects our code from being modified inadvertently. As an example of this, suppose that we tried to redefine the class definition of `FootballClubPrinter` so that `T` is not constrained to be of type `IFootballClub`:

```
class FootballClubPrinter< T  >
  implements IFootballClubPrinter< T > {

}
```

Here, we have removed the constraint on the type `T` for the `FootballClubPrinter` class. TypeScript will automatically generate an error:

```
error TS2344: Type 'T' does not satisfy the constraint 'IFootballClub'.
```

This error points us to our erroneous class definition; the type `T`, as used in the code (`FootballClubPrinter<T>`), must use a type `T` that extends from `IFootballClub`, in order to correctly implement the `IFootballClubPrinter` interface.

# Creating new objects within generics

From time to time, generic classes may need to create an object of the type that is passed in as the generic type `T`. Consider the following code:

```
class FirstClass {
  id: number;
}

class SecondClass {
  name: string;
}

class GenericCreator< T > {
  create(): T {
    return new T();
  }
}

var creator1 = new GenericCreator<FirstClass>();
var firstClass: FirstClass = creator1.create();

var creator2 = new GenericCreator<SecondClass>();
var secondClass : SecondClass = creator2.create();
```

Here, we have two class definitions, `FirstClass` and `SecondClass`. `FirstClass` just has a public `id` property, and `SecondClass` has a public `name` property. We then have a generic class that accepts a type `T` and has a single function, named `create`. This `create` function attempts to create a new instance of the type `T`.

The last four lines of the sample show us how we would like to use this generic class. The `creator1` variable creates a new instance of the `GenericCreator` class using the correct syntax for creating variables of type `FirstClass`. The `creator2` variable is a new instance of the `GenericCreator` class, but this time is using `SecondClass`. Unfortunately, the preceding code will generate a TypeScript compile error:

```
error TS2304: Cannot find name 'T'.
```

According to the TypeScript documentation, in order to enable a generic class to create objects of type `T`, we need to refer to type `T` by its `constructor` function. We also need to pass in the class definition as an argument. The `create` function will need to be rewritten, as follows:

```
class GenericCreator< T > {
  create(arg1: { new(): T }) : T {
    return new arg1();
  }
}
```

Let's break this `create` function down into its component parts. First, we pass an argument, named `arg1`. This argument is then defined to be of type `{ new(): T }`. This is the little trick that allows us to refer to `T` by its `constructor` function. We are defining a new anonymous type that overloads the `new()` function and returns a type `T`. This means that the `arg1` argument is a function that is strongly typed to have a single `constructor` that returns a type `T`. The implementation of this function simply returns a new instance of the `arg1` variable. Using this syntax removes the compile error that we encountered before.

This change, however, means that we must pass the class definition to the create function, as follows:

```
var creator1 = new GenericCreator<FirstClass>();
var firstClass: FirstClass = creator1.create(FirstClass);

var creator2 = new GenericCreator<SecondClass>();
var secondClass : SecondClass = creator2.create(SecondClass);
```

Note the change in usage of the `create` function. We are now required to pass in the class definition for our type of `T`—`create(FirstClass)` and `create(SecondClass)` as our first argument. Try running this code to see what happens. The generic class will, in fact, create new objects of types `FirstClass` and `SecondClass`, as we expected.

# Asynchronous language features

In this section of the chapter, we will discuss some asynchronous language features, and in particular, promises and the `async` and `await` keywords.

The code samples in this section have been designed to run on Node version 4 and above, which provides an ECMAScript 6 runtime. You can determine which version of Node you are running by executing the following on the command line:

```
node --version
```

You need to ensure that the return value is v4 or greater to compile and run the code samples in this section. The information returned by the version of Node used in this section is:

```
V6.1.0
```

## Promises

Promises are a technique for standardizing asynchronous processing in JavaScript. Remember that there are many occasions where a function is called in JavaScript, but the actual results are only received after a period of time. These occasions typically arise when your code is requesting a resource of some sort, such as posting a request to a web server for some JSON data, or reading a file from disk. The standard JavaScript technique for asynchronous processing is the callback mechanism.

Unfortunately, when working with a lot of callbacks, our code can sometimes become rather complex and repetitive. Promises provide a way of simplifying this callback code. To start off our discussion on promises, let's take a look at some typical callback code, as follows:

```
function delayedResponseWithCallback(callback: Function) {
  function delayedAfterTimeout() {
    console.log(`delayedAfterTimeout`);
    callback();
  }
  setTimeout(delayedAfterTimeout, 1000);
```

```
}

function callDelayedAndWait() {
  function afterWait() {
    console.log(`afterWait`);
  }
  console.log(`calling delayedResponseWithCallback`);
  delayedResponseWithCallback(afterWait);
  console.log(`after calling delayedResponseWithCallback`);
}

callDelayedAndWait();
```

We start with a function named `delayedResponseWithCallback` that takes a single argument of type `Function`, named `callback`. If we consider the last line of this function, we see that it is calling `setTimeout` with a 1000 millisecond or a one second delay. This is to simulate a delay in processing, that is, an asynchronous function, within our code. The `setTimeout` function takes a function as its first parameter, which will be called after the one second delay. In this case, we are passing the function named `delayedAfterTimeout`, which simply logs a message to the console, and then calls our callback function.

The second function in this code snippet is called `callDelayedAndWait`. If we take a look at the last three lines of this function, we see that it is logging a message to the console, and then calling our `delayedResponseWithCallback` function. It is passing in the function `afterWait` as the callback function. The last line of the code executes our `callDelayedAndWait` function. The output of this code is as follows:

```
calling delayedResponseWithCallback
after calling delayedResponseWithCallback
delayedAfterTimeout
afterWait
```

What we can see from the output is the sequence of events that is happening in our code. When we execute the `callDelayedAndWait` function, it sets up a callback function, and then logs the text `"calling delayedResponseWithCallback"` to the console. It then invokes the `delayedResponseWithCallback` function, and then continues on to the next line, where it logs the text `"after calling delayedResponseWithCallback"`. After a one second delay, the function `delayedAfterTimeout` is invoked, which then logs the text `"delayedAfterTimeout"` to the console, and finally the `afterWait` function is invoked, logging the text `"afterWait"` to the console.

While these sort of callback functions are fairly standard in JavaScript, it can make our code difficult to read, as well as difficult to understand, especially as our code base grows larger and larger. Promises on the other hand, provide a fluent syntax for handling asynchronous calls.

# Promise syntax

A promise is an object that is created by passing in a function that accepts two callbacks. The first callback is used to indicate a successful response, and the second callback is used to indicate an error response. Consider the following function definition:

```
function fnDelayedPromise (
  resolve: () => void,
  reject : () => void)
{
  function afterTimeout() {
    resolve();
  }
  setTimeout( afterTimeout, 2000);
}
```

Here, we have defined a function named `fnDelayedPromise` that takes two functions as arguments. These functions are named `resolve` and `reject`, and they both return a void. Within the body of the `fnDelayedPromise` function, we are again calling `setTimeout` (on the last line of the function) to wait for two seconds before calling the `resolve` callback function.

We can now use this function to construct a promise object, as follows:

```
function delayedResponsePromise() : Promise<void> {
  return new Promise<void>(
    fnDelayedPromise
  );
}
```

Here, we have created a function named `delayedResponsePromise` that returns a `new Promise<void>` object. Within the body of the function, we are simply creating and returning a new promise object, and using our earlier function definition named `fnDelayedPromise` as the only argument within its constructor. Note that the type `void` that is used to create a promise is using generic syntax (`new Promise<void>`) to indicate some information on the return type of the promise. We will discuss the use of the generic `<void>` syntax a little later, when we explore how to return values from promises.

While this syntax may seem a little convoluted, in general practice, these two function definitions are combined in a single code block. The purpose of the previous two snippets has been to highlight two important concepts. Firstly, to use promises, you must return a new promise object. Secondly, a promise object is constructed with a function that takes two callback arguments.

Let's take a look at how these two steps are combined in general practice, as follows:

```
function delayedPromise() : Promise<void> {
  return new Promise<void>
  (
    ( resolve : () => void,
      reject: () => void
    ) => {
      function afterTimeout() {
        resolve();
      }
      setTimeout( afterTimeout, 1000);
    }
  );
}
```

Here, we have a function named `delayedPromise` that returns a new `Promise<void>` object. The first line of this function constructs the `new Promise` object, and passes in an anonymous function definition that takes two callback functions, named `resolve` and `reject`. The body of the code is then defined after the fat arrow `=>` , and is enclosed with matching curly braces `{` and `}`. The body of the code is defining a function named `afterTimeout` that will be called after a one second timeout. Note that the `afterTimeout` function is invoking the `resolve` function callback.

Note that this code snippet has been carefully formatted to clearly show the matching braces `(` and `)` and matching curly braces `{` and `}`. Remember that to use promises, we must construct and return a `new Promise` object, and the constructor of a promise object takes a function (or anonymous function) with two callback arguments.

# Using promises

Promises provide a simple syntax for handling these `resolve` and `reject` functions. Let's take a look at how we would use the promises defined in our previous code snippet, as follows:

```
function callDelayedPromise() {
  console.log(`calling delayedPromise`);
```

```
    delayedPromise().then(
      () => { console.log(`delayedPromise.then()`) }
    );
}

callDelayedPromise();
```

Here, we have defined a function named `callDelayedPrcmise`. This function logs a message to the console, and then calls our `delayedPromise` function. We are using fluent syntax to attach to the `then` function of the promise, and defining an anonymous function that will be called when the promise is resolved. The output of this code is as follows:

```
calling delayedPromise
delayedPromise.then()
```

This promise fluent syntax also defines a `catch` function that is used for error handling. Consider the following promise definition:

```
function errorPromise() : Promise<void> {
  return new Promise<void>
  (
    (   resolve: () => void,
        reject: () => void
    ) => {
      reject();
    }
  );
}
```

Here, we have defined a function named `errorPromise` using our promise syntax. Note that within the body of the promise function, we are calling the `reject` callback function instead of the `resolve` function. This `reject` function is used to indicate an error. Let's now use the `catch` function to trap this error, as follows:

```
function callErrorPromise() {
  console.log(`calling errorPromise`);
  errorPromise().then(
    () => { console.log(`no error.`) }
  ).catch(
    () => { console.log(`an error occurred`)}
  );
}

callErrorPromise();
```

Here, we have defined a function named `callErrorPromise` that is logging a message to the console, and then invoking the `errorPromise` promise. Using our fluent syntax, we have defined an anonymous function to be called within the `then` response (that is, on success), and we have also defined an anonymous function to be called within the `catch` response (that is, on error). The output of this code is as follows:

```
calling errorPromise
an error occurred
```

# Callback versus promise syntax

As a comparison of the two techniques we have discussed, let's take a look at a simplified version of the callback versus the promise syntax, as follows:

Our standard callback mechanism is as follows:

```
function standardCallback() {
  function afterCallbackSuccess() {
    // execute this code
  }
  function afterCallbackError() {
    // execute on error
  }
  // invoke async function
  invokeAsync(afterCallbackSuccess, afterCallbackError);
}
```

And our promise syntax is as follows:

```
function usingPromises() {
  // invoke async function
  delayedPromise().then(
    () => {
      // execute on success
    }
  ).catch (
    () => {
      // execute on error
    }
  );
}
```

As we can see, using promises introduces a fluent syntax for handling asynchronous programming.

# Returning values from promises

So far, we have defined all of our promise objects as `Promise<void>`. The void in this case indicates that our promises will not return any values. If we use `Promise<string>`, this indicates that our promises will return string values. Let's take a look at how to return values from promises, as follows:

```
function delayedPromiseWithParam() : Promise<string> {
  return new Promise<string>(
    (
      resolve: (str: string) => void,
      reject: (str:string ) => void
    ) => {
      function afterWait() {
        resolve("resolved_within_promise");
      }
      setTimeout( afterWait , 2000 );
    }
  );
}
```

Here, we have a function named `delayedPromiseWithParam` that constructs and returns our promise object as usual. Note, however, that the definition of both the `resolve` callback function and the `reject` callback functions now take a single string argument. This string argument ties into the generic type that has been defined for this promise, that is, `Promise<string>`. If we wanted to use a number type for our `resolve` and `reject` arguments, we would need to define our return type as `Promise<number>`.

The inner workings of the anonymous function are similar to what we have discussed before, with the exception that the call to `resolve` now includes a string as an argument.

Let's take a look at how this return value can be used, as follows:

```
function callPromiseWithParam() {
  console.log(`calling delayedPromiseWithParam`);
  delayedPromiseWithParam().then( (message: string) => {
    console.log(`Promise.then() returned ${message} `);
  } );
}

callPromiseWithParam();
```

Here, we have defined a function named `callPromiseWithParam`, that logs a message to the console, and then calls our `delayedPromiseWithParam` function. We then use the fluent syntax to attach an anonymous function to the `then` function of the promise. Note how our anonymous function now takes a single string parameter, named `message`. This corresponds to the promise callback of `resolve : (str: sring )`. The output of this code is as follows:

```
calling delayedPromiseWithParam
Promise.then() returned resolved_within_promise
```

As expected, our promise called the `resolve` callback, that is, `resolve("resolved_within_promise")`, which corresponds to our `then( (message: string) => { ... } )`.

Note that promises can only return a single value when calling either the `resolve` or `reject` callback functions. If you need to return a message that contains multiple fields, then you will need to use an interface, as follows:

```
interface IPromiseMessage {
  message: string;
  id: number;
}

function promiseWithInterface() : Promise<IPromiseMessage> {
  return new Promise<IPromiseMessage> (
  (
     resolve: (message: IPromiseMessage) => void,
     reject: (message: IPromiseMessage) => void
  )  => {
          resolve({message: "test", id: 1});
       }
  );
}
```

Here, we have defined an interface named `IPromiseMessage` that contains a `message` of type `string`, and an `id` of type `number`. Our function named `promiseWithInterface` now returns a `Promise<IPromiseMesssage>`, and the `resolve` and `reject` callback functions now use `IPromiseMessage` as the argument type. Our call to `resolve` must now construct an object with both a `message` property and an `id` property, in order to correctly implement the `IPromiseMessage` interface. Using interfaces in this way allows our promises to return any type of data.

# Async and await

As a further language enhancement when working with promises, TypeScript introduces two keywords that work together when using promises. These two keywords are `async` and `await`. The usage of `async` and `await` can be best described by considering some sample code, as follows:

```
function awaitDelayed() : Promise<void> {
  return new Promise<void> (
    ( resolve: () => void,
      reject: () => void ) =>
      {
         function afterWait() {
           console.log(`calling resolve`);
           resolve();
         }
         setTimeout(afterWait, 1000);
      }
  );
}
```

We start with a fairly standard function named `awaitDelayed` that returns a promise, similar to the examples that we have seen before. Note that in the body of the `afterWait` function, we log a message to the console before calling the `resolve` callback. Let's now take a look at how we can use this promise with the `async` and `await` keywords, as follows:

```
async function callAwaitDelayed() {
  console.log(`call awaitDelayed`);
  await awaitDelayed();
  console.log(`after awaitDelayed`);
}

callAwaitDelayed();
```

We start with a function named `callAwaitDelayed` that is prefixed by the `async` keyword. Within this function, we log a message to the console, and then call the previously defined `awaitDelayed` function. This time, however, we prefix the call to the `awaitDelayed` function with the keyword `await`. We then log another message to the console. The output of this code is as follows:

```
call awaitDelayed
calling resolve
after awaitDelayed
```

What this output is showing is that the `await` keyword is actually waiting for the asynchronous function to be called before continuing on with the program execution. This produces an easy to read, and easy to follow flow of program logic by automatically pausing execution until the promise is fulfilled.

# Await errors

Our promise objects generally define both a success condition as well as an error condition when calling asynchronous functions. In order to trap these error conditions when using async await syntax, we can use a `try...catch` block. To illustrate this, let's define a promise that returns an error, as well as an error message, as follows:

```
function awaitError() : Promise<string> {
  return new Promise<string> (
    ( resolve: (message: string) => void,
      reject: (error: string) => void ) =>
      {
         function afterWait() {
           console.log(`calling reject`);
           reject("an error occurred");
         }
         setTimeout(afterWait, 1000);
      }
  );
}
```

Here, we have a function named `awaitError` that is defining and returning a `Promise<string>`, and is using our standard promise syntax with a one second delay. The line to note here is inside the `afterWait` function, where we are calling the `reject` promise callback with an error message. Our corresponding `async await` function will be as follows:

```
async function callAwaitError() {
  console.log(`call awaitError`);
  try {
    await awaitError();
  } catch (error) {
      console.log(`error returned : ${error}`);
  }
  console.log(`after awaitDelayed`);
}

callAwaitError();
```

Here, we have an `async` function named `callAwaitError` that logs a message to the console, and then calls `await awaitError()` within a `try...catch` block. Note again that the program logic will pause when it reaches the `await` keyword for the asynchronous function to return before continuing on with code execution. In this case, however, the call to `await` will result in an error being thrown, which will be trapped by the `catch(error)` block. Within this block, we are logging the error message received to the console. The output of this code is as follows:

```
call awaitError
calling reject
error returned : an error occurred
after awaitDelayed
```

As can be seen by the output, the program execution is pausing on the `await awaitError()` asynchronous function to return. When an error occurs, the `catch` block is activated, and the `catch` argument `error` holds the error message generated within the promise.

# Promise versus await syntax

As a refresher of promise versus async await syntax, let's compare these two techniques side by side. Firstly, the `then` and `catch` syntax used by standard promises:

```
function simplePromises() {
  // invoke async function
  delayedPromise().then(
    () => {
      // execute on success
    }
  ).catch (
    () => {
      // execute on error
    }
  );
  // code here does NOT wait for async call
}
```

Note that in the promise code above, we are using `.then` and `.catch` to define anonymous functions to be called depending on whether the asynchronous call was successful or not. Another caveat when using promise syntax is that any code outside of the `.then` or `.catch` block will be executed immediately, and will not wait for the asynchronous call to complete.

Secondly, the new async await syntax :

```
async function usingAsyncSyntax() {
  try {
    await delayedPromise();
    // execute on success
  } catch(error) {
      // execute on error
  }
  // code here waits for async call
}
```

Here, our async await syntax allows for a very simple syntax that flows logically. We know that any call to `await` will block code execution until the asynchronous function has returned, including any code defined outside our `try...catch` block.

As can be seen by comparing the two styles side by side, using async await syntax simplifies our code, makes it more human readable, and as such, less error-prone.

# Await messages

The final topic we will discuss on async await is how to process messages that are returned within our promises. Consider the following promise definition:

```
function asyncWithMessage() : Promise<string> {
  return new Promise<string> (
    ( resolve: (message: string ) => void,
        reject: (message: string) => void
    ) => {
      function afterWait() {
        resolve("resolve_message");
      }
        setTimeout(afterWait, 1000);
      }
  );
}
```

Here, we have defined a standard function returning a promise after a one second delay. The code to note here is the call to `resolve` within the `afterWait` function that is sending a message back to the callback. In this case, it is returning a string value of `"resolve_message"`, which matches our `Promise<string>` syntax. Again, we can use interfaces to return multiple values within a promise. Our corresponding async await function that uses this promise is as follows:

```
async function awaitMessage() {
  console.log(`calling asyncWithMessage`);
  let message: string = await asyncWithMessage();
  console.log(`message returned: ${message}`);
}

awaitMessage();
```

Here, we have defined an `async` function named `awaitMessage` that is logging a message to the console, and then calling the `asyncWithMessage` function. Note how we retrieved the message returned by the promise by simply defining a variable to hold the return value of the `await` call. We are then logging the received message to the console. The output of this code is as follows:

```
calling asyncWithMessage
message returned: resolve_message
```

As we can see by this code sample, retrieving and processing messages that are returned when using the `await` keyword is very simple. All we need to do is define a variable to hold the return result of the `await` call, and then we have access to our message.

# Summary

In this chapter, we have had an in-depth discussion on decorators, generics, and asynchronous programming techniques using promises and async await. We have seen how decorators provide a way of injecting code into, or modifying class definitions. We have also explored using experimental metadata information when working with decorators and class definitions. Our discussion then turned to generics, what they are, and how they are used. We worked through generic interfaces, and creating objects within generic functions. Our final discussion revolved around asynchronous programming techniques using callbacks, promises, and the `async` and `await` keywords.

In the next chapter, we will look at the mechanism that TypeScript uses to integrate with existing JavaScript libraries–declaration files.

# 5
# Writing and Using Declaration Files

One of the most appealing facets of JavaScript development is the myriad of external JavaScript libraries that have already been published, such as jQuery, Knockout, and Underscore. We have already seen how TypeScript uses "syntactic sugar" to enhance our JavaScript development experience, but how do we apply this "sugar" to existing JavaScript or JavaScript libraries? The answer is relatively simple–declaration files.

A declaration file is a special type of file used by the TypeScript compiler. It is marked with a `.d.ts` extension, and is then used by the TypeScript compiler within the compilation step. Declaration files are similar to header files used in other languages; they simply describe the syntax and structure of available functions and properties, but do not provide an implementation. Declaration files, therefore, do not actually generate any JavaScript code. They are there simply to provide TypeScript compatibility with external libraries, or to fill in the gaps for JavaScript code that TypeScript does not know about. In order to use any external JavaScript library within TypeScript, you will need a declaration file.

In this chapter, we will explore declaration files, show the reasoning behind them, and build one based on some existing JavaScript code. If you are familiar with declaration files and how to use them, then you may be interested in the *Declaration Syntax Reference* section, which is designed as a quick reference guide to the module definition syntax. Since writing declaration files is a rather small part of TypeScript development, we do not write them very often.

We will be looking at the following topics in this chapter:

- Global variables
- Using JavaScript code blocks in HTML
- Writing your own declaration files
- Module merging
- Declaration syntax reference

# Global variables

Most modern websites use some sort of server engine to generate the HTML for their web pages. If you are familiar with the Microsoft stack of technologies, then you would know that ASP.NET MVC is a very popular server-side engine, used to generate HTML pages based on master pages, partial pages, and MVC views. If you are a Node developer, then you may be using one of the popular Node packages to help you construct web pages through templates, such as Jade, Handlebars or **Embedded JavaScript** (**EJS**).

Within these templating engines, you may sometimes need to set JavaScript properties on the HTML page as a result of your server-side logic. As an example, let's assume that you keep a list of contact e-mail addresses on your database, and then surface these to your HTML page through a JavaScript global variable named `CONTACT_EMAIL_ARRAY`. Your rendered HTML page would then include a `<script>` tag that contains this global variable and contact e-mail addresses. You may have some JavaScript that reads this array, and then renders the values in a footer. The following HTML sample shows what a generated script would end up looking like:

```
<body>
  <script type="text/javascript">
    var CONTACT_EMAIL_ARRAY = [
        "help@site.com",
        "contactus@site.com",
        "webmaster@site.com"
    ];
  </script>
</body>
```

This HTML has a <script> block and within this <script> block, some JavaScript. The JavaScript defines a variable named `CONTACT_EMAIL_ARRAY` that contains some strings. Let's assume that we wanted to write some TypeScript that can read this global variable. Consider the following TypeScript code:

```
class GlobalLogger {
  static logGlobalsToConsole() {
    for(let email of CONTACT_EMAIL_ARRAY) {
      console.log(`found contact : ${email}`);
    }
  }
}

window.onload = () => {
  GlobalLogger.logGlobalsToConsole();
}
```

This code creates a class named `GlobalLogger` with a single static function named `logGlobalsToConsole`. The function simply iterates through the `CONTACT_EMAIL_ARRAY` global variable, and logs the items in the array to the console.

If we compile this TypeScript code, we will generate the following errors:

```
error TS2304: Cannot find name 'CONTACT_EMAIL_ARRAY'
```

This error indicates that the TypeScript compiler does not know anything about the variable named `CONTACT_EMAIL_ARRAY`. It does not even know that it is an array. As this piece of JavaScript is outside any TypeScript code, we will need to treat it in the same way as external JavaScript.

To solve our compilation problem, and make this `CONTACT_EMAIL_ARRAY` variable visible to TypeScript, we will need to use a declaration file. Let's create a file named `globals.d.ts` and include the following TypeScript declaration within it:

```
declare var CONTACT_EMAIL_ARRAY: string [];
```

The first thing to notice is that we are using a new TypeScript keyword – `declare`. The `declare` keyword tells the TypeScript compiler that we want to define the type of something, but that the implementation of this object (or variable or function) will be resolved at runtime. We have declared a variable named `CONTACT_EMAIL_ARRAY` that is of type `string []`. This `declare` keyword does two things for us, it allows the use of the variable `CONTACT_EMAIL_ARRAY` within TypeScript code, and it also strongly types this variable to be an array of strings.

With this `globals.d.ts` file in place, our code compiles correctly. If we now run this in a browser, the console output of our browser log will look as follows:

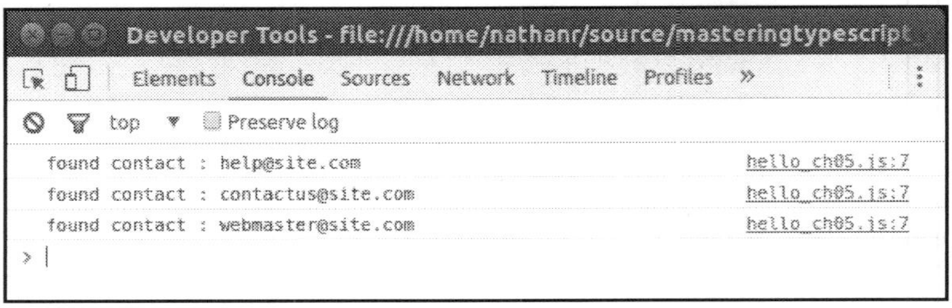


Using global variables in TypeScript

So, by using a declaration file named `globals.d.ts`, we have been able to describe the structure of an external JavaScript variable to the TypeScript compiler. This JavaScript variable is defined outside any of our TypeScript code, yet we are still able to work with the definition of this variable within TypeScript.

This is what declaration files are used for. We are basically telling the TypeScript compiler to use the definitions found within a declaration file within the compilation step, and that the actual variables themselves will only be available at runtime.

> Definition files also bring Intellisense or code completion functionality to our IDE for external JavaScript libraries and code.

# Using JavaScript code blocks in HTML

The samples we have just seen are an example of tight coupling between the generated HTML content (that contains JavaScript code in script blocks) on your web page, and the actual running JavaScript. You may argue, however, that this is a design flaw. If the web page needed an array of contact e-mails, then the JavaScript application should simply send an AJAX request to the server for the same information in JSON format. While this is a very valid argument, there are cases where including content in the rendered HTML is actually faster.

There used to be a time where the Internet seemed to be capable of sending and receiving vast amounts of information in the blink of an eye. Bandwidth and speed on the Internet were growing exponentially, and desktops were getting larger amounts of RAM and faster processors. As developers, during this stage of the Internet highway, we stopped thinking about how much RAM a typical user had on their machine. We also stopped thinking about how much data we were sending across the wire. This was because Internet speeds were so fast and browser processing speed was seemingly limitless.

And then came along the mobile phone and it felt like we were back in the 1990s with incredibly slow Internet connections, tiny screen resolutions, limited processing power, and very little RAM (and popular arcade gaming experiences such as Elevator Action `https://archive.org/details/Elevator_Action_1985_Sega_Taito_JP_en`). The point of this story is that as modern web developers, we still need to be mindful of browsers that run on mobile phones. These browsers are sometimes running on very limited Internet connections, meaning that we must carefully measure the size of our JavaScript libraries, JSON data, and HTML pages, to ensure that our applications are fast and usable, even on mobile browsers.

This technique of including JavaScript variables or smaller static JSON data within the rendered HTML page often provides us with the fastest way to render a screen on an older browser, or in the modern age, a mobile phone. Many popular sites use this technique to quickly render the general structure of the page (header, side panels, footers, and so on) before the main content is delivered through asynchronous JSON requests. This technique works well because it renders the page faster and gives the user faster visual feedback.

# Structured data

Let's enhance this simple array of contact e-mails with a little more relevant data. For each of these e-mail addresses, let's assume that we also want to include some text to render within the footer of our page, along with the e-mail addresses. Consider the following HTML script tag:

```
<script type="text/javascript">
  var CONTACT_DATA = [
    { DisplayText: 'Help',
    Email: 'help@site.com' } ,
    { DisplayText: 'Contace',
    Email: 'contactus@site.com' },
    { DisplayText: 'Webmaster',
    Email: 'webmaster@site.com' }
  ];
</script>
```

Here, we have defined a global variable named `CONTACT_DATA` that is an array of objects. Each object has a property named `DisplayText` and a property named `Email`. If we are to use this array within our TypeScript code, we will need to include a definition of this variable in our `globals.d.ts` declaration file, as follows:

```
interface IContactData {
  DisplayText: string;
  Email: string;
}

declare var CONTACT_DATA: IContactData[];
```

Here, we start with an interface definition named `IContactData` to represent the properties of an individual item in the `CONTACT_DATA` array. Each item has a `DisplayText` property that is of the type `string`, as well as an `Email` property which is also of the type `string`. Our `IContactData` interface, therefore, matches the original object properties of a single item in the `CONTACT_DATA` array. We then declare a variable named `CONTACT_DATA` and set its type to be an array of the `IContactData` interfaces.

This allows us to work with the `CONTACT_DATA` variable within TypeScript. Let's now create a class to process this data, as follows:

```
class ContactLogger {
  static logContactData() {
    for (let contact of CONTACT_DATA) {
      console.log(`DisplayText: ${contact.DisplayText}` +
        `, Email : ${contact.Email}`);
    }
  }
}

window.onload = () => {
  ContactLogger.logContactData();
}
```

Here, the class `ContactLogger` has a single static method named `logContactData`. Within this method, we loop through all of the items in the `CONTACT_DATA` array. As we are using the `for...of` syntax, the `contact` variable will be strongly typed to be of type `IContactData`, and therefore will have two properties–`DisplayText` and `Email`. We simply log these values to the console. The output of this code would be:

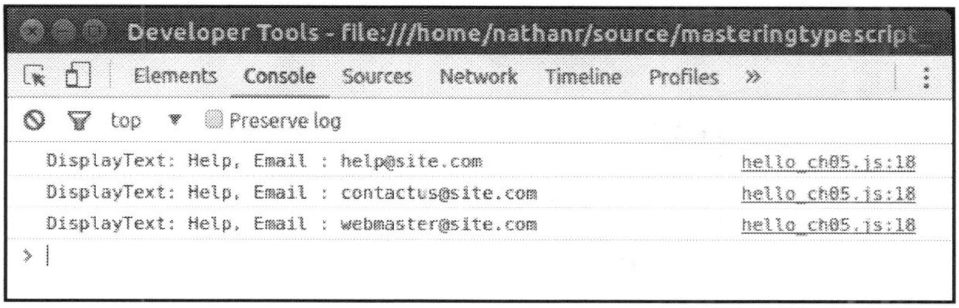


Using advanced global variables in TypeScript

# Writing your own declaration file

In any development team, there will come a time when you will need to either bug-fix, or enhance a body of code that has already been written in JavaScript. If you are in this situation, then you would want to try and write new areas of code in TypeScript, and integrate them with your existing body of JavaScript. To do so, however, you will need to write your own declaration files for any existing JavaScript that you need to reuse. This may seem like a daunting and time-consuming task, but when you are faced with this situation, just remember to take small steps, and define small sections of code at a time. You will be surprised at how simple it really is.

In this section, let's assume that you need to integrate an existing helper class, one that is reused across many projects, is well tested, and is a development team standard. This class has been implemented as a JavaScript closure, as follows:

```
ErrorHelper = (function() {
  return {
    containsErrors: function (response) {
      if (!response || !response.responseText)
        return false;

      var errorValue = response.responseText;

      if (String(errorValue.failure) == "true"
        || Boolean(errorValue.failure)) {
        return true;
      }
      return false;
    },
    trace: function (msg) {
      var traceMessage = msg;
      if (msg.responseText) {
        traceMessage = msg.responseText.errorMessage;
```

```
            }
            console.log("[" +
              new Date().toLocaleDateString()
              + "] " + traceMessage);
        }
    }
})();
```

This JavaScript code snippet defines a JavaScript object named `ErrorHelper` that has two methods. The `containsErrors` method takes an object named `response` as an argument. This `response` object is then checked for errors. An object does not have an error if the following are true:

- The `response` argument is undefined
- The `response.responseText` is undefined

An error condition, however, is returned if the following are true:

- The `response.responseText.failure` property is set to the string value of `"true"`
- The `response.responseText.failure` property is set to the boolean value of `true`

The `ErrorHelper` closure also has a function called `trace` that can be called with a string, or a `response` object similar to what the `containsErrors` function is expecting.

Unfortunately, this `ErrorHelper` function is missing a key piece of documentation. What is the structure of the object being passed into these two methods, and what properties does it have? Without some form of documentation, we are forced to reverse engineer the code to determine what the structure of the `response` object looks like. If we can find some sample usages of the `ErrorHelper` class, this may help us to guess this structure.

As an example of how this `ErrorHelper` is used, consider the following JavaScript code:

```
var failureMessage = {
  responseText : {
    "failure" :true,
    "errorMessage" : "Message From failureMessage"
  }
}

var failureMessageString = {
  responseText : {
    "failure" : "true",
    "errorMessage" : "Message from failureMessageString"
```

```
    }
  }

  var successMessage = {
    responseText : {
      "failure" : false
    }
  }

  if (ErrorHelper.containsErrors(failureMessage))
     ErrorHelper.trace(failureMessage);
  if (ErrorHelper.containsErrors(failureMessageString))
     ErrorHelper.trace(failureMessageString);
  if (!ErrorHelper.containsErrors(successMessage))
     ErrorHelper.trace("success");
```

Here, we start with a variable named `failureMessage` that has a single property `reponseText`. The `responseText` property in turn has two child properties–`failure` and `errorMessage`. Our next variable `failureMessageString` has the same structure, but defines the `responseText.failure` property to be of type string, instead of type boolean. Finally, our `successMessage` object just defines the `responseText.failure` property to be `false`, but it does not have an `errorMessage` property.

> In JavaScript JSON format, property names are required to have quotes around them, whereas in JavaScript object format, these are optional. Therefore, the structure `{"failure" : true}` is syntactically equivalent to the structure `{failure : true}`.

The last couple of lines of the preceding code snippet show how the `ErrorHelper` closure is used. All we need to do is call the `ErrorHelper.containsErrors` method with our variable, and if the result is `true`, log the message to the console via the `ErrorHelper.trace` function. Our output would be as follows:

ErrorHelper console output

# The module keyword

To test this JavaScript `ErrorHelper` closure using TypeScript, we will need an HTML page that includes both the `error_helper.js` file, and a TypeScript generated JavaScript file. Assuming that our TypeScript file is called `ErrorHelperTypeScript.ts`, our HTML page would then be as follows:

```
<!DOCTYPE html>
<html xmlns="http://www.w3.org/1999/xhtml">
<head>specify.
  <title></title>
  <script src="error_helper.js"></script>
  <script src="ErrorHelperTypeScript.js"></script>
</head>
<body>

</body>
</html>
```

This HTML is very simple, and includes both the existing `error_helper.js` JavaScript file, as well as the TypeScript generated `ErrorHelperTypeScript.js` file.

Within the `ErrorHelperTypeScript.ts` file, let's use the `ErrorHelper`, as follows:

```
window.onload = () => {
  var failureMessage = {
    responseText : {
      "failure" : true,
      "errorMessage" : "Error Message from Typescript"
    }
  }
  if (ErrorHelper.containsErrors(failureMessage))
     ErrorHelper.trace(failureMessage);
}
```

Here, we have a stripped down version of our original JavaScript sample. In fact, we can just copy and paste the original JavaScript code into our TypeScript file. We first create a `failureMessage` object with the correct properties, and then simply call the `ErrorHelper.containsErrors` method, and the `ErrorHelper.trace` method. If we were to compile our TypeScript file at this stage, we would receive the following error:

```
error TS2304: Cannot find name 'ErrorHelper'.
```

This error is indicating that there is no valid TypeScript type named `ErrorHelper`, even though we have the full source of `ErrorHelper` in our JavaScript file. TypeScript by default, will look through all the TypeScript files in our project to find class definitions, but it will not parse JavaScript files. We will need a new TypeScript definition file in order to correctly compile this code.

> This definition file is not included in the HTML file at all; it is only used by the TypeScript compiler and does not generate any JavaScript.

Without a set of helpful documentation on our `ErrorHelper` class, we will need to reverse engineer a TypeScript definition purely by reading the source code. This is obviously not an ideal situation, and is not recommended, but at this stage, it is all we can do. In these situations, the best starting point is simply to look at the usage samples and work our way up from there.

Looking at the usage of the `ErrorHelper` closure in JavaScript, there are two key pieces that should be included in our declaration file. The first is a set of function definitions for the `containsErrors` and `trace` functions. The second is a set of interfaces to describe the structure of the `response` object that the `ErrorHelper` closure relies upon. Let's start with the function definitions, and create a new TypeScript file named `ErrorHelper.d.ts` with the following code:

```
declare module ErrorHelper {
  function containsErrors(response);
  function trace(message);
}
```

This declaration file starts with the `declare` keyword that we have seen before, but then uses a new TypeScript keyword–`module`. The `module` keyword must be followed by a module name, which in this case, is `ErrorHelper`. This module name must match the closure name from the original JavaScript that we are describing. In all of our usages of the `ErrorHelper`, we have always pre-fixed the functions `containsErrors` and `trace` with the closure name `ErrorHelper` itself. This module name is also known as a namespace. If we had another class named `AjaxHelper` that also included a `containsErrors` function, we would be able to distinguish between the `AjaxHelper.containsErrors` and the `ErrorHelper.containsErrors` functions by using these namespaces, or module names.

The second line of our module declaration indicates that we are defining a function called `containsErrors` that takes one parameter. The third line of this module declaration indicates that we are defining another function named `trace` that also takes a single parameter. With this definition in place, our TypeScript code sample will compile correctly.

# Interfaces

Although we have correctly defined the two functions that are available to users of the `ErrorHelper` closure, we are missing the second piece of information about the functions available on the `ErrorHelper` closure–the structure of the `response` argument. We are not strongly typing the arguments for either of the `containsErrors` or `trace` functions. At this stage, our TypeScript code can pass anything into these two functions because it does not have a definition for the `response` or `message` arguments. We know, however, that both these functions query our parameters for a specific structure. If we pass in an object that does not conform to this structure, then our JavaScript code will cause runtime errors.

To solve this problem and to make our code more stable, let's define an interface for these parameters:

```
interface IResponse {
  responseText: IFailureMessage;
}

interface IFailureMessage {
  failure: boolean;
  errorMessage: string;
}
```

We start with an interface named `IResponse` that has a single property of `responseText`, the same name as the original JavaScript object. This `responseText` property is strongly typed to be of type `IFailureMessage`. The `IFailureMessage` interface is strongly typed to have two properties–`failure`, which is of type `boolean`, and `errorMessage`, which is of type `string`. These interfaces correctly describe the proper structure of the `response` argument for the `containsErrors` and `trace` functions. We can now modify our original declaration for these functions, as follows:

```
declare module ErrorHelper {
  function containsErrors(response: IResponse);
  function trace(message: IResponse);
}
```

The function definition for `containsErrors` and `trace` now strongly types the response argument to be of type `IResponse`, which we defined earlier. This modification to the definition file will now force any further usage of the `containsErrors` or `trace` functions to send in a valid argument that conforms to the `IResponse` structure. Let's write some intentionally incorrect TypeScript code and see what happens:

```
var anotherFailure: IResponse = {
  responseText: {
    success: true
  }
}
```

We start by creating a variable named `anotherFailure` and specify its type to be of type `IResponse`. Unfortunately, the `IResponse` interface does not have a property named `success`, and so we will generate the following TypeScript error:

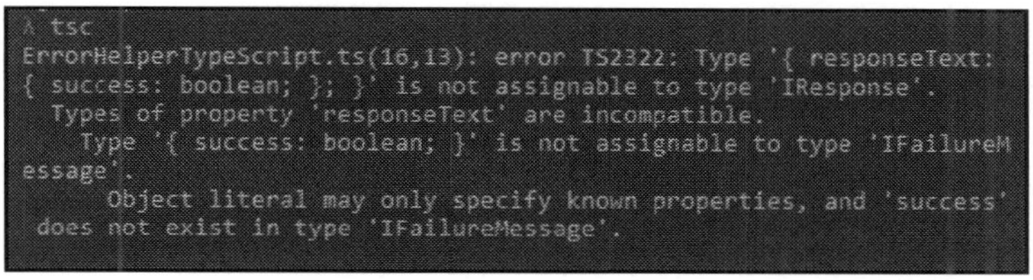

```
λ tsc
ErrorHelperTypeScript.ts(16,13): error TS2322: Type '{ responseText:
{ success: boolean; }; }' is not assignable to type 'IResponse'.
  Types of property 'responseText' are incompatible.
    Type '{ success: boolean; }' is not assignable to type 'IFailureM
essage'.
      Object literal may only specify known properties, and 'success'
 does not exist in type 'IFailureMessage'.
```

TypeScript error message with an invalid data structure

As can be seen from this fairly verbose but informative error message, the structure of the `anotherFailure` variable is causing all the errors. Even though we have correctly referenced the `responseText` property of `IResponse`, the `responseText` property is strongly typed to be of type `IFailureMessage`, which requires both a `failure` property and an `errorMessage` property; hence the error.

By creating a strongly typed declaration file for the existing `ErrorHelper` class, we can ensure that any further TypeScript usage of the existing `ErrorHelper` JavaScript closure will not generate runtime errors.

# Union types

We are not quite finished with the declaration file for the `ErrorHelper` just yet. If we take a look at the original JavaScript usage of the `ErrorHelper`, we will notice that the `containsErrors` function also allows for the `failure` property of `responseText` to be a string:

```
var failureMessage = {
  responseText : {
    "failure" : "true",
    "errorMessage" : "Error Message from Typescript"
  }
}
```

If we compile this code now, we will get the following compile error:

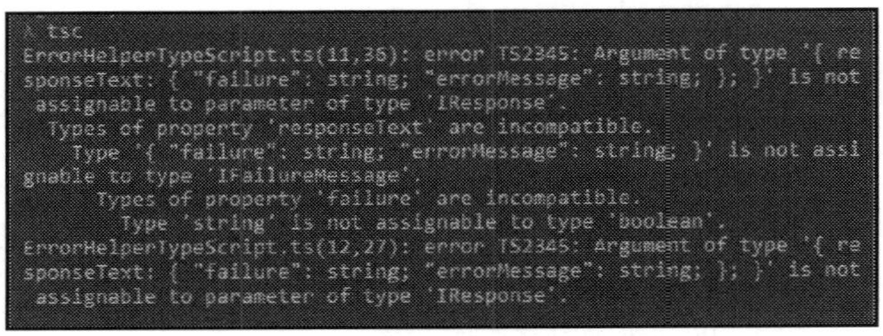


TypeScript error message with invalid property

In the preceding definition of the variable `failureMessageString`, the type of the `"failure"` property is `"true"`, which is of type `string`, and not `true`, which is of type `boolean`. In order to allow for this variant on the original `IFailureMessage` interface, we will need to modify our declaration file. The simplest way to allow for both types would be to use a type union, as follows:

```
interface IFailureMessage {
  failure: boolean | string;
  errorMessage: string;
}
```

Here, we have simply updated the `failure` property on the `IFailureMessage` interface to allow for both `boolean` and `string` types. Our code will now compile correctly.

This completes our definition file for the `ErrorHelper` JavaScript class.

# Module merging

As we now know, the TypeScript compiler will automatically search through all the `.d.ts` files in our project to pick up declaration files. If these declaration files contain the same module name, the TypeScript compiler will merge these two declaration files and use a combined version of the module declarations.

Suppose we have a file named `MergedModule1.d.ts` that contains the following definition:

```
declare module MergedModule {
  function functionA();
}
```

In addition, we have a second file named `MergedModule2.d.ts` that contains the following definition:

```
declare module MergedModule {
  function functionB();
}
```

The TypeScript compiler will then merge these two modules as if they were a single definition:

```
declare module MergedModule {
  function functionA();
  function functionB();
}
```

This will allow both `functionA` and `functionB` to be valid functions of the same `MergedModule` namespace and allow the following usage:

```
MergedModule.functionA();
MergedModule.functionB();
```

Modules can also merge with interfaces, classes, and enums. Classes, however, cannot merge with other classes, variables, or interfaces.

# Declaration syntax reference

When creating declaration files and using the `module` keyword, there are a number of rules that can be used to mix and match definitions. As a TypeScript programmer, you will generally only write module definitions every now and then, and on occasion, need to add a new definition to an existing declaration file.

This section, therefore, is designed to be a quick reference guide to this declaration file syntax, or a cheat sheet. Each section contains a description of the module definition rule, a JavaScript syntax snippet, and then the equivalent TypeScript declaration file syntax.

To use this reference section, simply match the JavaScript that you are trying to emulate from the JavaScript syntax section, and then write your declaration file with the equivalent definition syntax. We will start with the function overrides syntax as an example.

# Function overrides

Declaration files can include multiple definitions for the same function. If the same JavaScript function can be called with different types, you will need to declare a function override for each variant of the function.

### The JavaScript syntax

```
trace("trace a string");
trace(true);
trace(1);
trace({ id: 1, name: "test" });
```

### The declaration file syntax

```
declare function trace(arg: string | number | boolean );
declare function trace(arg: { id: number; name: string });
```

Each function definition must have a unique function signature.

# Nested namespaces

Module definitions can contain nested module definitions, which then translate to nested namespaces. If your JavaScript uses namespaces, then you will need to define nested module declarations to match the JavaScript namespaces.

### The JavaScript syntax

```
FirstNamespace.SecondNamespace.ThirdNamespace.log("test");
```

### The declaration file syntax

```
declare module FirstNamespace {
  module SecondNamespace {
    module ThirdNamespace {
      function log(msg: string);
    }
  }
}
```

# Classes

Class definitions are allowed within module definitions. If your JavaScript uses classes, or the new operator, then the newable classes will need to be defined in your declaration file.

### The JavaScript syntax

```
var myClass = new MyClass();
```

### The declaration file syntax

```
declare class MyClass { }
```

# Class namespaces

Class definitions are allowed within nested module definitions. If your JavaScript classes have a preceding namespace, you will need to declare nested modules to match the namespaces first, and then you can declare classes within the correct namespace.

### The JavaScript syntax

```
var myNestedClass = new OuterName.InnerName.NestedClass();
```

### The declaration file syntax

```
declare module OuterName {
  module InnerName {
    class NestedClass {}
  }
}
```

# Class constructor overloads

Class definitions can contain constructor overloads. If your JavaScript classes can be constructed using different types, or with multiple parameters, you will need to list each of these variants in your declaration file as constructor overloads.

### The JavaScript syntax

```
var myClass = new MyClass();
var myClass2 = new MyClass(1, "test");
```

### The declaration file syntax

```
declare class MyClass {
  constructor(id: number, name: string);
  constructor();
}
```

# Class properties

Classes can contain properties. You will need to list each property of your class within your class declaration.

### The JavaScript syntax

```
var classWithProperty = new ClassWithProperty();
classWithProperty.id = 1;
```

### The declaration file syntax

```
declare class ClassWithProperty {
  id: number;
}
```

# Class functions

Classes can contain functions. You will need to list each function of your JavaScript class within your class declaration, in order for the TypeScript compiler to accept calls to these functions.

### The JavaScript syntax

```
var classWithFunction = new ClassWithFunction();
classWithFunction.functionToRun();
```

### The declaration file syntax

```
declare class ClassWithFunction {
  functionToRun(): void;
}
```

Functions or properties that are considered as private do not need to be exposed via the declaration file, and can simply be omitted.

# Static properties and functions

Class methods and properties can be static. If your JavaScript functions or properties can be called without needing an instance of an object to work with, then these properties or functions will need to be marked as static.

### The JavaScript syntax

```
StaticClass.staticId = 1;
StaticClass.staticFunction();
```

### The declaration file syntax

```
declare class StaticClass {
  static staticId: number;
  static staticFunction();
}
```

# Global functions

Functions that do not have a namespace prefix can be declared in the global namespace. If your JavaScript defines global functions, these will need to be declared without a namespace.

### The JavaScript syntax

```
globalLogError("test");
```

### The declaration file syntax

```
declare function globalLogError(msg: string);
```

# Function signatures

A function can use a function signature as a parameter. JavaScript functions that use callback functions or anonymous functions, will need to be declared with the correct function signature.

### The JavaScript syntax

```
describe("test", function () {
});
```

### The declaration file syntax

```
declare function describe(
name: string, functionDef: () => void);
```

# Optional properties

Classes or functions can contain optional properties. Where JavaScript object parameters are not mandatory, these will need to be marked as optional properties in the declaration.

### The JavaScript syntax

```
var classWithOpt = new ClassWithOptionals();
var classWithOpt1 = new ClassWithOptionals(
  {id: 1});
var classWithOpt2 = new ClassWithOptionals(
  {name: 'test'});
var classWithOpt3 = new ClassWithOptionals(
  {id: 1, name: 'test'});
```

### The declaration file syntax

```
interface IOptionalProperties {
  id?: number;
  name?: string;
}
declare class ClassWithOptionals {
  constructor(options?: IOptionalProperties);
}
```

# Merging functions and modules

A function definition with a specific name can be merged with a module definition of the same name. This means that if your JavaScript function can be called with parameters and also has properties, then you will need to merge a function with a module.

### The JavaScript syntax

```
fnWithProperty(1);
fnWithProperty.name = "name";
```

### The declaration file syntax

```
declare function fnWithProperty(id: number);
declare module fnWithProperty { var name: string; }
```

# Summary

In this chapter, we have outlined what we need to know in order to write and use our own declaration files. We discussed JavaScript global variables in rendered HTML and how to access them in TypeScript. We then moved on to a small JavaScript helper function and wrote our own declaration file for this JavaScript. We finished off the chapter by listing a few module definition rules, highlighting the required JavaScript syntax, and showing what the equivalent TypeScript declaration syntax would be.

In the next chapter, we will look at how to use existing third-party JavaScript libraries, and how to import existing declaration files for these libraries into your TypeScript projects.

# 6
# Third-Party Libraries

Our TypeScript development environment would not amount to much if we were not able to reuse the myriad of existing JavaScript libraries, frameworks, and general goodness available today. As we have seen, however, in order to use a particular third-party library with TypeScript, we will first need a matching definition file.

Soon after TypeScript was released, Boris Yankov set up a GitHub repository to house TypeScript definition files for third-party JavaScript libraries. This repository, named **DefinitelyTyped** (`https://github.com/borisyankov/DefinitelyTyped`) quickly became very popular, and is currently the place to go for high-quality definition files. DefinitelyTyped currently has over 1500 definition files, built up over time from hundreds of contributors from all over the world. If we were to measure the success of TypeScript within the JavaScript community, then the DefinitelyTyped repository would be a good indication of how well TypeScript has been adopted. Before you go ahead and try to write your own definition files, check the DefinitelyTyped repository to see if there is one already available.

In this chapter, we will have a closer look at using these definition files, and cover the following topics:

- Downloading definition files
- Using NuGet within Visual Studio
- Using Typings
- Using Bower
- Using npm and @types
- Choosing a JavaScript framework
- Using TypeScript with Backbone
- Using TypeScript with Angular 1
- Using TypeScript with ExtJS

# Downloading definition files

The simplest method of including a definition file within your TypeScript project is to download the matching `.d.ts` file from DefinitelyTyped. This is a simple matter of finding the relevant file, and downloading the raw content. Let's assume that we wanted to start using jQuery within our project. We have found and downloaded the jQuery JavaScript library (v2.2.3), and included the relevant files within our project, under a directory named `lib`. To download the declaration file, simply browse to the `jquery` directory on DefinitelyTyped (`https://github.com/borisyankov/DefinitelyTyped/tree/master/jquery`). Then click on the `jquery.d.ts` file. This will open up a GitHub page with an editor view of the file. On the menu bar of this editor view, click on the **Raw** button. This will open a copy of the file, and from there, simply right-click, and **Save As** within your project directory structure. Create a new directory under the **lib** folder called `typings`, and save the `jquery.d.ts` file there.

Your project file should look something like the following:

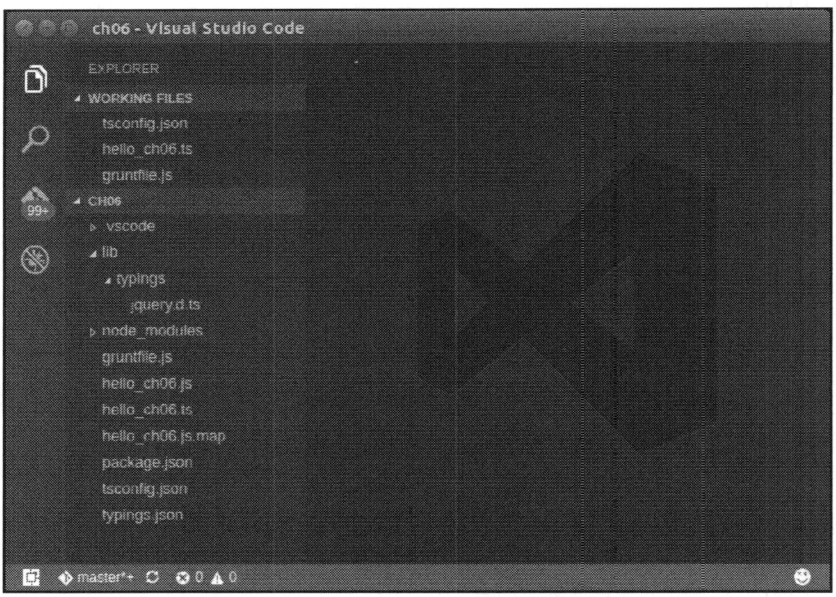


Visual Studio Code project structure with a downloaded jquery.d.ts file

We can now modify our index.html file to include the jquery JavaScript file, and begin writing TypeScript code that targets the jQuery library. Our index.html file will need to be modified as follows:

```
<html>
<head>
  <script src="lib/jquery-2.2.3.min.js"></script>
  <script src="app.js"></script>
</head>
<body>
  <h1>TypeScript html app</h1>
  <p>using jquery</p>
  <div id="content">

  </div>
</body>
</html>
```

The first <script> tag of this index.html file now includes a link to jquery-2.2.3.min.js, and the second <script> tag includes a link to the TypeScript generated app.js. Open up the app.ts TypeScript file, delete the exiting source, and replace it with the following TypeScript code:

```
console.log(`hello app.js`);

$(document).ready( () => {
  $("#content").html(`<h3>Hello TypeScript`);
  }
);
```

Here, we start by logging a message to the console, and then define an anonymous function to execute on the jQuery event of document.ready. The document.ready function is similar to the window.onload function we have been using previously, and will execute once jQuery has initialized. Within the body of this anonymous function, we are simply getting a handle to the DOM element named content using jQuery selector syntax, and then calling the html function to set its HTML value.

The `jquery.d.ts` file that we downloaded is providing us with the relevant module declarations that we need in order to compile jQuery within TypeScript. In other words, it contains TypeScript definitions for `$`, and all of the jQuery functions that are allowed when using the `$ (` function `)` syntax.

# Using NuGet

Instead of manually downloading each `.d.ts` declaration file for our project, we can also use NuGet. NuGet is a popular package management platform that will download required external libraries, and automatically include them within your Visual Studio or WebMatrix project. It can be used for external libraries that are packaged as DLLs such as StructureMap or it can be used for JavaScript libraries and declaration files. NuGet is also available as a command-line utility.

## Using the Extension Manager

To use the NuGet package manager dialog within Visual Studio, select the **Tools** option on the main toolbar, then select **NuGet Package Manager**, and finally select **Manage NuGet Packages for Solution**. This brings up the NuGet package manager dialog. On the left-hand side of the dialog, click on **Browse**. The NuGet dialog will then query the NuGet website and show a list of available packages. At the top left of the screen is a **search** box. Click within the **search** box, and type `jquery` to show all packages available within NuGet for jQuery, as shown in the following screenshot:

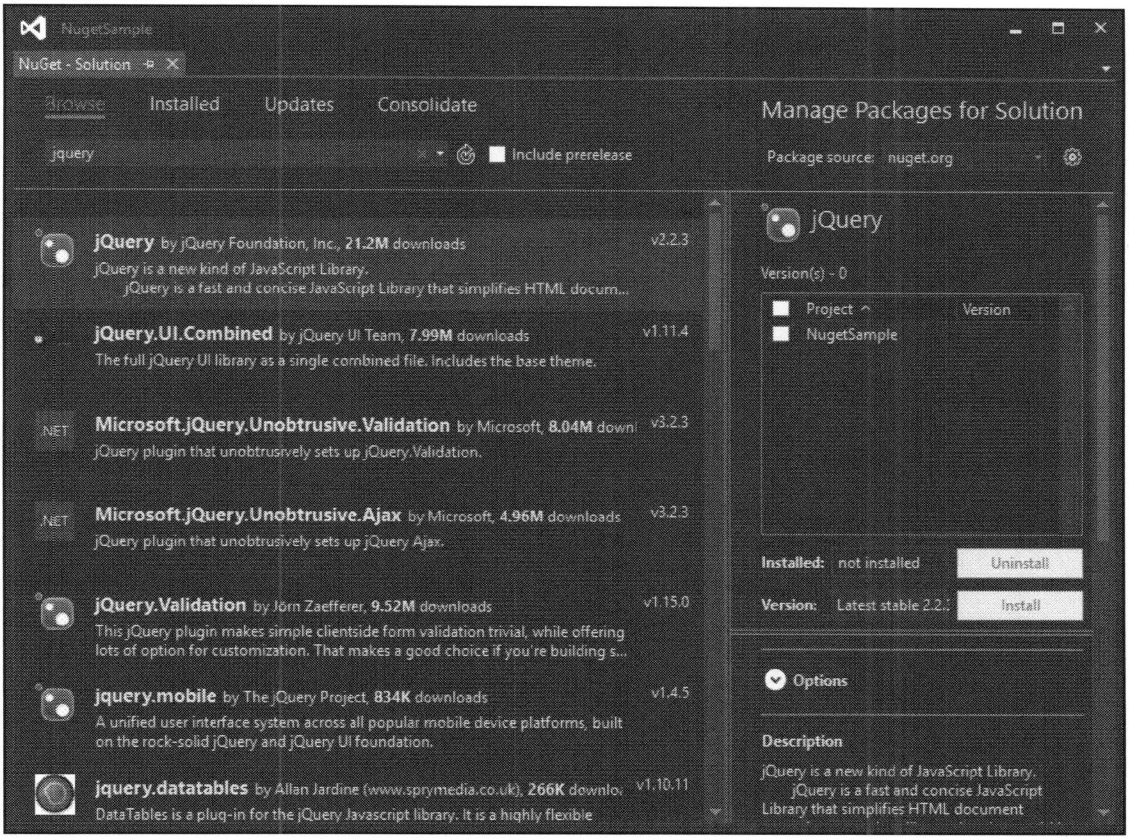


NuGet package manager dialog with results from a query on jQuery

Each package will have an **Install** button highlighted when you select the package in the **search results** panel. When a package is selected, the right-hand pane will show more details about the NuGet package in question. Note that the project details panel also shows the version of the package that you are about to install. Clicking on the **Install** button will download relevant files as well as any dependencies and include them automatically within your project.

> The installation directory that NuGet uses for JavaScript files is in fact called `Scripts` and not the `lib` directory that we created earlier. NuGet uses the `Scripts` directory as a standard, so any packages that contain JavaScript will install the relevant JavaScript files into the `Scripts` directory.

# Installing declaration files

You will find that most of the more popular declaration files that are found on the `DefinitelyTyped` GitHub repository have a corresponding NuGet package. These packages are named `<library>.TypeScript.DefinitelyTyped`, as a standard naming convention. If we type `jquery typescript` into the NuGet search box, we will see a list of these `DefinitelyTyped` packages returned. The NuGet package we are looking for is named `jquery.TypeScript.DefinitelyTyped`, created by Jason Jarret, and is, at the time of writing, at version 3.1.1.

> The `DefinitelyTyped` packages have their own internal version number, and these version numbers do not necessarily match the version of the JavaScript library that you are using.

Installing the `jQuery.TypeScript.DefinitelyTyped` package will create a `typings` directory under the `Scripts` directory, and then include the `jquery.d.ts` definition file. This directory naming standard has been adopted by the various NuGet package authors.

# Using the Package Manager Console

Visual Studio also has a command-line version of the NuGet package manager available as a console application, and it is also integrated into Visual Studio. Clicking on **Tools**, then **NuGet Package Manager**, and finally on **Package Manager Console**, will bring up a new Visual Studio window, and initialize the NuGet command-line interface. The command-line version of NuGet has a number of features that are not included in the GUI version. Type `get-help NuGet` to see the list of top-level command-line arguments that are available.

## Installing packages

To install a NuGet package from the console command line, simply type `install-package <packageName>`. As an example, to install the `jquery.TypeScript.DefinitelyTyped` package, simply type the following:

```
Install-Package jquery.TypeScript.DefinitelyTyped
```

This command will connect to the NuGet server, and download and install the package into your project.

On the toolbar of the **Package Manager Console** window are two drop-down lists, **Package Source** and **Default Project**. If your Visual Studio solution has multiple projects, you will need to select the correct project for NuGet to install the package into from the **Default Project** dropdown.

## Searching for package names

Searching for package names from the command line is accomplished with the `Find-Package` command. As an example, to find available packages that include the `definitelytyped` search string, run the following command:

```
Find-Package definitelytyped
```

## Installing a specific version

There are some JavaScript libraries that are not compatible with jQuery version 2.x, and will require a version of jQuery that is in the 1.x range. To install a specific version of a NuGet package, we will need to specify the `-Version` parameter from the command line. To install the `jquery v1.11.1` package, as an example, run the following from the command line:

```
Install-Package jQuery -Version 1.11.1
```

NuGet will either upgrade or downgrade the version of the package you are installing, if it finds another version already installed within your project. In the preceding example, we had already installed the latest version of jQuery (2.1.1) within our project, so NuGet will first remove `jQuery 2.1.1` before installing `jQuery 1.11.1`.

# Using Typings

As the number of publicly available declaration files for TypeScript started to grow and grow, a node-based command-line utility was released to help with management of declaration files. This package was called the TypeScript definition manager for `DefinitelyTyped`, or simply TSD. While TSD served a useful purpose for a few years, there were some breaking design changes needed in order to provide a suitable long-term solution. TSD has now been deprecated in favor of Typings.

Typings offers functionality similar to the NuGet Package Manager, but it is specifically geared towards TypeScript definition files. Whereas TSD relies on definition files from the `DefinitelyTyped` GitHub repository only, Typings allows definition files to be used from any source.

To install Typings, use `npm` as follows:

```
npm install typings -g
```

At the time of writing, this installed Typings version 2.0.0.

# Searching for packages

Typings allows for querying the package repository using the `search` keyword. To search for the `jquery` definition files, type the following:

```
typings search jquery
```

This command will search the `DefinitelyTyped` repository for any definition files with the name `jquery`. The results of this search show that there are a multitude of definition files, including `chai-jquery` and `jasmine-jquery`, as follows:

Search results for Typings search jquery

The output of the search command shows us the full name of the package, the source of the package, as well as the home page of the package itself. We will use the source of the package as a prefix when we install the definition file we need.

# Typings initialize

Before we start using Typings to download and install definition files, we need to create a `typings.json` file that will record our dependent definition files. This is done by simply typing the following:

```
typings init
```

This command will create the `typings.json` file as follows:

```
{
  "name": "using_typings",
  "dependencies": {}
}
```

# Installing definition files

To install a definition file – `jquery` as an example, use the `install` keyword as follows:

```
typings install dt~jquery --global --save
```

Note that we have prefixed the name of the definition file with the letters `dt~`. This matches the name of the source property that we saw when running our search query. This enables us to install definition files from sources other than DefinitelyTyped, if they are listed.

The `install` command will download the `jquery.d.ts` file into the following directory:

```
\typings\globals\query\index.d.ts
```

Typings will create the `\typings` directory based on the current directory where `typings install` was run, so make sure that you navigate to the same base directory in your project whenever you use Typings from the command line.

Typings also creates a `globals\index.d.ts` file that contains a reference path to all of the definition files that we have downloaded. Our project, therefore, only needs to include a reference to this base `globals\index.d.ts` file, and all other references paths will be automatically updated.

# Installing a specific version

There may be times where you require a specific version of a definition file to be included in your project, and may not simply want the latest version. Typings allows us to view the various versions of a definition file as follows:

```
typings view dt~jquery --versions
```

We can then install a specific version of the definition file as follows:

```
typings install dt~jquery@1.8.0 --global --save
```

# Re-installing definition files

One of the benefits of using Typings is that it can interrogate its `typings.json` file, and re-install any missing declaration files that are not within the project. This can be very handy if you are branching project source code into different directories, or if you are writing a number of projects that all have the same dependencies. Let's assume that you have the `typings.json` file as follows:

```
{
  "name": "using_typings",
  "dependencies": {},
  "globalDependencies": {
    "backbone": "registry:dt/backbone#1.0.0+20160316155526",
    "marionette": "registry:dt/marionette#0.0.0+20160317120654"
  }
}
```

This Typings file indicates that we have two global dependencies, that is, `backbone` and `marionette`. If we copy this file to a new directory, we can re-install these dependencies in our new directory by simply typing the following:

```
typings install
```

> Even if you are using Visual Studio and NuGet as a development environment, you may want to explore using Typings within your project instead of NuGet for definition files. Remember that not all definition files available via Typings are available via NuGet. Also, NuGet is a separate code repository, so it may take some time for package authors to update their definition files.

# Using Bower

Where Typings is used to download and manage TypeScript definition files, Bower is used to download and manage the actual JavaScript libraries themselves. The Bower command-line interface and overall functionality is very similar to Typings. Bower will also ensure that any dependencies a library has will be downloaded with the correct versions. As an example, let's use Bower to download the `backbone.js` library and its only dependency, `underscore.js`.

Installation of Bower is via the standard `npm` installation command, as follows:

```
npm install -g bower
```

Typings and Bower have a very similar command set; in fact the Typings command set was modeled after packages like Bower. So we can use the same workflow for initializing, searching, and installing JavaScript packages as we did with Typings, as follows:

```
bower init
```

This will ask a couple of questions about the current project, and then create a `bower.json` file to store installed packages and dependencies:

```
bower search backbone
```

This will search for Backbone libraries, similar to how Typings does:

```
bower install backbone --save
```

This will install `backbone.js` and its dependencies ( `underscore.js`), and save the dependencies list to the `bower.json` file.

Looking at the directory structure that Bower creates, you will notice that all libraries are downloaded by default to `./bower_components`. Each package then has its own directory, for example, Backbone and Underscore, and within each directory are the released JavaScript files. You will notice that Bower will download and install both the development versions and the minified versions all in one go.

# Using npm and @types

With the release of version 2.0 of the TypeScript compiler, we can now also install declaration files using npm. This means that there is no difference in our toolset in order to install project dependencies, as it is to include the declaration files. As an example, to install the Underscore library as a project dependency, we would type:

```
npm install underscore --save
```

And to install the declaration files for underscore, we can now type

```
npm install @types/underscore --save
```

Note the `@types` prefix used within the `npm` command. This special syntax instructs npm to install the declaration files for underscore, and is a very subtle but easily remembered syntax.

> This mechanism for including type definitions via npm has been adopted as the standard mechanism by TypeScript moving forward.

# Using third-party libraries

In this section of the chapter, we will begin to explore some of the more popular third-party JavaScript libraries, their declaration files, and how to write compatible TypeScript for each of these frameworks. We will compare Backbone, Angular (version 1), and ExtJS, which are all frameworks for building rich client-side JavaScript applications. During our discussion, we will see that some frameworks are highly compliant with the TypeScript language and its features, some are partially compliant, and some have very low compliance.

In the next chapter, we will explore some third-party JavaScript libraries that have been written explicitly with TypeScript in mind, or for which the TypeScript compiler has been modified to work with. In the remainder of this chapter, however, will focus on standard third-party libraries that were designed to support JavaScript.

# Choosing a JavaScript framework

Choosing a JavaScript framework or library to develop **Single Page Applications** (**SPAs**) is a difficult and sometimes daunting task. It seems that there is a new framework appearing every other month, promising more and more functionality for less and less code. To help developers compare these frameworks, and make an informed choice, Addy Osmani wrote an excellent article, named *Journey Through the JavaScript MVC Jungle.* (`http://www.smashingmagazine.com/2012/07/27/journey-through-the-javascript-mvc-jungle/`).

In essence, his advice is simple; it's a personal choice, so try some frameworks out, and see what best fits your needs, your programming mindset, and your existing skill set. The *TodoMVC* project (`http://todomvc.com`), which Addy started, does an excellent job of implementing the same application in a number of MV* JavaScript frameworks. This really is a reference site for digging into a fully working application, and comparing for yourself the coding techniques and styles of different frameworks.

Again, depending on the JavaScript library that you are using within TypeScript, you may need to write your TypeScript code in a specific way. Bear this in mind when choosing a framework, if it is difficult to use with TypeScript, then you may be better off looking at another framework with better integration. If it is easy and natural to work with the framework in TypeScript, then your productivity and overall development experience will be much better.

In this section, we will look at some of the popular JavaScript libraries, along with their declaration files, and see how to write compatible TypeScript. The key thing to remember is that TypeScript generates JavaScript – so if you are battling to use a third-party library, then crack open the generated JavaScript and see what the JavaScript code looks like that TypeScript is emitting. If the generated JavaScript matches the JavaScript code samples in the library's documentation, then you are on the right track. If not, then you may need to modify your TypeScript until the compiled JavaScript starts matching up with the samples.

When trying to write TypeScript code for a third-party JavaScript framework – particularly if you are working off the JavaScript documentation – your initial foray may just be one of trial and error. The rest of this chapter shows how three different libraries require different ways of writing TypeScript.

# Backbone

Backbone is a popular JavaScript library that gives structure to web applications by providing models, collections and views, amongst other things. Backbone has been around since 2010, and has gained a very large following, with a wealth of commercial websites using the framework. According to `Inforworld.com`, Backbone has over 1,600 Backbone related projects on GitHub that rate over three stars, meaning that it has a vast ecosystem of extensions and related libraries.

Let's take a quick look at Backbone written in TypeScript.

The Backbone environment can be set up with Bower and Typings as follows:

```
bower install backbone  --save
typings install dt~backbone-global  --global --save
typings install dt~jquery --global  --save
typings install dt~underscore -global --save
```

# Using inheritance with Backbone

From the Backbone documentation, we find an example of creating a `Backbone.Model` in JavaScript as follows:

```
var NoteModel = Backbone.Model.extend (
{
  initialize: function() {
    console.log("NoteModel initialized.");
  },
  author: function() {},
  coordinates : function() {},
  allowedToEdit: function(account) {
    return true;
  }
});
```

This code shows a typical usage of Backbone in JavaScript. We start by creating a variable named `NoteModel` that extends (or derives from) `Backbone.Model`. This can be seen with the `Backbone.Model.extend` syntax. The Backbone `extend` function uses JavaScript object notation to define an object within the outer curly braces `{ ... }`. In this example, the `NoteModel` object has four functions: `initialize`, `author`, `coordinates`, and `allowedToEdit`.

According to the Backbone documentation, the `initialize` function will be called once a new instance of this class is created. In our sample, the `initialize` function simply logs a message to the console to indicate that the function was called. The `author` and `coordinates` functions are blank at this stage, with only the `allowedToEdit` function actually doing something–`return true`.

If we were to simply copy and paste the preceding JavaScript into a TypeScript file, we would generate the following compile error:

```
error TS2341: Property 'extend' is private and only
accessible within class 'Model'.
```

When working with a third-party library, and a definition file from DefinitelyTyped, our first port of call should be to see what the definition file is expecting from our TypeScript code. After all, the JavaScript documentation says that we should be able to use the `extend` method as shown, so why is this definition file causing an error? If we open up the `backbone-global\index.d.ts` file, and then search to find the definition of the class `Model`, we will find the cause of the compilation error:

```
class Model extends ModelBase {

  /**
  * Do not use, prefer TypeScript's extend functionality.
  **/
  private static extend(
  properties: any, classProperties?: any): any;
```

This declaration file snippet shows some of the definition of the Backbone `Model` class. Here, we can see that the `extend` function is defined as `private static`, and as such, it will not be available outside the `Model` class itself. This, however, seems contradictory to the JavaScript sample that we saw in the documentation. Note, however, the comment in the code block–`Do not use, prefer TypeScript's extend functionality.`

This comment indicates that the declaration file for Backbone is built around TypeScript's `extends` keyword – thereby allowing us to use natural TypeScript inheritance syntax to create Backbone objects. The TypeScript equivalent to this code, therefore, must use the `extends` TypeScript keyword to derive a class from the base class `Backbone.Model`, as follows:

```
class NoteModel extends Backbone.Model implements INoteModel {
  initialize() {
    console.log(`TypeScript NoteModel initialize called.`);
  }
  author() {}
```

```
    coordinates() {}
    allowedToEdit(account) {
      return true;
    }
  }
```

We are now creating a class definition named `NoteModel` that `extends` the `Backbone.Model` base class. This class then has the functions `initialize`, `author`, `coordinates`, and `allowedToEdit`, similar to the previous JavaScript version. Our Backbone sample will now compile and run correctly.

With either of these versions, we can create an instance of the `NoteModel` object by including the following script within an HTML page:

```
<script >
  $(document).ready(function() {
    console.log('document.ready');
    var noteModel = new NoteModel();
  });
</script>
```

This JavaScript sample simply waits for the jQuery `document.ready` event to be fired, and then creates an instance of the `NoteModel` class. As documented earlier, the `initialize` function will be called when an instance of the class is constructed, so we would see a message logged to the console when we run this in a browser.

All of Backbone's core objects are designed with inheritance in mind. This means that creating new Backbone collections, views, and routers will use the same `extends` syntax in TypeScript. Backbone, therefore, is a very good fit for TypeScript, because we can use natural TypeScript syntax for inheritance to create new Backbone objects.

# Using interfaces

As Backbone allows us to use TypeScript inheritance to create objects, we can just as easily use TypeScript interfaces with any of our Backbone objects as well. Extracting an interface for the preceding `NoteModel` class would be as follows:

```
interface INoteModel {
  initialize();
  author();
  coordinates();
  allowedToEdit(account);
}
```

We can now update our `NoteModel` class definition to implement this interface as follows:

```
class NoteModel extends Backbone.Model implements INoteModel {
  // existing code
}
```

Our class definition now implements the `INoteModel` TypeScript interface. This simple change protects our code from being modified inadvertently, and also opens up the ability to work with core Backbone objects in standard object-oriented design patterns. We could, if we needed to, apply the Factory Pattern described in `Chapter 3`, *Interfaces, Classes and Inheritance*, to return a particular type of Backbone Model or any other Backbone object for that matter.

# Using generic syntax

The declaration file for Backbone has also added generic syntax to some class definitions. This brings with it further strong typing benefits when writing TypeScript code for Backbone. Backbone collections (surprise, surprise) house a collection of Backbone models, allowing us to define collections in TypeScript as follows:

```
class NoteCollection extends Backbone.Collection<NoteModel> {
  model = NoteModel;
  //model: NoteModel;
  //model: { new () : NoteModel }; // ok
}
```

Here, we have a `NoteCollection` that derives from, or `extends` a `Backbone.Collection`, but also uses generic syntax to constrain the collection to handle only objects of type `NoteModel`. This means that any of the standard collection functions such as `at()` or `pluck()` will be strongly typed to return `NoteModel` models, further enhancing our type safety and Intellisense.

Note the syntax used to assign a type to the internal `model` property of the collection class on the second line. We cannot use the standard TypeScript syntax `model: NoteModel`, as this causes a compile time error. We need to assign the `model` property to the class definition, as seen with the `model=NoteModel` syntax, or we can use the `{ new(): NoteModel }` syntax, as seen on the last line.

# Using ECMAScript 5

Backbone also allows us to use ECMAScript 5 capabilities to define getters and setters for `Backbone.Model` classes, as follows:

```
interface ISimpleModel {
  Name: string;
  Id: number;
}
  class SimpleModel extends Backbone.Model
    implements ISimpleModel {
    get Name()
      { return this.get('Name'); }
    set Name(value: string)
      { this.set('Name', value); }
    get Id()
      { return this.get('Id'); }
    set Id(value: number)
      { this.set('Id', value); }
  }
```

Here, we have defined an interface with two properties, named `ISimpleModel`. We then define a `SimpleModel` class that derives from `Backbone.Model`, and also implements the `ISimpleModel` interface. We then have ES5 getters and setters for our `Name` and `Id` properties. Backbone uses class attributes to store model values, so our getters and setters simply call the underlying `get` and `set` methods of `Backbone.Model`.

# Backbone TypeScript compatibility

As we have seen, Backbone allows us to use all of TypeScript's language features within our code. We can use classes, interfaces, inheritance, generics, and even ECMAScript 5 properties. All of our classes also derive from base Backbone objects. This makes Backbone a highly compatible library for building web applications with TypeScript. We will explore more of the Backbone object model in later chapters.

# Angular

AngularJS version 1 (or just Angular 1) has been a very popular JavaScript framework, which was built and distributed by Google. It has, however, been superseded by Angular 2, which uses TypeScript as its language of choice, and will be covered in the next chapter. This section will discuss writing Angular 1 code with TypeScript, as an example of a semi-compatible third-party library.

Angular takes a completely different approach to building JavaScript SPA's, introducing an HTML syntax that the running Angular application understands. This provides the application with two-way data binding capabilities, which automatically synchronizes models, views, and the HTML page. Angular also provides a mechanism for **dependency injection** (**DI**), and uses services to provide data to your views and models.

Let's take a look at a sample from the Angular v1.5.7 tutorial, found in *step 2*, where we start to build a controller named `PhoneListController`. The example provided in the tutorial shows the following JavaScript:

```
var phonecatApp = angular.module('phonecatApp', []);

phonecatApp.controller('PhoneListController', function ($scope)
{
  $scope.phones = [
    {'name': 'Nexus S',
     'snippet': 'Fast just got faster with Nexus S.'},
    {'name': 'Motorola XOOM™ with Wi-Fi',
     'snippet': 'The Next, Next Generation tablet.'},
    {'name': 'MOTOROLA XOOM™',
     'snippet': 'The Next, Next Generation tablet.'}
  ];
});
```

The preceding code snippet is typical of Angular 1 JavaScript syntax. We start by creating a variable named `phonecatApp`, and register this as an Angular module by calling the `module` function on the `angular` global instance. The first argument to the `module` function is a global name for the Angular module, and the empty array is a place-holder for other modules that will be injected via Angular's dependency injection routines.

We then call the `controller` function on the newly created `phonecatApp` variable with two arguments. The first argument is the global name of the controller, and the second argument is a function that accepts a specially named Angular variable named `$scope`. Within this function, the code sets the `phones` object of the `$scope` variable to be an array of JSON objects, each with a `name` and `snippet` property.

If we continue reading through the tutorial, we find a unit test that shows how the `PhoneListController` controller is used:

```
describe('PhoneListController', function(){
  it('should create "phones" model with 3 phones', function() {
    var scope = {},
      ctrl = new PhoneListController(scope);

    expect(scope.phones.length).toBe(3);
  });

});
```

The first two lines of this code snippet use a global function called `describe`, and within this function another function called `it`. These two functions are part of a unit testing framework named Jasmine. We will cover unit testing in a later chapter, but for the time being, let's focus on the rest of the code.

We declare a variable named `scope` to be an empty JavaScript object, and then a variable named `ctrl` that uses the `new` keyword to create an instance of our `PhoneListController` class. The `new PhoneListController(scope)` syntax shows that Angular is using the definition of the controller just like we would use a normal class in TypeScript.

Building the same object in TypeScript would allow us to use TypeScript classes, as follows:

```
var phonecatApp = angular.module('phonecatApp', []);

class PhoneListController  {
  constructor($scope) {
    $scope.phones = [
      { 'name': 'Nexus S',
        'snippet': 'Fast just got faster' },
      { 'name': 'Motorola',
        'snippet': 'Next generation tablet' },
      { 'name': 'Motorola Xoom',
        'snippet': 'Next, next generation tablet' }
    ];
  }
};
```

Our first line is the same as in our previous JavaScript sample. We then, however, use the TypeScript class syntax to create a class named `PhoneListController`. By creating a TypeScript class, we can now use this class as shown in our Jasmine test code–`ctrl = new PhoneListController(scope)`. The `constructor` function of our `PhoneListController` class now acts as the anonymous function seen in the original JavaScript sample:

```
phonecatApp.controller('PhoneListController', function ($scope) {
  // this function is replaced by the constructor
}
```

# Angular classes and $scope

Let's expand our `PhoneListController` class a little further, and have a look at what it would look like when completed:

```
class PhoneListCtrl  {
  myScope: IScope;
  constructor($scope, $http: ng.IHttpService, Phone) {
    this.myScope = $scope;
    this.myScope.phones = Phone.query();
    $scope.orderProp = 'age';
     _.bindAll(this, 'GetPhonesSuccess');
  }
  GetPhonesSuccess(data: any) {
    this.myScope.phones = data;
  }
};
```

The first thing to note in this class, is that we are defining a variable named `myScope`, and storing the `$scope` argument that is passed in via the constructor, into this internal variable. This is again because of JavaScript's lexical scoping rules. Note the call to `_.bindAll` at the end of the constructor. This Underscore utility function will ensure that whenever the `GetPhonesSuccess` function is called, it will use the variable `this` in the context of the class instance, and not in the context of the calling code. We will discuss the usage of `_.bindAll` in detail in a later chapter.

The `GetPhonesSuccess` function uses the `this.myScope` variable within its implementation. This is why we needed to store the initial `$scope` argument in an internal variable.

Another thing we notice from this code is that the `myScope` variable is typed to an interface named `IScope`, which will need to be defined as follows:

```
interface IScope {
  phones : IPhone[];
}
interface IPhone {
  name: string;
  snippet: string;
}
```

This `IScope` interface just contains an array of objects of type `IPhone` (pardon the unfortunate name of this interface, it can hold Android phones as well).

What this means is that we don't have a standard interface or TypeScript type to use when dealing with `$scope` objects. By its nature, the `$scope` argument will change its type depending on when and where the Angular runtime calls it, hence our need to define an `IScope` interface, and strongly type the `myScope` variable to this interface.

Another interesting thing to note on the constructor function of the `PhoneListController` class is the type of the `$http` argument. It is set to be of type `ng.IHttpService`. This `IHttpService` interface is found in the declaration file for Angular. In order to use TypeScript with Angular variables such as `$scope` or `$http`, we need to find the matching interface within our declaration file, before we can use any of the Angular functions available on these variables.

The last point to note in this constructor code is the final argument, named `Phone`. It does not have a TypeScript type assigned to it, and so automatically becomes of type `any`. Let's take a quick look at the implementation of this `Phone` service, which is as follows:

```
var phonecatServices = angular.module(
  'phonecatServices', ['ngResource']);

phonecatServices.factory('Phone',
  [ '$resource', ($resource) => {
      return $resource('phones/:phoneId.json', {}, {
        query: { method: 'GET',
          params: {
            phoneId: 'phones'
          },
          isArray: true
```

```
            }
          });
        }
      ]
    );
```

The first line of this code snippet again creates a global variable named `phonecatServices`, using the `angular.module` global function. We then call the `factory` function available on the `phonecatServices` variable, in order to define our `Phone` resource. This `factory` function uses a string named `'Phone'` to define the `Phone` resource, and then uses Angular's dependency injection syntax to inject a `$resource` object. Looking through this code, we can see that we cannot easily create standard TypeScript classes for Angular to use here. Nor can we use standard TypeScript interfaces or inheritance on these Angular classes.

## Angular TypeScript compatibility

When writing Angular code with TypeScript, we are able to use classes in certain instances, but must rely on the underlying Angular functions such as `module` and `factory` to define our objects in other cases. Also, when using standard Angular services, such as `$http` or `$resource`, we will need to specify the matching declaration file interface in order to use these services. We can therefore describe the Angular library as having medium compatibility with TypeScript.

# Inheritance – Angular versus Backbone

Inheritance is a very powerful feature of object-oriented programming, and is also a fundamental concept when using JavaScript frameworks. Using a Backbone controller or an Angular controller within the framework relies on certain characteristics, or functions being available. We have seen, however, that each framework implements inheritance in a different way.

As JavaScript does not have the concept of inheritance, each framework needs to find a way to implement it. In Backbone, this inheritance implementation is via the `extend` function of each Backbone object. As we have seen, the TypeScript `extends` keyword follows a similar implementation to Backbone, allowing the framework and language to dovetail each other.

Angular, on the other hand, uses its own implementation of inheritance, and defines functions on the Angular global namespace to create classes (that is `angular.module`). We can also sometimes use the instance of an application (that is `<appName>.controller`) to create modules or controllers. We have found, though, that Angular uses controllers in a very similar way to TypeScript classes, and we can therefore simply create standard TypeScript classes that will work within an Angular application.

So far, we have only skimmed the surface of both the Angular TypeScript syntax and the Backbone TypeScript syntax. The point of this exercise was to try and understand how TypeScript can be used within each of these two third-party frameworks.

Be sure to visit `http://todomvc.com`, and have a look at the full source-code for the Todo application written in TypeScript for both Angular and Backbone. They can be found on the **Compile-to-JS** tab in the example section. These running code samples, combined with the documentation on each of these sites, will prove to be an invaluable resource when trying to write TypeScript syntax with an external third-party library such as Angular or Backbone.

# ExtJS

ExtJS is a popular JavaScript library that has a wide variety of widgets, grids, graphing components, layout components, and more. With release 4.0, ExtJS incorporated a model, view, controller style of application architecture to their libraries. Although it is free for open-source development, ExtJS requires a license for commercial use. It is popular with development teams that are building web-enabled desktop replacements, as its look and feel is comparable to normal desktop applications. ExtJS, by default, ensures that each application or component will look and feel exactly the same, no matter which browser it is run in, and it requires little or no need for CSS or HTML.

The ExtJS team, however, has not released an official TypeScript declaration file for ExtJS, despite much community pressure. Thankfully, the wider JavaScript community has come to the rescue, beginning with Mike Aubury. He wrote a small utility program to generate declaration files from the ExtJS documentation (`https://github.com/zz9pa/extjsTypescript`).

Whether this work influenced the current version of the ExtJS definitions on DefinitelyTyped or not, remains to be seen, but the original definitions from Mike Aubury and the current version from brian428 on DefinitelyTyped are very similar.

# Creating classes in ExtJS

ExtJS is a JavaScript library that does things in its own way. If we were to categorize Backbone, Angular, and ExtJS, we might say that Backbone is a highly compliant TypeScript library. In other words, the language features of classes and inheritance within TypeScript are highly compliant with Backbone. Angular in this case would be a partially compliant library, with some elements of Angular objects complying with the TypeScript language features. ExtJS, on the other hand, would be a minimally compliant library, with little or no TypeScript language features applicable to the library.

Let's take a look at a sample ExtJS 4.0 application written in TypeScript. Consider the following code:

```
Ext.application(
  {
    name: 'SampleApp',
    appFolder: '/code/sample',
    controllers: ['SampleController'],
    launch: () => {

      Ext.create('Ext.container.Viewport', {
        layout: 'fit',
        items: [{
          xtype: 'panel',
          title: 'Sample App',
          html: 'This is a Sample Viewport'
        }]
      });

    }

  }
);
```

We start by creating an ExtJS application by calling the `application` function on the `Ext` global instance. The `application` function then uses a JavaScript object, enclosed within the first and last curly braces `{ }` to define properties and functions. This ExtJS application sets the `name` property to be `SampleApp`, the `appFolder` property to be `/code/sample`, and the `controllers` property to be an array with a single entry–`'SampleController'`.

We then define a `launch` property, which is an anonymous function. This `launch` function then uses the `create` function on the global `Ext` instance to create a class. The `create` function uses the `Ext.container.Viewport` name to create an instance of the `Ext.container.Viewport` class, which has the properties `layout` and `items`. The `layout` property can only contain one specific set of values, for example `'fit'`, `'auto'`, or `'table'`. The `items` array contains further ExtJS specific objects, which are created depending on what their `xtype` property suggests.

ExtJS is one of those libraries that are not intuitive. As a programmer, you will need to have one browser window open with the library documentation at all times, and use it to figure out what each property means for each type of available class. It also has a lot of magic strings in the preceding sample, the `Ext.create` function would fail if we mistyped the `'Ext.container.Viewport'` string, or simply forgot to capitalize it in the right places. To ExtJS, `'viewport'` is different to `'ViewPort'`. Remember that one of our solutions to magic strings within TypeScript is to use enums. Unfortunately, the current version of the ExtJS declaration file does not have a set of enums for these class types.

# Using type casting

We can, however, use the TypeScript language feature of type casting to help with writing ExtJS code. If we know what type of ExtJS object we are trying to create, we can cast the JavaScript object to this type, and then use TypeScript to check whether the properties we are using are correct for that type of ExtJS object. To help with this concept, let's just take the outer definition of the `Ext.application` into account. Stripped of the inner code, the call to the `application` function on the `Ext` global object would be reduced to this:

```
Ext.application(
  {
    // properties of an Ext.application
    // are set within this JavaScript
    // object block
  }
);
```

Using the TypeScript declaration files, type casting, and a healthy dose of ExtJS documentation, we know that the inner JavaScript object should be of type `Ext.app.IApplication`, and we can therefore cast this object as follows:

```
Ext.application(
  <Ext.app.IApplication> {
    // this JavaScript block is strongly
    // type to be of Ext.app.IApplication
  }
);
```

The second line of this code snippet now uses the TypeScript type casting syntax, to cast the JavaScript object between the curly braces `{ }` to a type of `Ext.app.IApplication`. This gives us strong type checking, and Intellisense, as shown in the following screenshot:

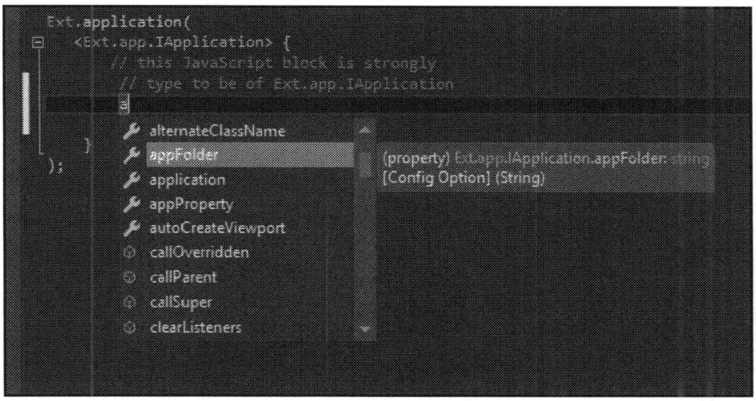


Visual Studio Intellisense for an Ext JS configuration block.

In a similar manner, these explicit type casts can be used on any JavaScript object that is being used to create ExtJS classes. The declaration file for ExtJS currently on Definitely Typed uses the same names for its object definitions as the ExtJS documentation uses, so finding the correct type should be rather simple.

The preceding technique of using explicit type casting is just about the only language feature of TypeScript that we can use with the ExtJS library, but this still highlights how strong typing of objects can assist us in our development experience, making our code more robust and resistant to errors.

# ExtJS-specific TypeScript compiler

If you are using ExtJS on a regular basis, then you may want to take a look at the work done by Gareth Smith, Fabio Parra dos Santos, and their team at `https://github.com/fabioparra/TypeScript`. This project is a fork of the TypeScript compiler that will emit ExtJS classes from standard TypeScript classes. Using this version of the compiler turns the tables on normal ExtJS development, allowing for natural TypeScript class syntax, the use of inheritance via the `extends` keyword, as well as natural module naming, without the need for magic strings. The work done by this team shows that because the TypeScript compiler is open-source, it can be extended and modified to emit JavaScript in a specific way, or to target a specific library. Hats off to Gareth, Fabio, and their team for their ground-breaking work in this area.

# Summary

In this chapter, we have had a look at third-party JavaScript libraries and how they can be used within a TypeScript application. We started by looking at the various ways of including community released versions of TypeScript declaration files within our projects, from downloading the raw files, to using package managers such as NuGet and Typings. We then looked at three types of third-party libraries, and discussed how to integrate these libraries with TypeScript. We explored Backbone, which can be categorized as a highly compliant third-party library, Angular 1, which is a partially compliant library, and ExtJS, which is a minimally compliant library. We saw how various features of the TypeScript language can co-exist with these libraries, and showed what TypeScript equivalent code would look like in each of these cases. In the next chapter, we will look at TypeScript specific third-party libraries, which are either built with TypeScript, or have complete TypeScript integration.

# 7
# TypeScript Compatible Frameworks

One of the watershed moments in the story of the TypeScript language came when it was announced that the Microsoft and Google teams had been working together on Angular 2. Angular 2 was a much anticipated update to the popular Angular (or Angular 1) framework. Unfortunately, this update needed a new set of language features in order to make the Angular 2 syntax cleaner and easier to understand. Originally, Google had proposed a new language named AtScript to facilitate these new language features, which were also closely aligned with the ECMAScript 6 and 7 proposals.

After several months of collaboration, it was announced that all of the necessary features of the AtScript language would be absorbed into the TypeScript language, and that Angular 2 would be written in TypeScript. This meant that the providers of new language features (TypeScript) and the consumers of the new language features (Angular 2) were able to agree on the requirements and immediate future of the language. This collaboration shows that the TypeScript language has had intense scrutiny from a renowned JavaScript framework team, and has passed with flying colors.

Angular 2, however, was not the first framework to adopt the TypeScript language, and many third-party JavaScript libraries also offer full support for TypeScript.

In this chapter, we will take a look at some of these more popular JavaScript frameworks that have full TypeScript language integration. We will compare the syntax used in each of these frameworks, by building the same sample MVC application using each framework. In doing so, we will have a side-by-side comparison that will show us how each of these frameworks has tackled the same design problems. Before we begin though, we will start with a general discussion on what an MVC framework is, and how it can help us in our development experience.

We will cover the following topics:

- What is an MVC framework?
- The benefits of using an MVC framework
- Outline of our sample application
- Using Backbone
- Using Aurelia
- Using Angular 2
- Using ReactJs

# What is MVC?

The acronym MVC stands for Model-View-Controller. It is a programming design pattern that aids in the design and implementation of user interfaces. User interfaces are inherently event driven, in other words, we display something on a screen, and then wait for the user to do something, which will generate some sort of event. This event may be to display a graph, or to hide a panel, or to log out of our application. Unfortunately, the exact sequence of events that a user of our application will follow cannot be completely pre-determined. It is this event-based paradigm that makes user interface design and programming rather more complex than a program that follows a defined sequence of steps.

The other complexity of user interfaces is to try and make components reusable. This means that a single component, such as a menu-bar for instance, should be able to be reused across multiple pages. Component reuse offers its own set of challenges, which generally center around which component is responsible for reacting to which events, and how components communicate when many of them are interested in the same event.

The Model-View-Controller design pattern breaks up the responsibilities of a user interface into three main components, as follows:

# The Model

The Model in MVC represents data. This is generally a very simple **Plain Old JavaScript Object** ( **POJO** ), that has certain properties. As an example of a Model, consider the following TypeScript class:

```
interface IModel {
  displayName: string;
  id: number;
}

class Model implements IModel {
  displayName: string;
  id: number;
  constructor(model : IModel) {
    this.displayName = model.displayName;
    this.id = model.id;
  }
}
let firstModel = new Model({ id: 1, displayName: 'firstModel'});
```

Here, we have defined an interface named `IModel` that has an `id` and a `displayName` property, and a class that implements this interface. We have provided a simple constructor to set these properties. The last line of this snippet creates an instance of this class, with the desired properties.

As can be seen from this snippet, the `Model` class is a very simple POJO that contains some data.

> Models often contain other models, building a nested structure of information. These models often map directly to the structures that are returned in JSON format from REST endpoints.

# The View

The View in MVC represents the visual representation of a Model. In web frameworks, this would typically be a snippet of HTML, as follows:

```
<div id="viewTemplate">
  <span><b> {id} </b></span>
  <span><h1> {displayName} </h1></span>
</div>
```

Here, we have an enclosing `div` that contains two spans. The first `span` is rendered in bold, and will display the `id` property from the model. The second `span` is rendered in `h1` style, and displays the `displayName` property from the model.

By separating the view elements of a user interface from the model, we can see that we are free to modify the view as much as we like, without even touching the code for the model. We could apply styles to each element through CSS, or even hide certain properties from the view completely.

This separation gives us the ability to design or modify the display portion independently of the model. This design work can even be handed off to a completely separate and independent team, who have specialist skills in user interface design. As long as the underlying model does not change, both parts of a model and view will work seamlessly together.

As an example of a View, consider the following code:

```
class View {
  template: string;
  constructor(_template: string) {
    this.template = _template;
  }
  render(model: Model) {
    // combine template and view
  }
}
```

Here, we have defined a class named `View` that has a single property, named `template`. When we construct this view, we give it the HTML template that it should use. This `View` class also has a `render` method, which has a single argument named `model`. The `render` method will combine the `template` and the `model`, and return the resulting HTML.

> The preceding examples are pseudo-code meant only for illustration purposes, and are not an example of using an MVC framework.

# The Controller

The Controller in an MVC framework does the job of coordinating the interaction between the Model and the View. A Controller will generally accomplish the following steps:

- Create an instance of a Model
- Create an instance of the View
- Pass the instance of the Model to the View
- Ask the View to render itself ( generate the actual HTML based on values in the Model )
- Attach the resulting HTML to the DOM tree

The Controller in MVC is also responsible for the logic of the application. This means that it can control which views are presented when, and what to do when certain events occur.

As an example of what a Controller could look like, consider the following code:

```
class Controller {
  model: Model;
  view : View;
  constructor() {
    this.model = new Model(
      {id : 1, displayName : 'firstModel'});
    this.view = new View($('#viewTemplate').html());
  }
  render() {
    $('#domElement').html(this.view.render(this.model));
  }
}
```

Here, we have defined a `Controller` class that has a `model` property and a `view` property. Our `constructor` function then creates an instance of the `Model` class with specific properties, and an instance of the `View`. The `View` instance is created with the template that is read from a DOM element named `viewTemplate`.

The `Controller` class also defines a `render` function, which sets the actual HTML of a DOM element named `domElement`. This HTML is the result of calling the `render` function on the `View` class, and passing in the `model` to be rendered.

> Again, this is pseudo-code for describing the responsibilities of a controller in MVC, and is not an actual example of using an MVC framework.

# MVC summary

The following diagram shows the three elements of the MVC design pattern:

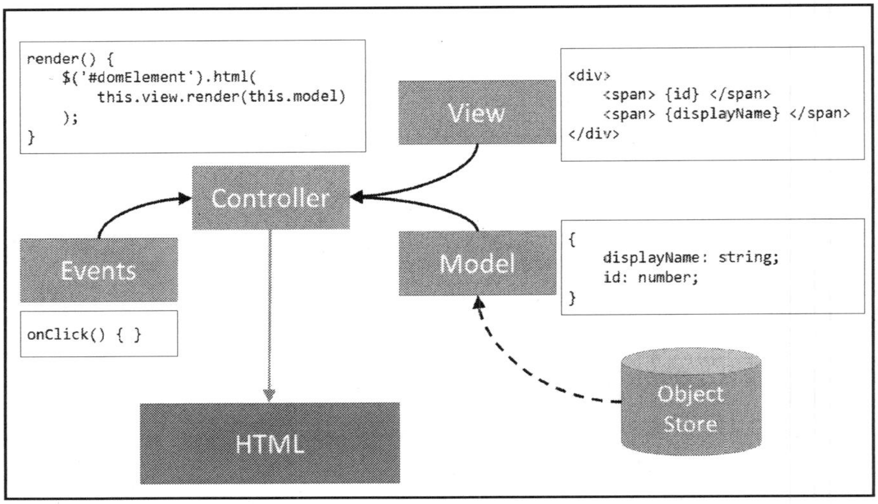


Model View Controller responsibilities

Models are simple objects holding properties, and are typically created from an object store or a database.

Views are HTML visual elements, incorporating model properties within their templates.

Controllers combine models and views, respond to events, and orchestrate generation of the resultant HTML.

# The benefits of using MVC

Using an MVC framework brings with it a number of tangible benefits, as follows:

- Decoupling of the various elements used to display information to the user
- Increased flexibility and reuse
- A single model may have multiple different views, which can be used at different times
- User interface design activities can be undertaken by a specialist team
- Changes to the data of a model can trigger events in a completely different controller without each component knowing about the other

- Views can contain other views in a nested fashion, enhancing reuse
- Changes in behavior of a component can be made without changing its visual representation (by changing the Controller and not the View)
- Rapid and parallel development
- Testability of individual components

# Sample application outline

To enable comparison of our various TypeScript frameworks, we will build the same application using each framework, which will accomplish the following:

- Use a view to display a model property
- Construct an array of data, with each array item being a single model instance
- Loop through the array and render each item in a list element
- Respond to a click event on each item rendered
- Display the model properties that were used to render the element

We will use the same dataset for our array in each of the four sample applications. This dataset is as follows:

```
interface IClickableItem {
  DisplayName: string;
  Id: number;
}

let ClickableItemCollection : IClickableItem[] = ( [
  { Id: 1, DisplayName : "firstItem"},
  { Id: 2, DisplayName : "secondItem"},
  { Id: 3, DisplayName : "thirdItem"},
]);
```

We start with an interface named `IClickableItem` that has an `Id` property of type `number`, and a `DisplayName` property of type `string`. We then define an array of `IClickableItem` objects, named `ClickableItemCollection`. The reason for using such an array is that it is a very common structure to work with when fetching data from a REST endpoint that returns JSON. If we can interpret a simple array like this, then we can easily substitute this array with JSON data later on.

Our resultant application will look as follows:

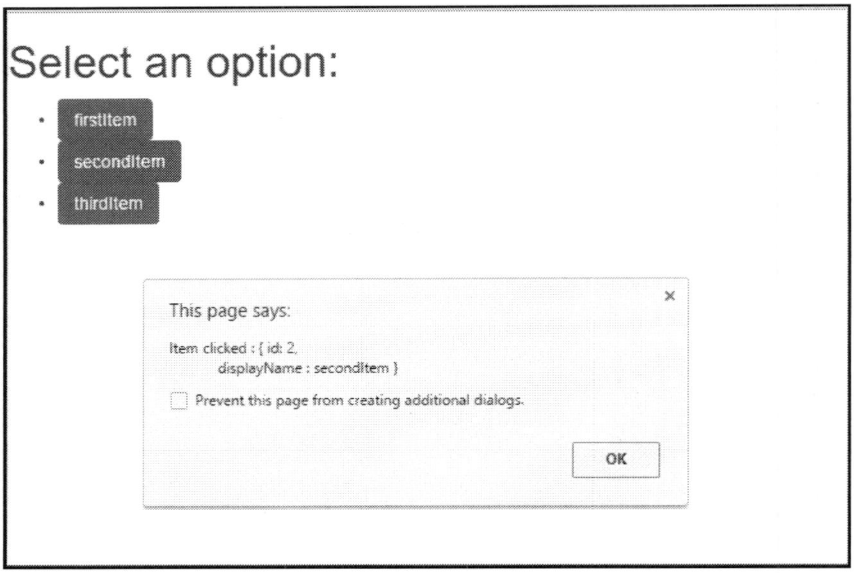


Sample application screenshot with alert information

Here, we have rendered a page that has three buttons, generated from our data array. When we click on any one of these buttons, an alert box will show with the properties of the underlying model.

# Using Backbone

We will start our exploration of TypeScript frameworks by building the sample application in Backbone. While it can be argued that Backbone is not a TypeScript framework per se, we have already seen how it can be used naturally with the TypeScript language syntax. Backbone is also one of the oldest frameworks around, and it is small, light, and extremely fast.

Backbone, however, requires writing a little more code than most frameworks, as it is really the bare-bones of an MVC framework. When working with Backbone, you will need to call rendering functions yourself, and also attach rendered HTML to the DOM tree manually.

The Marionette framework was built on top of Backbone in order to simplify and remove a lot of this repetitive code, and to introduce new concepts that were helpful when building web applications. Marionette is also extremely fast, as it adds a thin layer of functionality across the top of Backbone, while still using the underlying Backbone library.

# Rendering performance

If page rendering performance, CPU cycles, and RAM are critical factors in your applications, then you cannot go past Backbone for pure rendering speed.

In a recent project, our team was involved in speed testing Marionette and Backbone applications to determine if they were suitable for use on embedded devices. These embedded devices had 400-600Mhz CPUs, and 128-256Mb RAM. In comparison to a modern desktop, with a 3.6Ghz CPU and 8Gb of RAM, these are tiny machines indeed. This test application rendered a series of three HTML screens, each with varying complexity. The first page was a very simple page, the second had a variable menu structure, and the third had a rather complex, detailed informational view of some data. All code was written in TypeScript.

The processors and RAM available on each device were as follows:

- 400Mhz ARM9 with 128Mb RAM
- 400Mhz PowerPC with 256Mb RAM
- 624Mhz Marvell PXA300 256Mb RAM
- 6Ghz Core i7 8Gb RAM (desktop)

This test application ran a high-resolution timer, and sent messages via websockets to the HTML page. The timer started when a message was sent from the timing application to the web page. Once a message was received inside the web application, it decided which page to display. The page display mechanism used the Model View Controller pattern to render HTML to the browser. Once the HTML had been rendered to the screen, a message was sent back to the timing application to stop the clock. In this way, millisecond timing information could be obtained to determine how long it took to render HTML on each of these devices.

This test was repeated three times, to gain an average rendering time. The results were as follows, with all timings shown in milliseconds:

| | | **400Mhz ARM9 128Mb** | **400Mhz PowerPC 256Mb** | **624Mhz Marvel 256Mb** | **3.6Ghz Core i7 8Gb** |
|---|---|---|---|---|---|
| **Backbone** | Simple page | 187 ms | 131 ms | 187 ms | 5 ms |
| | Medium page | 241 ms | 151 ms | 267 ms | 11 ms |
| | Complex page | 380 ms | 370 ms | 379 ms | 17 ms |
| **Marionette** | Simple page | 525 ms | 349 ms | 501 ms | 7 ms |
| | Medium page | 1043 ms | 769 ms | 851 ms | 19 ms |
| | Complex page | 1532 ms | 847 ms | 1014 ms | 32 ms |

Looking at the results in this table, we can see that standard Backbone rendering on a slower CPU can take around 130 – 380 milliseconds. The same HTML being rendered from Marionette, however, starts at 350 milliseconds, and can go up to 1.5 seconds. This difference can be attributed to the higher CPU cycles that are taken up by the extra processing that Marionette is doing on top of Backbone.

These results tell us, then, that the more logic a framework contains, and therefore the more processing a framework does, the slower it will be on less powerful processors. So when assessing a framework that does a lot of magic behind the scenes, bear in mind that these features will chew up valuable CPU processing time, and may not be suitable for slower devices.

Our decision was to pursue Backbone as an MVC framework for these devices because it offered the fastest speed available. That said, on a modern computer with a fairly decent processor, the difference between 5 milliseconds of rendering time and 32 milliseconds is negligible.

# Backbone setup

Setting up a Backbone environment is fairly simple, and can be accomplished through `tsc`, and `npm` as follows:

Initialize the TypeScript environment with `tsc`:

```
tsc --init
```

Initialize `npm`, and install Backbone, Bootstrap, JBone, and the declaration files for Backbone using the `@types` syntax, as follows:

```
npm init
npm install backbone -save
npm install bootstrap --save
npm install jbone --save
npm install @types/backbone --save
```

JBone is an implementation of jQuery specifically built for Backbone. It includes all jQuery functionality that Backbone requires, and is significantly lighter and faster than the full jQuery library.

# Backbone models

For our sample application, we will build two Backbone models. One model will be for each item in our `IClickableItem` array, and the second model will be used to hold the entire array. Let's take a look at the `ItemModel`:

```
class ItemModel extends Backbone.Model implements IClickableItem {
  get DisplayName(): string
    { return this.get('DisplayName'); }
  set DisplayName(value: string)
    { this.set('DisplayName', value); }
  get Id(): number { return this.get('Id'); }
  set Id(value: number) { this.set('Id', value); }
  constructor(input: IClickableItem) {
    super();
    for (let key in input) {
      if (key) { this[key] = input[key]; }
    }
  }
}
```

Here, we have a class named `ItemModel` that is derived from `Backbone.Model`, and implements the `IClickableItem` interface. It is using ES5 getter and setter functions for the `Id` and `DisplayName` properties. Within these getter and setter functions, we are calling Backbones `model.get('<propertyName>')` and `model.set('<propertyName>')` functions. This is because Backbone stores object properties internally as attributes. Our `constructor` function is simply looping through each property in the `input` structure, and setting the relevant internal property name. This means that we can construct an `ItemModel` instance from a JavaScript static object as follows:

```
let itemModelInstance = new ItemModel(
  {Id: 1, DisplayName : 'test'});
```

The ability to construct an internal `ItemModel` in this way means that we can use any element of our `IClickableItem` array, and the resulting Backbone model will hydrate correctly.

The second Model we will construct is used to house all elements of our `IClickableItem` array, and is therefore a Collection of `ItemModel` instances, as follows:

```
class ItemCollection
  extends Backbone.Collection<ItemModel> {
  model = ItemModel;
}
```

This class, named `ItemCollection`, derives from `Backbone.Collection<ItemModel>`, and has a single property named `model`. This `model` property is set to the `ItemModel` class. We can therefore construct an `ItemCollection` as follows:

```
let itemCollection = new ItemCollection(
  ClickableItemCollection);
```

So, in a single line, we have created a `Backbone.Collection` of `ItemModel` instances from our original array.

# Backbone ItemView

For our sample application, we will also build two Views. One view will be used to render each item in our array, and the other view will be used to render the entire collection. The item view will therefore be nested inside the collection view.

Let's take a look at our item view:

```
class ItemView extends Backbone.View<ItemModel> {
  template: (json, options?) => string;
  constructor(
    options = < Backbone.ViewOptions<ItemModel> > {}
  ) {
      options.tagName = "li";
      options.events = <any>{'click': 'onClicked' };
      super(options);
      this.template = _.template(
        $('#itemViewTemplate').html()
      );
    }
    render() {
      this.$el.html(
        this.template(
            this.model.toJSON()
        )
      );
    return this;
  }
  onClicked() {
    alert(`Item clicked : { Id: ${this.model.get('Id')},
      DisplayName : ${this.model.get('DisplayName')} }`);
  }
}
```

Our `ItemView` class derives from `Backbone.View`, and uses generic syntax to strongly type the Model used by this view to the `ItemModel` class that we built earlier. The constructor function takes an optional argument named `options` that is of type `Backbone.ViewOptions<ItemModel>`. This options argument is also set to a blank object `{}` by default. By strongly typing this `options` argument, we ensure that the model used by this view is always of type `ItemModel`.

Our `constructor` function sets two properties on the `options` object. The first is called `tagName`, and Backbone will use this value as the outer HTML tag when it renders the HTML. The second `options` property is called `events`. Backbone events are used to tie DOM events back to functions on our view. This means that when the user clicks on an item, the `onClicked` function of this `ItemView` class will be fired. This `onClicked` function simply raises an alert popup.

The `options` object is then passed down to the base `Backbone.View` object via the `super` call.

The last line of the constructor sets up the template to be used for this view. Here, we are querying the HTML DOM tree for an element with the `id` of `itemViewTemplate`. Our HTML page will then need to include the following script in order for Backbone to be able to pick up this template:

```
<script type="text/template" id="itemViewTemplate">
  <button class="btn btn-primary"><%= DisplayName %>
  </button>
</script>
```

Note that Backbone uses Underscore's templating engine by default. In order to render a Model's property into the HTML, we use the `<%= PropertyName %>` syntax within the template.

The last function in our `ItemView` class that is of interest is the `render` function. This `render` function sets calls the `html` function of the `$el` internal property, and passes in the template function and a JSON representation of the internal model property. It also returns `this`, so that any code that uses it can chain commands onto the `render` function.

# Backbone CollectionView

The second view we will build is for the overall collection itself. This view is interesting in a couple of ways. Firstly, it will be constructed with two models. The first model is its own internal model, and will be used to render properties to the screen, and the second model is the collection to be used for each `ItemView`.

The second interesting thing about this view is that the `render` function will need to create individual instances of the `ItemView` class for each element in the collection, and combine the rendered HTML together with its own internal template. Our view is as follows:

```
class ItemCollectionView extends Backbone.View<ItemModel> {
  template: (json, options?) => string;
  constructor(options?: any) {
    if (!options)
      options = {};
      super(options);
      this.template = _.template(
        $('#itemCollectionViewTemplate').html()
      );
  }
  render() {
```

```
        this.$el.html(this.template(
          this.model.toJSON()));
        this.collection.each( (item) => {
          var itemView = new ItemView(
            { model : item});
          this.$el.find('#ulRegions')
            .append(itemView.render().el);
        });
        return this;
      }
    }
```

Here, we have created a view class named `ItemCollectionView` that again extends `Backbone.View<ItemModel>`. The `constructor` function is almost identical to the previous view, except that it is a little simpler, and just sets up the HTML template from the DOM element named `itemCollectionViewTemplate`. Our HTML, therefore, must include this as a snippet, as follows:

```
<script type="text/template" id="itemCollectionViewTemplate">
  <h1> <%= DisplayName %> </h1>
  <ul id="ulRegions">
  </ul>
</script>
```

This HTML snippet uses the `<%= PropertyName %>` syntax to render the `DisplayName` property from the model. We also have a `<ul>` element that will contain the rendered HTML for our child models.

Let's now take a look at the `render` function itself. The first line in the `render` function will render the main `ItemCollectionView` template and model, similar to what we have seen before. The second line of the `render` function will iterate through the `ItemCollection`, and create a new child `ItemView` for each collection element. Each of these child views are then rendered, and their resulting HTML appended to the `ulRegions` DOM element.

# Backbone application

Having created a model, a collection of models, and two views, we will now create a controller to bind these elements together. Backbone, however, does not have a specialist controller class, but we can use a standard TypeScript class to accomplish the work of a controller. This class will be named `ScreenViewApp`, as follows:

```
class ScreenViewApp {
  constructor() {
    console.log(`ScreenViewApp.constructor()`);
```

```
    }
    start() {
      let collectionModel = new ItemModel(
        {Id: 0, DisplayName: "Select an Option:"});
      let itemCollection =
        new ItemCollection(ClickableItemCollection);
      let itemCollectionView = new ItemCollectionView(
      {
        model: collectionModel,
        collection: itemCollection
      });
      $('#pageLayoutRegion').html(
        itemCollectionView.render().el
      );
    }
  }
```

Here, we have created a class named `ScreenViewApp` with a `constructor` and a `start` function. The `constructor` simply logs a message to the console. The body of the `start` function shows how we create the various elements that are used to render our application to the screen.

The first line of the `start` function creates an instance of the `ItemModel` with the `DisplayName` property set to `'Select an Option:'`. This property will be used to render the text at the top of the screen. We then create an instance of an `ItemCollection` class, and pass in the array of `IClickableItem[]` objects that we created earlier. This hydration of the `ItemCollection` class would generally be accomplished through a JSON request to a REST endpoint. The third line of this function then creates an instance of the `ItemCollectionView` class, and passes in an object with two properties, `model` and `collection`. The `model` property is the instance of the `ItemModel` named `collectionModel`, and the `collection` property is the instance of the `ItemCollection`, named `itemCollection`. In this way, we are passing both models to our view.

The final line of the `start` function simply calls the `html` function on the `pageLayoutRegion` DOM element to set the rendered HTML. Note that once a Backbone view has been rendered, the final HTML is placed within the `el` property of the view itself. With this class in place, we can then call the `start` function from our `index.html` page, as follows:

```
<script >
  window.onload = function() {
    app = new ScreenViewApp();
    app.start();
  }
</script>
```

```
<div id="pageLayoutRegion">
</div>
```

Here, we create an instance of the `ScreenViewApp` class within the `window.onload` function, and then call `start`. Below this `<script>` tag, we have placed a `<div>` with the `id` of `pageLayoutRegion`, where the resultant HTML will be placed.

As we noted at the start of this section, Backbone requires us to write a little more code than other frameworks in order to finish off our application. On the flip side of this coin, though, is that the code itself is very readable and logical, and contains no magic whatsoever. It is therefore very simple to pick up and write, and it requires a very small learning curve in order to use.

# Using Aurelia

Aurelia was one of the first SPA frameworks to offer full TypeScript integration. It is a framework that specifically uses ECMAScript 6 features to enhance the development experience. One of the most astounding features of the Aurelia framework is the small amount of code that you need to write in order to get things done. Aurelia understands that if you are writing a standard class, then you probably want to use the class properties to render some HTML.

# Aurelia setup

The simplest way to set up a development environment is to use Aurelia's command-line interface, named `aurelia-cli`, which can be installed as follows:

```
npm install aurelia-cli -g
```

Once this has been installed, it can be invoked to create a new project as follows:

```
au new
```

This will take you through a simple set of questions, starting with the name of the base directory that you would like to use. The next question is whether to use ESNext or TypeScript as your development language, and the last question is whether or not to download all project dependencies. Selecting TypeScript and then yes to download dependencies will take a few minutes to set up the default project structure. Once this is complete, a new directory will be created based on the project name you selected at the start of the process.

The aurelia-cli program has a number of options. To compile your project, type:

```
au build
```

To run your newly created Aurelia application, type:

```
au run
```

This will invoke the Aurelia compilation and bundling steps, and then set up an http-server to serve the application, by default on port `9000`. Browsing to `http://localhost:9000` will show the default Aurelia screen, as follows:

Aurelia welcome page

# Development considerations

Aurelia is a large framework that takes up a considerable amount of disk space. The directory size of the default application is around 150Mb worth. It also does a lot of heavy lifting under the hood. When working with Aurelia, just bear in mind that this may impact the performance of your application.

# Aurelia performance

When you first load your sample Aurelia application in a web browser, you will notice a considerable pause before the page is shown. To dive a little deeper into this initial lag, we can open up the developer toolbar in Chrome to see what is happening behind the scenes.

If we reload the web page with our developer toolbar, and take a look at the network traffic, we will notice that Aurelia is doing a lot of heavy lifting in the background, as follows:

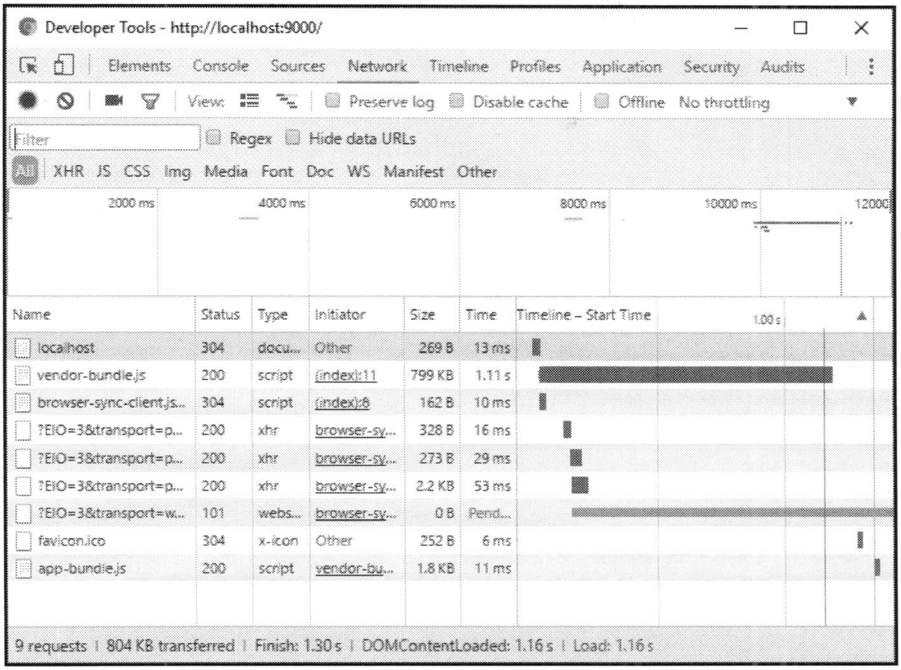


Chrome developer tools showing Aurelia network requests

Our trusty developer tools are showing us (on the summary bar at the bottom) that the web page itself is doing 9 separate file requests to the server, and that the total time taken to render the page was 1.16 seconds. Using the Microsoft Edge web browser, this load time increases to around three seconds, and using Firefox, this load time increases to between four and five seconds. This is a far cry from the 18 milliseconds that it takes to load our Backbone sample application.

Just bear in mind that in a production application, there may be an initial delay from when a user first browses to your home page, and when the page is finally rendered. An Aurelia application is considerably faster on Chrome than it is on Firefox or Microsoft Edge.

# Aurelia models

Aurelia is built based on the ECMAScript 2016 standard. This means that a standard class can be used as a model. There are no getters and setters as we needed in Backbone, nor are there any special constructors required to hydrate the model. Classes can contain other classes, and therefore it is very easy to define complex and nested models. Let's create our array of `ClickableItems` in the `src/app.ts` file as follows:

```
export class App {
  message: string = 'Select an Option:';
  items: ClickableItem[] = [
    { id: 1, displayName : "firstItem"},
    { id: 2, displayName : "secondItem"},
    { id: 3, displayName : "thirdItem"},
  ];
}

export class ClickableItem {
  displayName: string;
  id: number;
}
```

Here, we have modified the class named `App`, and added a new property named `items` that is simply an array of `ClickableItem` elements.

And that's all there is to it.

In Aurelia, standard classes are used as models.

# Aurelia views

Aurelia uses a naming convention to tie classes to their views. Our class is named `App`, and therefore the Aurelia runtime will search within the same directory as the class to find an HTML template with the same name. It will therefore tie `app.ts` to `app.html`, and use `app.html` as a template.

We will modify this `app.html` with the following snippet:

```
<template>
  <h1>${message}</h1>
  <ul>
    <li repeat.for="item of items">
      <button >${item.displayName}</button>
    </li>
```

```
    </ul>
  </template>
```

Here, we have wrapped an HTML fragment within a `<template>` tag. Within this template, we have an `<h1>` tag that uses the `${propertyName}` syntax to render the model's property named `message`. We then have a `<ul>` tag, and within this an `<li>` tag.

The `<li>` tag in this instance is the interesting part of this template. Note how we have injected an attribute named `repeat.for="item of items"`. This syntax is specific to Aurelia, and will loop through the `items` property of the `App` class, and repeat the `<li>` tag for each individual item. This will then be made available to the `<li>` tag via a variable named `item`. We could have called this `arrayItem`, in which case our code would need to be `repeat.for="arrayItem of items"`.

Within the `<li>` tag, we are simply creating a `<button>` tag, and using the data-binding syntax of `${item.displayName}` to render the `displayName` property of each array member.

# Aurelia bootstrap

With our view and models in place, we can turn our attention to the `index.html` file at the root of the project directory. This `index.html` file is as follows:

```
<!DOCTYPE html>
<html>
<head>
  <title>Aurelia</title>
</head>

<body aurelia-app="main">
  <script
    src="scripts/vendor-bundle.js"
    data-main="aurelia-bootstrapper"></script>
</body>
</html>
```

This is a very simple HTML file, which simply includes a page title file within the `<head>` tag, and then defines a `<body>` tag. There are a couple of interesting things to note about this HTML.

Firstly, the `<body>` tag has an extra attribute, named `aurelia-app`. This attribute is telling Aurelia that it should look for a `main.js` file in the `src` directory, as the initial starting point for the application.

This `index.html` file could not be simpler. It has a simple naming convention to find and initiate the `main` class from the `src` directory. Unfortunately, reading through the `main.ts` file, there does not seem to be any obvious links to the `app.ts` file, or the `App` class itself. It seems that Aurelia uses this standard naming convention as a way of finding and bootstrapping the Aurelia environment.

> There is always a slight drawback when using naming conventions like these, where specific magic strings are embedded within HTML attributes. When things are working, all well and good, but when you inadvertently mistype an attribute name, your entire web page may stop rendering completely. Sometimes, there is precious little information available to help track down these sorts of errors, as nothing is logged to the browser console. This can also easily happen if you rename a file, or rename a class as part of a refactoring exercise.

With these precious few lines of code in place, we have a running, working demo application.

# Aurelia events

The last requirement of our sample application is to display an alert when a user clicks on one of our buttons. In order to do this, we will need to add a function to our `App` class, and then bind the `onclick` DOM event to this function. Let's modify our `app.html` template first, as follows:

```
<li repeat.for="item of items"
  click.delegate="onItemClicked(item)">
  <button >${item.displayName}</button>
</li>
```

Here, we have added a `click.delegate` attribute to the `<li>` tag, and within it, are calling a function named `onItemClicked` with `item` as an argument. Note that this delegate is not defined within the `<li>` tag, but rather at the `<li>` tag level. This means that the `onItemClicked` function needs to be attached to our `App` class, and not our `ClickableItem` class. This is slightly different to our Backbone implementation, where each individual `ItemView` received the `onclick` event.

With this in place, we can modify our `App` class as follows:

```
export class App {
  message: string = 'Select an Option:';
  items: ClickableItem[] = [
```

```
    { id: 1, displayName : "firstItem"},
    { id: 2, displayName : "secondItem"},
    { id: 3, displayName : "thirdItem"},
  ];
  onItemClicked(event: ClickableItem) {
    alert(`App.onItemClicked , event.id
    ${event.id} - ${event.displayName}`);
  }
}
```

Here, we have added an `onItemClicked` function with a single argument named `event`, which is of type `ClickableItem`. Within this function, we are raising a simple `alert` to display the properties of the item that was clicked.

As we have seen, building Model, View, and Controller code within Aurelia is a very simple exercise. Using the power of ECMAScript 2016 classes, and simple HTML templates, we are able to get a lot of work done with very little code.

# Angular 2

As mentioned at the start of this chapter, Angular 2 is a complete rewrite of Angular 1, and uses TypeScript as its language of choice. In this section of the chapter, we will take a look at how the Model View Controller design pattern is used within Angular 2.

# Angular 2 setup

Similar to Aurelia's command-line development environment setup, Angular 2 also has a command-line project setup tool, named the Angular-CLI. This can be installed using `npm` as follows:

```
npm install -g angular-cli
```

Once the command-line interface has been installed globally, we can set up an Angular 2 development environment by using the Angular-CLI as follows:

```
ng new my-app
```

The Angular-CLI is named ng, and here we have specified that it should create a new project in a new directory named my-app. Within this new directory, the Angular-CLI will have downloaded and installed all necessary components of an Angular 2 application. To start a development web server, and see the application running, we issue the following command:

```
npm start
```

This start command will compile all of our application source code, and start a web server on port 4200. Browsing to http://localhost:4200 will then run our application. One of the benefits of using the Angular 2 development environment is that it will watch your source files for changes, and immediately re-compile the application when a file has changed. If you leave your browser instance open, then Angular 2 will also force a browser refresh once the application has been compiled, allowing immediate feedback on source code changes.

Keep an eye out on the console where you are running npm start from. This will show any TypeScript compilation errors that occur when you save your files.

# Angular 2 models

Angular 2 models are built the same way as Aurelia models, in that they are simple classes. Let's start by editing the file named app/app.component.ts, and add our Angular models as follows:

```
export class ClickableItem {
  displayName: string;
  id: number;
}

let ClickableItemArray : ClickableItem[] = [
  { id: 1, displayName : "firstItem"},
  { id: 2, displayName : "secondItem"},
  { id: 3, displayName : "thirdItem"},
];

// existing @Component code
export class AppComponent {
  title = 'hello angular !';
  items = ClickableItemArray;
}
```

Here, we have our standard `ClickableItem` class, which has the `displayName` and `id` properties. We are then creating an array named `ClickableItemArray` to hold our array items, as we have seen before. Our final class is called `AppComponent`, and has a `title` property and an `items` property, similar to our model class for Aurelia.

# Angular 2 views

Angular uses a class decorator named `@Component` to specify that a class can act as an HTML component. Let's take a closer look at this decorator:

```
import { Component } from '@angular/core';

// existing ClickableItem code

@Component({
  selector: 'app-root',
  templateUrl: './app.component.html',
  styleUrls: ['./app.component.css']
})
export class AppComponent {
  title = 'hello angular !';
  items = ClickableItemArray;
}
```

This code starts with an `import` statement to define the `Component` decorator from a library named `'@angular/core'`. This `import` statement is part of the modular syntax that we will cover in a later chapter. It basically gives us the ability to easily reference other classes from the Angular framework.

The `@Component` decorator defines three properties, `selector`, `templateUrl`, and `styleUrls`. The `selector` property is used to reference an HTML DOM element where the View will render into, similar to a standard jQuery selector. The `templateUrl` property specifies where the template HTML file for this component is found, and the `styleUrls` property is used to include CSS files used by the component.

Let's take a look at the `app.component.html` file that contains our template:

```
<h1>
  {{title}}
</h1>

<ul>
  <li *ngFor="let item of items">
    <button>
```

```
            {{item.displayName}}
        </button>
      </li>
    </ul>
```

Within this template, we are using the Angular syntax of `{{propertyName}}` to reference properties within our model. This is similar to the `${propertyName}` syntax that Aurelia uses. Our template, again similar to Aurelia, has an `<h1>` element to display the `title` property, and then has the usual `<ul>` and `<li>` tags.

Within the `<li>` tag, we are again looping through the `items` property of the `AppComponent` model to render each array item to the DOM. Angular uses the `*ngFor` keyword within its template to indicate a loop construct. The `"let item of items"` is again referencing each array element within the template via the `item` variable name. As we saw with Aurelia, if we changed this to `"let arrayItem of items"`, then we would need to reference each array element through the `arrayItem` variable.

The template that will be used for each array element is to render a `<button>` tag, and display the value of the `item.displayName` property.

With these changes in place, our Angular 2 application will render the array of `ClickableItem` elements within the HTML page.

# Angular performance

If we open up our handy developer tools and take a look at the number of network requests and time taken to load our page, we will notice that Angular is doing a total of around eight requests, and is refreshing the page in Chrome in around 517 milliseconds. Using Firefox, this is around 960 milliseconds, and in Microsoft Edge, around 2000 milliseconds. This is a good deal quicker than Aurelia, certainly for a development environment.

# Angular events

The last step in this sample application is to wire up our DOM `onclick` events and show an alert with details from the underlying model. As with Aurelia, this will require a slight modification to our template, and the addition of a click handler on our model. Let's start by updating the template in the `app.component.html` file as follows:

```
<ul>
  <li *ngFor="let item of items"
    (click)="onSelect(item)">
```

```
          <button>
            {{item.displayName}}
          </button>
      </li>
    </ul>
```

Here, we have simply added a `(click)="onSelect(item)"` attribute to the `<li>` tag used to render each item to the DOM. Note the slight difference between Aurelia and Angular syntax used here. Where Aurelia uses `click.delegate`, Angular simply uses `(click)`, surrounded by parentheses. We can now define the `onSelect` function within our `AppComponent` class as follows:

```
export class AppComponent {
  title = "Select an option :";
  items = ClickableItemArray;
  onSelect(selectedItem: ClickableItem) {
    alert(`onSelect : id=${selectedItem.id}
    displayName=${selectedItem.displayName}`);
  }
}
```

Here, we have defined an `onSelect` function that has a `ClickableItem` object as an argument. Within this function we are simply raising an alert to display the properties of the model that was used to create the element. As we saw with Aurelia, this handler is also at the `AppComponent` level and not at the `ClickableItem` as it was with Backbone. The reason for this is again that the controlling class, that is, the class that defines the `*ngFor` loop, is the `AppComponent` itself.

With this event handler in place, our sample application is up and running in Angular 2.

# Using React

The final TypeScript framework that we will take a look at in this chapter is React. The React framework is open source, and maintained by Facebook. React uses a specific in-line syntax for combining HTML templates and JavaScript code, named JSX. There are no string templates, or HTML snippets in React, as all templates are mixed in with normal JavaScript code in an XML-like syntax. TypeScript included support for React/JSX syntax in release 1.6. To use the new JSX syntax, however, we will need to create our TypeScript files with a `.tsx` extension, instead of the normal `.ts` file extension.

# React setup

The process that React uses to generate JavaScript from JSX files creates an extra step in the normal development workflow. Our TypeScript `.tsx` files, once compiled, will generate JavaScript files that are interspersed with JSX syntax. Once these files have been created, they need to pass through the JSX interpreter to generate standard JavaScript files. For this reason, it is recommended to use a bundling tool such as Webpack to perform this extra compilation step. Using Webpack will also combine our compiled `.tsx` files with the React libraries correctly.

To start a new project, we will follow a few steps, as follows:

```
npm init
```

The preceding command initiates `npm` for our project.

```
npm install -g webpack
```

This installs `webpack` as a global Node module.

```
npm install --save react react-dom
```

This installs the `react` and `react-dom` libraries (instead of using bower).

```
npm install --save-dev ts-loader source-map-loader
```

This installs the `ts-loader` and `source-map-loader` Node modules.

```
npm link typescript
```

This links our global installation of `typescript` for use by `webpack`.

Once these steps are complete, we can install the React declaration files via the `@types` syntax as follows:

```
npm install @types/react --save
npm install @types/react-dom --save
```

We can now create a `tsconfig.json` file via `tsc --init`, and then modify it slightly as follows:

```
{
  "compilerOptions": {
    "outDir": "./dist/",
    "module": "commonjs",
    "target": "es5",
    "noImplicitAny": true,
```

```
    "sourceMap": true,
    "jsx" : "react"
  },
  "exclude": [
    "node_modules"
  ]
}
```

Here, we have added an `"outDir"` property set to `"./dist/"`, which will be the directory that compiled JavaScript files will be written to – as well as a `"jsx"` property, which is set to `"react"`, to indicate that we are using JSX syntax in our compilation step.

The final configuration file we need for our development environment is a `webpack.config.js` file, as follows:

```
module.exports = {
  entry: "./app/index.tsx",
  output: {
    filename: "./dist/bundle.js",
  },

  // Enable sourcemaps for debugging webpack's output.
  devtool: "source-map",

  resolve: {
    // Add '.ts' and '.tsx' as resolvable extensions.
    extensions: ["", ".webpack.js",
        ".web.js", ".ts", ".tsx", ".js"]
  },

  module: {
    loaders: [
      // All files with a '.ts' or '.tsx' extension
      // will be handled by 'ts-loader'.
      { test: /\.tsx?$/,
        loader: "ts-loader" }
    ],

    preLoaders: [
      // All output '.js' files will have any
      // sourcemaps re-processed by 'source-map-loader'.
      { test: /\.js$/,
        loader: "source-map-loader" }
    ]
  },

  externals: {
```

```
        "react": "React",
        "react-dom": "ReactDOM"
      },
    };
```

This file is fairly well documented, so we will not describe each option here. One of the properties to note, however, is the `"entry"` property at the top of the file, specifying the `"./app/index.tsx"` file. This `index.tsx` file will be used as the initial startup file for the React bootstrapping process. The other property to note is the `"output"` property, specifying that the results of the bundling process should be written to the `"./dist/bundle.js"` file.

With our configuration files in place, we can compile and bundle all code simply by typing:

```
webpack
```

Running `webpack` at this stage will create an error, as we have not created the `app/index.tsx` file as yet. To resolve this error, simply create a blank `index.tsx` file in the `app` directory.

# React views

React models, similar to Aurelia and Angular models, are simple TypeScript classes. As we have covered these models in both of the previous sections, we will jump straight in and take a look at how React composes views.

Firstly, let's create an `app/ReactApp.tsx` source file. Within this file, we will create two views. The first view will be a view for each individual element of the `ClickableItemArray`, and will be named `ClickItemView`. The second view will be named `ArrayView`, and will render the entire array. This is similar to the two views that we created in Backbone, and does not rely on template array binding, as seen in the use of the `*ngFor` syntax, used in Angular. We will start with the `ClickItemView` as follows:

```
import * as React from 'react';

export class ClickableItem {
  displayName: string;
  id: number;
}

export class ClickItemView
  extends React.Component<ClickableItem,{}> {
  constructor() {
```

```
        super();
      }
      render() {
        return (
            <li><button> {this.props.displayName}</button></li>
        );
      }
    }
```

We start with an import statement to import all classes from the `'react'` module, and which specifies a namespace named `React` for these imports. Once again, this `import` statement is part of the modularization syntax that we will cover in a later chapter. We then define our `ClickableItem` model to serve as our data model, as we did in both Aurelia and Angular previously.

This code snippet also defines a class named `ClickItemView`, which is our React item view. In React, all views are referred to as modular, composable components, and so our `ClickItemView` class derives from or `extends` the `React.Component` base class. This base class uses generic syntax to define two required parameters for the generic type. The first of these parameters is the model to which the view refers to – which in this instance, is the `ClickableItem` model. The second object is the default state in which this model will take. As we do not require a default state at this stage, we will leave this as a blank object.

Our `ClickItemView` has both a `constructor` and a `render` function. The `constructor` function simply calls `super` to initiate the base `React.Component` class. The `render` function, however, is a little more interesting.

All React `render` functions must return a snippet of HTML. However, taking a closer look at this HTML snippet, we notice that it is not being handled as a `string`. In other words, React components can include HTML elements within their `render` function as if they were part of the standard language. This feature is the reason why React files need to be defined with the special `.tsx` extension. By using the `.tsx` extension, we are notifying the TypeScript compiler that we are mixing native HTML and TypeScript code within the same file.

The `render` function returns an `<li>` tag, and within this a `<button>` tag. Within the `<button>` tag, we see the React templating syntax that is used to inject the model's `displayName` property, through the `{this.props.displayName}` syntax.

The second view we will define is the view that will be used to render the entire `ClickableItemArray`. As mentioned earlier, React is similar to Backbone, in that we will define a view for every individual array item, and then another view for the whole collection. This view will be named `ArrayView`, as follows:

```
export interface IArrayViewProps {
  items: ClickableItem[],
  title: string
};

export class ArrayView extends
  React.Component<IArrayViewProps, {}> {
  render() {

    let buttonNodes =
      this.props.items.map(function(item) {
      return (
        <ClickItemView {...item}/>
      );
    });

    return <div>
      <h1>{this.props.title}</h1>
        <ul>
          {buttonNodes}
        </ul>
      </div>
    ;
  }
}
```

We start with an interface named `IArrayViewProps`, which describes the properties we will use within our `ArrayView` view. This `IArrayViewProps` interface has two properties, a `title` property, which will be used to render the page title, and an `items` property, which contains the data from the `ClickableItem` array.

Our `ArrayView` class extends `React.Component`. Again, the generic syntax for React components requires two arguments, an object describing the properties of the view, and an object describing its initial state. The only function in this view is the `render` function. The `render` function is divided into two sections.

The first section is the definition of a variable name, `buttonNodes`, which calls the `map` function on the `items` property, as seen in the call to `this.props.items.map`. This `map` function will loop through each item in the `items` array, and return an HTML snippet. The snippet returned is an HTML element named `ClickItemView`. This element name is the same as the class name of the `ClickItemView` class that we defined earlier. Note how the `ClickItemView` element specifies a variable list of attributes, as seen in the `{...item}` syntax. This syntax is a shorthand way of passing all properties of the array element to the `ClickItemView`.

The second section of the `render` function returns the HTML snippet for the entire `ArrayView`. This consists of an `<h1>` tag, which renders the `title` property via the `{this.props.title}` syntax. The next tag is a `<ul>` tag, and within this, the `{buttonNodes}` variable. This HTML snippet, therefore, will include the results of our `map` function as defined by the `buttonNodes` variable. In this way, React allows us to use any TypesScript variable or function within our HTML templates in a simple and intuitive manner.

# React bootstrapping

In order to see the results of our view definitions rendered in our sample application, we will need to bootstrap our React code, similar to what we did for Aurelia. To do this, we will modify the `app/index.tsx` file as follows:

```
import * as React from "react";
import * as ReactDOM from "react-dom";

import { ArrayView, ClickableItem }
  from "./ReactApp";

let ClickableItemArray : ClickableItem[] = [
  { id: 1, displayName : "firstItem"},
  { id: 2, displayName : "secondItem"},
  { id: 3, displayName : "thirdItem"},
];

ReactDOM.render(
  <ArrayView items={ClickableItemArray}
    title="Select an option:" />,
  document.getElementById("example")
);
```

Here, we are defining three `import` statements at the start of the file. The first two import statements make all classes from the `"react"` library and `"react-dom"` library available under the namespace `React` and `ReactDOM`, respectively. The third `import` statement makes the `ArrayView` and `ClickableItem` classes available from the `ReactApp.tsx` file that we created earlier.

We then create a variable named `ClickableItemArray`, which is our array of `ClickableItem` objects. Finally, we call the `ReactDOM.render` function, to render an element to the DOM of the `ArrayItem` type. Note how we have specified two attributes for this `ArrayItem` element.

The first attribute is named `items`, and the value of this item is the instance of the array we created named `ClickableItemArray`. Again, React is allowing us to use the `{variableName}` syntax to inject the value of the `ClickableItemArray` variable into the DOM. The second attribute in this snippet is named `title`, and is set to the string value of `"Select an option: "`. After we have defined these DOM elements, note how we include a comma, and then a call to `document.getElementById`.

This syntax is React's way of selecting a DOM element within the HTML page, and injecting the generated HTML. The `id` of the element is `"example"`, and as such will match a `<div id="example">` element within our HTML.

We will now need to create an `index.html` file in order to bootstrap and render our React application. This `index.html` file (at the root directory of our project) is as follows:

```
<!DOCTYPE html>
<html>
<head>
    <meta charset="UTF-8" />
    <title>Hello React!</title>
</head>
<body>
    <div id="example"></div>

    <!-- Dependencies -->
    <script src=
        "./node_modules/react/dist/react.js">
    </script>
    <script src=
        "./node_modules/react-dom/dist/react-dom.js">
    </script>

    <!-- Main -->
    <script src="./dist/bundle.js"></script>
```

```
</body>
</html>
```

This file includes `<script>` tags within the `<body>` element to load both the `react.js` and `react.dom.js` file, and then the bundled `./dist/bundle.js` file that Webpack creates. Note, however, that the `<body>` element includes a `<div>` tag with the `id="example"` before including the script tags for React. This is slightly different to most frameworks, where the script tags are defined as part of the `<head>` tag. Unfortunately, changing this order will generate errors with the framework, and render a blank page.

Our React application is now ready to run. Simply fire up a browser, and open the `index.html` file in your source directory. Note that where Aurelia and Angular require a web server to be running within your development environment, React and Backbone do not.

# React events

We can now turn our focus onto registering an event handler for the button click event. Again, the React framework is all about creating self-contained components, and so the click handlers in React will be attached to the View that is responsible for rendering our array items, similar to what we saw when working with Backbone. We will therefore modify our `ClickItemView` in the `app/ReactApp.tsx` file as follows:

```
export class ClickItemView
extends React.Component<ClickableItem,{}> {
  constructor() {
    super();
    this.handleClick =
      this.handleClick.bind(this);
  }
  render() {
    return (
      <li><button onClick={this.handleClick}>
      {this.props.displayName}</button></li>
    );
  }
  handleClick() {
    alert(`handleClick() { id : ${this.props.id}
    displayName : ${this.props.displayName} }`);
  }
}
```

Our `ClickItemView` class has been modified in three places. Firstly, we have created a new function named `handleClick`, which will create an `alert` showing the properties of the model that were used to create this view. This `alert` function is accessing the model properties via the `this.props.propertyName` syntax.

The second modification we have made to this class is in the `render` function. We have modified the template HTML snippet to include an `onClick` attribute, and bound this to the `{this.handleClick}` function. This is similar to the modifications we made for Aurelia ( `click.delegate="functionToCall"` ), and Angular `(click)=functionToCall` ), to bind the DOM `onclick` event to our function call.

The third modification we have made to this class is in the `constructor` function. After the call to `super`, we are calling `this.handleClick = this.handleClick.bind(this);`. This strange looking syntax is actually binding any call to the `handleClick` function to use the instance of the class that was created to render this array item as the correct `this`. Remember that when an `onclick` event is received by the `ClickItemView` class, it has been generated by the DOM event, and so the value of `this` will be as set by the context of the button (the calling context). Binding to `this` means that the `this` variable within the class will not reference the calling context, but rather the context of the entire class. This means that the `this` parameter is correctly referencing the class instance instead of the calling context, and that we can access other properties and functions within the class correctly.

With these DOM listeners in place, our application is complete and working with the React framework.

# Summary

In this chapter, we took a deep dive look into what an MVC framework is, and discussed each of its elements. We discussed the role and responsibilities of the Model, the View, and the Controller in MVC, and how they interact together to create user interfaces. We also had a brief discussion on the benefits of using MVC frameworks. We then took a look at four MVC frameworks that either have very tight integration with TypeScript, or have been written with TypeScript in mind. We implemented the same basic application in each of these frameworks, and compared the differences in concepts and syntax between Backbone, Aurelia, Angular 2, and React. We also discussed some performance implications to think about when working with each of these frameworks. In our next chapter, we will take a look at automated testing – unit testing, integration testing, and acceptance testing for our TypeScript applications.

# 8
# Test Driven Development

In our last chapter, we took an in-depth look at the MVC design pattern, and built a sample application using four different frameworks that all use this pattern. We saw that each framework does things slightly differently in terms of models and views, and that each framework had the notion of a controller component, or an application component. The basic principles of the MVC design pattern have given rise to other similar patterns, for instance **Model View Presenter** (**MVP**) and **Model View View Model** (**MVVM**). When discussing this group of patterns together, they have been described by some as **Model View Whatever** (**MVW**), or **Model View Something** (**MV***).

Some of the benefits of this MV* style of writing applications include modularity and separation of concerns. But this MV* style of building applications also brings with it a huge advantage–the ability to write testable JavaScript. Using MV* allows us to unit test, integration test, and acceptance test almost all of our beautifully hand-crafted JavaScript. This means that we can test our rendering functions to ensure that DOM elements are correctly shown on the page. We can also simulate button clicks, drop-down selects, and animations. We can also extend these tests to page transitions, including login pages and home pages. By building a large set of tests for our application, we will gain confidence that our code works as expected, and allow us to re-factor our code at any time.

In this chapter, we will look at test driven development in relation to TypeScript. We will discuss some of the more popular testing frameworks, write some unit tests using these frameworks, and then discuss test runners and continuous integration techniques.

The topics that we will be looking at in this chapter are:

- Test driven development
- Unit, integration, and acceptance tests
- Jasmine
- Jasmine runners
- Continuous integration

# Test driven development

TDD is a development process, or a development paradigm that starts with tests, and drives the momentum of a piece of production code through these tests. Test driven development means asking the question–how do I know that I have solved the problem?, instead of just–how do I solve the problem?

The basic steps of a test driven approach are the following:

- Write a test that fails
- Run the test to ensure that it fails
- Write the code to make the test pass
- Run the test so see that it passes
- Run all tests to see that the new code does not break any others
- Repeat

Using test driven development practices is really a mindset. Some developers follow this approach, and write tests first, while others write their code first and their tests afterwards. Then there are some that don't write tests at all. If you fall into the last category, then hopefully the techniques you learn in this chapter will help you to get started in the right direction.

There are so many excuses out there for not writing unit tests. Things like the test framework was not in our original quote, or it will add 20% to the development time, or the tests are outdated so we don't run them anymore. The truth is, though, that in this day and age, we cannot afford not to write tests. Applications grow in size and complexity, and requirements change over time. An application that has a good suite of tests can be modified far more quickly, and will be much more resilient to future requirement changes than one that does not have tests. This is when the real cost savings of unit testing become apparent. By writing unit tests for your application, you are future-proofing it, and ensuring that any change to the code base does not break existing functionality.

We also want to write our applications to stand the test of time. The code we write now could be in a production environment for years, which means that sometimes you will need to make enhancements or bug fixes to code that was written years ago. If an application has a full suite of tests surrounding it, then making modifications can be done with confidence that the changes made will not break existing functionality.

TDD in the JavaScript space also adds another layer to our code coverage. Quite often, development teams will write tests that target only the server-side logic of an application. As an example, in the Visual Studio space, these tests are often written to only target the MVC framework of controllers, views, and underlying business logic. It has always been fairly difficult to test the client-side logic of an application – in other words the actual rendered HTML and user-based interactions.

JavaScript testing frameworks provide us with tools to fill this gap. We can now start to unit-test our rendered HTML, as well as to simulate user interactions such as filling in forms, and clicking on buttons. This extra layer of testing, combined with server-side testing, means that we have a way of unit testing each layer of our application from server-side business logic, through server-side page rendering, right through to user interactions. This ability to unit test frontend user interactions is one of the greatest strengths of any JavaScript MV* framework. In fact, it could even influence the architectural decisions you make when choosing a technology stack.

# Unit, integration, and acceptance tests

Automated tests can be broken up into three general areas, or types of tests–unit tests, integration tests, and acceptance tests. We can also describe these tests as either black box or white box tests. White box tests are tests where the internal logic or structure of the code under test is known to the tester. Black box tests, on the other hand, are tests where the internal design and or logic are not known to the tester.

# Unit tests

A unit test is typically a white box test where all of the external interfaces to a block of code are mocked or stubbed out. If we are testing some code that does an asynchronous call to load a block of JSON, for example, unit testing this code would require mocking out the returned JSON. This technique ensures that the object under test is always given a known set of data. When new requirements come along, this known set of data can grow and expand, of course. Objects under test should be designed to interact with interfaces, so that those interfaces can be easily mocked or stubbed in a unit test scenario.

# Integration tests

Integration tests are another form of white box tests that allow the object under test to run in an environment close to how it would in real code. In our preceding example, where some code does an asynchronous call to load a block of JSON, an integration test would need to actually call the REST services that generate the JSON. If this REST service relied upon data from a database, then the integration test would need data in the database that matched the integration test scenario. If we were to describe a unit test as having a boundary around the object under test, then an integration test is simply an expansion of this boundary to include dependent objects or services.

Building automated integration tests for your applications will improve the quality of your product immensely. Consider the case of the scenario that we have been using where a block of code calls a REST service for some JSON data. Someone could easily change the structure of the JSON data that the REST service returns. Our unit tests will still pass, as they are not actually calling the REST server-side code, but our application will be broken because the returned JSON is not what we are expecting.

Without integration tests, these types of errors will only be picked up in later stages of manual testing. Thinking about integration tests, implementing specific datasets for integration tests, and building them into your test suite will eliminate these sorts of bugs early.

# Acceptance tests

Acceptance tests are black box tests, and are generally scenario-based. They may incorporate multiple user screens or user interactions in order to pass. These tests are also generally carried out by the testing team, as it may require logging in to the application, searching for a particular set of data, updating the data, and so on. With some planning, and the wealth of tools already available, we can also automate these acceptance tests, so that they are run as part of an automated test suite. The more acceptance tests a project has, the more robust it will be.

> Note that in the test driven development methodology, every bug that is picked up by a manual testing team must result in the creation of new unit, integration, or acceptance tests. This methodology will help to ensure that once a bug is found and fixed, it never reappears again.

# Unit testing frameworks

There are many JavaScript unit testing frameworks available, and also a few that have been written in TypeScript. Two of the most popular JavaScript frameworks are Jasmine (`http://jasmine.github.io/`) and QUnit (`http://qunitjs.com/`). If you are writing node-based TypeScript code, then you might want to have a look at Mocha (`https://github.com/mochajs/mocha/wiki`).

Two of the TypeScript-based testing frameworks are MaxUnit (`https://github.com/KnowledgeLakegithub/MaxUnit`) and tsUnit (`https://github.com/Steve-Fenton/tsUnit`). Unfortunately, both MaxUnit and tsUnit are newcomers in this space, and therefore may not have the features that are inherent in the older, more popular frameworks. MaxUnit, for example, did not have any documentation at the time of writing, and tsUnit does not have a test reporting framework compatible with CI build servers. Over time these TypeScript frameworks may grow, but seeing how easy it is to work with third-party libraries, and using DefinitelyTyped declaration files, writing unit tests for either QUnit or Jasmine becomes a very simple process.

For the rest of this chapter, we will be using Jasmine 2.4 as our testing framework.

# Jasmine

Jasmine is a behavior-driven JavaScript testing framework. It has a very simple syntax, and can be extended easily. It is the recommended framework for Aurelia as well as Angular 2 unit and integration testing. Installation of Jasmine using `npm` is as follows:

```
npm install jasmine --save
```

The relevant declaration files for Jasmine can be installed by using `@types` as follows:

```
npm install @types/jasmine --save
```

# A simple Jasmine test

Jasmine uses a simple format for writing tests. Consider the following TypeScript code:

```
describe("tests/01_SimpleJasmineTests.ts ", () => {
  it("should fail", () => {
    let undefinedValue;
    expect(undefinedValue).toBeDefined();
  });
});
```

This snippet starts with a Jasmine function called `describe`, which takes two arguments. The first argument is the name of the test suite, and the second is an anonymous function that contains our test suite. The next line uses the Jasmine function named `it` to describe an actual test, which also takes two arguments. The first argument is the test name, and the second argument is an anonymous function that contains our test, in other words, whatever is within the `it` anonymous function is our actual test. This test starts by defining a variable, named `undefinedValue`, but it does not actually set its value. Next, we use the Jasmine function `expect`. Just by reading the code of this `expect` statement, we can quickly understand what the unit test is doing. It is expecting that the value `undefinedValue` should be defined, that is, not equal to `undefined`.

The Jasmine `expect` function takes a single argument, and returns what is known as a Jasmine matcher. This matcher, `expect( ... )` uses the fluent syntax to assess the value passed into `expect` against the matcher. The `expect` keyword is similar to the `Assert` keyword in other testing libraries. The format of the `expect` statements is very human-readable, making Jasmine expectations relatively simple to understand.

# Jasmine SpecRunner

In order to run this test, we will need an HTML page that includes all of the relevant Jasmine third-party libraries, as well as our test JavaScript file. We can create a `SpecRunner.html` file as follows:

```
<html>
<head>
  <link rel="stylesheet" type="text/css"
    href="../node_modules/jasmine-core/
      lib/jasmine-core/jasmine.css" />
  <script type="text/javascript"
    src="../node_modules/jasmine-core/
      lib/jasmine-core/jasmine.js" >
  </script>
```

```
    <script type="text/javascript"
      src="../node_modules/jasmine-core/
        lib/jasmine-core/jasmine-html.js" />
    </script>
    <script type="text/javascript"
      src="../node_modules/jasmine-core/
        lib/jasmine-core/boot.js" >
    </script>
    <script type="text/javascript"
      src="./01_SimpleJasmineTests.js" >
    </script>
  </head>
    <body>
    </body>
  </html>
```

This HTML page is simply including the required Jasmine files installed by `npm`, that is, `jasmine.css`, `jasmine.js`, `jasmine-html.js`, and `boot.js`. The last line includes the compiled JavaScript file from our TypeScript test file, `01_SimpleJasmineTests.js`.

If we open up this page in a browser, we should see one failing unit test:

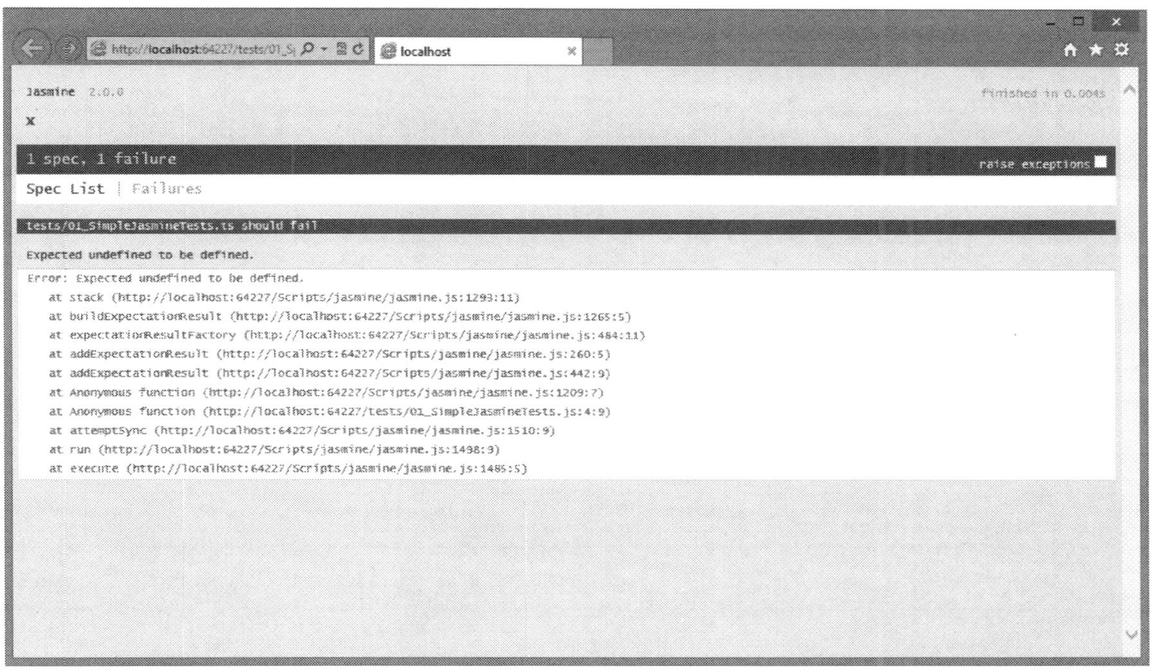


SpecRunner.html page showing Jasmine output

Excellent. We are following the test driven development process by firstly creating a failing unit test. The results are exactly what we expect. Our variable named `undefinedVariable` has not yet had a value assigned to it, and therefore will be `undefined`. If we follow the next step of the TDD process, we should write the code that makes the test pass. Updating our test as follows will ensure that the test will pass:

```
describe("tests/01_SimpleJasmineTests.ts ", () => {
  it("value that has been assigned should be defined", () => {
    let undefinedValue = "test";
    expect(undefinedValue).toBeDefined();
  });
});
```

Note that we have updated our test name to describe what the test is trying to accomplish, and to make the test pass, we are simply assigning the value `"test"` to our `undefinedValue` variable. Running the `SpecRunner.html` page now will show a passing test, as follows:

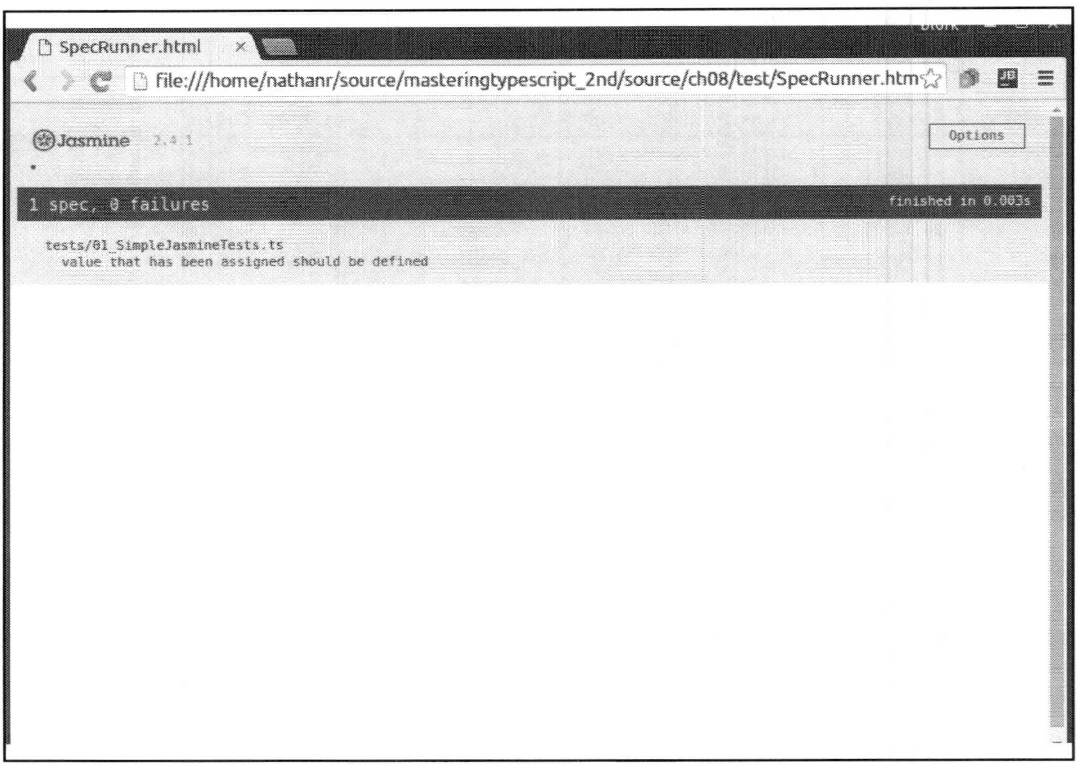


Jasmine spec runner showing passing tests

## Matchers

As seen in our first simple test, Jasmine uses a fluent syntax to allow us to attach Jasmine matchers after the `expect(...)` statement. In our first test, we used the `.toBeDefined` matcher. Jasmine, however, has a wide range of matchers that can be used within tests, and also allows us to write and include custom matchers. Let's take a quick look at some of these matchers:

```
it("expect value toBe(2)", () => {
  let twoValue = 2;
  expect(twoValue).toBe(2);
})
```

Here, we are using the `.toBe` matcher to test that the value of the `twoValue` variable is indeed `2`:

```
it("expect string toContain value ", () => {
  let testString = "12345a";
  expect(testString).toContain("a");
});
```

In this test, we are testing that the string `"12345a"` contains the value `"a"`:

```
it("expect true to be truthy", () => {
  let trueValue = true;
  expect(trueValue).toBeTruthy();
});
```

In this test, we are testing that the `trueValue` variable is set to the boolean value of `true`.

We can also reverse the value of any expectation by using the `.not` matcher as follows:

```
it("expect false not to be truthy", () => {
  let falseValue = false;
  expect(falseValue).not.toBeTruthy();
});
```

Here, we are using the `.not.` matcher, and then the `toBeTruthy` matcher to test that the `falseValue` variable is indeed `false`. We can also use the `.not` matcher on other combinations of matchers, as follows:

```
it("expect value not to be null", () => {
  let definedValue = 2;
  expect(definedValue).not.toBe(null);
});
```

This test is checking that the value of the `definedValue` variable is not `null`.

We can also check that two JavaScript objects are equal as follows:

```
it("expect objects to be equal", () => {
  let obj1 = {a : 1, b : 2};
  let obj2 = {b : 2, a : 1};

  expect(obj1).toEqual(obj2);
});
```

In this test, we have defined two objects, named `obj1` and `obj2` that have the same properties. The `toEqual` matcher will correctly identify that these two objects have the same properties and values, and are therefore considered equal.

Be sure to head over to the Jasmine website for a full list of matchers, as well as details on writing custom matchers.

# Test startup and teardown

As in other testing frameworks, Jasmine provides a mechanism to define functions that will run before and after each test, or as a test start-up and tear-down mechanism. In Jasmine, the `beforeEach` and `afterEach` functions act in this way, as can be seen from the following test:

```
describe("beforeEach and afterEach tests", () => {
  let myString;

  beforeEach(() => {
    myString = "this is a test string";
  });
  afterEach(() => {
    expect(myString).toBeUndefined();
  });

  it("should find then clear the myString variable", () => {
    expect(myString).toEqual("this is a test string");
    myString = undefined;
  });

});
```

In this test, we define a variable named `myString`, at the start of the test. As we know from JavaScript lexical scoping rules, this `myString` variable will then be available for use within the scope of the enclosing function, which is the `describe()` function. This means that the `myString` variable will be available within each of the following `beforeEach`, `afterEach`, and `it` functions. In our `beforeEach` function, this variable is set to a string value of `"this is a test string"`. Within the `afterEach` function, the variable is tested to see that it has been reset to `undefined`. The expectation within our test checks is that this variable has been set via the `beforeEach` function. At the end of our test, we then reset the variable to be `undefined`. Note that the `afterEach` function is also calling an `expect` – in this case to ensure that the test has reset the variable back to `undefined`.

> Version 2.1 of the Jasmine framework introduces a second version of setup and teardown, called `beforeAll` and `afterAll`. These functions, as can be derived from their names, will run once before or after all tests within the `describe()` grouping are run.

# Data driven tests

To show how extensible the Jasmine testing library is, JP Castro wrote a very short, but powerful utility to provide data-driven tests within Jasmine. His blog on this topic can be found here
(`http://blog.jphpsf.com/2012/08/30/drying-up-your-javascript-jasmine-tests/`), and the GitHub repository can be found here
(`https://github.com/jphpsf/jasmine-data-provider`). This simple extension allows us to write intuitive Jasmine tests that take a parameter as part of each test, as follows:

```
describe("data driven tests", () => {
  using("valid values", [
    "first string",
    "second string",
    "third string"
  ], (value) => {
      it(`${value} should contain 'string'`, () => {
        expect(value).toContain("string");
      });
    });
});
```

Note here the use of the `using` function within a `describe`. This `using` function takes three parameters–a string description of the value set, an array of values, and a function definition which is then calling our test itself.

This function definition uses the variable `value`, and will invoke our test with the value of this argument. Note also in the call to `it`, we are also changing the test name on the fly, to include the `value` parameter that is passed in. This is necessary in order for each test to have a unique test name.

Without a TypeScript definition of this `using` function, we will generate TypeScript errors, so let's define the structure of the `using` function as follows:

```
declare function using<T>(
  name: string,
  values : T [],
  func : (T) => void
);
```

This TypeScript declaration defines a function named `using`, and uses the generic syntax `<T>` to define three function arguments. The first argument is the name of the test, the second argument is an array of values of type `T`, and the third argument is a function that accepts an argument of type `T`. This function declaration ensures that the same type (`T`) is used for both the array of values, as well as the argument for the function itself.

Our data-driven tests now just need JP Castro's Jasmine extension, which is shown as follows in JavaScript:

```
function using(name, values, func) {
  for (var i = 0, count = values.length; i < count; i++) {
    if (Object.prototype.toString.call(values[i])
         !== '[object Array]')
    {
       values[i] = [values[i]];
    }
    func.apply(this, values[i]);
  }
}
```

This is a very simple function named `using`, that takes the three parameters that we mentioned earlier. The function does a simple loop through the array values, and passes in each array value to our test.

With this declaration in place, and the JavaScript `using` function, our code will compile correctly, and the tests will run through once for each value in the data array:

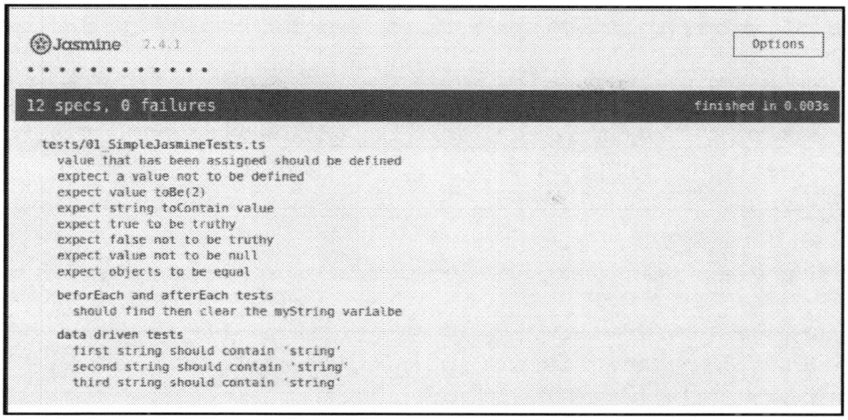


Jasmine spec runner showing data driven tests

# Using spies

Jasmine also has a very powerful feature that allows your tests to see if a particular function was called, and also to determine the actual parameters it was called with. This is known as spying on a function. When we create a spy, we are temporarily hijacking the function call in order to test these parameters. Let's take a look at a simple spy, as follows:

```
class MySpiedClass {
  testFunction(arg1: string) {
    console.log(arg1);
  }
}
describe("simple spy", () => {
  it("should spyOn a function call", () => {
    let classInstance = new MySpiedClass();
    let testFunctionSpy
      = spyOn(classInstance, 'testFunction');

    classInstance.testFunction("test");
    expect(testFunctionSpy).toHaveBeenCalled();
  });
});
```

We start with a class named `MySpiedClass`, which has a single function–`testFunction`. This function takes a single argument, and logs the argument to the console.

Our test starts by creating a new instance of `MySpiedClass`, and assigns it to a variable named `classInstance`. We then create a Jasmine spy named `testFunctionSpy`, by calling the `spyOn` function. This `spyOn` function takes two arguments–the class instance itself, and the name of the function to spy on. In this test, the class instance is named `classInstance`, and the function we wish to spy on is named `testFunction`. Once we have a spy created, we can call the function, and set an expectation on whether the function was called. This is the essence of a spy. Jasmine will watch the `testFunction` function of the instance of `MySpiedClass` to see whether or not it was called.

> Jasmine spies, by default, block the call to the underlying function. In other words, they replace the function you are trying to call with a Jasmine delegate. This is part of the hijacking process we mentioned earlier. If you need to spy on a function, but also need the body of the function to still execute, you must specify this behavior using the `.and.callThrough()` fluent syntax.

While this is a very trivial example, spies become very powerful in a number of different testing scenarios. Classes or functions that take callback parameters, for example, would need a spy to ensure that the callback function was in fact invoked.

# Spying on callback functions

Let's see how we can test that a callback function was invoked correctly using this spying technique. Consider the following TypeScript code:

```
class CallbackClass {
  doCallBack(id: number, callback: (result: string) => void ) {
    let callbackValue = "id:" + id.toString();
    callback(callbackValue);
  }
}

class DoCallBack {
  logValue(value: string) {
    console.log(value);
  }
}
```

Firstly, we define a class named `CallbackClass` that has a single function, `doCallback`. This `doCallback` function takes an `id` argument, of type `number`, and also a `callback` function. The `callback` function must take a `string` as an argument, and return `void`.

The second class that we have defined, named DoCallBack has a single function named logValue. This function signature matches the callback function signature required on the doCallback function we defined earlier. Using Jasmine spies, we are now able to test the logic of the doCallBack function. This function must create a string based on the id argument that was passed in, and then invoke the callback function. Our tests must therefore accomplish two things. Firstly, we need to ensure that the string generated within the doCallback function is formatted correctly, and secondly we need to ensure that our callback function was indeed invoked with the correct parameters. Our Jasmine test for this functionality is as follows:

```
describe("using callback spies", () => {
  it("should execute callback with the correct string value",
    () => {
      let doCallback = new DoCallBack();
      let classUnderTest = new CallbackClass();

      let callbackSpy = spyOn(doCallback, 'logValue');
      classUnderTest.doCallBack(1, doCallback.logValue);

      expect(callbackSpy).toHaveBeenCalled();
      expect(callbackSpy).toHaveBeenCalledWith("id:1");

    });
});
```

This test code firstly creates an instance of the CallbackClass class, and also an instance of the DoCallBack class. We then create a spy on the logValue function of the DoCallBack class. Remember that the logValue function is passed into the doCallBack function as the callback function parameter. We are therefore creating a spy on the logValue function of the DoCallBack class. When we invoke the doCallback function on the CallbackClass instance, this should therefore call our logValue function correctly.

Our expect statements on the last two lines verify that this callback chain has indeed been executed correctly. The first expect statement simply checks that the logValue function was invoked, and the second expect statement checks that it was called with the correct parameters.

# Using spies as fakes

Another benefit of Jasmine spies is that they can act as fakes. In other words, instead of calling a real function, the call is essentially hijacked, and then delegated to the function that is specified as part of the Jasmine spy – a fake function. These fake functions can also return values which can be very useful for generating small mocking frameworks. Consider the following test:

```
class ClassToFake {
  getValue() : number {
    return 2;
  }
}
describe("using fakes", () => {
  it("calls fake instead of real function", () => {
    let classToFake = new ClassToFake();
    spyOn(classToFake, 'getValue').and.callFake ( () => {
        return 5;
    });
    expect(classToFake.getValue()).toBe(5);
  });
});
```

We start with a class named `ClassToFake` that has a single function, `getValue`, which returns `2`. Our test then creates an instance of this class. We then call the Jasmine `spyOn` function to create a spy on the `getValue` function, and then use the `.and.callFake` syntax to attach an anonymous function as a fake function. This fake function will return `5` instead of the original `getValue` function that would have returned `2`. The test then checks to see whether the call to the `getValue` function on the `ClassToFake` instance will return `5`. In this test, Jasmine will substitute our new fake function for the original `getValue` function, and therefore return `5` instead of `2`.

There are a number of variants of the Jasmine fake syntax, including methods to throw errors, or return values – again consult the Jasmine documentation for a full list of its faking capabilities.

# Asynchronous tests

The asynchronous nature of JavaScript, made popular by AJAX and jQuery, has always been one of the draw-cards of the language, and is the principle architecture behind node-based applications. Let's take a quick look at an asynchronous class, and then describe how we should go about testing it. Consider the following TypeScript code:

```
class MockAsyncClass {
  executeSlowFunction(success: (value: string) => void) {
    setTimeout(() => {
        success("success");
    }, 1000);
  }
}
```

This MockAsyncClass has a single function, named executeSlowFunction, which takes a function callback named success. Within the executeSlowFunction code, we are simulating an asynchronous call with the setTimeout function, and only calling the success callback after 1000 milliseconds (1 second). This function is therefore simulating an asynchronous function, as it will only execute the callback after a full second.

Our test for this executeSlowFunction may look as follows:

```
describe("asynchronous tests", () => {
  it("failing test", () => {
    let mockAsync = new MockAsyncClass();
    let returnedValue : string;
    mockAsync.executeSlowFunction((value: string) => {
      returnedValue = value;
    });
    expect(returnedValue).toEqual("success");
  });
});
```

Firstly, we instantiate an instance of the MockAsyncClass, as well as a variable named returnedValue. We then call executeSlowFunction with an anonymous function for the success parameter. This anonymous function sets the value of returnedValue to whatever was passed in from the MockAsyncClass. Our expectation is that the returnedValue should equal "success", but if we run this test now, our test will fail with the following error message:

```
Expected undefined to equal 'success'.
```

What is happening here is that because executeSlowFunction is asynchronous, JavaScript will not wait until the callback function is called before executing the next line of code. This means that the expectation is being called before executeSlowFunction has had a chance to call our anonymous callback function (setting the value of returnedValue). If you put a breakpoint on the expect(returnValue).toEqual("success") line, and another breakpoint on the returnedValue = value line, you will see that the expect line is called first, and the returnedValue line is only called after a full second.

## Using done()

Jasmine version 2.0 has introduced a new syntax to help us with these sorts of asynchronous tests. In any `beforeEach`, `afterEach`, or `it` function, we pass an argument named `done` (which is a function), and then invoke it at the end of our asynchronous code. Let's rewrite our previous test for `executeSlowFunction` as follows:

```
describe("asynch tests with done", () => {
  let returnedValue;

  beforeEach((done) => {
    returnedValue = "no_return_value";
    let mockAsync = new MockAsyncClass();
    mockAsync.executeSlowFunction((value: string) => {
      returnedValue = value;
      done();
    });
  });

  it("should return success after 1 second", (done) => {
    expect(returnedValue).toEqual("success");
    done();
  });
});
```

In this version of our asynchronous test, we have moved the `returnedValue` variable outside of our test, and have included a `beforeEach` function to run before our actual test. This `beforeEach` function firstly resets the value of `returnValue`, and then sets up the `MockAsyncClass` instance. Finally, it calls the `executeSlowFunction` on this instance.

Note how the `beforeEach` function takes a parameter named `done`, and then calls `done()` after the `returnedValue = value` line has been called. Notice too, that the second parameter to the `it` function also now takes a `done` parameter, and calls `done()` when the test is finished.

So what have we accomplished here? We have modified our original test, and split it into two halves. The first half is the `beforeEach` function, which invokes our `executeSlowFunction`, storing the return value in the `returnValue` variable. Our actual test, therefore, is waiting for the `done()` function to execute, and then runs the remainder of the test. This test structure means that we are invoking our asynchronous function, and only executing our test and expectations once the asynchronous function has been executed.

> From the Jasmine documentation–The spec will not start until the `done` function is called in the call to `beforeEach`, and this spec will not complete until its `done` function is called. By default, Jasmine will wait for five seconds before causing a timeout failure. This can be overridden using the `jasmine.DEFAULT_TIMEOUT_INTERVAL` variable.

# Jasmine fixtures

Many times, our code is responsible for either reading in, or, in most cases, manipulating DOM elements from JavaScript. This means that any running code that relies on a DOM element could fail if the underlying HTML does not contain the correct element, or group of elements. In order to test functions that modify the DOM in any way, we will need to provide either a copy of, or the real DOM elements in order for our tests to pass.

One of the extension libraries for Jasmine, named `jasmine-jquery`, allows us to do exactly this. The `jasmine-jquery` library lets us inject HTML elements into the DOM before our tests execute, and will then automatically remove them from the DOM after the test is run.

We can install this library using `npm` as follows:

```
npm install jquery --save
npm install jasmine-jquery --save
```

With the equivalent `@types` declaration files as follows:

```
npm install @types/jasmine-jquery --save
```

Let's take a look at an example of a class that modifies a DOM element, as follows:

```
class ModifyDomElement {
  setHtml() {
    let elem = $('#my_div');
    elem.html('<p>Hello World</p>');
  }
}
```

This `ModifyDomElement` class has a single function, named `setHtml` that is using jQuery to find a DOM element with the ID of `my_div`. The HTML of this div is then set to a simple `"Hello world"` paragraph. Obviously, this class requires the existence of a DOM element named `my_div` in order to function correctly. Let's now take a look at how we can use the `setFixtures` function from the `jasmine-jquery` library within a test to set up this DOM element, as follows:

```
describe("fixture tests", () => {
  it("should modify a dom element", () => {
    setFixtures('<div id="my_div"></div>');
    let modifyDom = new ModifyDomElement();
    modifyDom.setHtml();
    var modifiedDomElement = $('#my_div');
    expect(modifiedDomElement.length).toBeGreaterThan(0);
    expect(modifiedDomElement.html()).toContain("Hello");
  });
});
```

The test starts by calling the `jasmine-jquery` function, `setFixtures`. This function will inject the HTML provided as a string parameter directly into the DOM for the duration of the test. The test then creates an instance of the `ModifyDomElement` class, and calls the `setHtml` function, which will modify the `my_div` element.

The remainder of the test uses the jQuery `$` function to find a DOM element with an `id` of `my_div`, and stores this in the variable named `modifiedElement`. The `modifiedElement` variable is then passed onto our two expectations. Note the first expect statement tests to see if the `length` property of the `modifiedDomElement` variable is `> 0`. This is the easiest way of figuring out if the element was in fact found in the DOM. If it was found, we are then checking the internal HTML of the element, to ensure that it contains the string `"Hello"`.

> The fixture methods provided by `jasmine-jquery` also allow for loading raw HTML files off disk, instead of having to write out lengthy string representations of HTML. This is also particularly useful if your MV* framework uses HTML file snippets. In addition, `jasmine-jquery` also has utilities for loading JSON from disk and purpose build matchers that work with jQuery. Be sure to check out the documentation at (`https://github.com/velesin/jasmine-jquery`).

# DOM events

There will be times when the code you are writing must respond to DOM events, such as `onclick` or `onselect`. Generally, developers will build this sort of code by testing manually, but there will come a time when these tests need to be automated. Luckily, writing tests that need these DOM events can also be simulated by using jQuery, `jasmine-jquery`, and spies as follows:

```
describe("click event tests", () => {
  it("should trigger an onclick DOM event", () =>{
    setFixtures(`
        <script>
        function handle_my_click_div_clicked() {
          // do nothing at this time
        }
        </script>
        <div id='my_click_div'
        onclick='handle_my_click_div_clicked()'>
          Click Here</div>`);
    var clickEventSpy = spyOnEvent('#my_click_div', 'click');
    $('#my_click_div').click();
    expect(clickEventSpy).toHaveBeenTriggered();
  });
});
```

This test is again calling the `setFixtures` function from the `jasmine-jquery` library. This `setFixtures` function is doing two things. Firstly, it is defining a function within a `<script>` tag named `handle_my_click_div_clicked`. Secondly, it is defining a `<div>` with an ID of `my_click_div`, and then attaching the DOM event of `onclick` to call the `handle_my_click_div_clicked()` function. This single function call is therefore setting up all of the required HTML for the `onclick` event. Without this `<script>` tag, running our tests will produce an error:

```
ReferenceError: handle_my_click_div_clicked is not defined
```

Our test then sets up a Jasmine spy named `clickEventSpy`. This spy uses the `jasmine-jquery` function named `spyOnEvent`, which takes two parameters–a jQuery selector for the element to spy on, and a DOM event name.

We are then using jQuery to trigger the event by calling `$('#my_click_div').click()`. Remember that the default behavior of a spy is to hijack the function definition, and call our spy instead. The last line of this test is our expectation, where we are expecting the spy to have been triggered. The `toHaveBeenTriggered` function is a Jasmine matcher that is provided by the `jasmine-jquery` library.

> jQuery and DOM manipulation provide us with a way of filling in forms, clicking on **submit**, **cancel**, **ok** buttons, and generally simulating user interaction with our application. We can easily write full acceptance or user acceptance tests within Jasmine using these techniques, further solidifying our application against errors and change.

# Jasmine runners

Firing up a web page in order to run our tests every time we make a change to one of our tests can quickly become labor intensive and error-prone. We have already explored the use of Grunt in our build tools in order to detect file changes and automatically recompile our TypeScript files when a file is saved. In this section, we will explore a few test runners that will detect changes to our test suite, and automatically rerun our tests without intervention. Using test runners gives us instant feedback on the status of all tests, as we are writing our code and saving changes.

# Testem

Testem is a node-based test runner. It is run from the command line, and opens up a simple interface to view test results. Testem will automatically detect changes to JavaScript files, and execute tests on the fly, providing instant feedback during the unit testing phase. Testem also has a very handy feature that allows multiple browsers to connect to the same Testem instance. This allows us to connect an instance of Chrome, Firefox, IE, Opera, Safari, QupZilla, or pretty much any type of browser to the same Testem runner. Testem will rerun our tests in each and every browser and present a summary view as follows:

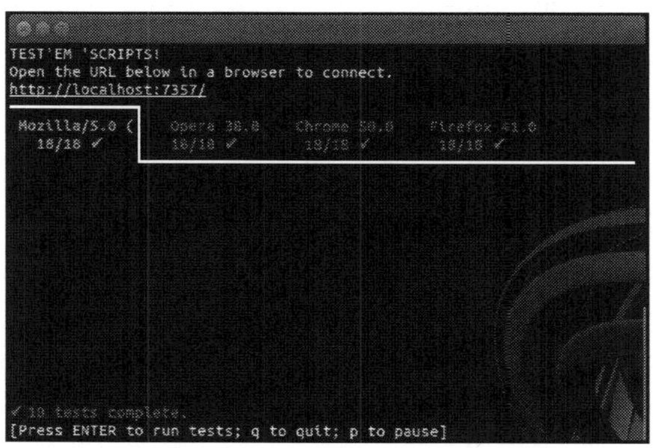


Testem command-line interface showing connected browsers

Testem also has a continuous integration setting that can be used on build servers. More info can be found at the GitHub repository (`https://github.com/airportyh/testem`)

Testem can be installed via node with the command (note that you may need to prefix with sudo on a Linux-based system):

```
npm install -g testem
```

Testem, by default, will try to load any JavaScript files in the current directory, parse them for any tests, and then run them when a browser is connected. Testem is therefore creating a simple HTML page in memory, and serving this page to our browsers. This simple style uses Jasmine 1.3 by default, so we will need to configure Testem to use Jasmine 2 by creating a simple `testem.yml` file in our test directory as follows:

```
{
  "framework" : "jasmine2",
  "src_files": [
    "jquery.js",
    "jasmine-jquery.js",
    "UsingExtension.js",
    "test1.js"
  ]
}
```

This file is a simple JSON format file that specifies two properties, `framework` and `src_files`. The `framework` property indicates that we are using Jasmine 2 as our test framework, and the `source_files` property includes some extra JavaScript files that are needed for our tests, along with the `test1.js` file itself. With this `testem.yml` file in place, we are able to run our full test suite using Jasmine 2.0, jQuery, and our data-driven tests.

Testem has a number of powerful configuration options that can be specified in the configuration file. Be sure to head over to the GitHub repository for more information.

Note that Testem is a good choice for unit testing, but is not a good choice for integration or acceptance testing. The nature of the framework means that Testem is building an HTML page on the fly-based on our configuration file. During integration testing, we generally want the HTML pages to be created by a web server.

# Karma

Karma is a test runner built by the AngularJS team, and features heavily in the Angular tutorials. It is a unit-testing framework only, and the AngularJs team recommends end-to-end or integration tests to be built and run via Protractor. Karma, like Testem, runs its own instance of a web server in order to serve pages and artifacts required by the test suite, and it has a large set of configuration options. It can also be used for unit-tests that do not target Angular. To install Karma to work with Jasmine 2.0, we will need to install a few packages using `npm`:

```
npm install -g karma-cli
npm install karma --save-dev
npm install karma-jasmine --save-dev
npm install karma-chrome-launcher
```

To run Karma, we will need a configuration file. By convention, this is generally called `karma.conf.js`. A sample Karma configuration file is as follows:

```
module.exports = function (config) {
  config.set({
    basePath: '../',
    files: [
      'test/UsingExtension.js',
      'node_modules/jquery/dist/jquery.js',
      'node_modules/jasmine-jquery/lib/jasmine-jquery.js',
      'test/01_SimpleJasmineTests.js'
    ],
    autoWatch: true,
    frameworks: ['jasmine'],
    browsers: ['Chrome'],
    plugins: [
            'karma-chrome-launcher',
            'karma-jasmine'
    ]
  });
};
```

We start by defining a function that takes a single parameter named `config`, and assign this function to the `module.exports` property. All configuration parameters are then set with a call to `config.set`. The `basePath` parameter specifies what the root path is, and if it is relevant to the directory that the `karma.config.js` file resides in. The `files` array contains a list of files to be included in the generated HTML. Here, we have specified the list of files that we need in order to successfully run our tests.

The `autoWatch` parameter keeps Karma running in the background watching files for changes, similar to what Testem does. The `frameworks` parameter specifies that we will be using jasmine as a test framework. Karma allows for a variety of browsers to be specified within the `browsers` parameter. In this sample, we are only using Chrome. The final parameter is named `plugins`, and includes the plugin required for launching Chrome, as well as the plugin for Jasmine. Once this `config` file is in place, simply run `karma start` as follows:

```
karma start <path to karma.config.js>.
```

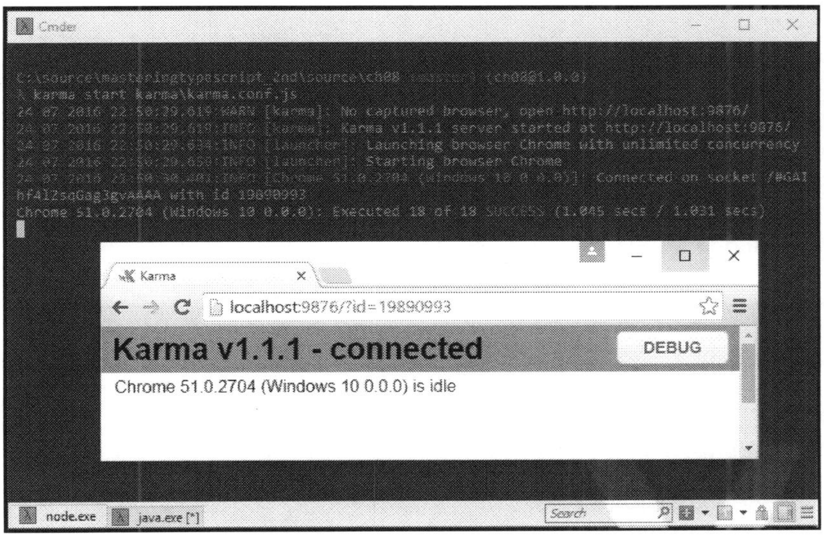


Karma output from a simple test

# Protractor

Protractor is a node-based test runner that tackles end-to-end, or integration and acceptance testing. Unlike Testem and Karma, which create a webpage for unit testing purposes, Protractor is used to programmatically control a web browser. Just like manual testing, Protractor has the ability to browse to a specific page, and then interact with the page from JavaScript. As a simple example, suppose that your website has a login page, and all further functionality requires a valid login. Using Protractor, we can start each test by browsing to the login page, entering valid credentials, and then continue to browse to each page that is part of our test suite.

Using Protractor, we can also check metadata properties within the HTML page – such as the page title, or we can fill in forms and click on buttons. Protractor can be installed with npm as follows:

```
npm install -g protractor
```

We will get to running Protractor a little later, but first, let's discuss the engine that Protractor uses under the hood to drive the browser.

# Using Selenium

Selenium is a driver for web browsers. It allows programmatic remote-control of web browsers, and can be used to create automated tests in Java, C#, Python, Ruby, PHP, Perl, and even JavaScript. Protractor uses selenium under the covers to control web browser instances. To install the selenium server for use with Protractor, run the following command:

```
webdriver-manager update
```

To start the selenium server, run the following command:

```
webdriver-manager start
```

If all goes well, selenium will report that the server has started, and will detail the address of the selenium server. Check your output for a line similar to the following:

```
RemoteWebDriver instances should connect to: http://127.0.0.1:4444/wd/hub
```

Note that you will need Java to be installed on your machine, as the web driver-manager uses Java to start the selenium server.

Once the server is running, we will need a configuration file for Protractor (similar to karma), that by convention is named `protractor.conf.js`. The contents of this file are as follows:

```
exports.config = {
  seleniumAddress: 'http://localhost:4444/wd/hub',
  specs: ['*.js']
}
```

Here, we are simply assigning some properties to the `exports.config` object. The first property that we are setting is `seleniumAddress`, which is the instance of the selenium server, as we saw earlier. The second property, named `specs`, is the list of tests to run. This `specs` property is therefore looking for any `.js` files in the same directory as the `protractor.conf.js` file.

Now for the simplest of tests:

```
describe("simple protractor test", () => {
  it("should navigate to google and find a title", () => {
    browser.driver.get('http://www.google.com');
    expect(browser.driver.getTitle()).toContain("Google");
  }) ;
});
```

Our test starts by opening the page at `'http://www.google.com'`. It then expects to see that the title of the page is set to `'Google'`. We can now run Protractor to execute this test as follows:

```
protractor .\protractor\protractor.conf.js
```

If you keep an eye on your screen, you will see Protractor starting a new instance of a Chrome browser session, and then navigate to the Google home page. It will then execute the expectation. Our command-line output is as follows:

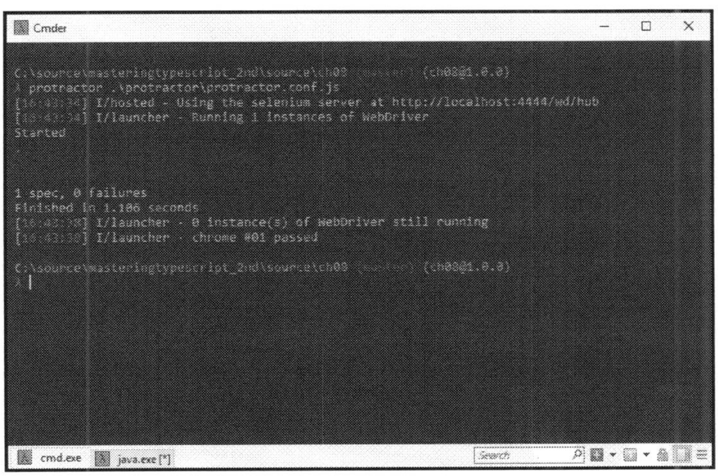

Protractor test results

# Using continuous integration

When writing unit tests for any application, it quickly becomes important to set up a build server and run your tests as part of each source control check in. When your development team grows beyond a single developer, using a continuous integration build server becomes imperative. This build server will ensure that any code committed to the source control server passes all known unit tests, integration tests, and automated acceptance tests. The build server is also responsible for labeling a build, and generating any deployment artifacts that need to be used during deployment. The basic steps of a build server would be as follows:

- Check out the latest version of the source code, and increase the build number
- Compile the application on the build server
- Run any server-side unit tests
- Package the application for deployment
- Deploy the package to a build environment
- Run any server-side integration tests
- Run any JavaScript unit, integration, or acceptance tests
- Mark the change set and build number as passed or failed
- If the build failed, notify those responsible for breaking it

The build server should fail if any one of the preceding steps fails.

## Benefits of CI

Using a build server to run through the preceding steps brings huge benefits to any development team. Firstly, the application is compiled on the build server – which means that any tools or external libraries will need to be installed on the build server. This gives your development team the opportunity to document exactly what software needs to be installed on a new machine in order to compile or run your application.

Secondly, a standard set of server-side unit tests can be run before the packaging step is attempted. In a Visual Studio project, these would be C# unit tests built with any of the popular .NET testing frameworks–MsTest, nUnit, or xUnit.

Next, the entire application's packaging step is run. Let's assume for a moment that a developer has included a new JavaScript library within the project, but forgotten to add it to source control. In this case, all of the tests will run on their local computer, but will break the build because of a missing library file. If we were to deploy the site at this stage, running the application would result in 404 errors – file not found. By running a packaging step, these sorts of errors are quickly found.

Once a successful packaging step has been completed, the build server should deploy the site to a specially marked build environment. This build environment is only used for CI builds, and must therefore have its own database instances, web service references, and so on, set up specifically for CI builds. Again, actually doing a deployment to a target environment tests the deployment artifacts, as well as the deployment process. By setting up a build environment for automated package deployment, your team is again able to document the requirements and process for deployment.

At this stage, we have a full instance of our website up and running on an isolated build environment. We can then easily target specific web pages that will run our JavaScript tests, and also run integration or automated acceptance tests – directly on the full version of the website. In this way, we can write tests that target the real life website REST services, without having to mock out these integration points. So in effect, we are testing the application from the ground up. Obviously, we may need to ensure that our build environment has a specific set of data that can be used for integration testing, or a way of generating the required datasets that our integration tests will need.

# Selecting a build server

There are a number of continuous integration build servers out there, including TeamCity, Jenkins, and **Team Foundation Server** (**TFS**).

## Team Foundation Server

TFS is a Microsoft product that will require a license for the server component, as well as a per-developer license. TFS needs a specific configuration on its build agents to be able to run instances of a web browser, as this is by default disabled. It also uses Windows Workflow Foundation to configure build steps, which takes a fair amount of experience and knowledge to modify.

## Jenkins

Jenkins is an open-source, free to use CI build server. It has wide community usage, and many plugins. Installation and configuration of Jenkins is fairly straight-forward, and Jenkins will allow processes to run browser instances, making it compatible with browser-based JavaScript unit tests. Jenkins build steps are command line-based, and it sometimes takes a little nous to configure build steps correctly.

## TeamCity

A very popular, and very powerful build server that is free to set up is TeamCity. TeamCity allows for free installation if you have a small number of developers ( < 20 ), and a small number of projects ( < 20). A full commercial license is only around $1,500.00, which makes it affordable for most organizations. Configuring build steps in TeamCity is much easier than in Jenkins or TFS, as it uses a wizard-style of configuration depending on the type of build step you are creating. TeamCity also has a rich set of functionality around unit-tests, with the ability to show graphs per unit-test, and is therefore considered best of breed for build servers.

# Integration test reporting

We have seen how to create and run tests using Jasmine, Testem, Karma, and Protractor. Each of our samples have successfully reported the number of tests executed, and the success or failure of the test suite. We have used simple configuration files and simple HTML files to set up and execute our tests.

In a real-world application, however, it is often necessary to run server-side logic or use server-side HTML rendering. For instance, most applications will require some sort of authentication, or login, before allowing calls to custom REST endpoints via JavaScript. Unfortunately, calling any of these REST endpoints from a normal HTML page will return 401 (Unauthorized) errors. For cases like these, we should run our tests against the full website.

This means that we will need a way of capturing the results of our test suite, for reporting back to our CI server. For these reporting purposes, Jasmine includes the ability to use custom test reporters, over and above the standard `HtmlReporter` that we have used previously. The GitHub project, jasmine-reporters (`https://github.com/larrymyers/jasmine-reporters`), has a number of pre-built test reporters that cater for the most popular build servers.

We can use these jasmine reporters with Protractor by updating the `protractor.conf.js` file, after installing the jasmine-reporters package via npm:

```
npm install jasmine-reporters --save-dev
```

Our updates to the `protractor.conf.js` file are as follows:

```
exports.config = {
  seleniumAddress: 'http://localhost:4444/wd/hub',
  specs: ['*.js'],
  onPrepare: function() {
    var jasmineReporters = require('jasmine-reporters');
    jasmine.getEnv().addReporter(
      new jasmineReporters.TeamCityReporter());
  }
}
```

Here, we have included an `onPrepare` property in our configuration settings, in order to run an anonymous function. This function simply creates a variable named `jasmineReporters` via a call to `require`, and then adds a new `TeamCityReporter` to the Jasmine runtime environment. The `require` function call is part of a module loading mechanism that we will cover in a later chapter.

Running our tests with Protractor will now output messages to the command line that TeamCity understands, as follows:

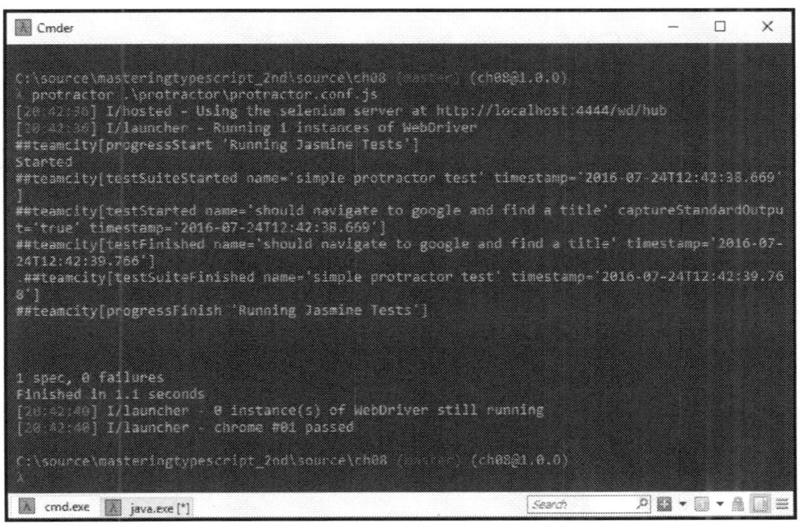


Protractor output using TeamCity format

# Summary

In this chapter, we have explored test driven development from the ground up. We have discussed the theory of TDD, explored the differences between unit, integration, and acceptance tests, and had a look at what a continuous integration build server process would look like. We then explored Jasmine as a testing framework, learned how to write tests, used expectations and matchers, and also explored jasmine extensions to help with data-driven tests and DOM on through fixtures. Finally, we had a look at test runners, discussed where and when they are best used, and used Protractor to drive web pages through selenium and report the results back to a build server.

In the next chapter, we will explore how to create tests for our three TypesScript frameworks–Aurelia, Angular 2, and React.

# 9

# Testing Typescript Compatible Frameworks

In `Chapter 7`, *Typescript Compatible Frameworks*, we discussed TypeScript compatible frameworks, and explored how Backbone, Aurelia, Angular 2, and React use the MVC or the MV* design patterns to write models, views, and controllers. We implemented the same sample application in each of these frameworks, in order to be able to compare the similarities between them and note the subtle differences. Then, in our last chapter, we started exploring test-driven-development, and discussed the use of Jasmine 2.0 as a test framework. We also explored using various test runners, including Testem and Karma, and finally explored Protractor for running integration, or end-to-end tests.

In this chapter, we will essentially be combining our work from the previous two chapters, and discussing how to unit and integration test each of our TypeScript compatible frameworks. For each of these frameworks, then, we will cover the following topics:

- Updates to the sample application to facilitate testing
- Setting up a unit testing framework
- Writing unit tests
- Setting up integration testing framework
- Writing integration tests

# Testing our sample application

You will recall that our sample application had the following features:

- Using a view to display a model property
- Constructing an array of data, with each array item being a single model instance
- Looping through the array and render each item in an `<li>` and `<button>` element
- Responding to a click event on each button element:
- Displaying the model properties that were used to render the element

If we were to outline some of the tests we could write, we would ideally like our tests to cover the following scenarios:

- Model tests:
    - Where internal models are used and assigned default values, test that these default values are created as expected
    - Where models are created from raw JavaScript objects, check that the models are created correctly
    - Where complex model objects are created, that is, models that contain other models, check that these are created correctly
- Application state:
    - Where the application starts up in a specific state, that is, internal variables are set to default values, verify that these have been set correctly
- Rendering tests:
    - Check that view objects are rendering the correct HTML to the DOM correctly, given a known model
- DOM event tests:
    - Check that DOM events, such as clicking on a button, are handled correctly
- Acceptance tests:
    - Browse to the required URL
    - Ensure that nothing has been selected
    - Click on a button to select the item
    - Verify that the screen shows which item has been selected

# Modifying our sample for testability

You will recall that our sample application shows an alert box when a button has been clicked. Unfortunately, if we run this version of our application within an automated unit test suite, we will need to trap the alert, and programmatically click on the **OK** button.

In general testing terms, alerts are something to be avoided. If an alert suddenly appears when it is not expected, this can cause your entire test suite to fail, as the browser is paused waiting for human intervention. There are, however, techniques to work with alert boxes if and when absolutely required. Bear in mind, though, that alert boxes are so 1990s, and any web designer will want a much more appealing modal dialog box instead.

Let's rather make a few changes to our application to display the currently selected item in a separate `<div>` at the bottom of the page. This has the added benefit that we are now storing the state of which button was last clicked within our application. We could therefore, use this technique to build a tabbed panel user interface, for example. Our updated sample application is as follows:

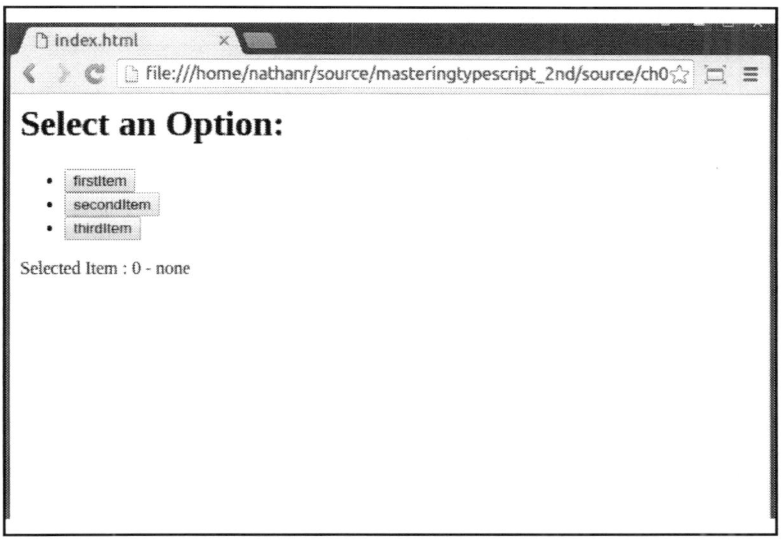


Updated sample application page layout

Here, we can see that we have created a DOM element at the bottom of the page to show the selected item's `Id` and `DisplayName` properties. Note that, when the page is first rendered, this will show the text **Selected Item : 0 – none**, to indicate that nothing has been selected as yet.

In order to accomplish this logic, we will therefore need to set an initial state for our application, somewhere within the application startup. This initial application state will also use a test to ensure that this property is set correctly.

# Backbone testing

In this section, we will take a look at modifying our existing Backbone sample application to include the necessary changes, as well as writing a set of Jasmine tests to cover all of our unit testing requirements.

# Complex models

The first change that we will need to make to our Backbone application is to introduce a complex model (that is, a model that contains other models). Remember that, in the initial version, we had a single model, named `ItemModel`. This `ItemModel` was used to store information about a single button, that is, its `Id` and `DisplayName`. We then created an `ItemView` that would take an `ItemModel`, and render it to a `<button>` element within the DOM. We then created an `ItemCollection` to house an array of `ItemModels`, and an `ItemCollectionView` to render the entire collection. Let's overlay these models and views onto our screen as follows:

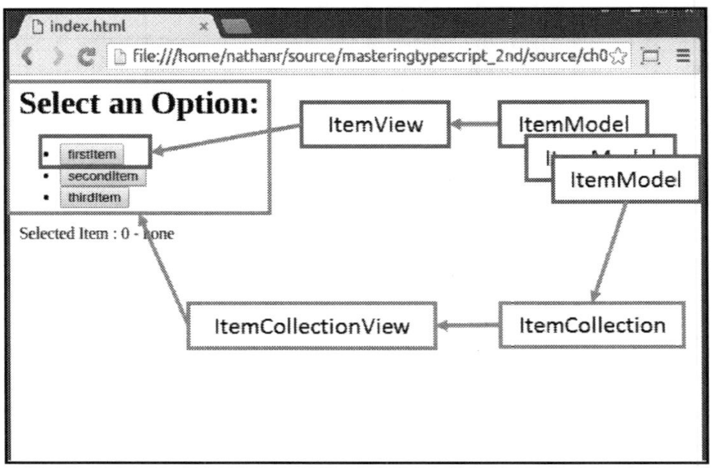


Backbone model, collection, and view overlay

Here, we can see that the `ItemView` is used to render a single `<li>` element (containing a `<button>`) into the DOM. The underlying Backbone model used for each of these `ItemViews` is an `ItemModel`. An array of `ItemModels` is stored in an `ItemCollection`. This `ItemCollection` is used by the `ItemCollectionView` to render all of the buttons on the screen.

Our modifications to the original application include creating a complex model and an associated view, as follows:

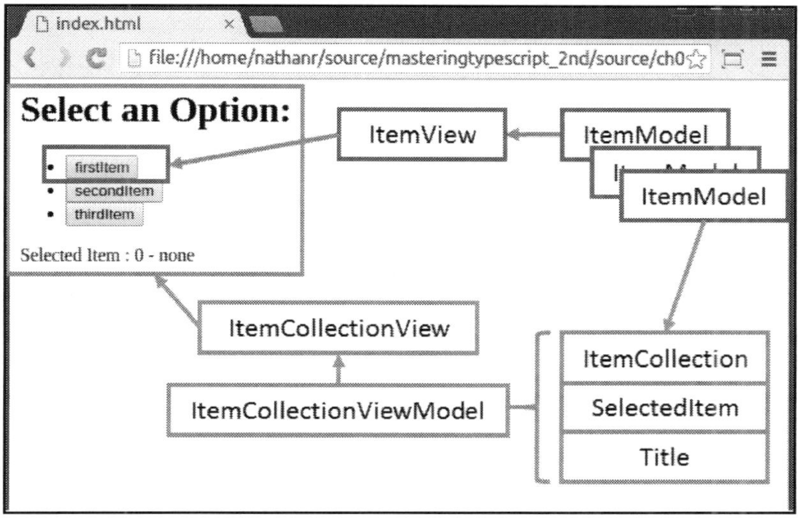


Updated sample application with model and view overlays

Here, we are reusing the `ItemView` / `ItemModel` combination as before. Note, however, that the `ItemCollection` is now housed within a complex model named `ItemCollectionViewModel`. This complex model also contains a property named `SelectedItem`, as well as a property named `Title`. The `Title` property will contain the text **Select an Option:**, and the `SelectedItem` property will be used to render the currently selected item into the DOM. We will also modify our `ItemCollectionView` slightly to render an `ItemCollectionViewModel` correctly.

Let's take a look at the complex model, the `ItemCollectionViewModel` class, as follows:

```
interface IItemCollectionViewModel {
  Title: string;
  SelectedItem : IClickableItem;
}

class ItemCollectionViewModel extends Backbone.Model
  implements IItemCollectionViewModel
{
  get Title(): string
  { return this.get('Title'); }
  set Title(value: string)
  { this.set('Title', value); }
  get SelectedItem(): IClickableItem
  { return this.get('SelectedItem'); }
  set SelectedItem(value: IClickableItem)
  { this.set('SelectedItem', value); }
  constructor(input: IItemCollectionViewModel) {
    super();
    for (var key in input) {
      if (key) { this[key] = input[key]; }
    }
  }
}
```

We start with an interface named `IItemCollectionViewModel` that has two properties–`Title` of type `string` and `SelectedItem` of type `IClickableItem`. We then define an `ItemCollectionViewModel` that extends `Backbone.Model`, and implements this interface. This is a standard `Backbone.Model`, and therefore must have `get` and `set` functions for each of our properties. This model also uses our standard constructor. Note, however, that we have not included a `Collection` property. This is due to the way that Backbone view classes are constructed. To understand this, let's take a look at the way an `ItemCollectionView` is constructed:

```
let collectionModel = new ItemCollectionViewModel( {
  Title:
    'Select an Option:',
  SelectedItem :
    Id: 0, DisplayName: "none"}});

let itemCollection =
  new ItemCollection(ClickableItemCollection);

let itemCollectionView = new ItemCollectionView(
{
  model: collectionModel,
```

```
    collection: itemCollection
});
```

Here, we are constructing an `ItemCollectionViewModel`, named `collectionModel`, and setting its internal `Title` and `SelectedItem` properties. We then create an instance of an `ItemCollection`, named `itemCollection`. The interesting point to note about this code sample is that we are then creating an `ItemCollectionView`, and passing in an object with two properties, named `model` and `collection`. All `Backbone.Views` have both a `model` and a `collection` property, allowing them to render either a single model, or a collection of models, or both. In our case, we are using the new complex model to render the `Title` and `SelectedItem` properties, and then using the existing Backbone `collection` property to render the `ItemCollection`.

# View updates

This change in our underlying model allows us to modify the view template for our `ItemCollectionView`, as follows:

```
<script type="text/template" id="itemCollectionViewTemplate">
  <h1> <%= Title %> </h1>
  <ul id="ulRegions">
  </ul>
  <div> Selected Item :
    <%= SelectedItem.Id %> -
    <%= SelectedItem.DisplayName %> </div>
</script>
```

Here, our updated HTML now includes the `Title` property rendered within an `<h1>` tag, and the `<div>` tag at the bottom of the template to show the `Id` and `DisplayName` properties of the `SelectedItem` property.

# DOM event updates

We can now turn our attention to what happens when we click on a button. Previously, we simply fired an alert dialog box from our `ItemView`, showing the value of the underlying model, as follows:

```
onClicked() {
  alert(`Item clicked : { Id: ${this.model.get('Id')},
    DisplayName : ${this.model.get('DisplayName')} }`);
}
```

What we need to implement now is a way for the `ItemView` to notify our `ItemCollectionView` that a particular `onClicked` event has happened. Thankfully, Backbone provides us with a very simple message bus that can be used for this purpose. In order to use the Backbone event bus, we will create a simple TypeScript class that has a static property through which we can fire event messages onto the bus, as follows:

```
class EventBus {
  static Bus = _.extend({}, Backbone.Events);
}
```

This class, named `EventBus`, has a single static property, named `Bus`, that uses the underscore `extend` function to combine a blank JavaScript object `{}` with the `Backbone.Events` object. This is all that is required to include a fully-fledged event bus within our application.

Firing an appropriate event from the `onClicked` function then simply becomes:

```
onClicked() {
  EventBus.Bus.trigger("item_clicked", this.model);
}
```

Here, we are firing an event named `item_clicked`, and attaching the model that was used within our `ItemView` as a parameter to the `trigger` function. Listening for this event within the `ItemCollectionView` consists of two parts. Firstly, we need to register for this event in our constructor as follows:

```
class ItemCollectionView extends
  Backbone.View<ItemCollectionViewModel> {
    constructor(options?: any) {
      // ... existing code

      this.listenTo(EventBus.Bus,
        "item_clicked", this.handleEvent);
    }
```

Every Backbone object has access to a function named `listenTo`. We have included a call to this `listenTo` function within our constructor with three arguments. The first argument is the object that will generate events that we are interested in, which in our case is the global `EventBus.Bus` object. The second argument is the event that we are interested in, and the third argument is the function to call when this event is raised.

The function call to handle this event is named `handleEvent`, so we will now need to implement this `handleEvent` function within our `ItemCollectionView`, as follows:

```
handleEvent(e) {
  this.model.SelectedItem = new ItemModel(e);
  this.render();
}
```

Here, we have defined a function named `handleEvent` on our `ItemCollectionView` object, which takes a single parameter named `e`. When this event is fired, we simply need to update the `SelectedItem` property of our model (which is of type `ItemCollectionViewModel` ) and then call our `render` function to update the DOM.

That's all there is to it. As we have seen, implementing an event bus, firing events, and listening for events are very simple processes indeed.

# Model tests

We can now turn our attention to writing unit tests for our Backbone models. When we construct a Backbone model, we use a POJO within the constructor to assign values to each of the models properties. So, given the following interface:

```
interface IClickableItem {
  DisplayName: string;
  Id: number;
}
```

We construct a new instance of our `ItemModel` class, as follows:

```
itemModel = new ItemModel({Id : 1, DisplayName : 'testDisplay'});
```

Remember that, internally, Backbone stores these POJO values as attributes on the class instance itself, which leads us to boilerplate code when writing a TypeScript version of a `Backbone.Model`, as follows:

```
class ItemModel extends Backbone.Model implements IClickableItem {
  get DisplayName(): string
    { return this.get('DisplayName'); }
  set DisplayName(value: string)
    { this.set('DisplayName', value); }
  get Id(): number { return this.get('Id'); }
  set Id(value: number) { this.set('Id', value); }
  constructor(input: IClickableItem) {
    super();
    for (var key in input) {
```

```
            if (key) { this[key] = input[key]; }
        }
    }
}
```

Each property in our interface (in this case, `IClickableItem` ) must define a pair of `get` and `set` functions, and use Backbone's `this.get` or `this.set` functions to store these properties correctly. As we are writing code to get this done, we need to write unit tests to ensure that this works correctly.

Our initial set of unit tests are as follows:

```
describe('ItemModel tests', () => {
  let itemModel : ItemModel;
  beforeEach( () => {
    itemModel = new ItemModel(
      {Id : 1, DisplayName : 'testDisplay'}
    );
  });
  it('should assign an Id property', () => {
    expect(itemModel.Id).toBe(1);
  });
  it('should assign a DisplayName property', () => {
    expect(itemModel.DisplayName).toBe('testDisplay');
  });
});
```

Here, we are defining a variable to hold an instance of our `ItemModel`, named `itemModel`. Note that its definition is outside the `beforeAll` function, and so it is available to each of our unit tests. Our `beforeEach` function initializes an instance of the `ItemModel` class, with default values, for each of our tests to reuse.

The first test, named `'should assign an Id property'`, is checking that the `Id` property returns the same value as was used in the constructor. Likewise, we have another test for the `DisplayName` property.

We can now extend these tests to verify that the `set` functions work correctly, as follows:

```
it('should set an Id property', () => {
  itemModel.Id = -10;
  expect(itemModel.Id).toBe(-10);
});
it('should set a DisplayName property', () => {
  itemModel.DisplayName = 'updatedDisplay';
  expect(itemModel.DisplayName).toBe('updatedDisplay');
});
```

As an added set of tests, we can even bypass the `set` and `get` functions, and verify that the underlying Backbone functions also set the properties correctly, as follows:

```
it('should call set on Id property', () => {
  itemModel.set('Id', -10);
  expect(itemModel.get('Id')).toBe(-10);
});
it('should call set on a DisplayName property', () => {
  itemModel.set('DisplayName', 'updatedDisplay');
  expect(itemModel.get('DisplayName')).toBe('updatedDisplay');
});
```

Here, we are testing that the internal `set` and `get` Backbone functions accomplish exactly the same thing as using the TypeScript property getter and setter syntax.

# Complex model tests

We can use the same techniques to test that complex models are instantiated correctly. Consider the following test suite:

```
describe('ItemCollectionViewModel tests', () => {
  let itemCollectionViewModel : ItemCollectionViewModel;
  beforeAll( () => {
    itemCollectionViewModel = new ItemCollectionViewModel(
      {
      Title :
        'testTitle',
      SelectedItem :
        { Id : 0, DisplayName : 'testDisplay'}
      }
    );
  });
```

Here, we are creating an instance of our complex model, named `itemCollectionViewModel`. The interesting bit is the construction of this complex model with a POJO. We are calling the constructor in our `beforeAll` function, and simply nesting POJOs within each other. We are setting the `Title` property, and then setting the `SelectedItem` property to another POJO that has the `Id` and `DisplayName` properties.

> These POJOs are using the same structure as what we expect to be returned in JSON format from the backend REST endpoints. Defining object tests like these can therefore easily extend into integration tests, which will call an actual web service and rehydrate our models from POJOs.

Our unit tests for this complex model can then simply traverse the available properties to ensure that everything is set correctly, as follows:

```
it('should assign a Title property', () => {
  expect(itemCollectionViewModel.Title).toBe('testTitle');
});
it('should assign a SelectedItem.Id property', () => {
  expect(itemCollectionViewModel.SelectedItem.Id).toBe(0);
});
it('should assign a SelectedItem.DisplayName property', () => {
  expect(itemCollectionViewModel.SelectedItem.DisplayName)
    .toBe('testDisplay');
});
```

Our first test checks the value of the `Title` property, and then the following tests check the value of the `SelectedItem` property (which is a child Backbone model).

# Rendering tests

Once we are happy that our Backbone models are hydrating correctly, we can turn our attention to their views and write some tests to ensure that they render these model properties correctly to the DOM. We will use Jasmine's `setFixtures` function to set up our Backbone templates, as follows:

```
describe('ItemView rendering tests', () => {
  let itemModel : ItemModel;
  beforeEach( () => {
    setFixtures(
      `<div id="itemViewElement"></div>
      <script type="text/template" id="itemViewTemplate">
        <button id='itemButton'>
          <%= DisplayName %>
        </button>
      </script>
      <script type="text/template"
        id="itemCollectionViewTemplate">
      </script>
    `);

    itemModel = new ItemModel(
      {Id : 1, DisplayName : 'testDisplay'});
});
```

Here, we have created and instantiated an `ItemModel` instance named `itemModel` for reuse within each test. We are also calling `setFixtures` in order to inject the HTML `<script>` tags that we will require into the DOM. The `<script>` tag that our `ItemView` will use is the `itemViewTemplate` script, which defines the following HTML:

```
<button id='itemButton'> <%= DisplayName %> </button>
```

This template uses the `DisplayName` property of the `ItemModel` instance inside a `<button>` tag. Note, however, that within the actual `ItemView` constructor, we are specifying a `tagName` property, as follows:

```
options.tagName = "li";
```

This `tagName` property means that a single `ItemView` HTML snippet – once it has been rendered – will contain the `<button>` element (from our HTML snippet) within an `<li>` element (from our `tagName` property). Within the HTML snippet, Backbone will also substitute our `DisplayName` property, and therefore render the following HTML:

```
<li>
  <button id="itemButton"> testDisplay </button>
</li>
```

Our test, therefore, will look for these HTML elements once the `ItemView` has been rendered, as follows:

```
it('should render a li and button element', () => {
  let itemView = new ItemView({model : itemModel});
  let renderedHtml = itemView.render().el;
  console.log(renderedHtml.outerHTML);
  expect(renderedHtml.outerHTML).toContain('<li>');
  expect(renderedHtml.innerHTML).toContain(
    '<button id="itemButton">');
  expect(renderedHtml.innerHTML).toContain('testDisplay')
});
```

In this test, we are creating an instance of the `ItemView` class, and instantiating it with our model. We then call the `render` function on the `itemView` instance, and store the value of the `el` property into a variable named `renderedHtml`. This `el` property is what will be attached to the DOM, and contains the HTML that has been generated as a result of the `render` function.

Our test then checks for the existence of an `<li>` element and a `<button>` element, and that the `<%= DisplayName %>` substitution has occurred correctly.

Our view tests, therefore, have accomplished the following:

- Created an instance of an `ItemModel`
- Created an instance of an `ItemView`, using the `ItemModel`
- Called the `render` function on the `ItemView`
- Verified that the rendered HTML contains the correct elements

# DOM event tests

The next set of functionality within our application that we will need to test is our DOM events. The basic flow of these tests is as follows:

- Construct an instance of an `ItemView`, with its corresponding `ItemModel`
- Render the HTML
- Find the `<button>` element, and simulate a DOM `click` event
- Ensure that the `onClicked` function of the `ItemView` is called
- Ensure that the `onClicked` function triggers an event bus message, and that the `ItemCollectionView` receives this event bus message

Our first test will simulate a click event, and use a Jasmine spy on the `onClicked` function of the `ItemView`, as follows:

```
it('should trigger onClicked', () => {
  let clickSpy = spyOn(ItemView.prototype, 'onClicked');
  let itemView = new ItemView({model : itemModel});
  itemView.render();
  itemView.$('#itemButton').trigger("click");

  expect(clickSpy).toHaveBeenCalled();

});
```

The first line of this test uses the `spyOn` function from Jasmine to attach a spy to the `onClicked` function of our `ItemView`. Note, however, that we are specifying `ItemView.prototype` as the input to our `spyOn` function. Remember that, when our Backbone view was constructed, we specified via the `options.events` property what functions to bind to DOM events. By the time we have completed running the constructor, we cannot then attach a spy to this function (as it is already bound to the DOM event). The solution, therefore, is to bind to the view `prototype` before the actual view is constructed.

Once we have a spy in place, we can construct the view and call the `render` function. Once the `render` function has been called, we can use standard jQuery DOM searches on the view and trigger a click, as seen in the following line:

```
itemView.$('#itemButton').trigger("click");
```

Here, we are using a fluent syntax and jQuery `$` functions to find the element with an `id` of `itemButton`, and `trigger` a DOM click event.

Our test passes, as the DOM click event calls our `onClicked` function of the `ItemView`.

The final test we need to build is one to ensure that the message bus is working correctly. Remember that, when an `ItemView` element is clicked, it will trigger an event on the message bus, and include its model properties as part of this message. On the other side of the message bus, the `ItemCollectionView` is listening for this event, and it will update the DOM to show our currently selected item.

Our test, therefore, is as follows:

```
it('should listen to onClicked in ItemCollectionView', () => {
  let clickSpy = spyOn(ItemCollectionView.prototype,
    'handleEvent');
  let itemCollectionView = new ItemCollectionView();

  let itemView = new ItemView({model : itemModel});
  itemView.render();

  itemView.$('#itemButton').trigger("click");

  expect(clickSpy).toHaveBeenCalled();

});
```

In this test, we start with a Jasmine spy on the `handleEvent` function of the `ItemCollectionView.prototype`. This `handleEvent` function is the end result of the message bus publish and subscribe mechanism. Our `ItemCollectionView` is listening for the event, and when the event is received the `handleEvent` function is called. So if this function is called, we know that the message bus communication is working between an `ItemView` (publisher) and an `ItemCollectionView` (subscriber). The rest of this test is similar to what we have seen in our previous DOM click event tests.

## Backbone testing summary

As we have seen, when testing Backbone applications, we are able to do a wide range of unit tests using Jasmine and Jasmine-jQuery alone. We are able to create model tests, view rendering tests, and even DOM event tests without leaving the Jasmine environment.

# Aurelia testing

In this section, we will take a look at the changes required to our Aurelia test application in order for it to store and display the currently selected item on our HTML page. We will then dive into writing unit tests that will check the internal state of our application, and write some DOM rendering tests. Finally, we will create a set of integration tests that use Protractor to click on a button within our page, and ensure that the HTML page is updated correctly.

## Aurelia components

In order to render the currently selected item to the DOM, and replace the alert that we have been using, we will build an Aurelia component. A component is essentially a view and view-model pairing. The view-model code is written as a standard TypeScript class, and the view is written as a standard HTML template. Aurelia has a particular naming convention that ties these two elements together, as we have seen with the `app.ts` and `app.html` resources that we built earlier. Aurelia will take care of data-binding between our view and view-model automatically, as long as they conform to this naming standard, which will allow us to write minimal code in order to accomplish our goal.

## Aurelia component view-model

Let's start by creating a local variable within our `App` class to hold the currently selected item, as follows:

```
import {ClickableItem} from './ClickableItem';

export class App {
  message: string = 'Select an Option:';
  currentElement: ClickableItem;
  items: ClickableItem[] = [
    { idValue: 1, displayName : "firstItem"},
    { idValue: 2, displayName : "secondItem"},
```

```
        { idValue: 3, displayName : "thirdItem"},
      ];
      constructor() {
        this.currentElement = { idValue: 0, displayName : 'none'};
      }
      onItemClicked(event: ClickableItem) {
        this.currentElement = event;
      }
    }
```

Here, we have made a few changes to our initial `app.ts` file. Firstly, we have added a line at the top of the file that imports a new class, named `ClickableItem`, from the `'./ClickableItem'` file. This import syntax is used for modularization, which allows us to easily reference classes that are in other TypeScript source files. We will cover modularization in depth in the next chapter.

The second change we have made is to add a local variable named `currentElement` (of type `ClickableItem`), where we can store the currently selected item. We have also created a `constructor` function for our class, and within this constructor we have set the `currentElement` to `{ 0, none }`. Effectively, we are setting the initial state of the application to have nothing selected.

The third change we have made is to modify the `onItemClicked` function that handles the DOM click event. Instead of creating an `alert`, we are now simply setting the `currentElement` property of the class to the item that was passed into the function.

Let's now turn our attention to the `ClickableItem` component itself. As mentioned earlier, a component consists of a view-model and a view. Our view-model will be created in a separate TypeScript file named `ClickableItem.ts`. This filename matches the `import {} from` statement at the top of the `app.ts` file (`'./ClickableItem'` – without the `.ts` extension). The source code for our `ClickableItem.ts` file is a simple TypeScript class, as follows:

```
import {bindable} from 'aurelia-framework';

export class ClickableItem {
  @bindable displayName: string;
  @bindable idValue: number;
}
```

Again, we are importing the `bindable` function from the `'aurelia-framework'` package at the top of the file so that we can use the `@bindable` property decorator within our class. We have then defined a simple class, named `ClickableItem`, which has two properties, named `displayName` and `idValue`. Each of these properties has been decorated with the `@bindable` property decorator. This decorator instructs Aurelia to bind the value of each decorated property to the view.

# Aurelia component view

Now that we have a view-model defined, we can create a `ClickableItem.html` file that will serve as the HTML template for the view, as follows:

```
<template>
  <div id="selectedElement">
    Selected Element: ${idValue} - ${displayName}
  </div>
</template>
```

This HTML template defines a `<div>` element with an `id` of `selectedElement`. Within this element are two substitution tags–`${idValue}` and `${displayName}`. These tags use the standard Aurelia tag substitution syntax, and their names match the properties of our view-model.

# Rendering a component

The final change to our application will be to include this `ClickableItem` component view as a sub-component into our existing app view. To do this, we will modify our `app.html` template, as follows:

```
<template>
  <require from="./ClickableItem"></require>
  <h1>${message}</h1>
    <ul>
    <li repeat.for="item of items"
        click.delegate="onItemClicked(item)" >
      <button id="select_button_${$index}" >
        ${item.displayName}
      </button>
    </li>
  </ul>

  <clickable-item
```

```
        id-value="${currentElement.idValue}"
        display-name="${currentElement.displayName}" >
      </clickable-item>
    </template>
```

The first change to our template is the addition of the `<require from="./ClickableItem">` tag. This tag instructs the view to load the HTML template found at `./ClickableItem.html`, and include this template for use within the `app.html` file itself.

The second change to our app template is the addition of the `<clickable-item>` tag at the bottom of the file. This tag has two attributes, named `id-value` and `display-name`. Aurelia will use the value of the App's properties to pass into the component's view-model. In other words, the value of the `App.currentElement.idValue` variable will be bound to the `id-value` attribute. Likewise, the value of the `App.currentElement.displayName` variable will be bound to the `display-name` attribute.

# Aurelia naming conventions

A very important convention to bear in mind when building and testing Aurelia components is the naming syntax that is used within a view-model (TypeScript class) and a view (HTML template). As we have seen earlier, Aurelia does a lot of heavy-lifting when automatically binding views and view-models. The key to this automated binding feature is the naming convention.

If we create a TypeScript class named `ClickableItem`, then this class name must be referred to in any HTML files as `<clickable-item>`. This naming convention is referred to as kebab-case. Aurelia imposes this syntax convention as a result of HTML restrictions, where upper case and lower case names are equivalent. In other words, an attribute name `TestAttribute='value'` is syntactically equivalent to `testattribute='value'`. To overcome this upper and lower case restriction, Aurelia has provided an automatic attribute-to-JavaScript-property binding convention that uses kebab-case. Each new uppercase letter must be converted to lowercase, and separated by a hyphen ( `-` ).

A simple way of remembering this naming convention is in the name TypeScript (note the uppercase T and uppercase S in the word TypeScript). So a TypeScript class named `MyTypeScriptClass` will be referred to in HTML views as `my-type-script-class`.

This naming convention also applies to HTML element attributes. So an attribute that is bound to a TypeScript property named `MyTypeScriptProperty` will need to be named `my-type-script-property` within any HTML view.

One more caveat in this naming convention syntax has to do with the `${ ... }` Aurelia syntax, which is used for parameter substitution. Remember that anything inside a `${ ... }` block is considered to be JavaScript, and so it does NOT use the kebab-case naming convention. Therefore, to reference a TypeScript property named `myPropertyName`, we need to use it as is within a `${ ... }` block, that is, `${myPropertyName}`.

Every Aurelia developer has been bitten by this syntax naming convention at some point in time. Once you have been bitten, however, and spent a few hours trying to figure out why your application simply does not render, it will become second-nature ( or should that be SecondNature ?) to go back and re-check ( ReCheck ?) these naming rules.

# Aurelia test setup

With our application changes completed, we can now focus on unit testing our Aurelia application. Before we do this, however, we will need to set up an Aurelia test environment.

One of the questions that the Aurelia command-line interface asks when setting up a new Aurelia application (`au new`) is whether or not to configure unit testing. If we answer yes to this question, then all of the testing configuration files and dependencies are installed automatically. In the interests of time, we will not investigate how to retrospectively add unit testing capabilities to an existing Aurelia application, but will instead assume that this has already been configured.

To run Aurelia unit tests, simply type:

```
au test
```

This will invoke the built-in Karma test runner, and execute any tests found in the `/test/unit` directory that match the filename convention of `*spec.js`.

> The `au build` command must be executed before any tests are compiled and included in a new test run. Aurelia provides the `--watch` command line argument, which will automatically re-execute the current command if modifications to files on disk are detected. This means that running `au test --watch` will compile and rerun any Karma unit tests automatically when our TypeScript source files are modified. This is a very useful feature that provides instant feedback when writing unit tests.

# Aurelia unit tests

Our first set of unit tests will need to verify that the `App` class (our entry point) has been constructed correctly, that is, it is in the correct state. When the application is first loaded, it will render a title, three buttons, and also indicate that no item has been selected. These HTML elements are bound to the `message`, `currentElement`, and `items` properties of the `App` class itself. Let's create an `app.spec.ts` file in the `/test/unit` directory, and write a test to verify that these properties have been set correctly, as follows:

```
import {App} from '../../src/app';
describe('App tests', function () {
  var application : App;
  beforeAll( () => {
    application = new App();
  });
  it('message property contains Select', function () {
    expect(application.message).toContain('Select');
  });
});
```

The first line of this test uses the `import` statement to import the `App` class from the `'../../src/app'` file. Note that the `../../` reference is necessary because any `import` statement that uses that path is relevant to the file that is doing the import.

We then use the standard Jasmine `describe` syntax to set up a test suite, and configure a variable named `application` to hold an instance of the `App` class. Our first test verifies that the `message` property of the `App` class (on construction) contains the phrase `"Select"`. This test is therefore checking the initial state of the `App` class when first constructed. We can then check each of the internal variables as follows:

```
it('has a property named items', function () {
  expect(application.items).toBeDefined();
});
it('has an array of clickable items', function () {
  expect(application.items.length).toBe(3);
});
it('sets currentElement property in constructor', function () {
  expect(application.currentElement).toBeDefined();
});
it('sets currentElement.idValue to 0', function () {
  expect(application.currentElement.idValue).toBe(0);
});
it('sets currentElement.displayName to none', function () {
  expect(application.currentElement.displayName).toBe('none');
});
```

Here, we have a few tests for the `items` variable, which is an array of length `3`, and a few tests for the `currentElement` variable, which should be set to `idValue = 0` and `displayName = 'none'`. These tests are verifying that, when an App instance is created, the initial state of the class is set correctly.

# Rendering tests

Our next round of tests will cover rendering elements to the DOM. Aurelia provides a set of helper classes, similar to Jamine's `setFixture` functionality, in order to attach HTML to the DOM and render views using these temporary DOM elements. Our test suite, therefore, needs to include the following two import statements at the top of the file:

```
import {StageComponent} from 'aurelia-testing';
import {bootstrap} from 'aurelia-bootstrapper';
```

These import statements include a class named `StageComponent`, and a function named `bootstrap`. The `StageComponent` class is the helper utility that Aurelia provides in order to house an instance of our item-under-test, which in our case is an instance of the `App` class. The `bootstrap` function is the standard method of creating and bootstrapping an Aurelia application.

Our test setup, then, is as follows:

```
var application;
beforeEach(function () {
  application = StageComponent
    .withResources('app')
    .inView(
      '<h1 id="messageHeader">${message}</h1>' +
      '<ul id="ulItemList">' +
      '<li repeat.for="item of items" ' +
      'click.delegate="onItemClicked(item)">' +
      '<button id="select_button_${$index}">' +
      '${item.displayName}</button>' +
      '</li>' +
      '</ul>' +
      '<clickable-item id-value="${currentElement.idValue}" ' +
      ' display-name="${currentElement.displayName}" ' +
      ' >
      </clickable-item>').boundTo(new App());
});
```

Here, we have defined a variable named `application` to house an instance of our `StageComponent` class. The creation of the `StageComponent` class uses a fluent style to effectively chain together three commands–`withResources`, `inView`, and `boundTo`. The `withResources` function call registers our `app` code with the `StageComponent`, and the `inView` defines the HTML DOM that we need for our tests. The final `boundTo` function call creates a new instance of the class `App`, and binds this new instance to the `StageComponent`.

Our first test must verify that the `message` property of the `App` class is rendered correctly to the DOM, as follows:

```
it('should render message property', (done) => {
  application.create(bootstrap).then( () => {
    var messageHeader =
      document.querySelector('#messageHeader');
    expect(messageHeader).toBeDefined();
    expect(messageHeader.innerHTML).toContain('Select');
    done();
  });
});
```

The first thing to note about this test is the use of the `(done)` parameter on the `it` function. Aurelia uses Jasmine's asynchronous testing features whenever we use `StageComponent`. We must therefore remember to pass in the `done` parameter as part of our test function, and also to call the `done` function once our test has completed.

The test itself starts by calling the `create` function on the instance of the `StageComponent` (which houses our `App` test instance), passing in the `bootstrap` function. This `create` function returns a promise named `then`, where we can define the actual content of our test. Once we are inside the promise, all of Aurelia's bootstrapping and binding has already taken place. We are then able to query the DOM via the `document.querySelector` function. In this test, we find the `#messageHeader <div>`, and check that the HTML rendered contains the string `'Select'`.

Our next test will verify that the array of buttons has been rendered to the DOM as follows:

```
it('should render buttons', function (done) {
  application.create(bootstrap).then(function () {
    var ulItemList = document.querySelectorAll(
      '#ulItemList > li > button');
    expect(ulItemList).toBeDefined();
    for (var i = 0; i < ulItemList.length; i++) {
      var itemElement = ulItemList[i];
      expect(itemElement.innerHTML).toContain('Item');
```

```
        }
        done();
      });
    });
```

In this test, we are using the `document.querySelectorAll` function to return an array of button elements. Note the CSS selector syntax that we have used–`#ulItemList > li > button`. This CSS selector will return each `button` element within an `li` element that are children of the `ulItemList` element. We are then looping through each element returned, and checking that the `innerHTML` property contains the word `'Item'`. Remember that the button text displayed on the page was `firstItem`, `secondItem`, and `thirdItem`, so each of these buttons will contain the word `'Item'`. While this may not be a definitive test, it shows how we are able to use standard CSS selectors to return more than one child item.

We have one other unit test to write. When an instance of the `App` class is first created, the `currentElement` property is set to a default value of `{ 0 , none }`. We would like to verify that this child component (of type `ClickableItem`) is rendered to the DOM the first time that the page is loaded. Our test is as follows:

```
    it('should render none as selected item', (done) => {
      application.create(bootstrap).then( () => {
        var clickableItem = document.querySelector(
         'clickable-item');
        console.log(clickableItem.innerHTML);
        expect(clickableItem.innerHTML).toContain('none');
        done();
      });
    });
```

Here, we are constructing an instance of our application, as we have done in our other tests, and are then using the `querySelector` to find the `<clickable-item>` element. We expect that the `innerHTML` element will contain the word `'none'`. Unfortunately, this test always fails. If we take a look at the DOM that is generated via the `StageComponent`, we will notice that the `<clickable-item>` element is in fact empty:

```
    <clickable-item class="au-target" au-target-id="25"></clickable-
item></div>
```

This problem indicates that the scope of a unit test within Aurelia does not extend to child components, as we initially expected.

# Aurelia end-to-end tests

In order to complete our Aurelia testing, and simulate DOM clicks that will correctly update the page to show which item is selected, we will need to switch to an integration test strategy, and configure Protractor to run some end-to-end tests.

As we discussed in the last chapter, Protractor needs a configuration file in order to set up our end-to-end testing environment. Our `protractor.conf.js` file, in the root of our project directory, is as follows:

```
exports.config = {
  directConnect: true,

  // Capabilities to be passed to the webdriver instance.
  capabilities: {
    'browserName': 'chrome'
  },

  //seleniumAddress: 'http://0.0.0.0:4444',
  specs: ['test/e2e/dist/*.js'],

  plugins: [{
    path: './node_modules/aurelia-tools/plugins/protractor.js'
  }],

  // Options to be passed to Jasmine-node.
  jasmineNodeOpts: {
    showColors: true,
    defaultTimeoutInterval: 30000
  }
};
```

There are two interesting properties in this `config` file to make note of. Firstly, the `specs` property contains the path to our integration `test` directory. In this instance, we have specified `test/e2e/dist/*.js`. This means that Protractor will search for all `.js` files in the `test/e2e/dist` directory to find end-to-end test suites.

The second property to make note of is the `plugins` property. This specifies that the `protractor.js` file from Aurelia must be loaded as a plugin in order to provide Aurelia specific extensions for Protractor.

With this `protractor.conf.js` file in place, there are a few more steps that we need to go through to integrate Protractor with our Aurelia project. These steps involve the following:

- Installing dependencies
- Including an `aurelia.protracotor.js` bootloader
- Adding an e2e task to the Aurelia task list
- Adding an e2eTestRunner to `aurelia_project/aurelia.json`

Our first setup step is to install the `del` and `gulp-protractor` dependencies as follows:

```
npm install del --save
npm install gulp-protractor --save
```

With these dependencies in place, we will need to create an `aurelia-protractor.js` file to act as a bootloader in the project root directory. The source for this file is included in the downloadable content for this chapter, and will not be discussed here.

We will also need two files in the `aurelia_project/tasks` directory, named `e2e.json` and `e2e.ts`. Again, these files are included in the downloadable content and are boilerplate configuration files, so they will not be included here.

The final step in configuring Protractor with Aurelia is to edit the `aurelia_project/aurelia.json` file and include the following configuration:

```
"e2eTestRunner": {
  "id": "protractor",
  "displayName": "Protractor",
  "source": "test/e2e/src/**/*.ts",
  "dist": "test/e2e/dist/",
  "typingsSource": [
    "typings/**/*.d.ts",
    "custom_typings/**/*.d.ts"
  ]
},
```

Here, we have included an `e2eTestRunner` configuration section that looks in the `test/e2e/src` directory for any test specification files to run as end-to-end tests.

At the time of writing, the aurelia-cli is at version 0.17.0, and does not set up or configure end-to-end test configuration. This means that we need to go through this process of setting up Protractor within an Aurelia project. Future versions of the aurelia-cli may include this configuration as a default.

With these configuration changes in place, we can start our Aurelia application from the command-line as usual, as follows:

```
au run
```

Once our development web site is running, we can start our Protractor tests by issuing a similar command from the command-line as follows:

```
au e2e
```

This command is using the Aurelia-CLI to start a task named `e2e`, which corresponds to the `e2e.ts` and `e2e.json` files that we created in the `aurelia_project` directory.

Now that we have Protractor running, we can focus on writing some end-to-end tests.

Our first end-to-end test suite is as follows:

```
describe('Aurelia end-to-end tests', () => {

  beforeEach( () => {
    browser.get('http://localhost:9000');
    browser.sleep(1000);
  });

it('should load page', () => {
  expect(browser.getTitle()).toBe('Aurelia');
});

it('should find an h1 element with Select an Option', () => {
  expect(element(by.css('h1')).getText()).toContain("Select");
});
```

Here, we have set up the default starting page in our `beforeEach` function, and specified that the browser should sleep for a second before running any of our tests. This sleep is necessary in order to give Aurelia time to bootstrap our application correctly.

Our first test verifies that the title of the page is `'Aurelia'`, and the second test verifies that the <h1> element contains the text `'Select'`. All well and good so far. We can now create a test to verify that the <clickable-item> element was rendered correctly with the text `'Selected Element : 0 - none'`, as follows:

```
it('should find 0 as selected element', () => {
  expect(element(by.id('selectedElement'))
    .getText()).toBe('Selected Element: 0 - none');
});
```

This test could not be simpler. We find an element on the page by using its `id` property, and verify that the text it contains is correct. This test is the one that we had problems with in the unit testing phase when we were trying to use `StageComponent`. By using Protractor, we are able to allow Aurelia to render the entire page, and then check that our DOM elements have been rendered correctly.

Our final test is to click on a button and verify that the DOM has been updated correctly, as follows:

```
it('clicking a button should update selected element', () => {
  element(by.id('select_button_0')).click();
  browser.sleep(500);
  expect(element(by.id('selectedElement'))
    .getText()).toBe('Selected Element: 1 - firstItem');
});
```

Here, we find the first `button` element on the page and call the `click` function. Once clicked, we need to have the browser sleep for a very short period of time, in order to allow Aurelia to process the click event. Finally, we verify that the `selectedElement` DOM element has been updated correctly.

## Aurelia test summary

This concludes our section on Aurelia unit and integration testing. We have seen that Aurelia provides an `au test` option to run Karma for unit testing purposes, and that all configuration and dependencies are automatically installed for us by the Aurelia command line setup. We explored how to create a child component, how to test initial application state, and then completed our test suite with an end-to-end test using Protractor.

# Angular 2 testing

In this section, we will take a look at unit and integration tests for our existing Angular 2 application, similarly to what we did with Backbone and Aurelia. Before we start with testing, however, we will need to make some small changes to our application in order to display the currently selected item on the page.

# Application updates

Our changes for Angular 2 are very simple, compared to the changes we made using Backbone or Aurelia. In order to track the currently selected item within our application, we will need to do three things:

1. Create a property to store our currently selected item.
2. Modify our `onSelect` function to update this property.
3. Update our view template to show this on the page.

Our first change is within the `AppComponent` class, as follows:

```
export class AppComponent {
  title = "Select an option :";
  items = ClickableItemArray;
  selectedItem : ClickableItem;
  constructor() {
    this.selectedItem = {id: 0, displayName: "none"};
  }
  onSelect(selectedItem: ClickableItem) {
    this.selectedItem = selectedItem;
    console.log(`onSelect : ${this.selectedItem.id}`);
  }
}
```

Here, we have made three changes. Firstly, we have added a `selectedItem` property to store the currently selected item. Secondly, we have created a `constructor` function that sets the `selectedItem` property to hold an initial value of `{ 0 - none }`. Thirdly, we have updated our `onSelect` function to simply set the internal `selectedItem` property to the item that was passed into our `onSelect` function.

Next, we will need to update our component template to include a `<div>` element to show the currently selected item on the page. Our `app.component.html` file is as follows:

```
<h1>{{title}}</h1>
<ul>
  <li *ngFor="let item of items; let i = index"
    (click)="onSelect(item)">
    <button id='select_button_{{i}}'>
        {{item.displayName}} {{i}}
    </button>
  </li>
</ul>
<div *ngIf="selectedItem">
  <div id='selectedItemText'>
```

```
        Selected : {{selectedItem.id}} -
          {{selectedItem.displayName}}
      </div>
    </div>
```

The only change to this template is the inclusion of a `<div>` element at the end of the template. This `<div>` starts with the `*ngIf="selectedItem"` statement. Any element can be optionally shown or hidden using the `*ngIf` syntax. What this effectively means, is that if the `selectedItem` property has a value, we then render the `<div>`. If it does not have a value, then this `<div>` will not be shown.

Within our `*ngIf <div>` element, we have another `<div>`, with an `id` of `selectedItemText`. This `<div>` will render the value of the `selectedItem.id` and `selectedItem.displayName` properties, similarly to how we show the currently selected item with Backbone and Aurelia.

These are the only changes required for our Angular 2 application in order to display the currently selected item. Simple, right?

# Angular 2 test setup

When creating a project using the Angular-CLI (by issuing the `ng new` command), the default project setup already includes all of the boilerplate code to run unit tests using Karma, and end-to-end tests using Protractor. This default setup is a very handy feature of Angular 2, shortening the development effort of configuring a test environment and giving us the ability to dive right in and write tests from the beginning of a project.

To run unit tests using Karma, we can type the following from the command line:

```
ng test
```

This command line option will compile and package our application, and run any tests that it finds within the `src` directory. Any TypeScript file where the name matches `*.spec.ts` will be designated as a test file, and any tests within this file will be executed. In addition, running Karma in this way will also automatically watch our files for changes, and re-compile and re-run our tests as changes are detected.

The Angular 2 default project creates `.spec.ts` files within the source directory, right alongside the components under test. This means that, within the `src/app` directory, we will find both `app.component.ts` and `app.component.spec.ts`. While this is the default setting, there is no reason why we cannot split the `.spec.ts` files into their own directory. In other words, the `src/app` directory can contain the `app.component.ts` file, and the `src/test` directory can contain the `app.component.spec.ts` file. We will use this second approach in the remainder of the chapter.

# Angular 2 model tests

To start off with, we will create a series of tests that will check the internal state of the `AppComponent` class once instantiated, in a file named `src/test/app.component.spec.ts`, as follows:

```
import { AppComponent } from '../app/app.component';

describe("tests/app.component.tests.ts ", () => {

  let appComponent;
  beforeAll( () => {
    appComponent = new AppComponent();
  });

  it("should construct an AppComponent", () => {
    expect(appComponent).toBeDefined();
  });
  it('should set title', () => {
    expect(appComponent.title)
      .toContain('Select an option');
  });
  it('should set selectedItem.id', () => {
    expect(appComponent.selectedItem.id).toBe(0);
  });
  it('should set selectedItem.displayName', () => {
    expect(appComponent.selectedItem.displayName)
      .toBe('none');
  });
});
```

Here, we start by importing the `AppComponent` class from the file in the `src/app` directory. We then create an instance of the `AppComponent` class in our `beforeAll` startup function, and then check the internal state of the `AppComponent` class once it has been created. Our first test simply verifies that the `constructor` has succeeded, and that the `appComponent` variable itself is defined. The next three tests verify that the `title`, `selectedItem.id`, and `selectedItem.displayName` properties have been set as expected.

These tests are very simple and straightforward: create an instance of a class, and check that the internal properties have been set correctly.

# Angular 2 rendering tests

In order to test that our DOM elements have been rendered correctly, we will need to use Angular 2's `TestBed` class, which is similar to Aurelia's `StageComponent` functionality. To use the `TestBed` class, we will need to structure our tests in a specific way, and in particular, configure the `TestBed` class to construct an instance of our `AppComponent` as follows:

```
describe('AppComponent rendering tests', () => {
  beforeEach(() => {
    TestBed.configureTestingModule({
      declarations: [
        AppComponent
      ],
    });
    TestBed.compileComponents();
  });
```

Here, we have a `beforeEach` function that makes a call to the static function of the `TestBed` class, named `configureTestingModule`. This function takes a configuration object as its only parameter, and within this configuration object, we specify a `declarations` property that is an array. This declarations array currently only contains our `AppComponent` module.

The `configureTestingModule` function is used to create a test environment for our module, in which the module under test can interact with a controlled version of the DOM. Placing this setup code in a `beforeEach` function ensures that the test environment is set up correctly before each test, and destroyed correctly after each test. Our test environment, and DOM structure therefore, cannot be polluted by other tests, running either before or after.

With this test setup in place, we can now write a unit test to ensure that the currently selected item is rendered onto the page, as follows:

```
it('should render 0 - none to the DOM', async(() => {
  const fixture = TestBed.createComponent(AppComponent);
  fixture.detectChanges();
  const element = fixture.debugElement.nativeElement;
  let selectedDiv = element.querySelector(
    '#selectedItemText');
  expect(selectedDiv.innerHTML).toContain('0 - none');
}));
```

This test starts by calling the static `createComponent` function on the `TestBed` class. Note that we are passing the name of the `AppComponent` class into the `createComponent` function, and essentially asking the Angular 2 engine to create an instance of this class in a test sandbox for us. The `createComponent` function returns a fixture variable, within which our component is rendered and through which we can work with the DOM in our test. Note how we call the `fixture.detectChanges` function. This function essentially forces a DOM refresh, and must be called whenever we are expecting the DOM to change.

Next, our test creates a variable named `element`, from the `fixture.debugElement.nativeElement` property. It is through this `element` variable that we then start to query and verify the DOM. We are using the `querySelector` function on the `element` variable in order to find a DOM element with the id of `selectedItemText`. Our test has only one expectation that the `selectedItemText` div has text that contains the words `'0 - none'`. Note how we are using the asynchronous testing capability of Angular by marking the entire test function as an `async` function. This means that Angular will pause test execution until the `beforeEach` function has completed the construction of our test environment, before executing the unit test.

# Angular 2 DOM testing

We can now create a test that will simulate a `click` event, and ensure that the `selectedItemText` div has been updated as we expected, as follows:

```
it('should update DOM when button clicked', async(() => {
  const fixture = TestBed.createComponent(AppComponent);
  fixture.detectChanges();
  const element = fixture.debugElement.nativeElement;
  let button_1 = element.querySelector('#select_button_0');
  button_1.click();

  fixture.detectChanges();
```

```
    let selectedDiv = element.querySelector('#selectedItemText');
    expect(selectedDiv.innerHTML).toContain('firstItem');
  }));
```

This test is similar to our previous test, in that it also uses the standard `createComponent` function of the `TestBed` class. The body of the test does two interesting things. Firstly, we use the `querySelector` to find a specific instance of a button (`1 - firstItem`), and then simply call the `click` function on the button. After calling the `click` function, we then need to call `fixture.detectChanges` again in order for the test harness to update the DOM following the button click event. Once this is done, we verify that our button click has correctly updated the `innerHTML` of the `selectedItemText` element.

# Angular 2 testing summary

The application changes that we needed to make to our Angular 2 application were very simple, compared to Backbone and Aurelia. Angular 2 also included all of the configuration for running both Karma unit tests and Protractor acceptance tests. Unlike Aurelia, however, Angular provided the necessary elements within its test environment for us to write DOM rendering and DOM event tests without having to switch to Protractor.

> The sample source code for this chapter includes end-to-end tests that also simulate button clicks through Protractor as an example of writing integration and acceptance tests.

# React testing

In the final section of this chapter, we will explore the necessary changes to our React sample application, and build a set of unit tests. These tests will verify that our initial application state is correct, as well as check that the page has been updated correctly after firing DOM click events, similar to what we have done with the other frameworks.

# Multiple entry points

Our React sample application uses Webpack as a compilation and bundling tool in order to convert our TypeScript files into usable React components. During Webpack's bundling process, we need to specify the entry point of our application, and also specify the output filename. Therefore, given an entry point of `/app/index.tsx`, and an output filename of `/dist/bundle.js`, all of our TypeScript code files will end up in the `bundle.js` file.

This is all well and good, but when creating tests our entry point is not the application itself, but instead the test specification. This means that we need to configure Webpack to generate different bundles, based on different entry points. This can be accomplished fairly simply with an update to the `webpack.conf.js` file, as follows:

```
module.exports = {

  entry : {
    app: "./app/index.tsx",
    test: "./test/react.app.tests.tsx",
    e2e: "./test/e2e/react.app.e2e.tests.tsx"
  },

  output: {
    filename: "./dist/[name].js",
  },
```

Here, we have modified our `entry` property from a single file (`entry : "./app/index.tsx"`), to a series of entry files named `app`, `test`, and `e2e`. This allows our browser application to use one `.tsx` file as an entry point, and our test application to use another. We have also included an entry point for end-to-end testing, in the `/test/e2e` directory.

The second modification we have made is to use the `[name]` of the entry point as the output of the Webpack bundling process. This means that we will end up with three bundled packages, `app.js`, with an entry point of `/app/index.tsx`, `test.js`, with an entry point of `/tests/react.app.tests.tsx`, and `e2e.js`, with an entry point of `/test/e2e/react.app.e2e.tests.tsx`.

# React modifications

We will now need to modify our React application in order to show the currently selected item on the page, as we have done with the other frameworks. Our original implementation used a parent view to render the header, and then a child view to render each button. This allowed our child view (`ClickItemView`) to handle the `onClick` event, and display an alert using its current model properties.

As we saw with Backbone, in order for a child item to notify its parent when an event has occurred, we could use a message bus. The preferred option when working with React message buses is to use Flux, but implementations can easily work with `Postal.js` or any other message bus. The use and implementation of Flux, or `Postal.js`, for that matter, is enough to cover a completely new chapter, so for the time being we will refactor our React code so that a message bus is not necessary.

The first update we need to make is to the `IArrayViewProps` interface to include a new property named `selectedItem`. This property will hold the details of the currently selected item, and it mirrors the modifications we made to our other applications. Secondly, we need to set this value in the `ArrayView` constructor, as follows:

```
export interface IArrayViewProps {
  title: string,
  items: ClickableItem[],
  selectedItem?: ClickableItem
};

export class ArrayView extends
  React.Component<IArrayViewProps, {}> {
    selectedItem: ClickableItem;
    constructor() {
      super();
      this.selectedItem = { id: 0, displayName: 'none'};

    }
```

Here, we have added a `selectedItem` property to the `IArrayViewProps` interface, and specified that it is optional. We have made this property optional, so that we do not need to pass in the value of this property in the DOM, but can rather defer the setting of the property in our constructor.

The real changes to this React application are within our `render` function. Previously, within our `render` function, we defined a `buttonNodes` variable as follows:

```
let buttonNodes =
  this.props.items.map(function(item) {
    return (
      <ClickItemView {...item}/>
    );
  });
```

This `buttonNodes` variable used the child component named `ClickItemView`, and was then used inside the `ArrayView` template as follows:

```
return <div>
  <h1>{this.props.title}</h1>
    <ul>
      {buttonNodes}
    </ul>
</div>;
```

Our updated version of the `ArrayView` template removes the `ClickItemView` as follows:

```
render() {

  return ( <div>
    <h1>{this.props.title}</h1>
      <ul>
        {this.props.items.map( function(item,i) {
          return (
            <li key={i} onClick={this.handleClick.bind(
              this, i, item)}>
              <button id={'select_button_' + item.id} >
              {item.displayName}</button>
            </li>
          );
        }, this)}
      </ul>

    <div id="selectedItem">Selected : {this.selectedItem.id} -
      {this.selectedItem.displayName}</div>
    </div>
  );
}
```

Here, we have essentially injected the functionality of the `ClickItemView` directly into the template for the `ArrayView`. There are two important changes to the template to make note of. Firstly, we have added a new parameter named `i` to the `map` function, which holds the index of the current array item. Secondly, we have updated the `onClick` handler, which is now calling the `bind` function with three parameters–`this`, `i`, and `item`. The `this` parameter now references the `ArrayView` class itself, so that the `onClick` DOM event is routed through to the ArrayView's `handleClick` function. The `i` parameter references the index of the array element we are rendering, and the `item` parameter contains the model for the array element.

We have also updated the <button> element to include an id attribute that uses the item's id property to generate a unique id. In this way, we will be able to reference each of the buttons via its id attribute, which will be select_button_1, select_button_2, or select_button_3.

Note that the this.props.items.map function takes two parameters – a function to execute for each array element, and also an instance to bind to. We have passed this as the instance to bind to, in order to ensure that the handleClick function will bind to the ArrayView class's implementation of the handleClick function itself.

The final change to this template is to add a <div> for the currently selected item, which has an id attribute of selectedItem and displays the values of the selectedItem.id and selectedItem.displayName properties at the bottom of the page.

All we need now is to define the handleClick function on the ArrayView, as follows:

```
handleClick(i : number, props: any) {
  this.selectedItem = props;
  this.forceUpdate();
}
```

This function will handle the onClick DOM event from any one of the rendered <button> elements, and does two things. Firstly, it sets the selectedItem property to the incoming props argument, and secondly it calls the forceUpdate function. The forceUpdate function will force an update to the DOM tree and will re-render the selectedItem template, in order to show the currently selected item on the page.

# Unit testing React components

With our application modifications in place, we can now focus on setting up a unit testing environment, and writing some tests. Thankfully, setting up a unit testing environment is as simple as creating a SpecRunner.html file that includes Jasmine files, React files, and our test specs, as follows:

```
<html>
<head>
  <link rel="stylesheet" type="text/css"
    href="./bower_components/
    jasmine-core/lib/jasmine-core/jasmine.css" />
  <script type="text/javascript"
    src="./bower_components/
    jasmine-core/lib/jasmine-core/jasmine.js" >
  </script>
```

```
    <script type="text/javascript"
      src="./bower_components/
      jasmine-core/lib/jasmine-core/jasmine-html.js" />
    </script>
    <script type="text/javascript"
      src="./bower_components/
      jasmine-core/lib/jasmine-core/boot.js" >
    </script>

        <!-- Dependencies -->
      <script src=
        "./node_modules/react/dist/react.js">
      </script>
      <script src=
        "./node_modules/react-dom/dist/react-dom.js">
      </script>

    <script src="./dist/test.js"></script>

  </head>
  <body>
  </body>
```

Here, we have included the standard Jasmine library files, including `jasmine.css`, `jasmine.js`, `jasmine-html.js`, and `boot.js`. We then included the two React dependencies, in `react.js` and `react-dom.js`. Finally, we included the test specifications, which we bundled into the `/dist/test.js` output file.

# React model and view tests

We can now start to write some tests for our React application. Remember that we modified the `webpack.config.js` file to specify that the `/test/react.app.tests.tsx` file should serve as our entry point for tests. We will now need to create this file, and write some tests as follows:

```
import * as React from "react";
import * as ReactDOM from "react-dom";
import * as TestUtils from "react-addons-test-utils";
import {ArrayView, ClickableItem} from '../app/ReactApp';

describe('ArrayView model tests', () => {
  it('should create a new ArrayView', () => {
    var app = new ArrayView();
    expect(app).toBeDefined();
    expect(app.selectedItem.id).toBe(0);
```

```
      expect(app.selectedItem.displayName).toBe('none');
    });
  });
```

Here, we are importing the `React` and `ReactDOM` namespaces from their respective files. We then import a class named `TestUtils` from the `'react-addons-test-utils'` file. We will use `TestUtils` in our rendering tests a little later. `TestUtils` is very similar in functionality to Aurelia's `StageComponent` or Angular's `TestBed`, in that it will help us to create the DOM tree for testing. Finally, we have imported the `ArrayView` and `ClickableItem` classes from our `ReactApp` file.

This test is a React model test. In our React application, we are only setting the value of the `selectedItem` in our constructor, and so this is really the only model test we need in order to verify that the application is in the correct initial state. If the `app` is defined, and the `app.selectedItem`'s properties are set correctly, then this test will pass.

We can now turn our attention to view rendering tests, as follows:

```
describe('ArrayView tests', () => {
  let renderer : any;

  let ClickableItemArray : ClickableItem[] = [
    { id: 1, displayName : "firstItem"},
    { id: 2, displayName : "secondItem"},
    { id: 3, displayName : "thirdItem"},
  ];

  beforeEach( () => {
    renderer = TestUtils.renderIntoDocument(
      <ArrayView items={ClickableItemArray}
      />);
  });

  it('should render none selected', () => {

    let domNode = ReactDOM.findDOMNode(renderer);
    let selectedItem = domNode.querySelector('#selectedItem');
    expect(selectedItem.textContent)
      .toBe('Selected : 0 - none');

  });
```

Here, we have defined two variables for use within our test suite. The first is named `renderer` and is of type `any`, and the second is an instance of a `ClickableItem` array, with some default values. Note the `beforeEach` function. In this function, we are setting the value of the `renderer` variable to the result of a call to `TestUtils.renderIntoDocument`. This `renderIntoDocument` function takes a React template as its only argument, and returns a handle to the generated DOM as a result of the rendering process. Note too, the template that it is using:

```
<ArrayView items={ClickableItemArray}
  />
```

This template is the same as the one that is used in our application's `index.tsx` file:

```
ReactDOM.render(
  <ArrayView items={ClickableItemArray}
      />,
);
```

The only difference between our test rendering step and our application's rendering step is, that in testing, we call `TestUtils.renderIntoDocument`, and in the web page we call `ReactDOM.render`. The actual template itself, however, is exactly the same.

This template, therefore, will create an instance of the `ArrayView` class, and will then set two parameters on the new class, named `items` and `title`. The `items` property is set to the instance of the `ClickableItemArray` that we created in our test setup, and the `title` property is set to `'Select an option:'`.

Our test, then, starts by defining a variable named `domNode`, and sets this to the result of the call to `ReactDOM.findDOMNode(renderer)`. This call is what we are using to extract the DOM out of the test environment that is created by `TestUtils.renderIntoDocument`. Once we have the `domNode` variable set, we can then use standard `querySelectors` to find elements rendered by our test. Within our test, we then query for the element with an `id` of `selectedItem`, and verify that this has been set to `'0 - none'`.

Looking at the syntax of React's unit testing framework, it seems to be very simple and intuitive to use. When setting up a rendering test with Aurelia, we need to call:

```
StageComponent.withResources(...).inView(...).boundTo(...),
```

And then use the following:

```
application.create(bootstrap).then( () => {})
```

With Angular 2, we needed:

```
beforeEach ( () => {} )
```

before we could use:

```
TestBed.createComponent(...)
```

Whereas, in React, we simply call the following line of code:

```
TestUtils.renderIntoDocument(...)
```

and then use this:

```
ReactDOM.findDOMNode(...)
```

# React DOM event tests

Our DOM event tests for React are a simple extension to the view tests that we have already worked through, as follows:

```
it('click select_button_1 should update dom', () => {

  let domNode = ReactDOM.findDOMNode(renderer);

  let button_1 = domNode.querySelector('#select_button_1');
  TestUtils.Simulate.click(button_1);
  let selectedItem = domNode.querySelector('#selectedItem');
  expect(selectedItem.textContent).toContain('1 - firstItem');

});
```

Here, we are setting our `domNode` variable to the result of the call to `ReactDOM.findDOMNode`, as we saw earlier. We are then querying the DOM for a button with an `id` of `select_button_1`. Once this button has been found, we again use our `TestUtils` class, and call the `Simulate.click` function in order to simulate a DOM click event on the instance of the button. Once `TestUtils.Simulate` has done its work, we simply query the `domNode` again for the currently selected `<div>` item, and verify that its value has indeed changed.

# Summary

In this chapter, we covered a fair bit of ground. We took an in-depth look at how to unit test and integration test each of our TypeScript compatible frameworks. Our tests meant that we needed to rework our application structure slightly, in order to facilitate testing correctly. Through this process, however, we learned a few interesting things.

Backbone has a very simple and powerful message bus implementation. We can write model, view rendering, and DOM event tests for Backbone without leaving our unit testing framework.

Aurelia uses a kebab-case naming convention for mapping between HTML attributes and JavaScript class names. Aurelia only renders an item-under-test, and therefore needs end-to-end tests written for holistic DOM render testing, and DOM click events.

Angular 2 is the simplest framework for setting up a test harness, and once set up can be used for model and view rendering, and DOM click event testing. Angular 2 also allows for dependency injection during a test setup.

React also has a simple test harness setup and a natural unit test syntax. React allows for model and view rendering, and DOM event testing within the same simple syntax. Protractor can be used on all frameworks, regardless of their underlying implementation.

In our next chapter, we will take an in-depth look at modularization, using both CommonJs (using Node) and AMD style module loading (using Require). We will also explore the SystemJs methods of module loading, which is a combination of both CommonJs and AMD into a single format.

# 10
# Modularization

Modularization is a popular technique used in modern programming languages that allows programs to be built from a series of smaller libraries, or modules. Writing programs that use modules encourages programmers to write code that conforms to the design principle called **Separation of Concerns**. The basic principle of Separation of Concerns is that we should program against a defined interface. This means that the code that is implementing this interface can be refactored, improved, enhanced, or even completely replaced without the rest of the program being affected. This also helps when testing our code, as the code that is providing the implementation of an interface can easily be stubbed or mocked out in a test scenario.

JavaScript, prior to ECMAScript 6, did not have a concept of modules. Popular frameworks and libraries, such as **Node** and **Require** implemented their own module loading syntax libraries to fill this gap. Unfortunately, two different approaches to module loading, and in particular the module loading syntax, were adopted by the JavaScript community. These two syntax styles were known as CommonJs (used in Node), and AMD, or Asynchronous Module Definition (used in Require). Fortunately, TypeScript has always supported both CommonJs and AMD code generation.

Now that the ECMAScript 6 module syntax has been published, TypeScript has adopted and implemented it, and will automatically generate the correct module syntax for either CommonJs or AMD based on a single compiler option.

In this chapter, we will explore what modules are, take a look at the ECMAScript 6 syntax for modules, and highlight the differences between CommonJs and AMD module syntax. We will then take a closer look at how Require uses AMD module syntax, and how SystemJs allows for using CommonJs module syntax in a browser. We will then explore CommonJs modules in regards to Node, and build a simple Node application using the Express framework.

We will be covering the following topics in this chapter:

- Module basics
- AMD module loading
- System.Js module loading
- Using Express with Node

# Module basics

So what is a module? Essentially, a module is a separate TypeScript file that exposes classes, interfaces, or functions for reuse in other parts of the project. Creating modules helps to structure your code files into logical groups. As your application becomes larger and larger, it makes sense to have each of your Models, Views, Controllers, helper functions, and so on, in separate source files so that they can be easily found. Consider the following directory tree:

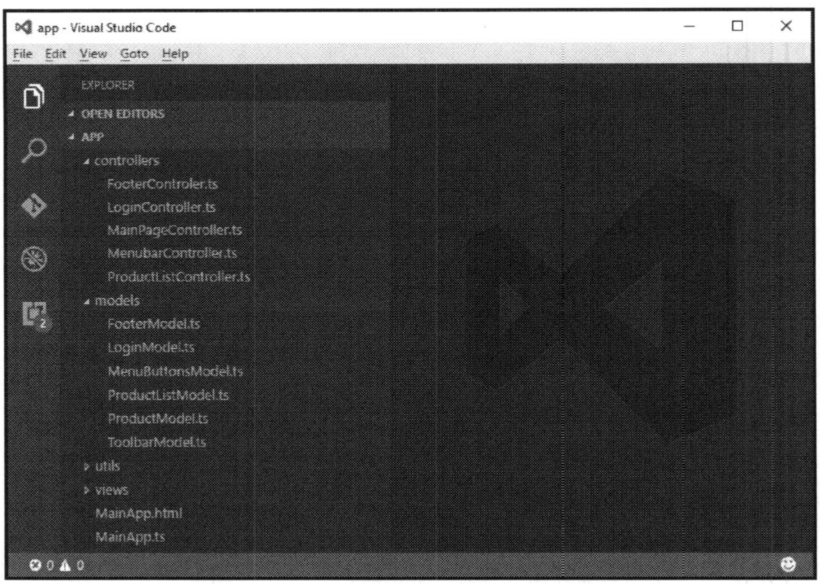


Sample project showing multiple modules in multiple directories

In this project structure, we have a separate directory for `controllers`, `models`, `utils`, and `views`. Within each of these directories, we have several files. Each filename is a clear indication of what we expect the file to contain. A `FooterController.ts` file, for example, is expected to contain a controller class that handles the footer of our application. This structure makes our programming lives much simpler.

The problem with so many source files is that each file needs to be referenced by our HTML page in order for the application to work. Given the preceding directory structure, our HTML page would need to name each file as a source script, as follows:

```
<html>
  <head>
    <script src="./Main.js"></script>
    <script src="./controllers/FooterController.js"></script>
    <script src="./controllers/LoginController.js"></script>
    <script src="./controllers/MainPageController.js">
    </script>
    <script src="./controllers/MenuBarController.js"></script>
    <script src="./controllers/ProductListController.js">
    </script>
    <!--all other files here ..-->

    <script src="./views/ToolbarView.js"></script>

  </head>
  <body>
  </body>
</html>
```

Including each JavaScript file in the HTML page is both time-consuming and error-prone. To overcome this issue, there are two options available – either use a bundling process, or use a module loader. Bundling essentially means that we run a post-compile step to copy (or bundle) all of the source files into a single file, so that we only need to include a single file in our HTML page. While this is a valid solution to our problem, it means that the HTML page must load this bundled file all in one go before the web page is ready to render. If this bundled file is large, it means that our browser will need to wait until the file is loaded, which could impact on our overall page loading time.

Module loaders, on the other hand, allow the browser to load all files simultaneously in separate threads, meaning that our page loading time is significantly reduced. Module loaders also allow for each of our individual JavaScript source files to define which files they have a dependency on. In other words, if our HTML page loads the `Main.js` file, and the `Main.js` file specifies that it needs the `FooterController.js` file as well as the `MainPageController.js` file, the module loader will ensure that these two files are loaded before executing the logic in the `Main.js` file. This technique essentially allows us to define a dependency tree per source file.

> Once a source file has been loaded by a module loader, any file that has a dependency on this file will not need the browser to reload the file from the website. This keeps the number of requests to the web server down to a minimum, and speeds up our page loading time.

# Exporting modules

There are two things we need in order to write and use modules. Firstly, a module needs to be exposed to the outside world in order to be consumed. This is called exporting, and uses the keyword `export`. This means that, within a particular source file, you may have functions and classes that are considered internal, and should not be made available to the outside world. Only components that are designed to be used outside of the source file should be exported. As an example of this, consider a module written in a file named `lib/Module1.ts`:

```
export class Module1 {
  print() {
    print(`Module1.print()`);
  }
}

function print(functionName: string) {
  console.log(`print() called with ${functionName}`);
}
```

Here, we have a class named `Module1`, and a function named `print` within the same source file. The `Module1` class, however, has added the keyword `export` to its class definition, and as such the `Module1` class will be available for use by the outside world.

The `print` function, however, does not use the `export` keyword. This means that the `print` function is only available for use within the `Module1.ts` source file and is not available for use by the outside world. This function is therefore private in scope. The `Module1` class is very simple, and defines a `print` function. Within this `Module1.print` function, a call is made to the private `print` function defined at the end of the file.

The `export` keyword, therefore, is exposing the entire `Module1` class for use to the outside world.

# Importing modules

In order to consume a module that has been exported, any source file that needs this module must import the module using the `import` keyword. In our preceding sample, if we wish to consume the `Module1` class, we would need to import it as follows:

```
import {Module1} from './lib/Module1';

let mod1 = new Module1();
mod1.print();
```

Here, we are in a file named `main.ts`, which sits at the root of the project. The first line of this file uses the `import` statement to import the definition of the `Module1` class from the `lib/Module1` file. Note the syntax of this `import` statement. Following the `import` keyword, is a name in braces `{Module1}` and then a `from` keyword, followed by the filename of the module itself. The module name `{Module1}` matches the name of the exported class in the `'./lib/Module1'` file. Note too, that we do not specify a `.ts` or a `.js` extension when importing modules. The module loader will take care of mapping our `import` statement to the correct module filename on disk.

Once the module has been imported, we can use the class definition of `Module1` as normal. In the last two lines of the preceding code snippet, we are simply creating an instance of the `Module1` class, and calling the `print` function. The output of this code is as follows:

```
print() called with Module1.print()
```

As we are running in a default Node environment, we will need to invoke our compiled `main.js` file by running `node main` from the command line.

# Module renaming

When importing a module, we can rename the exported module name as follows:

```
import {Module1 as m1} from './lib/Module1';
let m1mod1 = new m1();
mod1.print();
```

Here, we have imported the same module from `'./lib/Module1'`, but have used the `as` keyword when specifying the module name, that is, `{Module1 as m1}`. This means that we can now refer to the class named `Module1` (as according to our export definition), as simply `m1`. The last two lines of this code sample show how we can now create a class (of type `Module1`) by using the new `m1` name. The output of this code sample is exactly the same as the previous code:

```
print() called with Module1.print()
```

We can also have multiple names for an exported module, but these names need to be specified within the module itself. Consider the following module definition:

```
export class Module1 {
  print() {
    print(`Module1.print()`);
  }
}

export {Module1 as NewModule};
```

Here, on the last line of this code snippet, the `Module1` class has also been exported with the name `NewModule`. This allows a consumer to use either the name `Module1` or `NewModule` when importing the module, as follows:

```
import {NewModule} from './lib/Module1';
let nm = new NewModule();
nm.print();
```

Here, we are importing the `Module1` class using the name `NewModule`, and then using the `NewModule` class name to create an instance of the `Module1` class. The output of this code is exactly the same as we saw previously:

```
print() called with Module1.print()
```

# Default exports

When a module file only exports a single item, we can mark this item as a default export. This is accomplished with the `default` keyword. Consider a module file named `lib/Module2.ts`, as follows:

```
export default class Module2Default {
  print() {
    console.log(`Module2Default.print()`);
  }
}
export class Module2NonDefault {
  print() {
    console.log(`Module2NonDefault.print()`);
  }
}
```

Here, we have marked the `Module2Default` class as the default export for this module. Note that we can only have a single default export per module, but we are able to export other items within the file using standard export syntax. This can be seen in the second export of the `Module2NonDefault` class.

If a module has a default export, we can use a simpler syntax for importing it, as follows:

```
import Module2Default from './lib/Module2';

let m2default = new Module2Default();
m2default.print();
```

Here, we have removed the `{ ... }` braces, and are importing the default export as `Module2Default`. The name that we use in the import statement can be anything, and it can be renamed in our import statement as follows:

```
import m2rn from './lib/Module2';

let m2renamed = new m2rn();
m2renamed.print();
```

Here, we are importing the default export from the `'./lib/Module2'` file, as seen previously, but we are renaming it to `m2rn`. Note that, just as we used renamed module names earlier, we will need to refer to the module by the new name, as seen in the usage of this module, that is, `new m2rn()`.

While it may serve a purpose in some cases, renaming modules on import can make our code more difficult to read. As a habit, try to keep the module names on import the same as the module names that have been exported. This helps when reading our code, knowing exactly which module we are referring to in the original file.

## Exporting variables

As we have with other exported elements, we are also able to export variables that have been defined within a module. Consider the following export in `lib/Module1.ts`:

```
var myVariable = "This is a variable.";
export { myVariable }
```

Here, we are defining a variable named `myVariable`, and setting the value within the `Module1.ts` file. We are then exporting the variable itself, by wrapping the variable name in braces, that is, `{ myVariable }`. We can then import and use this variable as follows:

```
import { myVariable } from './lib/Module1';
console.log(myVariable);
```

While this may seem a little strange, and at first sight is breaking object-oriented coding principles, this technique is used by numerous frameworks to inject functionality into existing singleton instances. We will explore this technique later in this chapter, when we discuss setting up routes with the Express engine.

# AMD module loading

The module exporting and importing syntax that we have used thus far uses what is known as the CommonJs syntax, and is the default mechanism for module loading when using Node. Traditionally, this module loading syntax was not available for use within a browser, and as such, an alternative to CommonJs became popular, named Asynchronous Module Definition, or AMD. One of the most prevalent libraries to use AMD is Require.js, or simply Require. In this section, we will reuse the source code for the modules we created in Node, and recompile them for use with AMD. We will then show how to use Require to load these modules in the browser.

# AMD compilation

In order to compile our code to use the AMD module syntax, we will need to change the module setting in our `tsconfig.json` file, as follows:

```
{
  "compilerOptions": {
    "module": "amd",
    "target": "es5",
    "noImplicitAny": false,
    "sourceMap": false
  },
  "exclude": [
    "node_modules"
  ]
}
```

Here, we have specified the `"module"` parameter to be `"amd"`, instead of `"commonjs"`. This change specifies to the TypeScript compiler that the output of the compilation step must generate JavaScript code that uses the AMD module syntax. Let's take a look at what this means in terms of our module files.

Consider the following TypeScript module definition, as found in our `lib/Module3.ts` file:

```
export class Module3 {
  print() {
    console.log(`Module3.print()`);
  }
}
```

Here, we are exporting a class named `Module3`. When we compile this class with the CommonJs module option, TypeScript generates the following JavaScript file:

```
"use strict";
var Module3 = (function () {
  function Module3() {
  }
  Module3.prototype.print = function () {
    console.log("Module3.print()");
  };
  return Module3;
}());
exports.Module3 = Module3;
```

In this generated JavaScript file, we have the standard closure pattern being used to define a JavaScript class named `Module3`. Note the last line of the file, however. TypeScript has generated an `exports.Module3 = Module3;` line, which will attach our `Module3` class to the `exports` variable. This is the standard way to create modules when using JavaScript.

If we modify our compile options to `"amd"`, instead of `"commonjs"`, TypeScript will generate the following JavaScript for the same `lib/Module3.ts` file:

```
define(["require", "exports"], function (require, exports) {
  "use strict";
  var Module3 = (function () {
    function Module3() {
    }
    Module3.prototype.print = function () {
        console.log("Module3.print()");
    };
    return Module3;
  }());
  exports.Module3 = Module3;
});
```

Looking closely at this file, the inner class definition for the `Module3` closure and the `exports.Module3 = Module3;` line are exactly the same as we saw earlier. The entire class definition has, however, been wrapped in a function named `define`. This is the difference between CommonJs and AMD modules. AMD uses a `define` function that takes two parameters–an array of strings, and a function definition.

The array of strings, that is, `["require","exports"]`, is in fact a dependency array that specifies which libraries must be loaded before attempting to load this module. The function definition is called once the dependent libraries have been loaded. In addition, each of the items specified in the dependency array then become parameters that are available within the callback function. Hence `function(require, exports)` allows access to the `require` and `exports` arguments within the callback function. By having access to the `exports` global variable, we can now attach our `Module3` class definition to the `exports` variable that has been passed in as an argument.

> We have not changed our `Module3.ts` TypeScript file in any way in order to support both CommonJs and AMD module loading syntax. The TypeScript compiler has taken care of the module definitions automatically for us.

# AMD module setup

Now that we have our modules compiling in AMD syntax, we can focus our attention on loading and using them in a browser. In order to load and use AMD modules in a browser, we will make use of the Require.js module loader. Require.js, or simply Require, is a standard JavaScript framework, and as such can be installed via npm. Once installed within our project, we will also need the relevant declaration files. We can install Require using `npm` as follows:

```
npm install requirejs --save
```

And then install the declaration files as follows:

```
npm install @types/requirejs --save
```

With the Require.js framework and our declaration file in place, we can now configure Require to load our AMD modules.

# Require configuration

Require uses a global configuration file, typically called `RequireConfig.js`, that serves as the entry point to our browser application. Let's go ahead and create a TypeScript file, named `RequreConfig.ts`, as follows:

```
require.config( {
  // baseUrl: "."
});

require(['main'], (main) => {
  console.log(`inside main`);

});
```

Here, we start with a call to the `require.config` function, passing in a configuration object that sets some default values. We have commented the `baseUrl` property, and as such are calling the `require.config` function with a blank object. We will delve a little deeper into the available configuration parameters a little later in this chapter.

Following our call to `require.config`, we are then calling the `require` function with two arguments. The `require` function is very similar to the `define` function that we saw earlier. The first parameter to `require` is an array of strings, which list the files to be loaded, and the second parameter is a callback function. As with the `define` function, each dependency listed in the first array of strings will be available within the callback function as a parameter.

In our code sample, then, the only dependency listed is `main`, which translates to our `main.js` file. Note that Require will automatically append the `.js` extension when attempting to load JavaScript files. Once the `main.js` file has been loaded, it will be available within the function definition as the argument `main`.

# AMD browser configuration

The only remaining task, then, is to incorporate this `RequireConfig.js` file into our browser HTML, as follows:

```
<html>
<head>
<script
  type="text/javascript"
  src="./node_modules/requirejs/require.js"
  data-main="./RequireConfig" >
</script>
</head>
<body>
</body>
</html>
```

This is a very simple HTML file that only has a single `<script>` tag to load the `"./node_modules/requirejs/require.js"` file. This will cause the browser to load the `require.js` module loader. Note, however, that this script tag has an attribute named `data-main`. This `data-main` attribute is used by Require to load the initial configuration file, which in our case is `RequireConfig.js`. Again, Require will automatically append the `.js` extension for files, so this attribute is simply specified as `data-main="./RequireConfig"`.

Once the `require.js` file has been loaded, the `RequireConfig.js` file will be loaded and executed, and this will begin the module loading process.

If we use the **Network** tab on our **Developer Tools** within the browser, we will see how Require is loading and parsing each of our module files, and automatically downloading them for use, as follows:

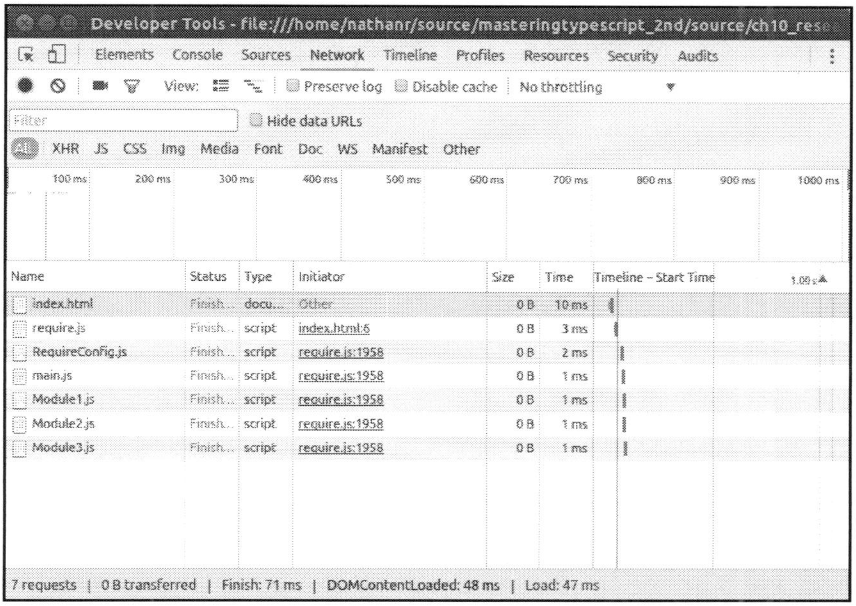


Network toolset showing modules loading in correct order

The browser starts by loading the `index.html` file, the `require.js` file, and then we see that it is loading our `RequireConfig.js` file. Within our `RequireConfig.js` file, we specified that we needed to load `main.js`, so this is the next file that Require will load. This `main.js` file then used the `import` module syntax to import the files `lib/Module1` and `lib/Module2`. We can see then, that these two files are being loaded next by Require. Interestingly, our `lib/Module1` file also imports the `lib/Module3` file, so Require also loads this file.

As can be seen by the network diagnostics, Require is recursively parsing each of our module files, starting with `RequireConfig.js`, and dynamically loading all modules that it finds. In this way, we are free to define modules as and when we please all by simply using the `export` and `import` module syntax. As long as we import our dependencies within a module, the module loader will automatically load these files on our behalf.

## AMD module dependencies

When working with modules, it is often the case that one module must be loaded before another. When module B needs to have module A loaded already, we can say that module B has a dependency on module A. When building a standard HTML page, this dependency is fairly easy to get right. All we need to do is ensure that the `<script>` tag for module A is included in the web page above the `<script>` tag for module B. Unfortunately, this is not so easy when using AMD module loading.

With AMD module loading, each module is loaded independently and asynchronously. This means that the order in which we specify our modules is not enough. What we need in this case is to be able to describe the dependencies between modules, so that the AMD module loader can co-ordinate these module requests.

The Require AMD module loader uses settings in the call to `require.config` to specify dependencies, along with other module characteristics. As an example of this configuration, let's set up a Jasmine testing environment using AMD module loading.

If you recall in the previous chapter, we set up a `SpecRunner.html` file for unit testing of Backbone samples. This `SpecRunner.html` file loaded three base files, as follows:

```
<script type="text/javascript"
  src="./<path_to_jasmine>/jasmine.js" >
</script>
<script type="text/javascript"
  src="./<path_to_jasmine>/jasmine-html.js" />
</script>
<script type="text/javascript"
  src="./<path_to_jasmine>/boot.js" >
</script>
```

The Jasmine framework has three component files that need to be loaded in the correct order–`jasmine.js` first, then `jasmine-html.js`, and finally `boot.js`. Loading `boot.js` before `jasmine.js` will generate runtime errors, and therefore `boot.js` has a dependency on `jasmine.js`. Let's take a look at the `RequireConfigSpecRunner.ts` file, which shows what the `require.config` file looks like for a Jasmine environment:

```
require.config( {
  baseUrl: ".",
  paths: {
    'jasmine' :
      './node_modules/jasmine-core/lib/
      jasmine-core/jasmine',
    'jasmine-html' :
      './node_modules/jasmine-core/lib/
```

```
        jasmine-core/jasmine-html',
      'jasmine-boot' :
        './node_modules/jasmine-core/lib/
        jasmine-core/boot'
    },
    shim : {
      'jasmine': {
        exports: 'window.jasmineRequire'
      },
      'jasmine-html' : {
        deps: ['jasmine'],
        exports: 'window.jasmineRequire'
      },
      'jasmine-boot' : {
        deps: ['jasmine-html'],
        exports: 'window.jasmineRequire'
      }
    }
  });
```

Here, we have included two new properties in our call to `require.config`, namely `paths` and `shim`. We will discuss the `shim` property in a moment, but for the time being let's focus on the `paths` property. The `paths` property contains a property entry for each of our Jasmine files. The important thing to note here, though, is that these are named entries, and that the name of the entry must be used throughout the rest of the Require configuration. If we take a look at the first entry, which is named `'jasmine'`, and points to `'./node_modules/jasmine-core/lib/jasmine-core/jasmine'`, the name of this entry is therefore `'jasmine'`, and all references to this file must use the `'jasmine'` name from here on out. We could easily have named this `'jasminejs'`, or `'jjs'`, as long as the name of the entry is used consistently throughout the Require configuration. The `'jasmine-boot'` entry is a perfect example of this naming scheme, as the actual file is simply named `boot.js`, and not `jasmine-boot.js`, but the named entry is `'jasmine-boot'`.

Also note that Require will append the `.js` file extension to each of these entries when it loads the file from disk.

The next configuration block is the `shim` property. This `shim` property contains an entry for each of our named libraries. The `shim` entry for each of these libraries may contain an `exports` and or a `deps` entry. The `exports` entry is used to specify the JavaScript global namespace that this library will attach to. As a simple example of what this exports property should contain, consider the following `shim` entries for jQuery, Underscore, and Backbone (note that these are not included in our current `require.config`, but are shown here for illustration purposes):

```
'jquery' : {
  exports: '$'
},
'underscore' : {
  exports: '_'
},
'backbone' : {
  exports: 'Backbone'
}
```

The jQuery library's `exports` property is simply `'$'`. This means that the jQuery library is being attached to the `$` namespace by Require, which allows us to use any jQuery function by prefixing it with `$`, as in `$('#elementId')`. Likewise, the Underscore library uses the _ character as its namespace, and it is used by simply calling `_.bind( ... )`. As a final example, the Backbone library uses the `Backbone` namespace, and is used by calling `new Backbone.Model`, for example. Each of these libraries therefore defines the global namespace in the `exports` property.

Along with the `exports` property in our `shim` configuration, each of our modules can also specify a `deps` entry, which is an array of strings. The `deps` entry is used to describe module dependencies. If we start at the bottom of the `shim` entries, we will see that the `'jasmine-boot'` entry specifies the `'jasmine-html'` entry as a dependency. Likewise, the `'jasmine-html'` entry specifies `'jasmine'` as a dependency. Require will therefore take note of these dependencies, and load our modules in order.

The `deps` property is an array of strings, which means that a single entry can specify multiple dependencies.

## Bootstrapping Require

As we saw with our minimal implementation earlier, the module loading process is kicked off with an initial call to the `require` function. Assuming that we have a very simple Jasmine test in the `test/SimpleTest.ts` file, we can bootstrap our test environment at the bottom of the `RequireConfigSpecRunner.js` file as follows:

```
var specs = [
  'test/SimpleTest'
];

require(['jasmine-boot'], (jasmineBoot) => {
  require(specs, () => {
    (<any>window).onload();
  });
});
```

This setup is interesting for a few reasons. Firstly, we have defined a variable named `specs` that is a simple string array. It contains a single entry, namely `'test/SimpleTest'`, which is a reference to our Jasmine test suite. Note, then, where this `specs` variable is used. It is used in a call to `require`, which is nested inside an outer call to `require`. This outer call is telling `require` that it must load the `'jasmine-boot'` module before executing the callback function. As the `'jasmine-boot'` module's `shim` entry specifies a dependency path, this callback function will only execute once all dependencies have been met.

Once the outer callback function is executed, the body of this function is again calling the `require` function, but this time with an array that lists all Jasmine files within our suite. This inner call to require will already have the dependent modules loaded (that is, the Jasmine files) before it is executed. Once all modules in the `specs` array have been loaded, the callback function then simply calls `window.onload()`, which will kick off the Jasmine test run.

Also note that the `window` global variable needs to be cast to a type of `<any>` in order to allow TypeScript compilation.

With this Require configuration and bootstrapping code in place, we can fire up our browser and run the `SpecRunner.html` file to execute all tests. Again, firing up our developer network tools, we can see the order in which each of our modules is loaded:

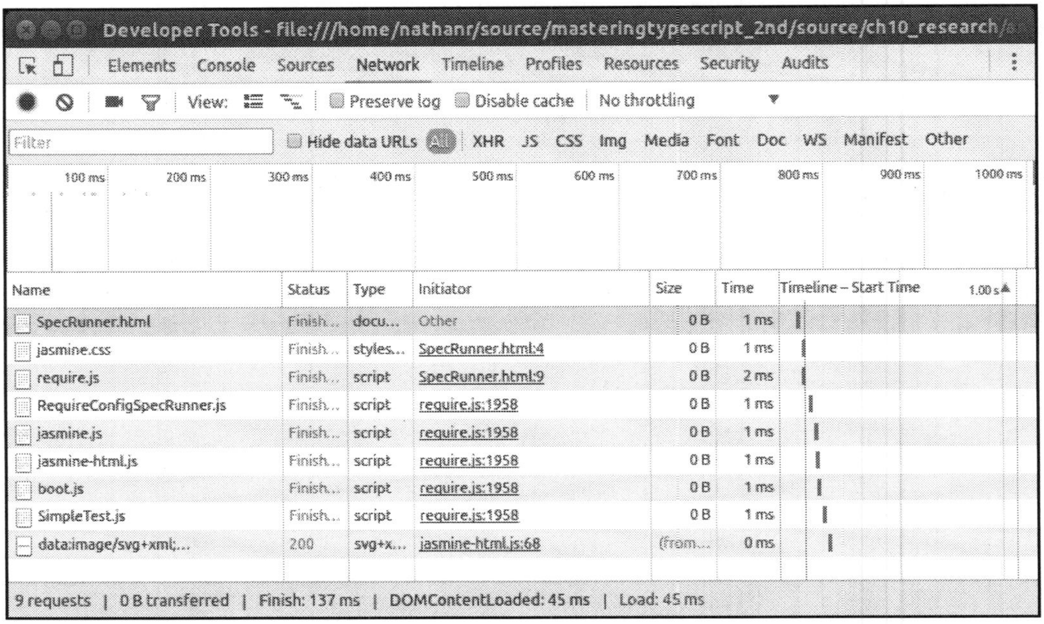


Network developer tools showing Jasmine module loading

# Fixing Require config errors

Quite often, when developing AMD applications with Require, we can start to get unexpected behavior, strange error messages, or simply blank pages. These strange results are generally caused by the configuration for Require, either in the `paths`, `shim`, or `deps` properties. Fixing these AMD errors can be quite frustrating at first, but generally, they are caused by one of two things–incorrect dependencies or `file-not-found` errors.

To fix these errors, we will need to open the debugging tools within the browser that we are using, which for most browsers is achieved by simply hitting F12.

## Incorrect dependencies

Some AMD errors are caused by incorrect dependencies in our `require.config`. These errors can be found by checking the console output in the browser. Dependency errors would generate browser errors similar to the following:

```
ReferenceError: jasmineRequire is not defined
ReferenceError: Backbone is not defined
```

This type of error might mean that the AMD loader has loaded Backbone, for example, before loading Underscore. So, whenever Backbone tries to use an Underscore function, we get a `not defined` error, as shown in the preceding output. The fix for this type of error is to update the `deps` property of the library that is causing the error. Make sure that all prerequisite libraries have been named in the `deps` property, and the errors should go away. If they do not, then the error may be caused by the next type of AMD error, a `file-not-found` error.

## 404 errors

File not found, or 404 errors are generally indicated by console output similar to the following:

```
Error: Script error for: jquery
http://requirejs.org/docs/errors.html#scripterror
Error: Load timeout for modules: jasmine-boot
http://requires.org/docs/errors.html#timeout
```

To find out which file is causing the preceding error, switch to the **Network** tab in your debugger tools and refresh the page. Look for 404 (file not found) errors, as shown in the following screenshot:

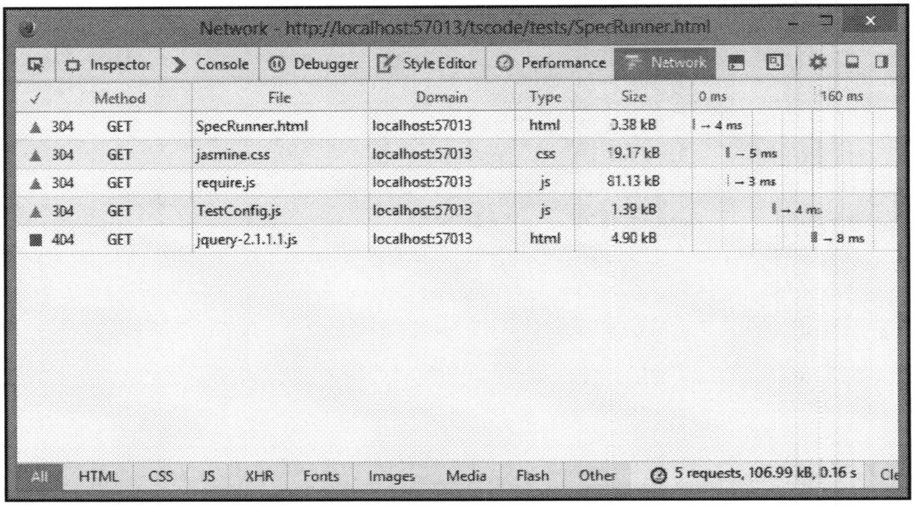


Firefox Network tab with 404 errors

In this screenshot, we can see that the call to `jquery.js` is generating a `404` error, as our file is actually named `/Scripts/jquery-2.1.1.js`. These sorts of errors can be fixed by adding an entry to the `paths` parameter in `require.config`, so that any call to `jquery.js` is replaced by a call to `jquery-2.1.1.js`.

Require has a good set of documentation for common AMD errors (`http://requirejs.org/docs/errors.html`) as well as advanced API usages, including circular references (`http://requirejs.org/docs/api.html#circular`), so be sure to check the site for more information on possible AMD errors.

# SystemJs module loading

SystemJs is a module loader that understands both CommonJs module format, AMD module format, and even the new ES6 module format. It works in both Node and the browser, and as such describes itself as a universal module loader. Before SystemJs came along, Node-based solutions used CommonJs format, and browser-based solutions used AMD format.

Now we can use CommonJs format in the browser, and even mix and match module syntax. In this section, we will take a look at how to configure SystemJS for loading CommonJs modules in the browser.

# SystemJs installation

SystemJs can be installed using npm as follows:

```
npm install systemjs --save
```

The relevant declaration files can be installed using `@types` as follows:

```
npm install @types/systemjs --save
npm install @types/es6-shim --save
```

Note that we have installed two declaration files here, namely `systemjs` and `es6-shim`. This is because SystemJs uses Promises for asynchronous loading, but the definition of the Promise object is not included in the SystemJs declaration file. The `es6-shim` package provides es6 functionality for browsers that do not support es6, and part of this includes Promises. The declaration file for es6-shim, therefore, provides a definition of the Promise object.

# SystemJs browser configuration

In order to use SystemJs within our browser, we will need to include the `system.js` source file, and then run a configuration script for SystemJs, similar to our `RequireConfig.js` file. Our HTML page is as follows:

```
<html>
<head>
</head>
<body>
  <script
    src="./node_modules/systemjs/dist/system.js">
  </script>
  <script src="./SystemConfig.js"></script>
</body>
</html>
```

Here, we have included two script files. One for the `system.js` framework itself, and then for a file named `SystemConfig.js`. This `SystemConfig.js` file is generated from the following `SystemConfig.ts` file:

```
SystemJS.config({
  packages : {
    'lib' : { defaultExtension: 'js' }
  }
});
SystemJS.import('main.js');
```

Our SystemJs configuration file starts with a call to the `SystemJS.config` function, and includes a configuration object. Within this object, we have only specified one property, named `packages`. This `packages` property specifies a `lib` property, and within this a single property named `defaultExtension : 'js'`. SystemJs uses the `packages` property to specify options for each of our source directories, or packages. The `lib` property therefore relates to all files contained within the `./lib` directory. The `defaultExtension` property tells SystemJs that all modules within the `./lib` sub-directory have a default extension of `.js`.

This means that, when SystemJs encounters a module import, such as `import {Module1} from './lib/module1'`, it will append the default extension of `'.js'` to the module filename, and therefore load a file named `'./lib/module1.js'`.

The second part of our SystemJs configuration file is a call to the `SystemJS.import` function, specifying the `main.js` file as the starting point for our application. Once SystemJs has loaded the `main.js` file, it will begin to parse our code for all other imported modules, and then load them for use. If we view the **Network** tab in our browser **Developer Tools**, we will see the following files loading:

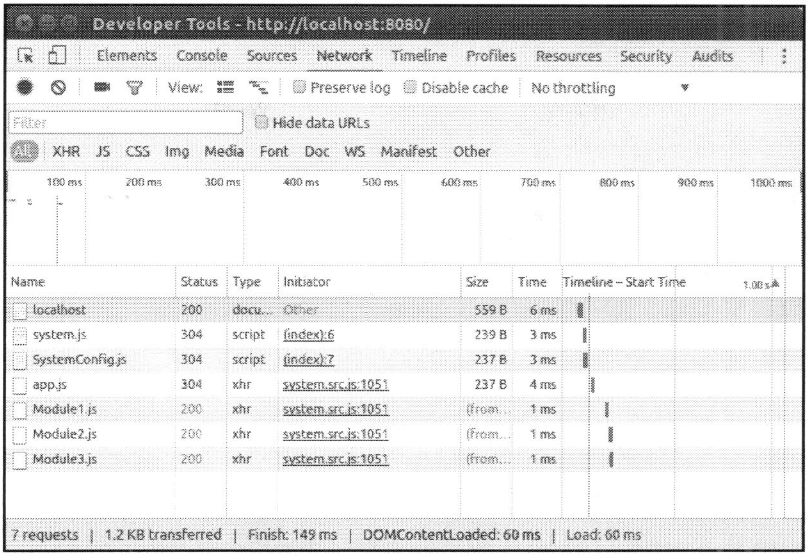


Network developer toolset showing SystemJs module loading

Note that, with both AMD modules and SystemJs modules, the Chrome browser assumes that these are being served from a running web server. If you attempt to load a page from disk, that is, by hitting *Ctrl–O* from Chrome, and navigate to your file on disk, you will receive a number of errors, as shown in the following screenshot:

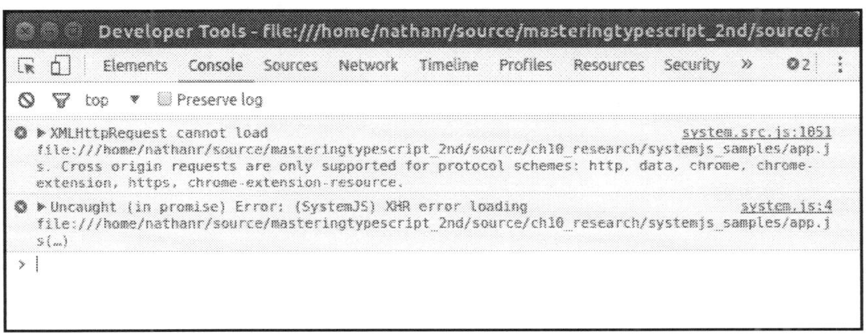


Console errors when attempting to load a SystemJs file from disk

Other browsers, such as FireFox, do not show these errors. Chrome does, however, supply a command-line option that allows this behavior, `--allow-file-access-from-files`. Alternatively, in order to load a page that uses SystemJs, simply run `http-server` from the root directory of your project, and then browse to the URL shown on the console. When `http-server` starts, it will show the IP address and port you should point your browser to, as follows:

```
Starting up http-server, serving ./
Available on:
  http://127.0.0.1:8080
  http://192.168.1.101:8080
```

# SystemJs module dependencies

So far, we have shown how to configure SystemJs to load modules as dependencies, when they are imported using `import` statements within our code. Let's finish this discussion on SystemJs by showing how to treat module dependencies, as we did with AMD. Similar to our AMD module dependency sample, we will build a unit testing framework with Jasmine and SystemJs. Remember that Jasmine has a specific module loading order. This means that the core `jasmine.js` file must be loaded before `jasmine-html.js`, and then when that is done we can load the `boot.js` module and run our tests.

Let's assume that we have two very simple test suites in the `test` directory, named `SimpleTest.ts`, and `SimpleTest2.ts`. These two files are just executing a sanity test. `SimpleTest.ts` is as follows:

```
describe('SimpleTest.ts : sanity test', () => {
  it('should pass', () => {
    expect(true).toBeTruthy();
  });

});
```

And `SimpleTest2.ts` is as follows:

```
describe('SimpleTest2.ts : sanity test 2', () => {
  it('should pass', () => {
    expect(true).toBeTruthy();
  });

});
```

In order to run these tests, we will also need a `SpecRunner.html` file, as follows:

```
<html>
<head>
  <link rel="stylesheet"
  type="text/css"
  href="./node_modules/jasmine-core/lib
  /jasmine-core/jasmine.css" />
</head>
<body>
  <script src="./node_modules/system.js/dist/system.js">
   </script>
  <script src="./SystemConfigSpecRunner.js"></script>
</body>
</html>
```

Here, we have a standard HTML file that loads the `jasmine.css` file and `system.js` itself. Note that we are then loading the `SystemConfigSpecRunner.js` file that holds our configuration. This `SystemConfigSpecRunner.ts` file is as follows:

```
SystemJS.config({
  baseUrl : '.',
  packages : {
    'lib' : { defaultExtension: 'js' }
    ,'test' : { defaultExtension: 'js' }
  },
  paths: {
    'jasmine' :
      './node_modules/jasmine-core/lib/
      jasmine-core/jasmine.js',
    'jasmine-html' :
      './node_modules/jasmine-core/lib/
      jasmine-core/jasmine-html.js',
    'jasmine-boot' :
      './node_modules/jasmine-core/lib/
      jasmine-core/boot.js'
  },
  meta : {
    'jasmine-boot' : {
      deps : ['jasmine-html']
      ,exports: 'window.jasmineRequire'
    },
    'jasmine-html' : {
      deps : ['jasmine']
      ,exports: 'window.jasmineRequire'
    },
    'jasmine' : {
      exports: 'window.jasmineRequire'
```

```
            }
        }
    });

    SystemJS.import('jasmine-boot').then( () => {
      Promise.all([
        SystemJS.import('test/SimpleTest'),
        SystemJS.import('test/SimpleTest2')
      ])
      .then(() => {
        (<any>window).onload();
      })
      .catch(console.error.bind(console));

    });
```

There are two parts to this configuration file. Firstly, we call `SystemJS.config` function with a configuration block, and then near the bottom of the file we call the function `SystemJS.import` to load and boot our Jasmine test environment. Let's focus on the configuration block to start off with.

Our configuration blocks start by specifying the `baseUrl` property as `'.'`. This tells SystemJs that all module requests are relative to the current directory. The next property is `packages` and, as we have seen before with SystemJs, this sets the default extension to `js` for the `'lib'` and `'test'` sub-directories.

The third property in our configuration block is the `paths` property. This property is very similar to the AMD version of the `paths` property, with one notable exception – the inclusion of the `.js` file extension on each of the path properties. As we saw with the Require version of the `paths` property, these paths are **named properties**, and as such the name given in the `paths` property (for example, `'jasmine'`) must be used consistently throughout the configuration block.

The next property that we need is the `meta` property. The format and usage of the `meta` property is exactly the same as the `shim` property used in Require, and accomplishes the same thing. The `meta` property is where our dependencies are set for each of the Jasmine libraries. As with the Require version, we specify both the `deps` property (for dependencies), and the `exports` property (for our global namespace).

# Bootstrapping Jasmine

Let's now take a closer look at the call to `SystemJS.import` at the bottom of the `SystemConfigSpecRunner.ts` file:

```
SystemJS.import('jasmine-boot').then( () => {
  Promise.all([
    SystemJS.import('test/SimpleTest'),
    SystemJS.import('test/SimpleTest2')
  ])
  .then(() => {
    (<any>window).onload();
  })
  .catch(console.error.bind(console));

});
```

Here we are bootstrapping the Jasmine environment by loading the Jasmine module named `'jasmine-boot'`. As with Require, SystemJs will find and load all dependencies that have been specified in our dependency tree for `'jasmine-boot'`, which in this instance includes both `'jasmine-html'` and `'jasmine'` itself. We then attach a fluent style `.then` function to execute once Jasmine has been loaded. Within this function we are then loading our two test suites with a call to `Promise.all`. This technique is similar to the one we used with Require, where we split the loading of test specs outside of our `SystemJs config` block, so that it is easier to add multiple tests without major modifications to the SystemJs configuration. The `Promise.all` function loads all spec files, and again uses a fluent syntax to attach a `then` function that will be executed when all files have been loaded. The function simply calls `window.onload()` and, as we saw with Require, which will force Jasmine to execute all tests. The final call is to `catch`, where we log any errors to the console.

Our SystemJs configuration is complete. With this in place, we can load our `SpecRunner.html` file to execute our Jasmine tests.

# Using Express with Node

In this section of the chapter, we will continue our exploration of modules by showing how to build a simple Node web server application. In order to accomplish this, we will make use of the ExpressJs (or simply Express) web framework for Node. Express provides us with a library of reusable Node modules to handle the basic functionality required for building a web server.

This includes routing, a template engine for generating web pages, libraries for handling sessions and cookies, authentication, and error messages (think 404 errors ), to name a few. Express provides a rich set of modules and APIs to cover everything you would need for a production web server application.

# Express setup

In order to build an Express application, we will need to install Express in our development environment, as well as include the various declaration files that are needed for TypeScript compilation. Express can be installed using `npm` as follows:

```
npm init
npm install express --save
```

Once Express has been installed, we will need the corresponding declaration files, as follows:

```
npm install @types/express --save
```

Express uses a series of other npm libraries whose declaration files are not included in the core `express.d.ts` declaration file. In order to allow for TypeScript compilation, we will need to install a few other declaration files as follows:

```
npm install @types/express-serve-static-core --save
npm install @types/serve-static --save
npm install @types/mime --save
npm install @types/node --save
```

We can now write the simplest of web applications for Express, in a file named `simple_app.ts`, as follows:

```
import * as express from 'express';

let app = express();

app.get('/', (req, res) => {
  res.send('Hello World');
});

app.listen(3000, () => {
  console.log(`listening on port 3000`);
});
```

We start by importing the Express module, `from 'express'`, and attaching it to a namespace named `express`. Note how we are now using a slightly modified version of the `import` keyword. Here, we have used the `import * as express` syntax in order to import all modules available within the Express library.

We then create a local variable named `app`, and assign a new instance of `express()` to it. The express module that we imported has a default constructor function that we are using to create our Express application.

We then call the `get` function on our `app` instance. This will set up what is known as a route handler in Express. The first argument is the string `'/'`, which tells Express that any HTTP request to `'/'` should be handled by our handler function, which is the second argument to the `get` function. Within this function, we are simply calling the `res.send` function to send the string `'Hello World'` to the HTTP request.

Express allows us to set up multiple route handlers, such that `'/login'` can be handled by a particular handler function, or `'/users'` by another. If no other handlers are specified, Express will route the request to the closest matching handler. This means that, if a handler for `'/login'` is defined; it will handle all requests that start with `'/login'`. In our sample application, we have only specified a handler for `'/'`, so all requests will be routed to this handler.

The final part of our application calls the `listen` function on the `app` instance, and essentially sets up the listening loop. The first argument is the port number to listen on, and the second is a function that is called on initial application startup. Here we are simply logging a message to the console.

We can compile and then run this Node Express application by typing:

```
tsc
node simple_app.js
```

Our Express application will start up on port `3000`, and wait for HTTP requests. Firing up a browser and pointing it to `http://locahost:3000` will trigger the request handler, rendering **Hello World** to the browser, as follows:

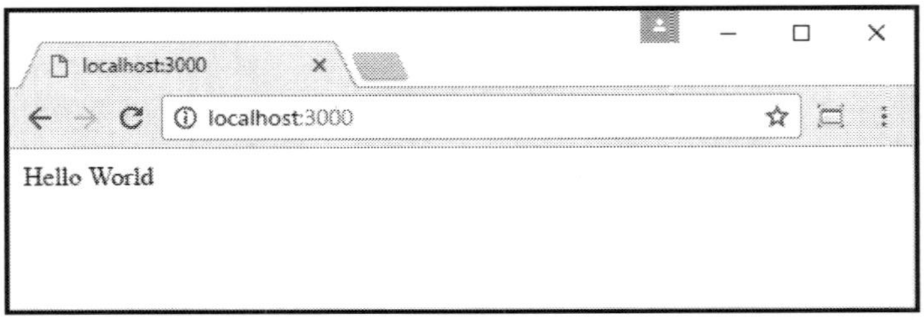


Simple Express application rendering on port 3000

# Using modules with Express

If we wrote all handlers for our application in a single file, with an `app.get` function for each application route, this would become a maintenance headache very quickly. What we really need to do is create a separate module for each of our request handlers, and then reference them from our main application. Luckily, this is very simple using the standard module syntax.

As an example of how to do this, let's create a handler function in a new module file. This file will be named `SimpleModuleHandler.ts`, as follows:

```
export function processRequest(req, res) {
  console.log(`SimpleModuleHandler.processRequest`);
  res.send('Hello World');
};
```

Here, we are exporting a function named `processRequest`, which is a request handler function. As such, it has two parameters, named `req` and `res`, that hold the HTTP request and response objects. This new handler function simply logs a message to the console, and then calls the `res.send` function to write a string to the response stream as we did earlier. Our `app.ts` file can then be modified to use this module as follows:

```
import * as express from 'express';
import * as simpleHandler from './SimpleModuleHandler';

let app = express();

app.get('/', simpleHandler.processRequest );
```

```
app.listen(3000, () => {
  console.log(`listening on port 3000`);
});
```

We have made two changes to our Express application. Firstly, we imported from the module file named `'./SimpleModuleHandler'`, and assigned all import functions to a namespace called `simpleHandler`. Secondly, we modified the `app.get` function call. The `app.get` function call now references the `processRequest` function from the imported module. This means that, when an HTTP request is received by our application, it will be processed by the `processRequest` function from the `SimpleModuleHandler` module. Running this application will now log a message to the console whenever a request is processed, as seen in the following console output:

```
> node simple_module_app.js
listening on port 3000
SimpleModuleHandler.processRequest
```

# Express routing

So far, we have learned that we can register a request handler against a particular HTTP request. In a more complex application, however, we would hand off all HTTP requests to a route hander to figure out which handler function to invoke. Having a global instance of a route handler allows us to easily attach new routes for our application.

Express provides a `Router` object to handle registration of new route handlers, as well as to manage application routing as a whole. Let's create two new modules in a directory named `routes`, named `Login.ts` and `Index.ts`. We will use the `Index.ts` module to handle requests to `'/'`, and the `Login.ts` module to handle requests to `'/login'`. This structure helps us to segregate application functionality into separate modules, and helps us to manage our code on the whole. In a production application, we may have a large number of distinct routes, each written within their own separate modules and each handling both `GET` and `POST` requests.

Our `Index.ts` file, then, is as follows:

```
import * as express from 'express';
var router = express.Router();

router.get('/', (req, res, next) => {
  res.send(`Index module processed ${req.url}`);
});

export { router } ;
```

Here, we start by importing the `express` module, as we have done before. We then call the `Router` function on the `express` module, and assign this to a local variable named `router`. This `Router` function acts as a kind of singleton instance, meaning that the call to `express.Router` returns the same router instance no matter where it was called from. In this way, we can attach new routes to the same global Express router handler, and specify both the path (`'/'`) and the route handler function ( `(req, res, next) => {}` ) for each route. In the preceding sample, our Index route handler function simply logs a message to the browser.

Note the last line of this module. We are exporting the variable named `router`, using the variable export syntax ( `export { router }` ). Remember that this `router` variable was set using the `express.Router()` function at the beginning of the module, and then used to attach a new route handler, in the call to `router.get`. As we have modified this global `router` instance, we need to re-export it for use by our application. This means that we are essentially attaching a new route handler to the Express router singleton instance.

Let's now take a look at the `Login.ts` module, which is almost identical:

```
import * as express from 'express';
var router = express.Router();

router.get('/login', (req, res, next) => {
  res.send(`Login module processed ${req.url}`);

});

export { router } ;
```

Here, the `Login.ts` module also modifies the global `express.Router` instance, and this time attaches a route handler for the `'/login'` path. Again, this handler simply logs a message to the browser. The final line in this module is again exporting the `router` variable via the `export { router }` statement. Express, then, is giving us the ability to chain multiple route handlers to the same `express.Router` instance by importing and then re-exporting the same `router` variable.

Let's now update our application to use these two route handlers, as follows:

```
import * as express from 'express';
let app = express();

import * as Index from './routes/Index';
import * as Login from './routes/Login';

app.use('/', Index.router);
```

```
app.use('/', Login.router);

app.listen(3000, () => {
  console.log(`listening on port 3000`);
});
```

Our application is now simply importing the `Index` and `Login` modules from their respective files, and then calling the `app.use` function to register our route handlers. Note how we are referencing the exported `router` local variable from each module, as seen in the call to `Index.router` and `Login.router`. These two lines, therefore, are registering our route handlers for our application to use.

With these routing modules in place, any web browser request to `'/'` will be handled by the `Index.ts` module, and any request to `'/login'` will be handled by the `Login.ts` module. In this way, we are starting to organize our code into logical modules, each responsible for a distinct area of application functionality.

# Express templating

Each of our route handlers are currently logging very simple messages to the browser. In a real-world application, however, we will need to render complete HTML pages. These pages would have a standard HTML structure, use CSS style sheets, and depending on the creativity of the design team, could easily become very complex. To support the complexity of generating HTML pages, most frameworks provide a templating engine.

Express also provides a complete template framework, which can use a choice of different template engines, including Pug, Mustache, Jade, Dust, and EJS to name a few. Introducing a template engine within our Express application is as simple as installing the template engine of choice, and configuring Express to use this template engine.

In this sample application, we will use the Handlebars engine. Handlebars uses standard HTML snippets, and introduces variables within the HTML templates using a simple double brace `{{` and `}}` syntax. Template engines such as Pug or Jade use their own custom formats to represent HTML elements, which are a mix of HTML keywords, class names, and variable substitution. As a quick comparison, consider a Handlebars template as follows:

```
<!DOCTYPE html>
<html>
<head>
  <title>{{title}}</title>
  <link rel='stylesheet' href='/stylesheets/style.css' />
</head>
```

```
<body>
  {{{body}}}
</body>
</html>
```

This template looks very much like standard HTML, with a few elements that will be substituted, such as `{{title}}` and `{{{body}}}`. A similar Jade template would be as follows:

```
doctype
html
head title #{title}
  link(rel='stylesheet', href='/stylesheets/style.css'
body
```

While this Jade template saves us a lot of typing, it does mean that we will need to learn and understand the various keywords and subtle syntax used in Jade in order to render valid HTML. Note how there are no recognizable HTML elements, which have instead been replaced by a custom Jade syntax. For the sake of simplicity, then, and to avoid learning a completely new syntax for HTML templates, we will use Handlebars as our template engine, as it uses recognizable HTML syntax, interspersed with substitution variables.

# Using Handlebars

Handlebars can be installed via npm as follows:

```
npm install hbs --save
```

Once Handlebars has been installed, all we need to do is add three lines to our application source file (`app.ts`), as follows:

```
import * as express from 'express';
let app = express();

import * as Index from './routes/Index';
import * as Login from './routes/Login';

import * as path from 'path';
app.set('views', path.join(__dirname, 'views'));
app.set('view engine', 'hbs');

app.use('/', Index.router);
app.use('/', Login.router);
```

Here, we have added an `import` for the module named `'path'`. The `path` module allows us to use several handy functions when working with directory path names. One of the variables exposed by the path module is the `__dirname` variable, which holds the full path name of the current directory. We are using this `__dirname` variable in a call to the `path.join` function, which will return the full pathname to the local `views` directory. We are then setting the `'views'` global Express parameter to this directory. Handlebars will by default use this global parameter to find the path where template files are stored.

Our last change to our `app.ts` file is to call `app.set` with the argument `'view engine'`, and the value `'hbs'`. This function call indicates to Express that it should use Handlebars as the template engine. These are the only changes we need to make to our Express application.

Now that we have registered a template library, we can update our `routes/Index.ts` router to use a Handlebars template, as follows:

```
import * as express from 'express';
var router = express.Router();

router.get('/', (req, res, next) => {

  res.render('index',
    { title: 'Express'
        //,username : userName
    }
  );
});

export { router } ;
```

Here, we have updated the route hander function to call `res.render` instead of `res.send`, as was used previously. This `res.render` function takes the name of the template as its first parameter, and then uses a POJO to use as input to the template engine.

If we run our web application at this stage, we will generate an error indicating that Handlebars cannot find the view named `"index"`, as follows:

```
Error: Failed to lookup view "index" in views directory
"/express_samples/views" at EventEmitter.render
(//express_samples/node_modules/express/lib/application.js:579:17)
at ServerResponse.render
(//express_samples/node_modules/express/lib/response.js:960:7)
at //express_samples/routes/Index.js:7:9
at Layer.handle [as handle_request]
```

We will now need to create an `index` view template. This template must exist in the `views` subdirectory, and as such will be named `views/index.hbs`. Handlebars uses the `.hbs` extension to specify Handlebars template files. This file is as simple as the following:

```
<h1>{{title}}</h1>
<p>Welcome to {{title}}</p>
```

Our `index.hbs` template file contains an `<h1>` element and a `<p>` element. Both of these elements use the `{{title}}` argument passed into the view template for parameter substitution.

Our rendered HTML page is now starting to look like the real thing; however, we still need the `<doctype>`, `<head>`, and `<body>` tags to be rendered in order for this to be valid HTML. Handlebars, similar to other rendering engines, allows us to specify a base layout template that will be used as the base layout for all pages. This is by default named `layout.hbs`, as follows:

```
<!DOCTYPE html>
<html>
  <head>
    <title>{{title}}</title>
    <link rel='stylesheet' href='/stylesheets/style.css' />
  </head>
  <body>
    {{{body}}}
  </body>
</html>
```

Here, we have defined the basic layout template to be used for each view. Handlebars will create HTML pages starting with this template, and then substitute any specific view template within the `{{{body}}}` tag. This base template has included a style sheet in the `<link>` tag in our `<head>` element, as we would expect in a standard HTML page. Note how the `<title>` element uses the `{{title}}` substitution parameter. Our login request handler renders this page with an object that includes a `title` property. Handlebars will therefore use this object to replace the `{{title}}` parameter with the passed in object value. Our resulting page is as follows:

Express application showing simple index page template

And our source HTML for this page is as follows:

Page source for simple Express index page

# Express POST events

Our Express application currently only renders an index page using the Handlebars template engine. Let's now extend our application to render a login form, and then process the results of a user completing the form, and posting this form back to our application.

We will therefore need our login route handler to accept both HTML `GET` actions, as well as HTML `POST` actions. In order to accomplish this, we will need to modify our application in a few areas. Firstly, we need an associated `login.hbs` view template to render the login form. Secondly, we will need to render this form on a `GET` request. Once the user has filled in the form, and POSTed it back to the application, we will need to parse this `POST` data. We will use a few Express modules to help with parsing.

Our new `login.hbs` view is created in the `views` directory, and it contains a simple HTML form, as follows:

```
<h1>Login</h1>
<p>
<form method="post">
  <p>{{ErrorMessage}}</p>
  <p>Username : <input name="username"></input></p>
  <p>Password : <input name="password"></input></p>
  <button type="submit">Login</button>
</form>
</p>
```

Here, we have created an HTML form that contains a few standard form elements. To start with, we have a `<p>` element to display the view property named `{{ErrorMessage}}`, which will be used to display any submission errors to the user. Following this, we have two input fields, named `username` and `password`, and a button named Login to `submit` the form.

Now that we have this view in place, we can update our `routes/Login.ts` file to render this view, as follows:

```
import * as express from 'express';
var router = express.Router();

router.get('/login', (req, res, next) => {
  res.render('login',
    {
        title: 'Express Login'
    }
  );
});

export { router } ;
```

Here, we have modified our route handler to simply render the `'login'` view, and set the `title` property to a string containing the value `'Express Login'`. Running our application now and navigating to `http://localhost:3000/login` will invoke our login request handler, and display our simple login form as follows:

Login form rendered to the browser as a result of the login.hbs template

Now that our login form has been rendered, we can focus on processing the form values when they have been submitted. Clicking on the `Login` button will cause the HTML page to generate a `POST` message to the login request handler. We therefore need to specify a handler that will pick up this `POST` message. In order to do this, we can modify our `Login.ts` handler, and include a new `POST` handler, as follows:

```
router.post('/login', (req, res, next) => {
  if (req.body.name.length > 0) {
    req.session['username'] = req.body.username;
    res.redirect('/');
  } else {
    res.render('login', {
      title: 'Express',
      ErrorMessage: 'Please enter a user name'
    });
    }
});
```

Here, we are calling the `post` method of the `router` module. As we saw with the `get` function, Express uses the `post` function to set up a `POST` event handler within our module.

This `post` handler is checking the `request.body.username` property to read the form data out of the posted form request. If the `username` property is valid, we store the value in the session property named `req.session['username']`, and redirect the browser to the default page. If the `username` property has not been entered, we simply re-render the login view, and display an error message.

Before we test this new login page, however, we will need to install and configure a few node modules, as follows:

```
npm install body-parser --save
npm install cookie-parser --save
npm install express-session --save
```

The `body-parser` module is used to parse form data as a result of a `POST` event, and attach this form data to the request object itself. This means that we can simply use `req.body` to de-reference the form's data.

The `cookie-parser` and `express-session` modules are used for session handling. In our login `POST` handler, we are setting a session variable to the `username` property of the form data. This will not work without these two modules.

The final change we need to make is to import these modules into our application, and run through any configuration that they need. We will therefore need to update our `app.ts` application file as follows:

```
// existing code
app.set('view engine', 'hbs');

import * as bodyParser from 'body-parser';
import * as cookieParser from 'cookie-parser';
import * as expressSession from 'express-session';

app.use(bodyParser.json());
app.use(bodyParser.urlencoded({ extended: false }));
app.use(cookieParser());
app.use(expressSession({ secret : 'asdf' }));

// existing code
app.use('/', Index.router);
```

Here, we are importing the new modules using our standard `import * as` module syntax. We are then running through four `app.use` function calls, in order to configure each of our modules. The `body-parser` module uses the `json()` function call to return middleware that Express will use to convert incoming requests into objects attached to `req.body`. The `body-parser` also needs to set the `urlencoded` property in order to allow for JSON-like objects to be exposed. These two settings will create a POJO available via the `req.body` property when receiving `POST` requests.

The `cookie-parser` module is configured by simply using the exported constructor function, and the `express-session` module is also configured in the same way. Note that both the `cookie-parser` and `express-session` modules are needed in order to store variables in the `req.session` object.

With these modules in place, our `POST` request handler will be able to query `req.body.username` to find the username that was entered, and `req.body.password` to find the corresponding password. It will also be able to store values in the session.

# HTTP request redirection

Now that we have a working login module to handle a simple login request, we can redirect the browser session back to our home page, and the `Index.ts` request handler via the call to `res.redirect('/')`. Let's update our `Index.ts` request handler to work with the `username` value that we have stored in the session, as follows:

```
router.get('/', (req, res, next) => {
  res.render('index',
    {   title: 'Express'
        ,username : req.session['username']
    }
  );
});
```

Here, we have simply added a new property to the object that is passed to our `index.hbs` template named `username`. The value of this property is retrieved from our session. We can now update our `index.hbs` view template as follows:

```
<h1>{{title}}</h1>
<p>Welcome to {{title}}</p>

{{#if username}}
  <p>User : {{username}} logged in.
{{else}}
  <p>Click <a href="/login">here to login</a></p>
{{/if}}
```

Here, we have added a code block within our Handlebars template that uses some JavaScript logic to render different HTML based on the `username` property. If the `username` property has a value, then we show that the user has logged in. If not, we render a link to the `'/login'` request handler to allow the user to log in. Our changes could not have been simpler.

Firing up our application now, we will see the home page, with a link to login, as follows:

Express home page showing a link to the login page

Following the link to login, we will then be presented with the **Login** screen, as follows:

Express login form

Once we have filled in the form and clicked on **Login**, the login request handler will process our request and then redirect our browser to the home page, as follows:

Express home page after logging in

Note, how the **Click here to login** link has disappeared according to our logic and the value of the username (from the session) is displayed, as the user is now logged in.

# Node and Express summary

In this section of the chapter, we explored modularization as it applies to Node and the Express engine. We started with a simple Express application, and built a simple request handler as a Node module. We then explored the routing capability of Express, and built two distinct modules, one to handle requests to our main page, and the other to handle login functionality. We then introduced Handlebars as a rendering engine, and built three views–a `layout.hbs` view that held the overall page structure, a view for the main page, and a view for the login page. We then worked with a `POST` request handler and showed how to parse form values and store a property in the user's session. Finally, we showed how redirection works, and tied these two pages together to implement login functionality in our application.

# Summary

In this chapter, we have had a look at using modules – both CommonJs and AMD. We explored the syntax used for modularization, and showed how to both `export` and `import` modules. We then explored the use of AMD module syntax using the Require library, and discussed how to take care of module dependencies. We then explored the use of CommonJs module syntax, and showed the equivalent structure for module dependencies using SystemJs. The final portion of this chapter worked with Node and Express modules, where we put together a sample application to render both an index and login page, and handle logins through session information.

In the next chapter, we will tackle object-oriented programming principles, and take a look at some useful design patterns.

# 11
# Object-Oriented Programming

In 1995, the **Gang of Four** (**GoF**), published a book named *Design Patterns: Elements of Reusable Object-Oriented Software*. In it, the authors, Erich Gamma, Richard Helm, Ralph Johnson, and John Vlissides, describe a number of classic software design patterns, which present simple and elegant solutions to common software problems. If you have never heard of design patterns such as a Factory pattern, Composite pattern, Observer pattern, or Singleton pattern, then reading through this GoF book is highly recommended.

The design patterns presented by the GoF have been reproduced in many different programming languages, including Java and C#. Vilic Vane has authored a book named *TypeScript Design Patterns*, in which each of these GoF patterns are implemented and discussed from a TypeScript perspective. In `Chapter 3`, *Interfaces, Classes, and Inheritance*, we took some time to build a classic Factory pattern implementation, which is one of the more popular design patterns described by the GoF. TypeScript, with its ES6 and ES7 language compatible constructs is a perfect example of an object-oriented language. With classes, abstract classes, interfaces, inheritance, and generics, TypeScript applications can now take full advantage of any of the GoF design patterns.

Describing the implementation of each of these GoF patterns in the TypeScript language is a subject that cannot be covered in a single chapter, and would do injustice to the excellent coverage of the GoF patterns covered by Vilic Vane. In this chapter, therefore, we will focus on the process of writing object-oriented code, and work through an example of two of the GoF design patterns that work very well together when dealing with complicated UI layouts. These are the **State** and **Mediator** design patterns, which focus on application state, and how objects interact with each other. We will build an Angular 2 application that uses a rather complex UI design and which includes some sophisticated CSS animated transitions. We will then start the process of reworking our original application to apply object-oriented design principles, and discuss how objects in our application interact. We will then implement the State and Mediator design patterns in order to encapsulate the logic that is used to determine what UI element should be shown when.

In this chapter, we will be covering the following topics:

- Object-oriented principles
- Using interfaces
- **SOLID** principles
- User interface design
- The State pattern
- The Mediator pattern
- Modular code

# Object-oriented principles

Any application that we build should be assessed in terms of object-oriented best practices. Robert Martin published what is known as the SOLID design principles, which is an acronym for five different object-oriented best practices. Following these practices will help to ensure that the code we write is easy to maintain, easy to understand, easy to extend, and resilient to change. In our current fast-paced world, we generally don't have the luxury of taking extraordinary amounts of time to modify our applications in order to keep up with ever changing requirements. The faster we can deliver updates to satisfy our business needs, the better chance we have of keeping ahead of our competition. Sticking to the SOLID design principles gives us a good foundation that will enable easy modifications to existing code, in order to satisfy these rapidly changing demands on our code base.

## Program to an interface

One of the primary notions that the GoF adhere to is the idea that programmers should *Program to an interface, not an implementation*. This means that programs are built using interfaces as the defined interaction between objects. By programming to an interface, client objects are unaware of the internal logic of their dependent objects, and are therefore much more resilient to change. By defining an interface, we are starting to cement an API that describes what functionality an object provides, how it should be used, and also how multiple objects interact with each other.

# SOLID principles

An extension of the program to an interface principle is what has been coined as the SOLID design principles, which are based on the ideas of Robert Martin. This is an acronym for five different principles, and it deserves a mention whenever object-oriented programming is discussed.

## Single responsibility

The idea behind the single responsibility pattern is that an object should have just a single responsibility. Do one thing, and do it well. We have seen examples of this principle in the various TypeScript compatible frameworks that we have worked with. As an example, a Model class is used to represent a single model. A Collection class is used to represent a collection of these models, and a View class is used to render models or collections.

If any one of our classes starts to become a super class, in other words it is doing many different types of things, then this is an indication that we are breaking this principle. As a simple example, if your source code file for a particular class starts to get very long – then this class is possibly doing too much. Think about what this class's primary responsibility is, and then break out the functionality of the class into smaller classes.

## Open closed

The Open-Closed principle states that an object should be open to extension, but closed for modification. In other words, once an interface has been designed for a class, changes over time to this interface should be achieved through inheritance, and not by modifying the interface directly.

Note that if you are writing libraries that are consumed by third parties via an API, then this principle is essential. Changes to an API should only be made through a new, versioned release, and should not break the existing API or interface, to ensure backwards compatibility of your API.

## Liskov substitution

The **Liskov Substitution Principle** (**LSP**) says that if one object is derived from another, then these objects can be substituted for each other without breaking functionality. While this principle seems fairly easy to implement, it can get pretty hairy when dealing with subtyping rules related to more complex types, such as lists of objects or actions on objects, which are commonly found in code that uses generics. In these instances, the concept of variance is introduced, and objects can be either covariant, contra-variant, or invariant. We will not discuss the finer points of variance here, but keep this principle in mind when writing libraries or code using generics.

## Interface segregation

The idea here is that many interfaces are better than one general-purpose interface. If we tie this principle with the single responsibility principle, we will start to look at our interfaces in terms of smaller pieces of the puzzle working together, rather than interfaces encompassing large portions of functionality.

## Dependency inversion

This idea states that we should depend on abstractions (or interfaces) rather than instances of concrete objects. Again, this is the same principle as programming to an interface, not an implementation.

# User interface design

As an example of the use of the SOLID design principles, let's build an application that uses a complex UI design, and see how these principles can help us break up our code into smaller, manageable modules, separated by interfaces.

In this section, we will build an Angular 2 application that will provide a left-to-right panel style page layout. We will use Bootstrap to provide a little styling, and some CSS-based transitions to slide panels in from the left or right. This will provide the user with a slightly different browsing experience to the common up-down scrolling design that most websites utilize.

# Conceptual design

Let's take a look at what this left-to-right design will look like conceptually:

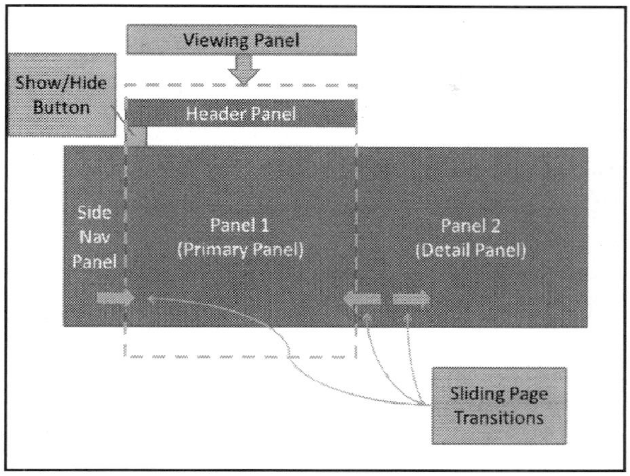


Conceptual view of the left-to-right UI panel design

The **Viewing Panel** will be our main page, with a **Header Panel** and a **Button** to control showing or hiding the side navigation pane on the left-hand side. When the left-hand side pane is opened, it will use a CSS animation in order to slide in from the left, and when it is closed it will again use an animation to slide back to the left. Likewise, when a button is clicked to show the second panel (Panel 2), this detail panel will slide in from the right, using a CSS animation, and will end up occupying the entire **Viewing Panel**.

The following screenshot shows the viewing panel with the header panel and left-hand side panel visible:

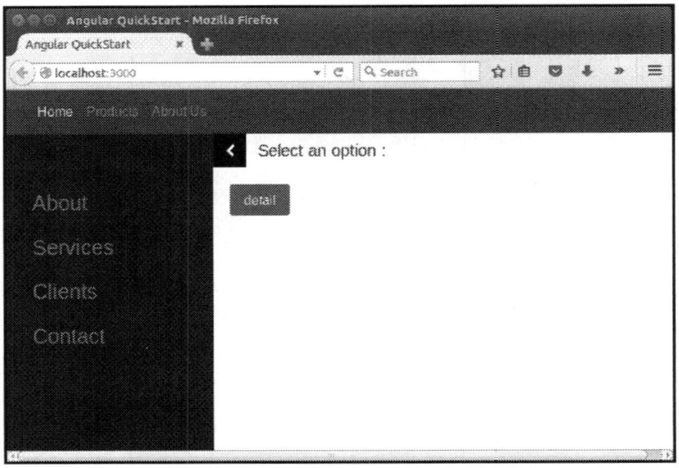


Main viewing panel with left-hand side panel visible

Here, we can clearly see the header panel at the top, the left-hand side menu panel, and two buttons. The first button is to the left of the **Select an option:** text, and it is simply a < arrow that will hide the left-hand side panel. Clicking on this button uses a CSS animation to slide the left-hand side panel to the left, so that it is out of the way. This can be seen in the following screenshot:

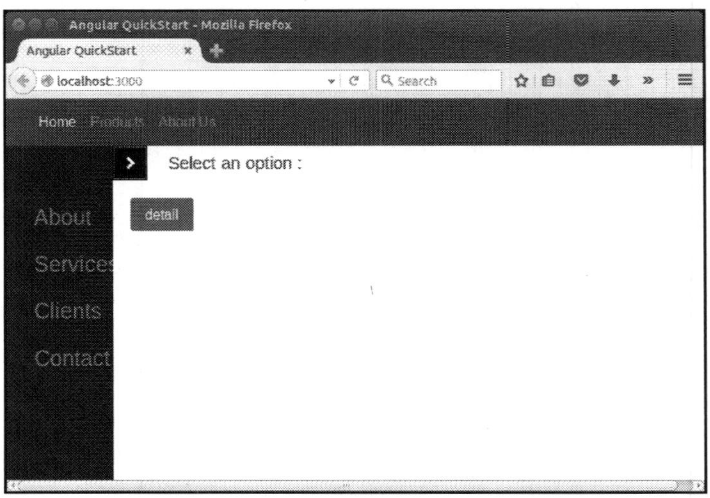


Animated transition for the left-hand side panel

Here, we have paused the CSS animation to show that the left-hand side panel is in the process of collapsing, and the main panel is being expanded to fill the entire view panel. Note that the show/hide left panel button has changed from a < arrow to a > arrow. This subtle change indicates to the user that the side panel can be expanded by clicking on the > button.

If the **detail** button is clicked, this will cause the left-hand side panel and the main page to slide to the left, revealing the second page through another CSS animation, as can be seen in the following screenshot:

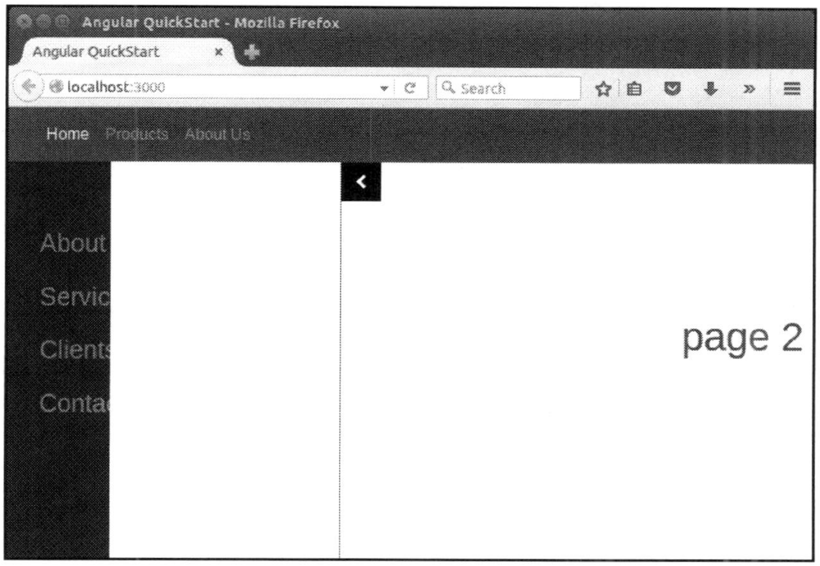


Animated page transition for the right-hand detail panel

Here, the second page is transitioning from the right-hand side, and both the left-hand side panel and the main page are sliding to the left.

# Angular 2 setup

Now that we have a conceptual view of what our application will look like, we can start implementing this layout, by setting up an Angular 2 application. As we have seen in earlier Angular 2 projects, we start by issuing an `ng new` command to use the Angular command line interface. This process will set up all of the required dependencies that Angular needs, and create an initial `app.component.ts` and `app.component.html` file for us.

Our `app/app.component.ts` file could not be simpler:

```
import { Component } from '@angular/core';

@Component( {
  selector : 'my-app',
  templateUrl : 'app/app.component.html',
  styleUrls: ['app/app.component.css']
})
export class AppComponent
{
  title = "Select an option :";
}
```

Here, we import the `Component` module as we have seen before, and then define three properties to pass to the `@Component` decorator. Note, however, that instead of specifying a `template` property, which normally contains HTML, we have specified a `templateUrl` property. This instructs Angular to load the named file from disk, and use it as the component template. Similarly, we have specified a CSS file to be used by our component via the `styleUrls` property. Our `AppComponent` class, then, just has a single property named `title`.

Using the `templateUrl` property to load a separate file containing our HTML template is an example of the dependency inversion principle. Our `AppComponent` class is dependent on an HTML template in order to render the component to the browser. When using the `template` property, we have a tight coupling between the HTML template, and the class itself. This means that any modification to the template requires recompilation of the module. By splitting the template out into a separate loadable file, we have broken this tight coupling, and the module class can be modified independently from its HTML template.

Our `app.component.html` file is currently very simple, as follows:

```
<div>
{{title}}
</div>

<div>
<button>detail</button>
</div>
```

Here, we have two `<div>` elements. The first contains our title, and the second contains a button.

# Using Bootstrap

Now that we have the basics of our Angular 2 application, we can flesh out the HTML that it will contain. In order to do this, we will use the Bootstrap framework. Bootstrap is an HTML-based, CSS driven method of building common web components that provide much of the functionality and styling needed in modern websites. From buttons to icons, to tabs or alerts, and almost everything in between, Bootstrap provides a simple syntax to add professional looking styling to our site. It has also been built as a responsive framework, meaning that it will automatically adjust to render optimally for mobile, tablet, or desktop devices. To include Bootstrap styling in our web page, we firstly need to install it via `npm` as follows:

```
npm install bootstrap --save
```

To include the boostrap.css file into our application, we can simply edit the `angular.cli.json` file in the base directory, and add an entry to the `styles` property as follows:

```
"styles": [
  "styles.css",
  "../node_modules/bootstrap/dist/css/bootstrap.min.css"
],
```

We can now start to flesh out the page design in our `app.component.html` page, starting with the navigation bar at the top of the screen, as follows:

```
<nav class="navbar navbar-inverse bg-inverse
  navbar-toggleable-sm">
  <a class="navbar-brand"> </a>
  <div class="nav navbar-nav">
    <a class="nav-item nav-link active">Home</a>
    <a class="nav-item nav-link">Products</a>
    <a class="nav-item nav-link">About Us</a>
  </div>
</nav>
```

Here, we have created a top navigation bar, by specifying a `<nav>` link, and have set some Bootstrap-specific CSS classes to create a dark `navbar` that occupies a band across the top of the page. Within this `<nav>` link, we have an `<a>` tag, which is just a blank element, and then we define a child `<div>` with three `<a>` links within it. These links are named `Home`, `Products`, and `About Us`, and they will be rendered as navigation links.

Note that the samples in this chapter use Bootstrap version `4.0.0-alpha.4`, which has some differences to earlier versions. If the preceding HTML navigation bar does not render correctly, then check your `package.json` file, and ensure that the bootstrap version is correct, as follows:

```
"dependencies": {
  .. other npm libraries ...
  "bootstrap": "^4.0.0-alpha.4",
  ... other npm libraries ...
}
```

# Creating a side panel

We can now take a look at creating our left-hand side panel. A great resource for HTML elements, CSS styling, and animations is the w3schools.com website. The how to section of the documentation provides a huge library of samples, including slideshows, modal boxes, progress bars, and responsive tables to name just a few. We will use a sample from the side navigation section, called `Sidenav Push Content`. This example shows how to create a side navigation screen that pushes the main content of the page over as it expands, instead of creating an overlay. We will start with some HMTL added to our `app.component.html` as follows:

```
<div id="mySidenav" class="sidenav">
  <a href="#">About</a>
  <a href="#">Services</a>
  <a href="#">Clients</a>
  <a href="#">Contact</a>
</div>
```

Here, we have described a `<div>` element with an `id` of `mySideNav`, and a CSS class of `sidenav`. This `<div>` contains four sub links. To turn this into an attractive side navigation bar, we will now need to edit our `app.component.css` file to add a few styles as follows:

```
/* The side navigation menu */
.sidenav {
  height: 100%; /* 100% Full-height */
  width: 250px; /* 0 width - change this with JavaScript */
  position: fixed; /* Stay in place */
  z-index: 1; /* Stay on top */
  top: 50px;
  left: 0;
  background-color: #111; /* Black*/
  overflow-x: hidden; /* Disable horizontal scroll */
  padding-top: 60px; /* Place content 60px from the top */
```

```
  transition: 0.3s;
}

/* The navigation menu links */
.sidenav a {
  padding: 8px 8px 8px 32px;
  text-decoration: none;
  font-size: 25px;
  color: #818181;
  display: block;
  transition: 0.3s
}

/* When you mouse over the navigation links, change their color */
.sidenav a:hover, .offcanvas a:focus{
  color: #f1f1f1;
}
```

With these few CSS styles in place, our side navigation panel starts to take shape, as can be seen in the following screenshot:

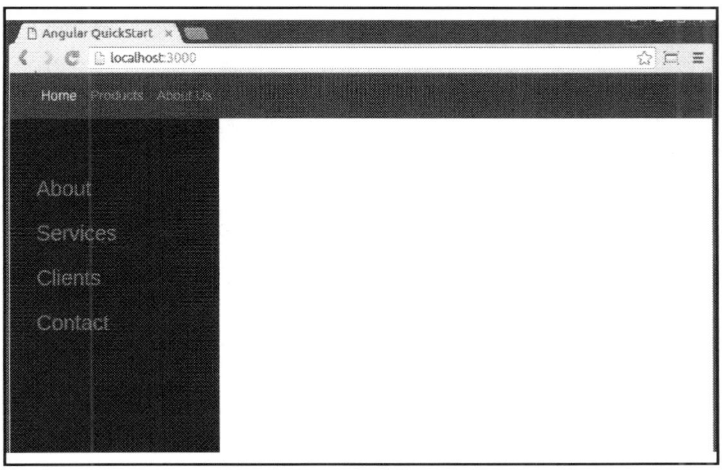


Simple side navigation bar with CSS styling

Here we have a nicely styled side navigation bar. Unfortunately, though, our main page content has disappeared behind the side navigation bar, meaning that we will need to apply a surrounding `<div>` and some styles to ensure that the left-hand panel pushes our main panel content over to the right. Our main panel content then becomes:

```
<div id="main" class="main-content-panel">
  <div class="row">
    <div class="col-sm-1">

      <button class="btn button-no-borders"
        (click)="showHideSideClicked()" >
        <span id="show-hide-side-button" class="fa "><</span>
      </button>
    </div>
    <div class="col-sm-11 ">
      <div class="row-content-header">{{title}}</div>
    </div>
  </div>

  <div class="main-content">
    <button class="btn btn-primary"
      (click)="buttonClickedDetail()">detail</button>
  </div>
</div>
```

Here, we have wrapped our main content in a `<div>` with an `id` of `"main"`, and a class of `"main-content-panel"`. This `<div>` is then broken down into a row that consists of two columns, of size `1` and `11`. This row houses our show/hide side panel button, and the `{{title}}` element. Beneath this header row is our main content, which simply includes a single button named `detail`. Our corresponding CSS for this section of HTML is as follows:

```
#main {
  margin-left: 250px;
  transition: .3s;
}

#main-body {
  transition: .3s;
}

.main-content {
  padding: 20px;
}

.row-content-header {
  padding: 5px;
```

```
    font-size: 20px;
  }
```

There are two key styles here that affect our page content. The first is the `margin-left: 250px` element of the `#main` style. This `margin-left` value is the CSS property that pushes our main content over to the right when the left-hand panel is visible. This property matches the corresponding side panel value of `.sidenav { width: 250px; }`. In other words, the side panel has a width of `250px`, and the main panel has a left margin of `250px`. These two values combined show the left-hand panel, and also push the main panel over to the right. We will adjust these two values from `250px` to `0px` in order to show or hide the left-hand panel.

The second key style is the `transition: .3s;` property that defines how long it takes to animate both the side panel collapsing and expanding, and the main panel being pushed to the right, or expanding to fill the screen. With these styles in place, we can now attach some code to kick off an animated page transition. To get this to work we need to register a click handler in the HTML, and then implement the click handler in our `app.component.ts` file. Firstly, let's examine the button click DOM event in the `app.component.html` file:

```
<button class="btn button-no-borders"
  (click)="showHideSideClicked()" >
  <span id="show-hide-side-button" class="fa "></span>
</button>
```

Here, we have defined a function named `showHideSideClicked`, which will be called whenever we click on the show/hide button. Our changes to `app.component.ts` are as follows:

```
export class AppComponent
{
  title = "Select an option :";
  isSideNavVisible = true;
  showHideSideClicked() {
    if (this.isSideNavVisible) {
      document.getElementById('main')
        .style.marginLeft = "0px";
      document.getElementById('mySidenav')
        .style.width = "0px";
      this.isSideNavVisible = false;
    } else {
      document.getElementById('main')
        .style.marginLeft = "250px";
      document.getElementById('mySidenav')
        .style.width = "250px";
      this.isSideNavVisible = true;
```

```
            }
        }
    }
```

Here, we have added a property to the `AppComponent` class named `isSideNavVisible`, and set it to `true` by default. This property is keeping track of whether the side navigation bar is visible or not. We have then implemented the `showHideSideClicked` function. If the side navigation bar is visible, we set the `marginLeft` style of the main panel to `0px`, and also set the `width` of the `mySideNav` element to `0px`. This essentially collapses the side panel, and makes the main panel fill the whole screen. If the side navigation bar is collapsed, we do the opposite, and also set the `isSideNavVisible` property at the same time. Running our application at this stage shows and hides the left-hand panel quite nicely, using the `transition: .3s` property to apply a visually appealing animation.

## Creating an overlay

We can now turn our attention to the second page, which will slide in from the right when we click on the detail button. Our HTML snippet is as follows:

```
<div id="mySidenav" class="sidenav">
... existing sidebar ...
</div>

<div id="myRightScreen" class="overlay">
  <button class="btn button-no-borders"
  (click)="closeClicked()">
    <span class="fa fa-chevron-left"></span>
  </button>
  <div class="overlay-content">
  <h1>page 2</h1>
  </div>
</div>
... existing main panel ...
<div id="main" class="main-content-panel">
```

Here, we have inserted a `<div>` element with an `id` of `myRightScreen`, and specified the CSS class of `overlay`. This is a simple `<div>` that contains a button at the top, with a click handler of `closeClicked`, and an `<h1>` element to show page 2. As with the side navigation bar, we will need some CSS styling to accomplish two things.

Firstly, we need to set the second page over to the right, and then we need a way to slide it in from the right when the detail button is clicked. Our CSS is as follows:

```
/* The Overlay (background) */
.overlay {
  height: 100%;
  width: 100%;
  position: fixed; /* Stay in place */
  z-index: 1; /* Sit on top */
  left: 0;
  top: 54px;
  overflow-x: hidden; /* Disable horizontal scroll */
  transition: 0.3s;
  transform: translateX(100%);
  border-left: 1px solid;
}
```

Again, there are two styles that are controlling how the second page is revealed. The first is the `transform: translateX(100%)` style, and the second is the `transition: 0.3s` style. The transform style in this case is essentially moving the X starting position of the `<div>` to `100%`. This means that by default, it is offset on the X axis `100%` of the page width, and therefore is not visible. The `transition: 0.3s` style is again just animating the show or hide of the panel.

Let's implement some of the click handlers on our page to see this in action. Firstly, we need to handle the click event of the detail button, as follows:

```
buttonClickedDetail() {
  document.getElementById('myRightScreen')
    .style.transform = "translateX(0%)";
  document.getElementById('main')
    .style.transform = "translateX(-100%)";
}
```

Here, we are doing two things. Firstly, we are setting the `transform` property of the second page to a value of `translateX(0%)`. This is doing the opposite of the `translateX(100%)`, and is setting the X starting position of the `<div>` to `0%`. With the translate CSS property in place, this gives us the sliding in from the right effect that we are after.

The second thing that we are doing in this function is to set the transform property of our main `<div>` to `translateX(-100%)`. Again, this has the effect of sliding the main panel over to the right. Before we test this transition, let's implement the `closeClicked` function that will close the right panel, as follows:

```
closeClicked() {
  document.getElementById('myRightScreen')
    .style.transform = "translateX(100%)";
  document.getElementById('main')
    .style.transform = "translateX(0%)";
}
```

Here, we are doing the opposite action to the `buttonClickedDetail` function, in order to slide the second page panel over to the right, and also reveal our main panel. These two functions are working in conjunction to set the `translateX` properties of both the `myRightScreen<div>` element, and the main `<div>` element.

If we fire up our page now, we will be able to click on the detail button, and see the second page slide in from the right.

# Coordinating transitions

So far, we have created a simple web application that has a main panel, a left-hand side panel and a second page panel, and added some CSS styles and transitions to create a visually pleasing page structure. Unfortunately, there are some issues with our current implementation. If we are on the main page, and our left-hand side panel is visible, then clicking on the detail button does not close the left hand panel before sliding in the right panel. This causes the second page to show on top of the left hand panel as follows:

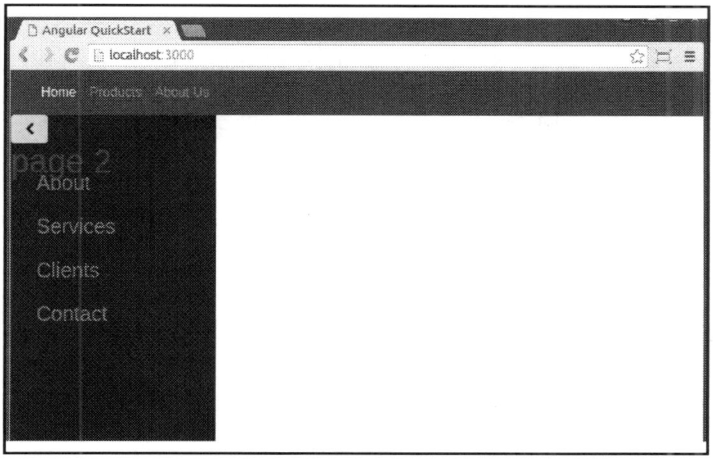


Right hand panel showing over the top of the left hand panel

To fix this, we could call the `showHideSideClicked` function that we already have, in order to hide the side panel first. This seems to fix the issue, but introduces another bug. If we have the side panel visible, and then show and hide the detail panel, the side panel remains closed. To fix this bug, we could call the `showHideSideClicked` function again when we close the right hand panel, but this solution unfortunately presents its own quirky bugs.

While we could rework the logic of our application to iron out all of these bugs, we are quickly getting into a frustrating cycle of trying to fix one thing, only to find it has another undesired side effect. What we really need is a mechanism to keep track of all of these visual elements, and control how the application reacts to user input. This is where the State and Mediator design patterns come to the rescue.

# The State pattern

The GoF describe two design patterns named the State pattern, and the Mediator pattern. The State pattern uses a set of concrete classes that are derived from a base class to describe a particular state. As an example, consider creating an `enum` to describe the states that a door can be in. At first glance, a door could be either `Open` or `Closed`. In this case, a simple `if...else` control flow would probably take care of any logic we wish to apply.

Consider, however, what happens to our control flow and logic if we needed a `Locked` and `Unlocked` state, or, if it were a sliding door for a `SlightlyAjar`, `HalfOpen`, `AlmostFullyOpen`, and `FullyOpen` state. The State design pattern allows us to easily define these states, and adjust our logic based on the current state of an object.

If we think about our application a little, we know that our screens will be in one or another particular state at any point in time. We are either on the main screen panel or on the second page panel. Also, the left-hand side panel is either visible or hidden. This combination give us three states:

- Main panel only
- Main panel with side navigation, or
- Detail panel

# State interface

The State pattern helps us to define these states in code. The basic principle of the State design pattern is that we create an interface, or an abstract base class that defines the properties of each state, and we then create concrete classes for each specialization. In our application, then, we have two main questions that we need to ask each state. These are:

- Is the side panel visible?
- Are we on the main panel or the detail panel?

Additionally, if we are on the main panel, then we also need to know whether to show the > arrow on the top left of the main panel, or the < arrow. This is tied to whether the side panel is visible or not. Our interface for these states is therefore the following:

```
export enum StateType {
  MainPanelOnly,
  MainPanelWithSideNav,
  DetailPanel
}

export enum PanelType {
  Primary,
  Detail
}

export interface IState {
  getPanelType() : PanelType;
  getStateType() : StateType;
  isSideNavVisible() : boolean;
  getPanelButtonClass() : string;
}
```

Here, we start with an `enum` for `StateType`, which lets us know which of the three states we are in. We then define the `PanelType enum` for whether we are on the `Primary` or `Detail` panels. Our interface, `IState`, has four functions. The `getPanelType` returns a `PanelType enum` value, and the `getStateType` function returns the `StateType enum` value. The `isSideNavVisible` function simply returns a `boolean` value indicating if the side navigation panel is visible or not. The final function, `getPanelButtonClass`, will return a class name for switching the show hide button from a chevron left ( < ) to a chevron right ( > ), depending on the state of the side panel.

With this interface in place, we have defined what questions we can ask each of our concrete state classes. Depending on whether we are on the main panel or the detail panel, the answers to this question will change slightly. This is the essence of the State design pattern. Define an interface that gives you the answers you need for all states, and then program to that interface. This shields any logic we build to consume these states from the definition of the states themselves. In other words, adding or removing a new state class will not affect any code we have written against the `IState` interface.

# Concrete states

Let's now examine the three concrete state classes as follows:

```
export class MainPanelOnly
  implements IState {
    getPanelType() : PanelType { return PanelType.Primary; }
    getStateType() : StateType { return StateType.MainPanelOnly; }
    getPanelButtonClass() : string { return 'fa-chevron-right';}
    isSideNavVisible() : boolean { return false; }
}
```

We start with a state class named `MainPanelOnly`, which is used to describe the state when the side navigation bar is not visible, and we are on the main viewing panel. This is a very simple class that implements the `IState` interface, and as such simply returns the correct values for each of the four functions. As we can see by the return values, we are on `PanelType.Primary`, the `IsSideNavVisible` function returns `false`, and we need an `'fa-chevron-right'` class to display on our show hide button. Our other two concrete states are very similar, as follows:

```
export class MainPanelWithSideNav
  implements IState {
  getPanelType() : PanelType { return PanelType.Primary; }
  getStateType() : StateType {
    return StateType.MainPanelWithSideNav; }
  getPanelButtonClass() : string { return 'fa-chevron-left';}
```

```
    isSideNavVisible() : boolean { return true; }
}

export class DetailPanel
    implements IState {
    getPanelType() : PanelType { return PanelType.Detail; }
    getStateType() : StateType { return StateType.DetailPanel; }
    getPanelButtonClass() : string { return '';}
    isSideNavVisible() : boolean { return false; }
}
```

Here, the `MainPaleWithSideNav` state class is the same as the `MainPanel` class, except that it returns true for the `isSideNavVisible` function, and `'fa-chevron-left'` for the panel button class. The `DetailPanel` state class returns `PanelType.Detail`, `false` for the `isSideNavVisible` function, and a blank class name for the panel button.

These three classes are very simple, and they are describing the state that the UI should be in when they are the current state. These classes help us to encapsulate the logic that is used in our application to manage the various UI elements on our screen.

# The Mediator pattern

Now that we can describe the various states that our UI is in, we can begin to apply the logic that is required to move between these states. The Mediator pattern is used to define how a set of objects interact. This pattern injects a Mediator object in between objects that affect each other, so that objects do not directly communicate with each other. This promotes loose coupling between objects that are involved in working together.

There are essentially two parts to the Mediator pattern. The first part is to define an interface that the Mediator can call in order to apply the changes that it needs. In our application, we will need the Mediator to be able to signal the UI to either show or hide the side navigation panel, and show or hide the detail panel. The Mediator also needs to switch the show hide button from a < chevron to a > chevron, depending on the current application state. Secondly, the Mediator needs a registry of all of the different states that are allowed, and will call the UI functions to apply changes based on the movement between these states.

By defining an interface for these interactions, we are following object-oriented best practices, and shielding the Mediator code from the actual implementation of the UI changing logic. We will therefore be able to code and test this Mediator logic without an actual UI in place.

Our interface for the Mediator class is, therefore, as follows:

```
export interface IMediatorImpl {
  showNavPanel();
  hideNavPanel();
  showDetailPanel();
  hideDetailPanel();
  changeShowHideSideButton(fromClass: string, toClass: string);
}
```

Here, we have distilled all of the UI changes required by our application into four functions. We can either show or hide the side navigation panel, show or hide the detail panel, and update the button CSS class.

Looking back at our work so far, we have simplified our business logic into two parts. Firstly, we have defined the states that our UI will be in at any point in time, and secondly we have defined the functions required to update our UI. We are already on the way to building a modular, object-oriented, easy to understand, and easy to maintain application. We will tackle the implementation of the Mediator logic a little later, after we have performed some housekeeping on our existing code.

# Modular code

Our application so far has all of its HTML, CSS, and business logic as part of the `AppComponent` class. Although we have already broken this class down into a separate `app.component.html` and `app.component.css` files, it really contains a number of separate components all in one. Let's take this opportunity to modularize our code, and create three separate classes. These will be:

- A `NavbarComponent` class to render and handle the navigation bar at the top of the screen
- A `SideNavComponent` class to render the left-hand side navigation panel
- A `RightScreenComponent` to handle the detail panel that slides in from the right

This means that the `AppComponent` class becomes the central application class, and it will be responsible for coordinating each of these components.

# Navbar component

Our first task is to create a `NavbarComponent` class that will have the sole responsibility of rendering the navigation bar at the top of the screen. To do this we will create a `navbar.component.ts` file and a `navbar.component.html` file in our `app` directory.

The contents of the HTML file are simply copied from our existing `app.component.html` file as follows:

```
<nav class=" navbar navbar-inverse bg-inverse
  navbar-toggleable-sm">
  <a class="navbar-brand"> </a>
  <div class="nav navbar-nav">
    <a class="nav-item nav-link active">Home</a>
    <a class="nav-item nav-link">Products</a>
    <a class="nav-item nav-link">About Us</a>
  </div>
</nav>
```

We can then create a `NavbarComponent` class as follows:

```
import { Component } from '@angular/core';
@Component( {
  selector: 'navbar-component',
  templateUrl: './app/navbar.component.html'
})

export class NavbarComponent {

}
```

This is a very basic Angular 2 class that references our HTML file, and specifies a selector property in the `@Component` decorator. To use this new component in our application, we will need to register this component with Angular, and then simply drop in a `<navbar-component>` tag in our current `app.component.html` file. Registration is accomplished by importing this component into our `app.module.ts` file, as follows:

```
import { AppComponent } from './app.component';

// include here to enable html to find correct component
import { NavbarComponent } from './navbar.component';

@NgModule({
  declarations: [
    AppComponent,
    NavbarComponent
```

```
  ],
  imports: [
    BrowserModule,
    FormsModule,
    HttpModule
  ],
  providers: [],
  bootstrap: [AppComponent]})
```

Here, we have added a module import statement to reference our `navbar.component` module, and then we have updated the `declarations` array of the `@NgModule` decorator. By updating the `declarations` array, we are registering the `<nabar-component>` tag for use within any HTML template. The final change we need to make is to include this new `<navbar-component>` tag into our `app.component.html` file. With these changes in place, our application will use the new `navbar.component` module when rendering the page.

# SideNav component

In a similar manner, let's now create a component for the left-hand side navigation panel, named `SideNavComponent`. This will need three source files named `sidenav.component.ts`, `sidenav.component.html`, and `sidenav.component.css`. The HTML file is again a simple cut and paste from our existing HTML file, as follows:

```
<div id="mySidenav" class="sidenav">
  <a href="#">About</a>
  <a href="#">Services</a>
  <a href="#">Clients</a>
  <a href="#">Contact</a>
</div>
```

The `SideNavComponent` class is as follows:

```
import { Component } from '@angular/core';

@Component( {
  selector: 'sidenav-component',
  templateUrl: './sidenav.component.html',
  styleUrls: ['./sidenav.component.css']
})

export class SideNavComponent {

  closeNav() {
    document.getElementById('mySidenav')
```

```
      .style.width = "0px";
    }
    showNav() {
      document.getElementById('mySidenav')
      .style.width = "250px";
    }

}
```

Again, we have a fairly simple Angular 2 class that registers the `selector` property, the HTML, and CSS files with the `@Component` decorator. Note, however, that we have created two functions in this class, named `closeNav` and `showNav`. These two functions set the `style.width` CSS property to `0px` and `250px`, respectively. What we have done here is to essentially encapsulate all of the functionality surrounding the side navigation bar into the `SideNavComponent` class. This is the single responsibility design principle – that a class should just have a single responsibility.

We can now register this component in the `app.module.ts` file, as we did with the `NavbarComponent`, and we can then drop the `<sidenav-component>` tag into our `app.component.html` file.

## RightScreen component

Let's now go ahead and create the last component in our application, which covers the right hand or detail screen, named `RightScreenComponent`. Again, we will create a `rightscreen.component.ts` file, an HTML file, and a CSS file for this component. We will not focus on the HTML and CSS files for this component yet, as they are a simple cut and paste from the existing HTML and CSS from our `app.component` files. Let's rather take a look at the Angular 2 class for this component, as follows:

```
import { Component, EventEmitter, Output } from '@angular/core';

@Component( {
  selector: 'rightscreen-component',
  templateUrl: './rightscreen.component.html',
  styleUrls: ['./rightscreen.component.css']
})

export class RightScreenComponent
{
  @Output() notify: EventEmitter<string>
    = new EventEmitter<string>();

  closeClicked() {
```

```
    this.notify.emit('Click from nested component');
  }

  closeRightWindow() {
    document.getElementById('myRightScreen')
      .style.transform = "translateX(100%)";
  }

  openRightWindow() {
    document.getElementById('myRightScreen')
      .style.transform = "translateX(0%)";
  }
}
```

This class is very similar to the other component classes that we have created, in that it species our `selector` tag, a `templateUrl`, and then the css file in the `@Component` decorator. We then define the class with three functions – `closeClicked`, `closeRightWindow`, and `openRightWindow`. The `closeRightWindow` and `openRightWindow` functions set the `style.transform` values for this component, as we have discussed earlier.

The really interesting part of this class is the `closedClicked` function, and the use of something called an `EventEmitter`. Note how we have imported both the `EventEmitter` class and the `Output` decorator in our `import` statement at the top of the file. Angular 2 uses the `@Output` property decorator and the `EventEmitter` generic class to enable components to notify other components when events occur.

Remember that this panel has a button on the top left-hand side that is used to close the panel and return to the main screen. The HTML for this button is as follows:

```
<button class="btn btn-default" (click)="closeClicked()">
  <span class="fa fa-chevron-left"></span>
</button>
```

We know that the Angular syntax for handling a DOM click event is to specify `(click)="<handlerFunction>"`. In our preceding HTML, this `<handlerFunction>` is called `closeClicked`, and therefore must be defined in our component class itself.

However, this `RightScreenComponent` class is only in control of its own HTML area, and cannot therefore include any functionality that is for the application itself. In this case, then, all we need to do is to raise an event stating that the close button has been clicked, and leave it up to another part of the application to react to this event and do something. Again, this ties into our design principle of single responsibility.

Let's take a closer look at this `EventEmitter` syntax:

```
@Output() notify: EventEmitter<string>
  = new EventEmitter<string>();

closeClicked() {
  this.notify.emit('Click from nested component');
}
```

We set up our event emitter by decorating the `notify` property with the `@Output` decorator. We then specify that the type of this property is `EventEmitter<string>`, and then immediately create an instance of the `EventEmitter` class. The `EventEmitter` is a generic class, meaning that we can substitute a `<number>`, or `<boolean>`, or even a complex class in this declaration.

As the `notify` property is an instance of an `EventEmitter` of type `string`, we can call `this.notify.emit` with a string argument in our `closeClicked` function. This takes care of emitting an event when a user clicks on this button within our `RightScreenComponent` class.

We now need to define an event handler for this event. As the `AppComponent` class is responsible for both creating and controlling this `RightScreenComponent`, we make a change to our `app.component.html` file to register for this notification event. The inclusion of the `<rightscreen-component>` tag now becomes:

```
<rightscreen-component (notify)='onNotifyRightWindow($event)'>
</rightscreen-component>
```

Here, we have added an attribute to our `<rightscreen-component>` tag to register for a `(notify)` event, and then called the `onNotifyRightWindow` function within our `AppComponent` class. The implementation of this function for the time being can just pop up an alert so that we can test that the firing and registering for this event is working correctly:

```
onNotifyRightWindow(message:string):void {
  alert('clicked');
}
```

We will hook up this event handler a little later to our Mediator class in order to trigger the switch to move to a different state.

## Child components

Our AppComponent class is the owner of our entire application. It renders the HTML used for the entire page, which includes the navbar, sidenav, rightscreen, and main panel components. As such, it is also the parent of these sub-components. In other words, all of these components are children of the AppComponent class, and are referred to as child components. What we need now is a way for the AppComponent class to reference the SideNavComponent and RightScreenComponent classes within the class itself. This is to tie in the instances of these classes that are created via the HTML tags, <sidenav-component> and <rightscreen-component>.

Angular provides the @ViewChild property decorator for this purpose. To use this decorator, our AppComponent class needs to be updated as follows:

```
import { Component, ViewChild } from '@angular/core';
import { SideNavComponent } from './sidenav.component';
import { RightScreenComponent } from './rightscreen.component'
.. @Component ...
export class AppComponent
{
  @ViewChild(SideNavComponent)
  private sideNav : SideNavComponent;
  @ViewChild(RightScreenComponent)
  private rightScreen: RightScreenComponent;
  .. the rest of the class ...
```

There a few changes that we need to make. Firstly, we need to import the ViewChild decorator from the @angular/core module, and then import the SideNavComponent and RightScreenComponent modules. Secondly, we need to create two private properties, named sideNav and rightScreen, to hold the instances of our child components.

We then use Angular 2's @ViewChild decorator with the class name that we wish to reference. This means that the @ViewChild(SideNavComponent) will connect the private sideNav property to the correct instance of the SideNavComponent class.

Similarly, we are asking Angular 2 to connect the instance of the RightScreenComponent class used in our HTML to the private rightScreen variable. In this way, our AppComponent class now has programmatic access to these two classes that were referenced in the HTML.

# Mediator interface implementation

Now that the `AppComponent` class has references to its child components, we can focus on the implementation of the `IMediatorImpl` interface, as follows:

```
showNavPanel() {
  this.sideNav.showNav();
  document.getElementById('main').style.marginLeft = "250px";
}
hideNavPanel() {
  this.sideNav.closeNav();
  document.getElementById('main').style.marginLeft = "0px";
}
showDetailPanel() {
  this.rightScreen.openRightWindow();
  document.getElementById('main').style.transform =
    "translateX(-100%)";
}
hideDetailPanel() {
  this.rightScreen.closeRightWindow();
  document.getElementById('main').style.transform =
    "translateX(0%)";
}
changeShowHideSideButton(fromClass: string, toClass: string) {
  if (fromClass.length > 0 && toClass.length > 0) {
    document.getElementById('show-hide-side-button')
      .classList.remove(fromClass);
    document.getElementById('show-hide-side-button')
      .classList.add(toClass);
  }
}
```

We start with the `showNavPanel` function, which calls the implementation of the `showNav` function on the `sideNav` child component, and then sets the `marginLeft` style on the main DOM element. Likewise, the `hideNavPanel` function does the opposite. The `showDetailPanel` function calls the implementation of the `openRightWindow` function on the `rightScreen` child component, and then sets the `transform` property on the main DOM element.

With this implementation in place, we can now focus on the Mediator class itself.

# The Mediator class

The Mediator class is responsible for coordinating the overall application state, and the interactions between our various UI classes. As such, it really needs to have three key ingredients. Firstly, it needs to have the concrete implementation of the `IMediatorImpl` interface so that it can call the various functions it needs to when the UI needs updating. We have just implemented the `IMediatorImpl` interface in our `AppComponent` class, so we will need to pass a reference to the `AppComponent` instance to the Mediator class.

Secondly, the Mediator class needs a concrete instance of each of our State classes so that it can recreate both the current state of the application, as well as the desired next state. It can then compare the current state and the desired next state to figure out what changes will need to occur to move from state to state.

Thirdly, the Mediator class needs to store the current state of the application. As it is responsible for moving from state to state, it makes sense for the Mediator to be the single source of truth for anything state related. Also, where UI functionality is dependent on the current state of the application, we can forward any queries about what to do through to the Mediator class to make a decision for us.

Bearing these elements in mind, let's take a look at the properties and constructor of our Mediator class, as follows:

```
export class Mediator {
  private _mainPanelState = new MainPanelOnly();
  private _detailPanelState = new DetailPanel();
  private _sideNavState = new MainPanelWithSideNav();

  private _currentState: IState;
  private _currentMainPanelState: IState;
  private _mediatorImpl: IMediatorImpl;

  constructor(mediatorImpl: IMediatorImpl) {
    this._mediatorImpl = mediatorImpl;
    this._currentState =
      this._currentMainPanelState
        = this._sideNavState;
  }
```

We start with the three concrete instances of our three State classes, named `_mainPanelState`, `_detailPanelState`, and `_sideNavState`. Following this, we have two properties, named `_currentState` and `_currentMainPanelState`, which are both of type `IState`. These properties will be used to store the current state of the application itself, and the main panel. Remember that if we switch from the main panel to the detail panel and then back again, the side navigation panel should reappear in the same state as we left it. This is what the `_currentMainPanel` state variable will be used for.

The next function we will implement within the Mediator class is a simple factory function to retrieve the concrete instance of a State object given the `StateType` as an input, as follows:

```
getStateImpl(stateType: StateType) : IState {
  var stateImpl : IState;
  switch(stateType) {
    case StateType.DetailPanel:
      stateImpl = this._detailPanelState;
      break;
    case StateType.MainPanelOnly:
      stateImpl = this._mainPanelState;
      break;
    case StateType.MainPanelWithSideNav:
      stateImpl = this._sideNavState;
      break;
  }
  return stateImpl;
}
```

This is a simple helper function that returns the correct implementation of a State object given a `StateType enum` value.

We can now focus on the heart of the Mediator class, managing the changes to the UI when we move from state to state, as follows:

```
moveToState(stateType: StateType) {
  var previousState = this._currentState;
  var nextState = this.getStateImpl(stateType);

  if (previousState.getPanelType() == PanelType.Primary &&
    nextState.getPanelType() == PanelType.Detail ) {
      this._mediatorImpl.showDetailPanel();
    }
  if (previousState.getPanelType() == PanelType.Detail &&
    nextState.getPanelType() == PanelType.Primary) {
      this._mediatorImpl.hideDetailPanel();
    }
```

```
        if (nextState.isSideNavVisible())
          this._mediatorImpl.showNavPanel();
        else
          this._mediatorImpl.hideNavPanel();

        this._mediatorImpl.changeShowHideSideButton(
          previousState.getPanelButtonClass(),
          nextState.getPanelButtonClass() );

        this._currentState = nextState;
        if (this._currentState.getPanelType() == PanelType.Primary ) {
          this._currentMainPanelState = this._currentState;
        }
      }
```

This function, named `moveToState`, contains all of the UI logic to handle our three application states. We start by declaring two variables, named `previousState` and `nextState`. The `previousState` variable is where we are now, and the `nextState` variable is where we want to be, as passed in via the `stateType` argument. Once we have these two State objects, we can start to compare their properties, and then call the `IMediatorImpl` interface functions accordingly.

Consider the first `if` statement. The logic here simply states the following:

- If we were on the primary panel, and we wish to move to the detail panel, then tell the UI to show the detail panel

The second `if` statement states the following:

- If we are on the detail panel, and wish to move to the primary panel, then tell the UI to hide the detail panel

Our third `if` statement states the following:

- If our State tells us that the side navigation panel should be visible, then show it, otherwise hide it

We then make a call to the UI to switch the show hide button from our current state icon to our future state icon. This will have the effect of switching the button from < to >, or vice versa, based on the properties of our two states.

Once we have finished updating the UI, we need to store our current state.

Finally, our last `if` statement states that if we are on the main panel, update the internal value of the `_currentMainPanelState`. We need to store this value so that when we switch to the detail panel and back again, we restore our side navigation bar correctly.

This function contains, in simple, human-readable statements, how to move from state to state. Our logic has boiled down into asking a few simple questions, and responding accordingly.

# Using the Mediator

The last step in the implementation of the State and Mediator design pattern is to trigger the change of state. This trigger could be purely within our code, or it could be as a result of actions on our UI. To begin with, we will need to create a new instance of the `Mediator` class, and register our `AppComponent` as the implementation for the `IMediatorImpl` interface, as follows:

```
export class AppComponent
  implements IMediatorImpl
{
  ... existing code ...
  mediator: Mediator = new Mediator(this);
```

Here, we are specifying that the `AppComponent` class implements the `IMediatorImpl` interface, and we are then defining a local variable named `mediator`. This local variable calls the `Mediator` constructor, passing in `this` (our `AppComponent` class instance). This call essentially registers our `AppComponent` class as the implementation of the `IMediatorImpl` interface that the `Mediator` uses to make changes to the UI.

Once we have registered our `AppComponent` class with the Mediator, we can use the Mediator to trigger a state change. As an example of this, let's ensure that when the application first starts up, we only show the main panel – or in other words, move to the `StateType.MainPanelOnly` state. To do this, we will need to tap into Angular's component rendering life cycle, and implement a function named `ngAfterViewInit`, as follows:

```
export class AppComponent
  implements IMediatorImpl, AfterViewInit
{
  ... existing code ...

  ngAfterViewInit() {
```

```
    this.mediator.moveToState(StateType.MainPanelOnly);
  }
```

Here, we have indicated that the `AppComponent` class implements the `AfterViewInit` interface. This interface defines a single function, named `ngAfterViewInit`, which we are using to move to the `MainPanelOnly` state. The `ngAfterViewInit` function is automatically called by the Angular framework after the initial view of the component has been initialized. This means that Angular has already parsed our component's HTML, created all child views, and has rendered the HTML to the browser. Only at this stage do we have a reference to our `SideNavComponent` child view, and our `RightScreenComponent` view, which are needed by the Mediator.

Our application now loads up, and is in the correct starting state.

# Reacting to DOM events

We are almost there in our implementation of the State and Mediator pattern. The final piece of the puzzle is hooking up our DOM click events to trigger a state change. Let's modify the `buttonClickedDetail` function as follows:

```
buttonClickedDetail() {
  this.mediator.moveToState(StateType.DetailPanel);
}
```

The `buttonClickedDetail` function is invoked when a user clicks on the detail button on our main panel. All that this event handler now needs to do is to call the `moveToState` function on the Mediator to move to the `DetailPanel` state. Very simple indeed.

We also need to modify the event handler function that is called when a user is on the detail panel, and click on the < button to return to the main panel. Remember that we hooked up an `EventEmitter` in the `RightScreenComponent` to an event handler in our `AppComponent` class named `onNotifyRightWindow`. We can now modify this handler as follows:

```
onNotifyRightWindow(message:string):void {
  this.mediator.moveToState(
    this.mediator.getCurrentMainPanelState());
}
```

Here, we are simply moving to the previous main panel state. Again, very simple indeed.

The last user interaction that we need to handle is when the user clicks on the show hide side navigation bar button. This button will either show or hide the side navigation bar. Remember that the effect of clicking on this button will be slightly different, depending on whether the side navigation bar is currently open or closed. The `AppComponent` class, therefore, should not be making this decision as it is based on the current state.

It makes sense, then, to simply trap this event from our `AppComponent` class, and then forward the decision making to our Mediator class, as the Mediator class holds all of the information needed about our current state.

Our event handler in our `AppComponent` class is as follows:

```
showHideSideClicked() {
  this.mediator.showHideSideNavClicked();
}
```

Here, we are simply calling the `showHideSideNavClicked` function on the Mediator class, which is implemented as follows:

```
showHideSideNavClicked() {
  switch (this._currentState.getStateType()) {
    case StateType.MainPanelWithSideNav:
      this.moveToState(StateType.MainPanelOnly);
      break;
    case StateType.MainPanelOnly:
      this.moveToState(StateType.MainPanelWithSideNav);
      break;
  }
}
```

This function simply queries the `_currentState` object, and switches to the `MainPanelOnly` state, or the `MainPanelWithSideNav` state accordingly.

Our implementation of the State and Mediator pattern is now complete.

# Summary

In this chapter, we have taken an in-depth look at building an Angular 2 application from the ground up. We have experimented with a left-to-right page transition design, and shown how to manipulate CSS styles and CSS transitions to create a visually appealing application. Unfortunately, our initial attempts in creating this application ended up with a lot of confusing and hard to fix local variables, as we attempted to keep all of the page elements under control.

We then took a step back, and discussed how the State and Mediator design pattern could help us to manage page transitions. We then refactored our application into meaningful components, and took a deep-dive look into how to apply the State and Mediator pattern to manage our application state, and complex page transitions.

In the next chapter, we will take a look at the concept of dependency injection, and how we can use the new language features of TypeScript to implement this powerful and simple object-oriented design paradigm.

# 12
# Dependency Injection

In our last chapter, we explored the concepts of object-oriented programming, and worked through the process of building an application that conformed to object-oriented design principles. While the Gang of Four described a set of design patterns to handle object construction and behavior, none of these patterns tackled the construction of large hierarchies of objects, or large systems. In recent years, another powerful set of design patterns has emerged that tackles exactly this problem.

When designing large systems, we should be thinking of groups of objects as services. We may need a service to handle connections to a database, or a service to retrieve customer information. This change in thinking helps our systems to be more loosely-coupled. When new features are required, we should be able to call upon and merge the functionality of various services in order to accomplish our task.

With this in mind, there are two design patterns that help us deal with locating and using services in a large application. The first of these is named **Service Location**, where we build a central **registry** of available services, and then request these services as needed. The second of these is an extension of the Service Location pattern, and is named dependency injection. With dependency injection (or DI), instead of asking for available services, these services are automatically injected into our code ready for us to use. In this chapter, we will work through an example where Service Location becomes very handy. We will build a service locator, and refactor our code to use this design pattern. We will then discuss the drawbacks of Service Location, and build a DI framework of our own, using TypeScript decorators.

In this chapter, we will look into the following topics:

- Object dependency
- Service Location
- Interface resolution

- Constructor injection
- Decorator injection
- Dependency injection

# Sending mail

To begin our discussion on dependency injection, let's create a simple Node application that sends e-mails. Sending mail is a common requirement of most systems, especially when you have a user registration process as part of your business application.

# Using nodemailer

There are a variety of Node-based packages that we can import to give us e-mail capability. In this chapter, we will use the `nodemailer` package, which can be installed as follows:

```
npm install --save nodemailer
```

Once installed, we will need a few declaration files using `@types`, as follows:

```
npm install @types/node --save
npm install @types/nodemailer --save
npm install @types/nodemailer-direct-transport --save
npm install @types/nodemailer-smtp-transport --save
npm install @types/nodemailer-bluebird --save
```

With the `nodemailer` package installed, and the relevant TypeScript declaration files in place, we can follow the examples on the Nodemailer website, and send an e-mail in three simple steps, as follows:

```
import * as nodemailer from 'nodemailer';

var transporter = nodemailer.createTransport(
  `smtps://<username>%40gmail.com:<password>@smtp.gmail.com`
);

var mailOptions = {
  from : 'from_test@gmail.com',
  to : 'to_test@gmail.com',
  subject : 'Hello',
  text: 'Hello from node.js'
};

transporter.sendMail( mailOptions, (error, info) => {
```

```
    if (error) {
      return console.log(`error: ${error}`);
    }
    console.log(`Message Sent ${info.response}`);
  });
```

Here, we have imported the `nodemailer` module, and then set up a `transporter` variable that contains a username and password for an account on Gmail. If you have a Gmail account, you can try this out fairly quickly. If not, you will need access to an SMTP server to actually send out e-mails. Most commercial e-mail systems will have a public SMTP server, similar to `smtp.gmail.com`, that you can use if you have a registered account.

Once we have a connection to the SMTP server, we set up a `mailOptions` variable that contains the details of our e-mail, such as the sender, recipient, subject, and e-mail body. These properties are named `from`, `to`, `subject`, and `text`, respectively. Finally, the call to the `sendMail` function on the `transporter` variable will send the actual e-mail.

Instead of having to call these functions every time we want to send a mail, let's create a reusable class that encompasses all of the setup code for us, as follows:

```
import * as nodemailer from 'nodemailer';

export class GMailService {
  private _transporter: nodemailer.Transporter;
  constructor() {
    this._transporter = nodemailer.createTransport(
      `smtps://<username>%40gmail.com:<password>@smtp.gmail.com`
    );
  }
  sendMail(to: string, subject: string, content: string) {
    let options = {
      from: 'from_test@gmail.com',
      to: to,
      subject: subject,
      text: content
    }

    this._transporter.sendMail(
      options, (error, info) => {
        if (error) {
          return console.log(`error: ${error}`);
        }
        console.log(`Message Sent ${info.response}`);
      });
  }
}
```

Here, we have built a class named `GMailService` that encapsulates the internal workings of the `nodemailer` package, and only exposes a simple function, named `sendMail`. The `sendMail` function has also reduced the number of parameters that we need in order to send an e-mail. Note that we have removed the `from` parameter, in favor of hardcoding this sender mail address within the class. This will ensure that all e-mails sent from our application will come from the same e-mail address. We will tackle the issue of hardcoding the sender's e-mail a little later, but at least this piece of information is now centralized into a single place.

We can use this class as follows:

```
import GMailService from './app/GMailService';

let gmailService = new GMailService();

gmailService.sendMail(
  '<test_user>@gmail.com',
  'Hello',
  'Hello from gmailService');
```

Here, we have simply created an instance of the `GMailService` class, and called the `sendMail` function to send a simple e-mail.

At this point, our `GMailService` class is working as expected, and is sending e-mails correctly. Unfortunately, the call to the `sendMail` function does not currently provide any feedback to the calling code. It would be far better if the `sendMail` function provided a mechanism to let us know if mail has been sent correctly or not. We should, therefore, refactor our `sendMail` function to expose the results of the actual e-mail send as follows:

```
sendMail(to: string, subject: string, content: string)
: Promise<void>
{
  let options = {
    from: '<fromaddress>@gmail.com',
    to: to,
    subject: subject,
    text: content
  }

  return new Promise<void> (
    (resolve: (msg: any) => void,
      reject: (err: Error) => void) => {
        this._transporter.sendMail(
          options, (error, info) => {
            if (error) {
              console.log(`error: ${error}`);
```

```
                reject(error);
            } else {
                console.log(`Message Sent
                  ${info.response}`);
                resolve(`Message Sent
                  ${info.response}`);
            }
        })
    }
  );
}
```

Here, we have modified the signature of the `sendMail` function to return a Promise. The implementation of this Promise essentially wraps the call to `this._transporter.sendMail` in a new Promise object, and calls either the `reject` callback, if there is an error, or the `resolve` callback if the e-mail was sent correctly.

By returning a Promise, we can now detect the result of the e-mail as follows:

```
gmailService.sendMail(
  "test2@test.com",
  "subject",
  "content").then( (msg) => {
    console.log(`sendMail result :(${msg})`);
} );
```

Here, we have simply used fluent syntax and called `then` on the Promise to execute a function after the `sendMail` function completes.

# Configuration settings

When writing code that is sending e-mails, it makes sense to use different settings for your e-mail services depending on the deployment environment. When developers are working with e-mail code, they should be able to use a local SMTP server, so that they can quickly verify e-mails that are sent to and from different e-mail accounts, without actually sending out e-mails. In a testing environment, testers should be able to specify which accounts they wish to use as the sending account, and what SMTP server to use.

In a **Factory Acceptance Testing** (**FAT**) environment, these e-mail settings may change once more, so that e-mails from any of the test environments do not affect the FAT environment. The final settings would, of course, be set for a production environment.

Changing settings depending on where the code is deployed is a common problem that is generally solved via a configuration file of some sort. Configuration values are read in from a file on disk, and these are used throughout the system. Different environments use different configuration files, and the system code does not need to be changed simply to change these settings.

In our code samples, there are currently two values that are good candidates for configuration settings. These are the SMTPS server connection string (which includes our username and password), and the from e-mail address that all e-mails are sent from.

These settings can easily be expressed as an interface, as follows:

```
export interface ISystemSettings {
  SmtpServerConnectionString: string;
  SmtpFromAddress: string;
}
```

Here, the `ISystemSettings` interface defines the two properties that will need to change when changing environments. The `SmtpServerConnectionString` will be used to connect to the SMTP server, and the `SmtpFromAddress` will be used to specify the originating address for all e-mails.

We can now modify our `GMailService` class to use this interface, as follows:

```
import * as nodemailer from 'nodemailer';
import { ISystemSettings } from './ISystemSettings';

export default class GMailService {
  private _transporter: nodemailer.Transporter;
  private _settings: ISystemSettings;

  constructor(settings: ISystemSettings) {
    this._settings = settings;
    this._transporter = nodemailer.createTransport(
        this._settings.SmtpServerConnectionString
    );
  }
  sendMail(to: string, subject: string, content: string)
  : Promise<void>
  {
    let options = {
      from: this._settings.SmtpFromAddress,
```

```
            to: to,
            subject: subject,
            text: content
        }
        // existing code
```

Here, we have imported the `ISystemSettings` interface, created a local variable named `_settings` to hold this information, and modified our `constructor` function to accept an instance of an object that implements the `ISystemSettings` interface.

This `ISystemSettings` interface is used in two places. Firstly, when we call the `nodemailer.createTransport` function, we use the `SmtpServerConnectionString` property. Secondly, when we construct the `options` object, we use the `SmtpFromAddress` property.

Using the `GMailService` class now means that we must provide both of these parameters when constructing the object, as follows:

```
let gmailService = new GMailService({
  SmtpServerConnectionString : 'smtp://localhost:1025',
  SmtpFromAddress : 'smtp_from@test.com'
});

gmailService.sendMail(
  "test2@test.com",
  "subject",
  "content").then( (msg) => {
    console.log(`sendMail result :(${msg})`);
} );
```

Here, we have constructed an object that conforms to the `ISystemSettings` interface, that is, it has both an `SmtpServerConnectionString` and an `SmtpFromAddress` property. This object is then passed into the `GMailService` constructor. Note how the setting for the `SmtpServerConnectionString` is now a local SMTP server, listening on port `1025`, and therefore does not require a fully-functional e-mail address with a username and password.

Running our code now will produce the following error:

```
error: Error: connect ECONNREFUSED 127.0.0.1:1025
```

This error is telling us that an e-mail could not be sent correctly, as there is no SMTP server running on localhost port `1025`.

# Using a local SMTP server

There are a number of local SMTP server implementations that we can use for development purposes. If you are working in a Windows environment, then take a look at **Papercut**. Papercut is a simple standalone executable that can be fired up to act as a local SMTP server. If you prefer Node-based solutions, then `smtp-sink` is a simple package that also provides a local SMTP server. Installation of `smtp-sink` is as simple as:

```
npm install -g smtp-sink
```

Once installed, it can be started by simply typing:

```
smtp-sink
```

The default options for `smtp-sink` will start an SMTP server on port `1025`, and a web server on port `1080`, where e-mails can be viewed by pointing a browser to `http://localhost:1080/emails`.

With `smtp-sink` running, our sample application will be able to send an e-mail to the local SMTP server.

# Object dependency

Our changes to the `GMailService` class have introduced an object dependency. In order for the `GMailService` class to function, it is now dependent on an instance of a class that provides the implementation of the `ISystemSettings` interface. `GmailService` is therefore dependent on `ISystemSettings`.

This dependency is actually a good thing. It means that we can provide different versions of classes that implement `ISystemSettings`, without making any changes to our `GmailService` code. This allows us to configure the environment that the `GMailService` runs within, whether in development, testing, FAT, or production.

It also allows us to test some boundary conditions. In other words, what happens if the SMTP server is not running, or not configured correctly ? Does the `GMailService` correctly report that an error has occurred? What actions does our code need to take when the service cannot send an e-mail correctly?

# Service Location

Our current implementation of the GMailService relies on the calling code to create an instance of the ISystemSettings interface, and pass this through in the constructor. When we write code that creates an instance of the GMailService, we are therefore forced to provide the ISystemSettings interface at the time of construction. This is a compile-time dependency. In other words, changing the instance of ISystemSettings requires changes to the source code, and then recompilation. It would be far better, however, if we set these options at runtime.

In order to accomplish this, the GMailService class needs to request the implementation of the ISystemSettings interface at runtime.

If a class itself requests the concrete object that is currently implementing an interface, then this process is called Service Location. In other words, the class itself is attempting to locate the service that is providing the implementation of an interface.

In order for this to work, however, we need a central registry that can answer the following question: "Give me the concrete class that is currently implementing this interface". This is the essence of the Service Location design pattern.

A service locator will need to do two things. Firstly, it needs to provide a mechanism to register implementations of a class against an interface. Secondly, it needs to provide a mechanism for a class to resolve the current implementation of an interface.

Let's implement a simple service locator, as follows:

```
export class ServiceLocator {
  static registeredClasses : any[] = new Array();
  public static register(
    interfaceName: string, instance: any)
  {
    this.registeredClasses[interfaceName] = instance;
  }
  public static resolve(
    interfaceName: string)
  {
    return this.registeredClasses[interfaceName];
  }
}
```

Here, we have defined a class named `ServiceLocator` that has a `register` function, a `resolve` function, and an internal array named `registeredClasses`. The `register` function takes two parameters–an `interfaceName` of type string, and a class instance of type `any`. The `register` function then simply adds the class instance to the `registeredClasses` array, using the `interfaceName` as a key.

The `resolve` function then returns the instance of the class based on the `interfaceName` that is passed in as a key.

This very simple `ServiceLocator` class can then be used as follows:

```
import { ServiceLocator } from './app/ServiceLocator';
import { ISystemSettings } from './app/ISystemSettings';

let smtpSinkSettings : ISystemSettings  = {
  SmtpServerConnectionString : 'smtp://localhost:1025',
  SmtpFromAddress : 'smtp_from@test.com'
};

ServiceLocator.register('ISystemSettings', smtpSinkSettings);

let currentSettings : ISystemSettings =
  ServiceLocator.resolve('ISystemSettings');

console.log(`current smtp from address :
  ${currentSettings.SmtpFromAddress}`);
```

Here, we have constructed an instance of an object to provide the two properties required by the `ISystemSettings` interface, and named it `smtpSinkSettings`. We then call the `register` function to register this object with the `'ISystemSettings'` key. Once an object has been registered, we can then call the `resolve` function of the `ServiceLocator` class to retrieve the currently registered object for this key. We then print the results to the console.

We can now update our `GMailService` class to use the `ServiceLocator` as follows:

```
export default class GMailService {
  private _transporter: nodemailer.Transporter;
  private _settings: ISystemSettings;

  constructor() {
    this._settings =
      ServiceLocator.resolve('ISystemSettings');
    this._transporter = nodemailer.createTransport(
      this._settings.SmtpServerConnectionString
    );
  }
```

```
        // existing code
```

Here, we have updated the `constructor` of the `GMailService` class to use the service locator pattern. Our internal `_settings` property still holds the instance of the `ISystemSettings` object, but the `GMailService` class itself is requesting the instance of the `ISystemSettings` interface, from the `ServiceLocator` class.

We can now construct an instance of the `GMailService`, as follows:

```
let gmailService = new GMailService();
```

Note how we have hidden the internal dependencies of the `GMailService` away from the user of the class by using the service locator pattern. The class itself requests the resources that it needs in order to perform its functions.

# Service Location anti-pattern

The ideas behind the service locator pattern were first introduced by Martin Fowler around 2004, in a blog titled *Inversion of Control Containers and the Dependency Injection pattern* (`http://martinfowler.com/articles/injection.html`). Since then, this pattern has been built and field-tested in a number of different languages and environments. In his book, *Dependency Injection in .NET*, Mark Seeman argues that the Service Location pattern is in fact an anti-pattern.

Mark's reasoning is that it is too easy to misunderstand the usage of a particular class when Service Location is used. In the extreme case, each function of a class may use different services, which means that the user of the class needs to read through the entire code-base to understand what dependencies a class has.

# Dependency injection

Mark Seeman argues that a better way of using Service Location is to list all of the dependencies of a class in the class constructor, and then hand over the process of constructing a class to something that understands how to resolve all of these dependencies. The process of constructing a class can be thought of as assembling a class instance, and filling in the available services.

In this way, when a class instance is requested, the dependencies of the class are resolved for us, and the assembler process simply gives us an instance of the class that works correctly. In other words, all of the dependencies that a class has are injected into the class by the assembler before the class is given to us.

This is the essence of the dependency injection design pattern.

# Building a dependency injector

In this section of the chapter, we will use the learnings we have gained in writing a service locator and combine this with TypeScript decorators in order to create a simple dependency injection framework. Before we do, however, let's discuss the problem of interface resolution.

## Interface resolution

As we know, the interface keyword is a TypeScript language construct that we use to define the shape of classes or objects. Wherever we need to define a custom type, and need the TypeScript compiler to ensure that properties and functions are available on an object, we use an interface. Interfaces are particularly handy when describing services, where any number of services could provide the same functionality to our code. In order to create a usable dependency injector, we need to be able to answer the question–"Given an interface, how do we obtain the service that is currently implementing it?".

In our current Service Location implementation, we are simply using string values to both `register` and `resolve` an interface, as shown in the two calls to the `ServiceLocator`:

```
ServiceLocator.register('ISystemSettings', smtpSinkSettings);
```

and

```
this._settings = ServiceLocator.resolve('ISystemSettings');
```

Unfortunately, using strings in these cases is something to be avoided. It is too easy to mistype the string itself, and to introduce runtime errors as a result. Again, we cannot use the interface name itself in this case, as interfaces are compiled away in the resulting JavaScript.

# Enum resolution

As we have seen in previous chapters, magic strings are a prime example where we can refactor our code to use an `enum`. As an example of this, let's consider a `ServiceLocator` built around an `enum`, as follows:

```
interface ISystemSettings {
}

interface IGMailService {
}

enum Interfaces {
  ISystemSettings,
  IGMailService
}

class ServiceLocatorTypes {
  public static register(
    interfaceName: Interfaces, instance: any) {}
  public static resolve(
    interfaceName: Interfaces) {}
}

ServiceLocatorTypes.register(Interfaces.ISystemSettings, {});

ServiceLocatorTypes.resolve(Interfaces.ISystemSettings);
```

Here, we start with two interfaces that we wish to use with our service locator, named `ISystemSettings` and `IGMailService`. Note that we have excluded the internal properties of these interfaces to simplify the code under discussion.

Next, we have defined an `enum` named `Interfaces`, which contains an entry for each of the interfaces that we wish to use. Our class definition (again without function implementations) for the `ServiceLocatorTypes` class simply shows the change to the `register` and `resolve` function signatures to use the `enum` named `Interfaces`.

The last two lines of this code snippet show how the `Interfaces` enum would be used when calling the `register` and `resolve` functions. By using an `enum` to store our interface names, we have eliminated the use of magic strings, and now have a central `enum` to describe all interfaces that will be used by the system.

## Class resolution

As an alternative to the enum implementation, we could also use special-purpose classes. This is best illustrated by looking at a code sample, as follows:

```
interface ISystemSettings { }
class IISystemSettings { }

interface IGMailService { }
class IIGMailService { }

class ServiceLocatorGeneric {
  public static register<T>(
    interfaceName: {new(): T;}, instance: any) {}
  public static resolve<T>(
    interfaceName: {new() : T}) {}
}

ServiceLocatorGeneric.register(IISystemSettings, {});

ServiceLocatorGeneric.resolve(IISystemSettings);
```

Here, we start with an interface named ISystemSettings, which is the interface that we wish to use with our service locator. We then define a class named IISystemSettings that has no functions or properties, but is only used for interface resolution. The naming of this class is important. By convention, we have named this class to be the same as the interface that we are describing, but have added an extra 'I' to the start of the name. This means that an interface named ITest would have a corresponding class named IITest, whose sole purpose is to provide a unique name (in place of an enum) when used with a dependency injection framework.

Our ServiceLocatorGeneric class has also modified the register and resolve function signatures to accommodate the use of a class name instead of an enum. We are now using generic syntax, and requiring that the interfaceName argument is of type { new() : T; }. Remember from our discussion on generics that, when using a function that needs to new() up an instance of a class when given a class name, it needs to be referenced by the class constructor.

This generic syntax then allows us to call the register and resolve functions by simply providing a class name, as seen in the last two lines of the code snippet. If we compare the enum style resolution to the class name resolution style, we end up with:

```
ServiceLocatorTypes.register(Interfaces.ISystemSettings, {});
```

As enum style resolution, and:

```
ServiceLocatorGeneric.register(IISystemSettings, {});
```

As class name resolution.

In the rest of this chapter, we will use class name resolution for a few reasons:

The definition of an interface and the class name used for interface resolution are defined in the same source file. With enum style resolution, interface definitions are scattered across the code base, but the enum instance is in a single file. This gives us two places to modify code when a new interface to be used in Service Location is needed.

Using class definitions means there is less code to type. While this may seem like a trivial reason, it also means that there is less code to read. As developers, we spend all day reading and writing code, and the less we need to read to get the message across, the better.

The double II interface naming standard is a visual trigger that indicates that this code is using Service Location. Whenever we read code, and see this double II prefix, we immediately know that Service Location is in play. This helps us distinguish between standard interfaces and Service Location based interfaces fairly quickly.

# Constructor injection

Earlier, we discussed the benefits and anti-patterns at play when using a service locator pattern, and picked up on Mark Seeman's ideas that dependency injection should only occur on class constructors. Our previous version of the GMailService class used Service Location within the constructor function as follows:

```
export default class GMailService {
  private _transporter: nodemailer.Transporter;
  private _settings: ISystemSettings;

  constructor() {
    this._settings =
      ServiceLocator.resolve('ISystemSettings');
    this._transporter = nodemailer.createTransport(
      this._settings.SmtpServerConnectionString
    );
  }
```

Here, we have specified a local `_settings` property of type `ISystemSettings`, and are using the `ServiceLocator` to resolve this internal property. The switch to a dependency injection pattern using constructor injection would be as follows:

```
export default class GMailServiceDi {
  private _transporter: nodemailer.Transporter;
  private _settings: ISystemSettings;

  constructor(_settings?: IISystemSettings) {
    this._transporter = nodemailer.createTransport(
      this._settings.SmtpServerConnectionString
    );
  }
```

There are a few points to note about this code. Firstly, we still have the private `_settings` property, which is typed to the `ISystemSettings` interface. This means that we can still refer to `this._settings` within the body of the code. Secondly, we have now included a parameter in our constructor–`_settings?: IISystemSettings`. We are therefore expecting the dependency injector to find the implementation of the `ISystemSettings` interface, or more correctly the class that is registered against the `IISystemSettings` key, and inject this into our class so that the private `_settings` property contains this implementation.

For our dependency injector to work, the name of the constructor parameter, and the name of the private property must both be the same.

Let's take a look at what the result of the constructor injection would look like, after the class itself has been processed by the dependency injector framework, as follows:

```
export default class GMailServiceDi {
  private _transporter: nodemailer.Transporter;
  // private _settings: ISystemSettings;
  get _settings() : ISystemSettings {
    return ServiceLocatorGeneric.resolve(IISystemSettings);
  }

  constructor(_settings?: IISystemSettings) {
    this._transporter = nodemailer.createTransport(
      this._settings.SmtpServerConnectionString
    );
  }
}
```

Here, we have an example of what the class should look like after injection. The `private _settings` property has been replaced by a `get` function of the same name, that is, `get _settings()`. This function internally calls our `ServiceLocator` to resolve the interface. By creating a simple `get` function, we have essentially injected our dependency.

# Decorator injection

In a previous chapter, we discussed the use of decorators, and how they are invoked when a class is defined. Decorators are not invoked when a class is instantiated, so their usage is limited to interrogating and manipulating class definitions. Decorators, as we know, can be applied to classes, properties, functions, and parameters. Let's build a simple class decorator, and see what information it gives us about a class.

Remember that there are three things about a class that we are interested in during this exercise. Firstly, we need to find the definition of the class constructor. Once we know what the constructor looks like, we need to find the list of parameters that the constructor uses. Each of these parameters will then become getters that use our service locator to resolve dependencies. The last piece of information we will need to find is the type that each constructor parameter is expecting. Once we have this information, we can build a simple getter function to return the correct type within our decorator.

# Using a class definition

Let's put together a simple class decorator, and see what information we can deduce from the class. Our decorator is as follows:

```
export function ConstructorInject(classDefinition: Function) {
  console.log(`classDefinition:`);
  console.log(`================`);
  console.log(`${classDefinition}`);
  console.log(`================`);
}
```

Here, we are simply logging the value of the `classDefinition` argument to the console.

Note that, to use decorators, our `tsconfig.json` file must include the options that turn on decorator functionality, as follows:

```
"experimentalDecorators": true,
"emitDecoratorMetadata": true
```

Let's now decorate our `GMailServiceDi` class with this decorator, and see what happens:

```
import { ConstructorInject } from './ConstructorInject';

@ConstructorInject
export default class GMailServiceDi {
  private _transporter: nodemailer.Transporter;
  private _settings: ISystemSettings;
  constructor(_settings?: IISystemSettings) {
  }
}
```

Here, we have imported our `ConstructorInject` decorator, and applied it to our `GmailServiceDi` class. Note that, for the sake of brevity, we have removed the body of the constructor code that configures the `_transporter` property. If we now create an instance of this class as follows:

```
import GMailServiceDi from './app/GMailServiceDi';
var gmailDi = new GMailServiceDi();
```

We would generate the following console output from our `ConstructorInject` decorator:

```
classDefinition:
================
class GMailServiceDi {
  constructor(_settings) {
  }
}
================
```

As we can see, the `classDefinition` parameter is populated with the full class definition. This definition, however, is not the TypeScript definition of our class, but is the JavaScript definition of our class. This means that we have lost the type information on each of our constructor parameters, as this information is compiled away. What we do have, however, is the name of the properties that this class uses in its constructor.

> The generated JavaScript will always include the constructor as the first function. If we add any other function at the top of the class definition, and write the constructor at the bottom of the class definition, TypeScript will always move the constructor function to the top of the class definition.

# Parsing constructor parameters

By having access to the full class definition, we can use simple string searching to find the properties of the class constructor. If we find the first open bracket character `'('`, and the next closed bracket character `')'`, we can extract a string that contains all of our constructor parameter names, as follows:

```
let firstIdx = classDefinition.toString().indexOf('(') + 1;
let lastIdx = classDefinition.toString().indexOf(')');
let arr = classDefinition.toString().substr(
  firstIdx, lastIdx - firstIdx);

console.log(`class parameters :`);
console.log(`${arr}`);
console.log(`==================`);
```

The output of this code is as follows:

```
=================
class parameters :
_settings
==================
```

We can test this code by inserting another parameter in our constructor, and checking the output. So if the `GmailServiceDi` class had two arguments, as follows:

```
constructor(_settings?: IISystemSettings, testParameter?: string) {
}
```

Then the parsing of the constructor would produce the following:

```
class parameters :
_settings, testParameter
==================
```

So by some simple string extrapolation, we are able to find out what property names are required by this class. We can then easily parse this array as follows:

```
let splitArr = arr.split(', ');

for (let paramName of splitArr) {
  console.log(`found parameter named : ${paramName}`);
}
```

Here, we are creating an array named `splitArray` from the string containing our parameter names, and logging each entry to the console. The output of this would be as follows:

```
found parameter named : _settings
found parameter named : testParameter
```

So we now have an array that specifies what the parameter names are for our constructor function.

# Finding parameter types

Now that we know what each of our constructor parameter names are, we need to match these with a parameter type. In order to do this, we will need to make use of the reflect-metadata package, as follows:

```
let parameterTypeArray =
  Reflect.getMetadata("design:paramtypes", classDefinition);
console.log(`parameterTypeArray:`);
console.log(`===================`);
console.log(`${parameterTypeArray}`);
console.log(`===================`);

for (let type of parameterTypeArray) {
  console.log(`found type : ${type.name}`);
}
```

Here, we are calling the `Reflect.getMetadata` function, and using the `"design:paramtypes"` argument to extract an array from the class definition. We then print this array to the console, and then loop through the array to print the `name` property of each element in the `"design:paramtypes"` array. The output of this code is as follows:

```
parameterTypeArray:
===================
class IISystemSettings {
},function String() { [native code] }
===================
found type : IISystemSettings
found type : String
```

This type information is exactly what we need to build a constructor injector. Note that the first parameter, which we know has the name `_settings`, is of type `IISystemSettings`. The second parameter, which is named `testParameter`, is of type `String`.

Before we continue, let's remove the `testParameter` parameter, which we were only using in a test case, in order to prove that we can parse more than one parameter.

# Injecting properties

We can now combine the results of both arrays to match the parameter name with the type name, as follows:

```
for (let i = 0; i < splitArr.length; i++) {
  let propertyName = splitArr[i];
  let typeName = parameterTypeArray[i];

  console.log(`
    parameterName : ${propertyName}
    is of type    : ${typeName.name}
  `);
}
```

Here, we are looping through the `splitArr` array (which contains our parameter names), and using the same index on the `parameterTypeArray` to match property names with type names. The result is as follows:

```
parameterName : _settings
is of type    : IISystemSettings

parameterName : testParameter
is of type    : String
```

With this information at hand, we can now use JavaScript to inject the property that we require, as follows:

```
Object.defineProperty(classDefinition.prototype, propertyName, {
  get : function() {
    return ServiceLocatorGeneric.resolve(
        eval(typeName)
    );
  }

});
```

Here, we are using the `Object.defineProperty` function that JavaScript provides to create a property at runtime and attach it to the definition of our class. The `defineProperty` function takes three parameters. The first parameter is the prototype of the class to be modified. The second parameter is the `propertyName` itself, and the third parameter is the definition of the property. Our property definition is a simple getter function that then calls the `ServiceLocatorGeneric.resolve` function, passing in the `typeName`. Note how we have called the `eval` function, passing it the `typeName` that we retrieved from our `parameterTypeArray`. This step is necessary in order to send the class definition to the service locator instead of a simple string.

# Using dependency injection

Now that we are injecting property functions through our `ConstructorInjector` decorator, we can now use our dependency injector framework as follows:

```
import GMailServiceDi from './app/GMailServiceDi';
import { ServiceLocatorGeneric } from './app/ServiceLocator';
import { IISystemSettings } from './app/ISystemSettings';

ServiceLocatorGeneric.register(IISystemSettings, {
  SmtpServerConnectionString : 'smtp://localhost:1025',
  SmtpFromAddress : 'smtp_from@test.com'
});

var gmailDi = new GMailServiceDi();

gmailDi.sendMail("test@test.com", "testsubject", "testContent"
).then( (msg) => {
   console.log(`sendMail returned : ${msg}`);
} ).catch( (err) => {
   console.log(`sendMail returned : ${err}`);
});
```

After importing the various modules into our sample, we call `ServiceLocatorGeneric.register` to register the object that is providing the `IISystemSettings` interface. We then simply create an instance of the `GmailServiceDi` class, with no parameters. At this stage, our dependency injector has done all of the work for us, and has injected the correct properties for immediate use.

Note how simple this object constructor is, that is, `new GMailServiceDi()`. It looks just like any other normal instantiation of an object. Once the class has been instantiated, we can call the `sendMail` function as we did before.

# Recursive injection

As a final test of our dependency injection framework, let's now inject the `GmailServiceDi` class into another class. This means that our new class will be dependent on the `IGmailServiceDi` interface, which is itself dependent on the `ISystemSettings` interface. This is an example of a recursive dependency tree.

We start by defining an interface for the `GmailServiceDi` class itself, as follows:

```
export interface IGMailServiceDi {
  sendMail(to: string, subject: string, content: string)
  : Promise<void>;
}

export class IIGMailServiceDi { }
```

Here, we have taken the definition of the `sendMail` function, which returns a Promise, and created an interface named `IGMailServiceDi`. We have also created the class that will be used as a type lookup by our dependency injection framework, named `IIGMailServiceDi`.

With these interfaces in place, we can create a class that is dependent on the `IGMailServiceDi` interface, as follows:

```
@ConstructorInject
class MailSender {
  private gMailService : IGMailServiceDi;
  constructor(gMailService?: IIGMailServiceDi) {}
  async sendWelcomeMail(to: string) {
    await(this.gMailService.sendMail(to, "welcome", ""));
  }
}
```

Here, we have created a class named `MailSender`, and used the `ConstructorInject` decorator to decorate the class. Our class has a private property named `gMailService`, which is of type `IGMailServiceDi`. This is the property that will be created by our dependency injection framework.

The constructor function simply uses the IIGMailService class to indicate that the private gMailService property should be injected. The MailSender class has a sendWelcomeMail function that uses an async await pattern to call the GmailServiceDi sendMail function.

To test this class, we simply need to create a new instance, and call the sendWelcomeMail function as follows:

```
let mailSender = new MailSender();
mailSender.sendWelcomeMail("test@test.com");
```

The output of this code is as follows:

```
ServiceLocator resolving : IIGMailServiceDi
ServiceLocator resolving : IISystemSettings
Message Sent 250
```

Here, we can see that the dependency injection framework is calling the ServiceLocator to resolve IIGMailServiceDi. This is during the constructor of the MailSender class. As the GmailServiceDi class is dependent on the ISystemSettings interface, a second call is made to resolve IISystemSettings.

# Summary

In this chapter, we discussed the service locator and dependency injection design patterns. We started by creating a class to send e-mails, and then created our own simple service locator that could resolve instances of classes given a string name. We then moved to a more resolute Service Location pattern that used class names instead of magic strings as the key to both registering and resolving instances of classes. We then discussed the pitfalls of the service locator pattern, and implemented a dependency injection framework using decorators.

In our next chapter, we will take a look at building applications that combine a web server such as Node and Express with our TypeScript-compatible frameworks, starting with Angular 2.

# 13
# Building Applications

Up until this point, we have been looking at various features of the TypeScript language, and have worked with some of the most popular TypeScript frameworks available. We have explored client-side frameworks such as Angular, Aurelia, React, and Backbone, as well as server-side frameworks such as Node and Express. In this chapter, we will combine the two, and look at how to serve a web application from Express for each of these frameworks. We will also explore how to interact between client-side and server-side code using REST endpoints.

In general, the server-side of an application is responsible for two things. Firstly, it will respond to an initial web page request, compile the HTML page, and send this page to the browser. Once the page is parsed by the browser, it may request additional resources from the server, including JavaScript files, CSS files, images, and the like. This process is called serving requests, and it is standard web technology.

The second major responsibility of any server-side application is to handle data interactions. This may take the form of additional HTTP `GET` requests, in order to serve data to the web page, or it may be in the form of HTTP `POST` requests, where the web server will need to process a message sent to it. In this chapter, we will build a simple RESTful API that will provide both `GET` and `POST` functionality. We will implement an Express route that will handle a `GET` request and return a JSON response, as well as a `POST` handler to receive and process a JSON `POST` request.

Once our server-side REST endpoints are in place, we will then explore the different methods that each framework uses to issue and consume these `GET` and `POST` requests. In any application there will come a time where a user will need to enter data into a form on a page, and our application will need to retrieve these values to generate a `POST` request. This process is called data binding. We will see how each framework accomplishes data binding in a slightly different manner.

To be able to compare the implementation of these techniques across our frameworks, we will implement a navigation bar, and a login page with each framework. The navigation bar will issue a `GET` request to our web server for a JSON data packet that will drive the rendering of the navigation buttons. In a similar manner, the login page will issue a `POST` request to our web server.

In this chapter, we will be covering following topics:

- The UI Experience
- Serving applications from Node
- Processing JSON on the server side
- Using forms based input
- Data binding
- Posting data to our server

Each of these topics will be implemented in our TypeScript compatible frameworks:

- Aurelia
- Angular 2, and
- React

Before we delve into these techniques, however, let's take a few moments to talk about web page design.

# The UI experience

At the start of every web-based project, the requirements around the UI start to be discussed. What will the application look like, what style will it use, and how will our users interact with the system? UI design is a specialist area, which can either make or break an otherwise good website. Likewise, the UI experience is all about ease of use, intuition, and simple workflow. As such, many companies employ specialist teams to either design the UI for look and feel, or to design the UI experience, including workflow. In general, the output of this exercise is a set of HTML pages and CSS files.

There will come a time, however, where every developer needs to put together a UI – so understanding the process and working with tools that are designed for design is a necessary step of building applications.

In this chapter, we will be using Bootstrap to provide the default styles for our pages, and **Brackets** for the design tools. Go ahead and install Bootstrap using npm as per usual:

```
npm init
npm install bootstrap --save
```

# Using Brackets

When working with HTML and CSS during the design phase, we are constantly editing and tweaking both the HTML files and the CSS stylesheet to get our pages to look good. One of the best tools for this job is an editor named Brackets. Brackets is an open source editor that is specifically targeted to web designers and frontend developers. It has many features that are geared around quick editing of HTML and CSS elements, including live preview, right-click to edit CSS, color pickers, and more. One of the handiest features, however, is live preview.

In live preview mode, a separate browser window is opened, and any changes made to your HTML or CSS files will automatically be refreshed within the browser. Having instant feedback when applying CSS styles or editing HTML is an incredible time saver. Brackets with a live preview window is shown in the following screenshot:

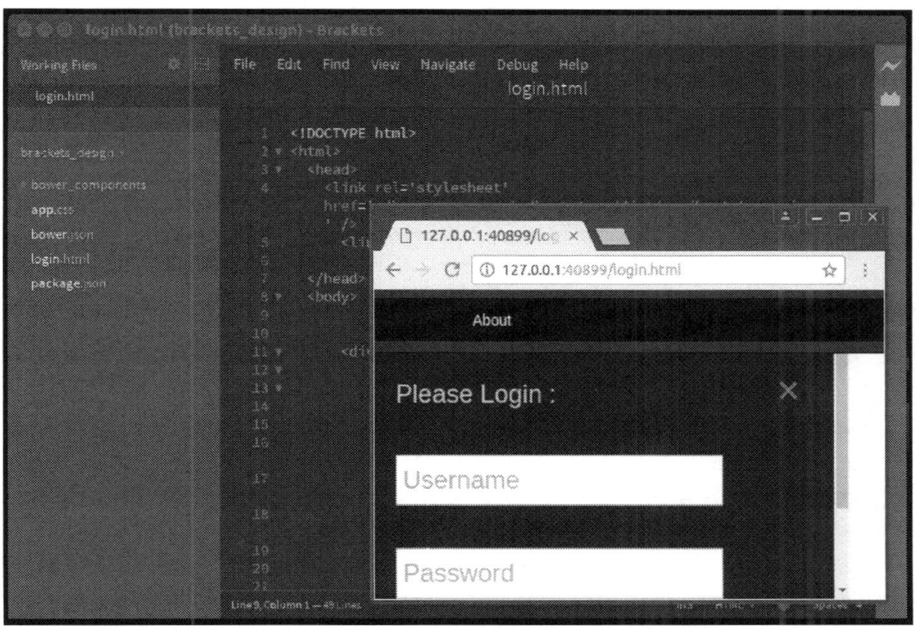


Brackets editor with a live preview browser window

Installing Brackets is as simple as downloading the installer from its website, `brackets.io`, and executing it. Once installed, we can enhance the default functionality through the use of Brackets extensions. Brackets has a really slick and simple extension manager, which helps to find and install available extensions. Brackets will also automatically notify us when updates to these extensions are available.

To install an extension, click on **File** | **Extension Manager**, or click on the lego block icon on the right-hand side vertical sidebar. We will be using a single extension named Emmet, but there are literally hundreds of available Brackets extensions. In the search bar, type `Emmet`, and then click on the **Install** button for the **Emmet** extension (authored by Sergey Chikuyonok), as shown in the following screenshot:

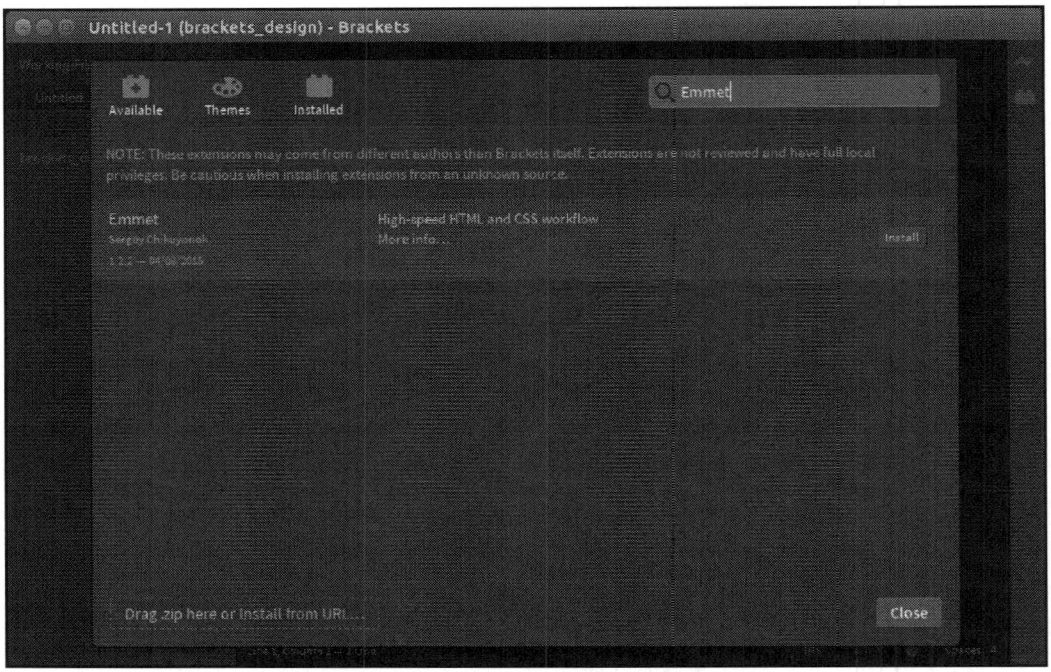


Brackets extension dialog

Brackets does not have the concept of a project per se, but instead just works off a root folder. Let's create a new folder on our filesystem, and then open this folder in Brackets using **File** | **Open Folder**.

# Using Emmet

Let's now create a simple HTML page, by using **File | New**, or simply *Ctrl+N*. Instead of writing our HTML file by hand, we will use Emmet to generate our HTML. Type in the following Emmet string:

```
html>head+body>h3{index.html}+div#content
```

Now hit *Ctrl+Alt+Enter*, or from the **File** menu, select **Emmet | Expand Abbreviation**.

Voila ! Emmet has generated the following HTML in a millisecond – not bad for one line of code:

```
<html>
<head></head>
<body>
  <h3>index.html</h3>
  <div id="content"></div>
</body>
</html>
```

Hit *Ctrl+S* to save the file, and enter `index.html` as the filename.

> Only once we have saved the file, does Brackets start to do syntax highlighting based on the file extension.

Let's take a closer look at the Emmet abbreviation string that we entered earlier. Emmet uses the > character to create a child, and the + character to denote a sibling. If we use `{ }` next to an element, then this means that the element's content will be set to the value provided inside the braces. So the Emmet string that we entered previously said–"Create an `html` tag with a child `head` tag. Then create another child tag of `html` named `body`. Within this `body` tag, create an `h3` tag with the content `index.html`, and then create a sibling `div` tag with the `id` of `content`". Head over to the Emmet website (`emmet.io`) for further documentation, and remember to keep a cheat-sheet handy (`docs.emmet.io.cheat-sheet`) when you are learning and working with Emmet string shortcuts.

Let's now add a script tag to our `index.html` file. Move your cursor in between the `<head></head>` tags, and type the following Emmet string:

```
link
```

Now hit Ctrl+Alt+Enter to have Emmet generate a full `<link>` tag, and conveniently place our cursor between the quotes ready for the filename. The filename that we are looking for is `bootstrap-min.css`. Go ahead and start by typing `./`. Note how Brackets understands that you are looking for a CSS file, and will automatically start providing Intellisense, or code-completion options to help you find the file, as follows:

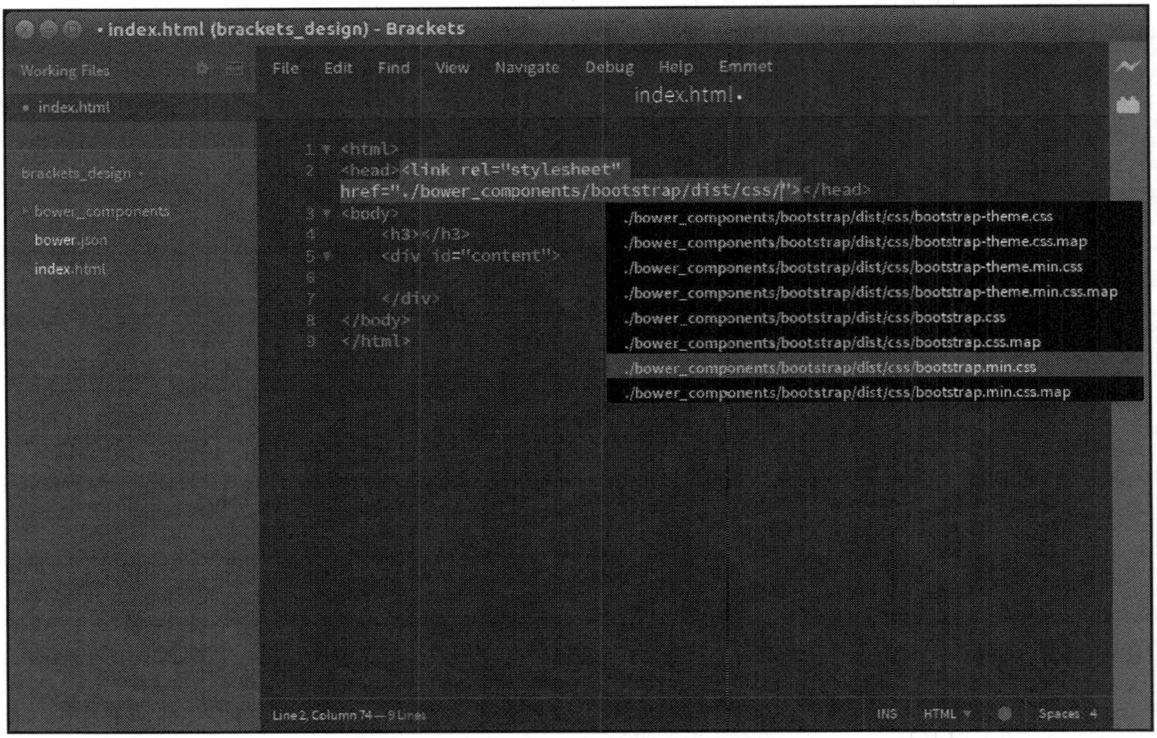


Brackets showing automatic file selection for a script file

With our `bootstrap.min.css` file included, we can start to flesh out the content of our HMTL page. At the beginning of the `<body>` tag, we can create a Bootstrap `navbar` with the following Emmet string:

```
nav.navbar.navbar-default.navbar-inverse
```

Which will generate the following HTML:

```
<nav class="navbar navbar-default navbar-inverse">
</nav>
```

Within this <nav> tag, we can create a <div> element with the class container-fluid as follows:

```
div.container-fluid
```

And within this generated <div>, an <a> element with the class navbar-brand as follows:

```
a.navbar-brand{Home}
```

Under this <a> element, we can create a list element as follows:

```
ul.nav.navbar-nav>li.nav-item.nav-link.active>a{About}
```

These Emmet commands will create the following HTML:

```
<nav class="navbar navbar-default navbar-inverse">
  <div class="container-fluid">
    <a href="" class="navbar-brand">Home</a>
    <ul class="nav navbar-nav">
      <li class="nav-item nav-link active">
        <a href="">About</a></li>
    </ul>
  </div>
</nav>
```

# Creating a login panel

With a navigation bar in place, let's now create a login panel that uses the same overlay CSS technique that we have used in our previous chapters. The HTML for this panel is as follows:

```
<div id="sideNav" class="login_sidenav">
  <form>
    <div class="container">
      <a href="#" class="closebtn" >&times;</a>
      <div class="row">Please Login :</div>
      <div class="row">
        <input class="sidenav-input"
        type="text" placeholder="Username">
      </div>
      <div class="row">
        <input class="sidenav-input" type="password"
         placeholder="Password">
      </div>
      <div class="row">
        <button class="btn btn-primary
```

```
            btn-lg">Login</button>
          </div>

        </div>
      </form>
    </div>
```

Here, we have created a `<div>` element with the `id` of `"sideNav"`, and a CSS class of `login_sidenav`. We then define a `<form>` element, with an `<input>` element for a `Username` and `password`, along with a `Login` button.

The corresponding CSS styles (defined in `app.css`) are as follows:

```
.login_sidenav {
  height: 100%; /* 100% Full-height */
  width: 450px; /* 0 width - change this with JavaScript */
  position: fixed; /* Stay in place */
  background-color: #111; /* Black*/
  overflow-x: hidden; /* Disable horizontal scroll */
  padding-top: 60px; /* Place content 60px from the top */
  color: lightgray;
}

.login_sidenav .row {
  padding: 20px;
  font-size: 24px;
}

.sidenav-input {
  padding: 5px;
  font-size: 24px;
  color: midnightblue;
}

.login_sidenav .closebtn {
  position: absolute;
  top: 60px;
  right: 25px;
  font-size: 36px;
  margin-left: 50px;
}

.login_sidenav a:hover, .offcanvas a:focus{
  color: #f1f1f1;
}

.login_sidenav a {
  padding: 8px 8px 8px 32px;
```

```
        text-decoration: none;
        font-size: 25px;
        color: #818181;
        display: block;
        transition: 0.3s
    }
```

This CSS, combined with our HTML page, results in the following screen:

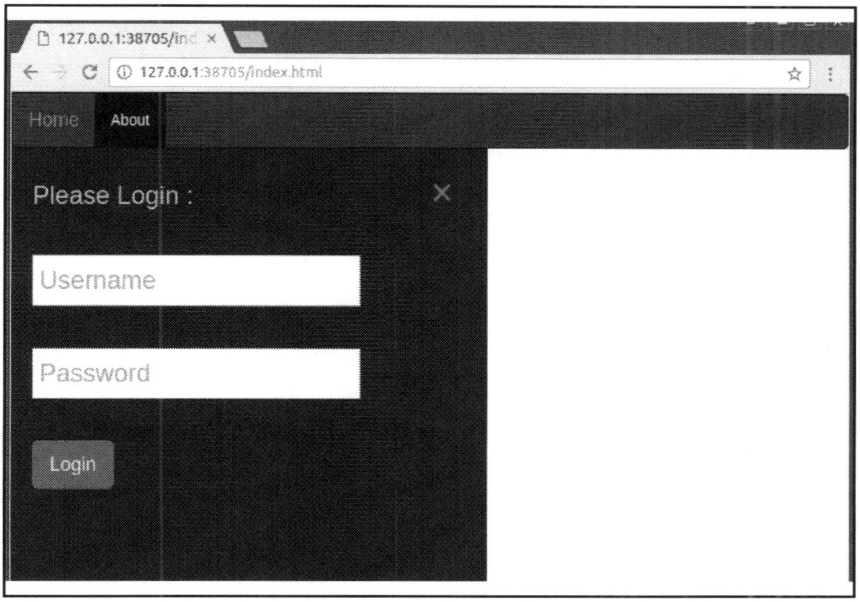


Our Brackets designed navigation bar and login screen.

Here, we can see that we have a navigation bar at the top of the page, and then a sidebar overlay that contains a login form. This form has two input elements, which are Username and Password, as well as a **Login** button.

With this HTML and CSS in place, we can use Brackets to quickly and easily create new styles, or tweak this layout to our hearts content. We have not invested a great deal of time or effort in creating these layouts either – we have simply been tweaking HTML and CSS. This design phase of a project can therefore be accomplished very quickly and only relies on minimal HTML and CSS knowledge. With template screens like these, we can also start conversations with customers to determine if the look and feel of the site is what is expected, without having to build an entire application.

Now that we have an initial design in place, we can start to implement these screens using our frameworks.

# An Aurelia website

In this section of the chapter, we will build an Aurelia application that is hosted by Node and Express. We will also implement the login screen using Aurelia, and work through sending and receiving JSON data from the Node website to the Aurelia application. First up, let's get Node and Aurelia working together.

To create our Aurelia application, we simply create a new directory on disk, change to this directory, and run the Aurelia command line interface to create an Aurelia environment:

```
mkdir node_aurelia
cd node_aurelia
au new .
```

At this stage, we can start up an Aurelia environment by simply typing `au run`, and pointing our browser at `http://localhost:9000`.

> At the time of writing, Aurelia was still using `typings` in order to register and download type information for the Aurelia compilation step. This means that Aurelia declaration files will be downloaded into the `typings` directory, and registered in the `typings.json` file. Aurelia has not switched to the updated `npm @types` declaration file syntax.

# Node and Aurelia compilation

The Aurelia environment will use TypeScript to compile all of our `.ts` files, and package them for use in the `app-bundle.js` file in the `scripts` directory. Note, however, that it will not compile any files in the root directory. If we create a `main.ts` file at the project root, Aurelia will not generate any `.js` files for this `main.ts` file, as it is explicitly looking for application files in the `app` directory. In order to do this, then, we will need to run `tsc` from the root directory.

Before we do this, however, we must update the `tsconfig.json` file to exclude the `aurelia_project` directory and the `custom_typings` as follows:

```
"exclude": [
  "node_modules",
  "aurelia_project"
],
```

Failing to do so will corrupt the Aurelia build process. If you run `tsc` without this change to `tsconfig.json`, you will receive numerous errors, as follows:

```
aurelia_project/generators/attribute.ts(2,52):
  error TS2307: Cannot find module 'aurelia-cli'.
aurelia_project/generators/binding-behavior.ts(2,52):
  error TS2307: Cannot find module 'aurelia-cli'.
aurelia_project/generators/element.ts(2,52):
  error TS2307: Cannot find module 'aurelia-cli'.
```

Make sure that you update the `tsconfig.json` file before running `tsc` from the command line.

Remember that to compile our Aurelia code, we need to issue the Aurelia build command:

```
au build
```

And to compile our Node modules, we need to issue the TypeScript build command:

```
tsc
```

# Serving the Aurelia application

We can now focus on the task of creating a Node application that will serve our Aurelia pages. Let's go ahead and create a simple Node application by creating a file named `main.ts` in the project root directory. This application will listen on port `3000`, just to ensure that we can run Node from the same project root directory as Aurelia, as follows:

```
import * as express from 'express';
let app = express();

app.listen(3000, () => {
  console.log(`express listening on port 3000`);
});
```

Here, we are simply creating a new Express application and listening on port `3000`. In order to compile and run this app, we will need to install Express, and also the various declaration files needed by TypeScript, as follows:

```
npm install --save express
typings install --save dt~express
typings install --save dt~serve-static
typings install --save dt~express-serve-static-core
typings install --save dt~mime
```

Before we compile this Express app, we also need to switch to `commonjs` module compilation. Edit the `tsconfig.json` file, and change the `module` value as follows:

```
"module": "commonjs",
```

With these settings in place, we can issue the `node main` command from the command line at the root of the project, and ensure that Express is running:

```
express listening on port 3000
```

# Aurelia pages in Node

We can now flesh out our Node implementation so that it serves up a page to include all Aurelia components, and run our Aurelia application. Aurelia already has an `index.html` page included in the project root directory, which is as follows:

```
<!DOCTYPE html>
<html>
  <head>
    <meta charset="utf-8">
    <title>Aurelia</title>
  </head>

  <body aurelia-app="main">
    <script src="scripts/vendor-bundle.js"
    data-main="aurelia-bootstrapper"></script>
  </body>
</html>
```

All we need to do is to generate this page from our Express application. In order to do this, we will need a few things. Firstly, we need a route object so that Express understands what to do when an HTTP `GET` request is sent through. Secondly, we will need to render a view using **Handlebars**, and thirdly, we will need to serve the Aurelia files themselves.

Let's start with a simple route object, in the `routes` directory, named `index.ts`, as follows:

```
import * as express from 'express';
var router = express.Router();

router.get('/', (req, res, next) => {

  res.render('index',
    { title: 'ExpressAurelia'
    }
  );
});

export { router } ;
```

This Express router is simply processing a `GET` request, and rendering the `'index'` page with the title of `ExpressAurelia`.

We can now create the corresponding views in the `views` directory, starting with `layout.hbs` to cover the layout for all pages, as follows:

```
<!DOCTYPE html>
<html>
<head>
<link rel='stylesheet'
  href='../node_modules/bootstrap/dist/css/bootstrap.min.css' />
<link rel='stylesheet'
  href='../css/app.css' />
<script src="../node_modules/underscore/
  underscore-min.js"></script>
<title>{{title}}</title>
</head>

  {{{body}}}

</html>
```

This `layout.hbs` Handlebars template is very simple, and it includes the `bootstrap.min.css` file, an `app.css` file, and a script link to `underscore.min.js`. As we have used Bootstrap in our Brackets design, we will need to include the Bootstrap CSS file for use by our HTML. We have also included an `app.css` file in the `/css` directory, where we can include specific application styles. The last link is to Underscore, which we will use later on. To install these files into our application, we simply need to call the following:

```
npm install bootstrap --save
npm install underscore --save
```

Our `index.hbs` file is as follows:

```
<body aurelia-app="main">
  <script src="scripts/vendor-bundle.js"
    data-main="aurelia-bootstrapper"></script>
</body>
```

Note that Aurelia uses a `<script>` tag within the `<body>` tag to bootstrap our Aurelia application. This is why our `layout.hbs` file did not include a `<body>` tag, but instead relies on each individual Handlebars template to generate this `<body>` tag.

Before we fire up our application, let's install Handlebars as follows:

```
npm install hbs --save
```

With our views and routes in place, we can update our `main.ts` file to register Handlebars, and serve the required Aurelia directories as follows:

```
import * as express from 'express';
import * as Index from './routes/index';
import * as path from 'path';

let app = express();

app.set('views', path.join(__dirname, 'views'));
app.set('view engine', 'hbs');

app.use('/', Index.router);

app.use('/scripts',  express.static(__dirname + '/scripts'));
app.use('/node_modules',
  express.static(__dirname + '/node_modules'));
app.use('/css',  express.static(__dirname + '/css'));

app.listen(3000, () => {
  console.log(`express listening on port 3000`);
});
```

Here, our `main.ts` file starts by importing the `'express'` and `'path'` modules, as well as our `'routes/index'` module. After creating the Express application, we call the `set` function on the `app` instance. The first call registers the `'views'` subdirectory for use with Handlebars, and the second call registers Handlebars as the rendering engine, as we have seen in earlier chapters.

We then register our router as a `GET` handler for the `'/'` base directory.

> The last three calls to the `app.use` function register the `/scripts`, `/node_modules`, and `/css` directories as static content. These calls will make any files within these directories available for serving by the application. The `/scripts` directory is where Aurelia generates the `vendor-bundle.js` file as a result of the Aurelia compilation step. Any directory that is serving static content must be registered in the same way before Express will serve this content.

With this simple configuration in place, we can start our Express application by running `node main` from the command line, and then browse to `http://localhost:3000`. This will start up and serve our Aurelia application.

So far, so good. We have successfully integrated Aurelia and Express, and are now serving our Aurelia application and all relevant CSS and associated files from Express.

# Aurelia components

Now that we have the basic Aurelia application being served by Express, we can build the necessary components in order to render our HTML page. Remember that the HTML and CSS for this page is according to the design output from our Brackets exercise. Our Aurelia `App` component will serve as our application's main controller, and will render our navigation bar. We will then create a new login component that will be responsible for the login panel.

Our `app.ts` file is as follows:

```
interface IMenuItem {
  ButtonName: string;
}

export class App {
  message = 'Hello World!';
  menuItems: IMenuItem[] = [
    {ButtonName : 'About'},
    {ButtonName : 'Contact Us'}
  ];
}
```

Here, we start with an interface named `IMenuItem` that has a single property named `ButtonName`. Our `App` class creates an array of these `IMenuItems`, in a property named `menuItems`. This property will be used to create a series of buttons within the navigation panel. Our `app.html` can now render these menu items as follows:

```
<template>

<nav class="navbar navbar-default
  navbar-fixed-top navbar-inverse">
    <div class="container-fluid">
      <a class="navbar-brand">Home</a>
      <ul class="nav navbar-nav">
        <li repeat.for="item of menuItems"
          class="nav-item nav-link active">

        <a href="#">${item.ButtonName}</a></li>
      </ul>
    </div>
</nav>

</template>
```

This Aurelia template for the `App` class is pretty much a copy and paste of the original Brackets HMTL that contains the navigation bar. The only change to the original HTML is to inject a `repeat.for` attribute to loop through the `menuItems` array, and render a new `<a href>` tag for each item in the array. With these simple updates in place, our page will now render a Bootstrap navigation bar.

# Processing JSON

Let's now update our Aurelia application so that the navigation buttons that we render in the navigation panel are not hard-coded within the `App` class, but are instead generated from a JSON array that is served from our Express application. In a typical large-scale web application, there will be many times that the web server will be responsible for generating content that the page must render. Our navigation items may be held within a database, for example, so that the website can change dynamically. In order to do this, the Aurelia application needs to request a JSON array from the Express application, and inject these values into the `App.menuItems` property.

As a start, let's ensure that our Express application serves up the JSON array when a `GET` request is made to the REST endpoint at `/menuitems`. This is easily accomplished by creating a new route in our `routes/index.ts` file as follows:

```
router.get('/menuitems', (req, res, next) => {
  res.json({ menuItems : [
    { ButtonName : 'About'},
    { ButtonName : 'Contact'},
    { ButtonName : 'Login'}
  ] });
});
```

Here, we simply register another `get` HTTP handler by calling `router.get`. The first parameter is the REST endpoint that we wish to expose, which in this case is `'/menuitems'`. Within the body of this handler, we simply call `res.json` with the JSON that we wish to return. We can test this handler by pointing our browser to `http://localhost:3000/menuitems`, which will return this simple JSON string.

With our REST endpoint in place, we can now modify our Aurelia `App` class to request this JSON as part of the `constructor`, and set the `menuItems` property once a response has been received. Our changes to `app.ts` are as follows:

```
import {HttpClient} from 'aurelia-http-client';

interface IMenuItem {
  ButtonName: string;
}

export class App {
  message = 'Hello World!';
  menuItems: IMenuItem[] = [];
  constructor() {
    let client = new HttpClient();

    client.get('/menuitems')
      .then((data) => {
        console.log(`data: ${data.response}`);
        let jsonResponse = JSON.parse(data.response);
        this.menuItems = jsonResponse.menuItems;
      });
  }
}
```

We start by importing the `HttpClient` module from `'aurelia-http-client'`. This module gives us access to Aurelia's `HttpClient` class that we will use as a client for our REST endpoints. Note that we have removed the hard-coded array items for the property `menuItems`, and have replaced it with an empty array.

Our `constructor` function creates an instance of the `HttpClient` class, named `client`, and then calls the `get` function with the name of our REST endpoint (`/menuitems`). The `HttpClient` class gives us a fluent style interface that we can use to attach a `then` function, which will be called once the response is received. Remember that calls back to a web server are asynchronous in nature. Within this `then` function, we are parsing the `response` property of the `data` object into a valid JSON object, and are then setting our `menuItems` property to the value of the `menuItems` array that was returned by the REST endpoint. This is all that is needed to process a RESTful `GET` request within an Aurelia class.

Before we attempt to compile our Aurelia application, we will need to install the `aurelia-http-client` module, and register it with Aurelia for use. To install this module, we simply use `npm` as usual:

```
npm install aurelia-http-client --save
```

Registration with Aurelia is accomplished by modifying the `aurelia_project/aurelia.json` file, and adding an entry for the `aurelia-http-client` in the dependencies array as follows:

```
"dependencies": [
  "aurelia-binding",
  "aurelia-bootstrapper",
  "aurelia-dependency-injection",
  "aurelia-event-aggregator",
  "aurelia-http-client",
  // other existing entries
```

We can now build and run our Aurelia application. The `App` class will now request the JSON from our `/menuitems` REST endpoint, and build our navigation buttons based on the response from our Express application.

# Aurelia forms

Aside from receiving data from a REST endpoint, applications generally need to post data to the server for processing. As an example of this, let's implement our login screen and see how we post data from Aurelia to our Express application. We will use the Brackets designed HTML within a new Aurelia component named `login`. Our `login` component is in the `src/login.ts` file as follows:

```
import {HttpClient} from 'aurelia-http-client';
export class Login {
  header = 'Please login';
  userName = "";
  password = "";

  onSubmit() {
    var postMessage = {
      userName: this.userName,
      password : this.password };

    let client = new HttpClient();
    client.post('/login', postMessage)
      .then( (message) => {
        console.log(`post returned : ${message.response}`);
      })
      .catch( (err) => {
        console.log(`err.response: ${err.response}`);
      })
      ;
  }
}
```

Here, we have created a class named `Login` that has three properties. The `header` property is used to render a message to the screen, and the `userName` and `password` properties will hold the values that the user has typed into the form. We have also defined an `onSubmit` function that will be triggered by the HTML form when the `Submit` button is clicked. This function creates a JSON object with the given `userName` and `password` values, and then calls the `post` method that is available via the `HttpClient` class. This post function call will `POST` the JSON packet to the `'/login'` REST endpoint, which will either return a success or failure response. The `success` response will be processed by the `then` function, and the error response will be caught by the `catch` function. For the time being, we are simply logging the response from the REST endpoint to the console.

The HTML template for the `login` component is as follows:

```
<template>
  <div id="sideNav" class="login_sidenav">
    <form role="form" submit.delegate="onSubmit()">
    <div class="container">
      <a href="#" class="closebtn" >&times;</a>
      <div class="row">${header}</div>
      <div class="row">
        <input
          class="sidenav-input"
          value.bind="userName"
          type="text"
          placeholder="Username">
      </div>
      <div class="row">
        <input
          class="sidenav-input"
          value.bind="password"
          type="password"
          placeholder="Password">
      </div>
      <div class="row">
        <button class="btn btn-primary btn-lg">Login
        </button>
      </div>
    </div>
    </form>
  </div>
</template>
```

Again, this is a copy and paste exercise from our Brackets HTML page, with a few minor changes to integrate with Aurelia. Firstly, we have defined the `<form>` tag with an attribute named `submit.delegate`. The value of this attribute is the `onSubmit` function that we defined earlier in our `Login` class. The `submit.delegate` attribute, therefore, binds the form submit event to the `onSubmit` function.

Within the form itself, we have a `<div>` with the class of `container`, and then three `<div>` elements with the class of `row`. The first of these uses standard Aurelia `${...}` syntax to render the value of the `Login` class `header` property into the DOM.

The two `<input>` elements use an attribute named `value.bind` to bind the text as input by the user to the properties on the `Login` class itself.

With our `login` component in place, we can update the `app.html` file to include this component as follows:

```
<template>

  <require from="./login"></require>
  <login></login>

// existing <nav> class
```

Here, we have used the `<require>` tag within the `app.html` file to indicate to Aurelia that it needs to load the `./login` component for use within the template. We then render the login component by simply adding a `<login>` tag.

# Posting data

Now that we have an Aurelia form in place, and are reading data as entered by the user, we will need to implement an Express handler for this HTTP `POST` event. This handler is written within the `routes/index.ts` file as follows:

```
import * as util from 'util';

router.post('/login', (req, res, next) => {
  console.log(`login received :
    ${util.inspect(req.body, false, null)}`);
  res.sendStatus(200);
});
```

Here, we have imported a module named `util`, and then registered an Express handler for a `POST` to the REST endpoint `/login`. Within this handler, we are simply logging the `body` of the request to the console, and then returning an HTTP response code of `200` (OK ). Within the `console.log` call, we are using the `util.inspect` function to give us a string representation of the `req.body` object. If we run our application now, and send a `POST` request to this handler, the `req.body` will unfortunately be `undefined`:

```
express listening on port 3000
login received : undefined
```

To resolve this issue, we will need to install and register the `'body-parser'` node module, as we did in an earlier chapter. The updates to our `main.ts` file are as follows:

```
// other includes
import * as bodyParser from 'body-parser';
// existing code
app.use(bodyParser.json());
app.use(bodyParser.urlencoded({ extended: false }));

app.use('/', Index.router);
```

Here, we have included the `'body-parser'` node module, and then called the `app.use` function to register it with the Express engine. With our changes in place, the `POST` handler for the REST endpoint `/login` will now correctly display the received JSON packet:

```
express listening on port 3000
login received: { userName: 'asdf', password: 'sadf' }
```

# Aurelia messaging

Now that we have the `login` module sending our login details to the Express application, we will need to notify the Aurelia application that a login event has occurred. In order to do this, we need a mechanism to raise an event within the `Login` component that the `App` component can subscribe to. Aurelia uses the modules in the `'aurelia-event-aggregator'` package to do this. Our changes to the `Login` module are as follows:

```
import {HttpClient} from 'aurelia-http-client';
import {EventAggregator} from 'aurelia-event-aggregator';
import {inject} from 'aurelia-framework';

@inject(EventAggregator)
export class Login {
  header = 'Please login';
  userName = "";
  password = "";
  ea: EventAggregator;
  constructor(EventAggregator) {
    this.ea = EventAggregator;
  }
  // onSubmit() code
```

Here, we have included the `EventAggregator` class from the `'aurelia-event-aggregator'` module, as well as the `inject` decorator from the `'aurelia-framework'` module. We are then decorating our class definition with the `@inject` decorator, with the name of the class we need to inject, which in this case is the `EventAggregator`. We have also created a local variable named `ea` that will hold the instance of the `EventAggregator` class, and then created a `constructor` function to set the local `ea` variable to the injected value.

Note how the dependency injection framework used within Aurelia has similarities to the dependency injection framework that we built in the last chapter. Aurelia, however, requires us to manually set the local variable in the `constructor` function, which we were able to do away with in our dependency injection framework. Aurelia also used the name of the class to tie the `@inject` decorator with the corresponding constructor parameter.

We can now send a message from the `Login` component with a single line of code, as follows:

```
client.post('/login', postMessage)
  .then( (message) => {
    console.log(`post returned : ${message.response}`);
    this.ea.publish('login_result', {success: true});
  })
  .catch( (err) => {
    console.log(`err.response: ${err.response}`);
  });
```

Here, we have called the `ea.publish` function on a successful HTTP `POST`, with a message subject of `'login_result'`, and a message body of `{ success: true }`. The subject and body of the messages can be literally anything, as long as both the publisher and the subscriber understand the subject and the body.

To receive, or listen to this message, we will make the following changes to our `App` module:

```
import {EventAggregator, Subscription} from 'aurelia-event-aggregator';
import {inject} from 'aurelia-framework';
@inject(EventAggregator)
export class App {
  message = 'Hello World!';
  menuItems: IMenuItem[] = [];
  ea: EventAggregator;
  constructor(EventAggregator?) {
    this.ea = EventAggregator;
    this.ea.subscribe('login_result', (response) => {
      console.log(`App.loginResult() : ${response.success}`);
```

```
    });
    // existing code
```

Again, we need to import the `EventAggregator` class and the `inject` decorator from their respective modules. Similar to the changes we made in the `Login` module, we have decorated the `App` class with the `@inject` decorator, and are injecting the `EventAggregator` through the `constructor` function.

We are then calling the `ea.subscribe` function to subscribe to a particular event name, and have written an anonymous function that will be called when the event is received. While this will work correctly, it would be better for our application if we called a class function instead of an anonymous function. Using anonymous functions in this way poses some problems when we get to unit testing our applications. Let's split this into a named function, as follows:

```
loginResult(response) {
  console.log(`App.loginResult() : ${response.success}`);
}
```

So that our subscription therefore becomes:

```
this.ea.subscribe('login_result', this.loginResult);
```

So far, so good. The problem with this solution, however, is that when the `loginResult` function is invoked from the event handler, it is running inside the scope of the event handler callback, and therefore has no access to the instance of `this` inside our `App` class instance. To see this in action, let's create a class variable on the `App` class named `isLoginVisible`, as follows:

```
@inject(EventAggregator)
export class App {
  message = 'Hello World!';
  menuItems: IMenuItem[] = [];
  ea: EventAggregator;
  isLoginVisible = true;
  constructor(EventAggregator?) {
    // existing code
    this.ea.subscribe('login_result', this.loginResult);
    // exising code
  }
  loginResult(response) {
    console.log(`App.loginResult() : ${response.success}`);
    this.isLoginVisible = false;
  }
}
```

Here we have created a variable named `isLoginVisible`, which is set to `true` when the `App` class is instantiated. Our `loginResult` function is now attempting to set this variable to `false` when a successful login result message is received. Running this code, however, will generate the following error message:

```
vendor-bundle.js:14688 ERROR [event-aggregator] TypeError: Cannot set
property
'isLoginVisible' of undefined(...)
```

What this error message is telling us, is that the `this` variable inside the `loginResult` function does not have a property named `isLoginVisible`. It is therefore a different `this` context than what we expected. To fix this issue, we can use a handy function from the Underscore library named `bindAll`.

Remember when we created our initial HTML files within Node, we included the `underscore.min.js` script in our `layout.hbs` file? This is where it is used.

Our fix to the perennial `this` scoping error is as follows:

```
_.bindAll(this, 'loginResult');
this.ea.subscribe('login_result', this.loginResult);
```

Here, we have called the underscore `bindAll` function to bind the instance of the `App` class' `this` variable to be used within the `loginResult` function. With this simple change in place, our code works as expected.

The last thing that we need to do is to use the `isLoginVisible` variable within the `app.html` template, as follows:

```
<login if.bind="isLoginVisible"></login>
```

Here, we are using the Aurelia `if.bind` function to either show or hide the `<login>` template based on the value of the `isLoginVisible` variable.

Our Aurelia application is now complete. We have successfully integrated a Node Express application with Aurelia, created a REST endpoint for serving up application data, and have shown a full `POST` workflow to implement a login screen. We have also set up a simple messaging service to coordinate events between components.

# An Angular 2 website

In this section of the chapter, we will integrate an Angular 2 application with Node and Express, similar to what we did for Aurelia. Again, we will show how to load JSON within an Angular component, and then build our login screen to accept input from our web form, and post it to our Express application. The good news is that apart from a few minor changes, most of the Express code that we built for use with Aurelia can be reused with Angular 2. First up, let's initialize our Angular application, and integrate it with Express.

## Angular setup

Setting up an Angular 2 application should be almost second nature at this stage. All we need to do is issue an `ng new` command with the name of our project. To use Express, we will need to install express using `npm` as follows:

```
npm install express --save
npm install hbs --save
npm install bootstrap --save
```

## Serving Angular 2 pages

As we did with Aurelia, we now need to set up our Express application, which includes the `main.ts` file, an `index.ts` file in the `routes` directory, and our `index.hbs` and `layout.hbs` files in the `views` directory. Let's start by building the `layout.hbs` file in the views directory.

The Angular 2 application that is set up via the Angular-CLI uses webpack within the compilation step to output all compiled JavaScript files into the `dist` directory. To find out what an Express `index.html` file should look like, we will need to issue an `ng build` command, and then take a look at the `dist/index.html` file that Angular has created. Using this file as a template, our `views/layout.hbs` file is as follows:

```
<!doctype html>
<html>
<head>
  <meta charset="utf-8">
  <title>{{title}}</title>
  <base href="/">
  <link rel='stylesheet'
     href='/node_modules/bootstrap/dist/css/bootstrap.min.css' />
```

```
    <meta name="viewport" content="width=device-width,
     initial-scale=1">
    <link rel="icon" type="image/x-icon" href="favicon.ico">
  </head>
  <body>
    {{{body}}}
    <script type="text/javascript"
      src="/dist/inline.bundle.js"></script>
    <script type="text/javascript"
      src="/dist/polyfills.bundle.js"></script>
    <script type="text/javascript"
      src="/dist/styles.bundle.js"></script>
    <script type="text/javascript"
      src="/dist/vendor.bundle.js"></script>
    <script type="text/javascript"
      src="/dist/main.bundle.js"></script></body>
  </html>
```

Here, we have simply copy and pasted the contents of the `dist/index.html` file provided by the Angular 2 sample, and made a few changes. We have modified the `<title>` tag to load the `{{title}}` property from the Handlebars model, and we have added a `{{{body}}}` parameter within the `<body>` tag. The only other changes to this file are two CSS links to include `bootstrap.min.css`.

The `index.hbs` file is even simpler:

```
<app-root>Loading...</app-root>
```

Here, we are using Angular syntax to load the Angular component that has the `app-root` selector.

We can now create our Express application in the `main.ts` file at the root of the project to serve these files, as follows:

```
import * as express from 'express';
let app = express();

import * as Index from './routes/index';

import * as path from 'path';
app.set('views', path.join(__dirname, 'views'));
app.set('view engine', 'hbs');

import * as bodyParser from 'body-parser';

app.use(bodyParser.json());
app.use(bodyParser.urlencoded({ extended: false }));
```

```
app.use('/', Index.router);

app.use('/node_modules',
  express.static(__dirname + '/node_modules'));
app.use('/dist',
  express.static(__dirname + '/dist'));

app.listen(3000, () => {
  console.log(`listening on port 3000`);
});
```

Here, we have a standard Express application that is setting up our routes, our Handlebars views, and the `body-parser` module. Our `app.use` function calls are very similar to Aurelia, which allows Express to load static files in the `node_modules`, and `dist` directories.

Before we compile our application, we will need to create the Express `routes/index.ts` file, which is exactly the same as we used with Aurelia, so we will not cover it here.

Compiling our Express application with `tsc main.ts`, and then running it with `node main` should load the default "app works!" web page.

Note that the only file in the project root directory that needs compiling is the `main.ts` file that serves as our Express application. Attempting to create a `tsconfig.json` file in the project root directory will conflict with the Angular compilation step that relies on `src` being the root directory for TypeScript files. This means that the compilation step for an Angular 2 and Express application is a three-step process. To compile our application, we need to issue the following commands:

```
ng build
tsc main.ts
tsc -p routes
```

The first command will build the Angular application, and output all files into the `dist` directory. The second command builds our `main.ts` file, which is the Express application that will serve the compiled files, and the third command will build any files in the `routes` directory. Now that we have Express serving our Angular application, we can focus on the Angular components.

# Angular 2 components

Our Angular application needs two components–a `navbar` component to render the navigation bar and a `login` component to render the login panel. As we wish to copy and paste our HTML from the Brackets design output, we will also create `.html` files for each of these components.

Let's start with the `src/app/navbar.component.ts` file, as follows:

```
import { Component, Injectable } from '@angular/core';
interface IButtonName {
  ButtonName : string;
}

@Component( {
  selector: 'navbar-component',
  templateUrl: './navbar.component.html'
})
@Injectable()
export class NavbarComponent {
  menuItems : IButtonName [] = [
    { ButtonName : 'About'},
    { ButtonName : 'Contact'}
  ];
}
```

Here, we are importing the `Component` and `Injectable` decorators from the `'@angular/core'` module. We will use the `Injectable` decorator a little later, but for now, this `navbar` component is very simple. We register an interface named `IButtonName` that is used by the `NavbarComponent` class to set up an internal variable named `menuItems`. The rest of the class is standard Angular syntax. Our `navbar.component.html` file is as follows:

```
<nav class="navbar navbar-default
  navbar-fixed-top navbar-inverse">
    <div class="container-fluid">
      <a class="navbar-brand">Home</a>
      <ul class="nav navbar-nav">
        <li *ngFor="let item of menuItems; let i = index" >
          <a href="#">{{item.ButtonName}}</a>
        </li>
      </ul>
    </div>
</nav>
```

This is again a copy and paste from our original HTML designed pages, with an `*ngFor` directive to loop through the `menuItems` array of the `NavbarComponent` class and to generate `<a>` tags for each array item, similar to what we did with Aurelia.

In order to render this navigation bar in our Angular application, we need to update our `app.component.html` file as follows:

```
<navbar-component></navbar-component>
```

Before we compile and run our application, however, we need to register this new `NavBarComponent` class in the `app.module.ts` file, as follows:

```
// exiting imports
import { AppComponent }  from './app.component';
import { NavbarComponent } from './navbar.component';

@NgModule({
  imports:      [ BrowserModule ],
  declarations: [ AppComponent, NavbarComponent ],
  bootstrap:    [ AppComponent ]
})
export class AppModule { }
```

Here, we have imported the `NavbarComponent` as per usual, and registered it for use in our templates by including it in the `declarations` array.

With these changes in place, our navigation bar will show up at the top of the page.

We will follow a similar approach for our `Login` component, and create a `login.component.ts` file and a `login.component.html` file. The `login.component.ts` file is as follows:

```
import { Component, Injectable } from '@angular/core';

@Component( {
  selector: 'login-component',
  templateUrl: './login.component.html'
})
@Injectable()
export class LoginComponent {
  userName: string ;
  password: string ;
  loginClicked() {
    console.log(`this.userName : ${this.userName}`);
    console.log(`this.password : ${this.password}`);
  }
}
```

Again, this is a standard Angular component named `LoginComponent` that has two properties, named `userName` and `password`, both of which are strings. We have also included a `loginClicked` function that will be called when the user clicks on the `Submit` button on our login page. At the moment, this function simply logs the values of the `userName` and `password` properties to the console.

Our `login.component.html` file is as follows:

```
<div id="sideNav"  class="login_sidenav" >
  <form>
  <div class="container">
    <a href="#" class="closebtn" >&times;</a>
    <div class="row">Please Login :</div>
    <div class="row">
      <input
      class="sidenav-input"
      type="text"
      placeholder="Username"
      name="userName"
      [(ngModel)]="userName"></div>
    <div class="row">
      <input
      class="sidenav-input"
      type="password"
      placeholder="Password"
      name="password"
      [(ngModel)]="password"></div>
    <div class="row">
      <button
      class="btn btn-primary btn-lg"
      (click)="loginClicked()">Login
      </button>
    </div>
  </div>
  </form>

</div>
```

Here, we have modified the HTML for use by our Angular component slightly. Note how the `userName` and `password` input elements have the `[(ngModel)]` attribute, as well as a `name` attribute. These attributes are what Angular uses to bind the values that our user inputs into our class variables. We have also attached a click handler to the `(click)` event of the `Login` button.

Before we compile and run our Angular application with these two components, however, we will need to register a few more modules in the `app.module.ts` file, as follows:

```
import { NgModule }       from '@angular/core';
import { BrowserModule } from '@angular/platform-browser';

import { HttpModule } from '@angular/http';
import { FormsModule }    from '@angular/forms';

import { AppComponent }   from './app.component';
import { NavbarComponent } from './navbar.component';
import { LoginComponent } from './login.component';

@NgModule({
  imports:       [ BrowserModule, HttpModule, FormsModule ],
  declarations: [ AppComponent, NavbarComponent, LoginComponent ],
  bootstrap:     [ AppComponent ]
})
export class AppModule { }
```

Here, we have imported the `HttpModule` and the `FormsModule` from their respective Angular modules. These two modules are required for form-based data binding, and for working with RESTful web services, which we will tackle next. Note how the `HttpModule` and the `FormsModule` components have been added to the `imports` array. Our `declarations` array has also been updated to include the `LoginComponent`.

We can now render the `login` component within our page by updating the `app.component.html` page, as follows:

```
<navbar-component></navbar-component>
<login-component></login-component>
```

This simple change will now render both the `login` component and the `navbar` component within our page.

# Processing JSON

As we did with Aurelia, let's now work on the `navbar` component to use our Express endpoint of `/menuitems` to load the array of `navbar` buttons, as follows:

```
import { Http, Response, Headers, RequestOptions }
  from '@angular/http';
// existing code
@Injectable()
export class NavbarComponent {
```

```
    menuItems : IButtonName [];

  constructor (private http: Http) {
    console.log('AppComponent constructor');
    this.http.get('/menuitems')
     .map(res => res.text())
     .subscribe(
       (data) => {
        let jsonResponse = JSON.parse(data);
        this.menuItems = jsonResponse.menuItems;
       },
       err => {
         console.log(`error : ${err}`);
       },
       () => {
         console.log(`success`);
       }
     );
    }

  }
```

Our updates to the `navbar` component start with an `import` of a few modules from `'@angular.http'`. We have also created a `constructor` function, and are using Angular's dependency injection framework to inject an instance of the `Http` class into the private variable `http`. Note how the syntax for Angular's dependency injection framework is closer to the framework that we developed in an earlier chapter. Angular uses both a variable name and the type of the variable to perform dependency injection.

Within the `constructor` function, we are using the `this.http` class to issue a `GET` request by calling the `get` function with our REST endpoint name. The `map` function converts the `response` received by the REST endpoint to text by calling the `res.text` function, and the `subscribe` function uses an Observable pattern to allow us to attach three functions. The first function we attach is the **happy path**, that is, the REST endpoint has returned a `200 OK` result, and a data packet. The second function is the error path, and the third function will be executed after either successful or error condition calls. For our happy path, we are converting the incoming `data` object to JSON, and then setting the internal `menuItems` variable to the array of button data that is returned.

Angular will automatically update the HTML DOM with the new values returned by the REST endpoint, as soon as we set the corresponding internal variables that have been bound to the HTML.

Before we test this code, we will need to update our `app.component.ts` class to import the `map` and `subscribe` functions, as follows:

```
import { Component } from '@angular/core';

import 'rxjs/add/operator/map';
import 'rxjs/operator/delay';
import 'rxjs/operator/mergeMap';
import 'rxjs/operator/switchMap';

@Component({
  selector: 'my-app',
  templateUrl: 'app/app.component.html'
})
export class AppComponent  { name = 'Angular'; }
```

Here, we have imported a few modules from the `rxjs` namespace. The reason for adding it into the app component instead of our `navbar` component is so that all modules have access to these functions.

Compiling and running our application now will show the three buttons in the `navbar` as served from our Express REST endpoint. So far, so good.

# Posting data

Let's now turn our attention to the `login` component, and use the same `Http` class from Angular to post our login data to our REST endpoint. We already have a `loginClicked` function in this class, so all we need to do is to create the correct HTTP packet and post it as follows:

```
constructor(private http: Http) {
}

loginClicked() {
  console.log(`this.userName : ${this.userName}`);
  console.log(`this.password : ${this.password}`);
  var headers = new Headers();
  headers.append('Content-Type', 'application/json');

  let jsonPacket = {
    userName : this.userName ,
```

```
        password : this.password };

      this.http.post('/login', jsonPacket , {
        headers: headers
      })
      .map(res => res.text())
      .subscribe(
        data => data,
        err => {
        console.log(`error : ${err}`);
        },
        () => {
        console.log(`success`);
        }
      );
    }
```

We start by adding a `constructor` function, as we did with the `navbar` component, to inject the `Http` module into a private variable named `http`. The bulk of the changes, however, are in the `loginClicked` function. In order to post data to a REST endpoint, we will need to create a `Headers` object, and append the `Content-Type` of `application/json` using the `headers` instance. We then construct a `jsonPacket` object, using our `userName` and `password` variables that have been updated as part of the data binding process. We then call the `post` method of the `Http` class using our endpoint name, the `jsonpacket`, and our `POST` headers. The `map` and `subscribe` functions are similar to our earlier `GET` request.

Our work with Angular in this section is complete. We have integrated a Node and Express web server to both serve Angular web pages, and serve as a REST endpoint. We have also successfully implemented a navigation bar component and a `login` component, and shown how to both consume and post data to REST endpoints with Angular. Back in `Chapter 11`, *Object-Oriented Programming*, we covered Angular events using the `EventEmitter`, so we will not cover it again here.

# An Express React website

In the last section of this chapter, we will take a look at integrating React and Express. As we have done with Aurelia and Angular, we will start by housing our Express and React components in the same directory, and then work through the Express layouts that we will need to serve a React site. We will then take a look at using REST endpoints within React.

# Express and React

As we have done before, setting up a React site is as simple as creating a `package.json` file with the relevant React components and a `tsconfig.json` file, and then creating a `webpack.config.js` file so that we can use webpack. Our `package.json` file is as follows:

```
{
  "name": "node_react",
  "version": "1.0.0",
  "description": "",
  "main": "index.js",
  "scripts": {
    "test": "echo "Error: no test specified" && exit 1"
  },
  "author": "",
  "license": "ISC",
  "dependencies": {
    "body-parser": "^1.15.2",
    "express": "^4.14.0",
    "hbs": "^4.0.1",
    "promise-polyfill": "^6.0.2",
    "react": "^15.4.0",
    "react-dom": "^15.4.0",
    "whatwg-fetch": "^2.0.1",
 "@types/body-parser": "0.0.33",
    "@types/core-js": "^0.9.35",
    "@types/express": "^4.0.35",
    "@types/react-dom": "^0.14.23",
    "@types/whatwg-fetch": "0.0.33"
  },
  "devDependencies": {
    "source-map-loader": "^0.1.5",
    "ts-loader": "^1.2.2"
  }
}
```

Here, we have the standard React components listed in the `dependencies` property, which are `react` and `react-dom`. We have also included our `express`, `hbs`, and `body-parser` modules that Express will use. Along with these Express modules, we also have `promise-polyfill` and `whatwg-fetch`. These two modules will be used by our React components to consume our REST endpoints. We also have a number of declaration files listed as `@types`. As usual, we have two `devDependencies` listed in `source-map-loader` and `ts-loader`, which React uses to provide TypeScript compilation via webpack.

Our `tsconfig.json` file is as follows:

```
{
  "compilerOptions": {
    "outDir" : "./dist/",
    "module": "commonjs",
    "target": "es5",
    "noImplicitAny": false,
    "sourceMap": false,
    "moduleResolution": "node",
    "jsx": "react"
  },
  "exclude": [
    "node_modules"
  ]
}
```

Here, we have specified an output directory in the `outDir` property set to `./dist`, and also set the `jsx` property to `react`.

Our `webpack.config.js` file has not changed since `Chapter 7`, *TypeScript Compatible Frameworks*.

# Serving the React application

With these files in place, we can reuse our Express `main.ts` file from our Aurelia application, with a single modification, as follows:

```
// existing code
app.use('/dist',
  express.static(__dirname  ));

app.listen(3000, () => {
  console.log(`express listening on port 3000`);
});
```

Here, we are specifying to Express that we need to serve the `/dist` directory as static files. Remember that when we run webpack from the command line to compile our React source, all sources are generated into the `dist` directory, meaning that we need a specific entry in our Express application to serve this directory and its contents.

Before we run the `webpack` command from the command line, we need to create two files. The first is the `app/index.tsx` file that serves as the entry-point to our React site, which at this stage can be an empty file. The second is the `routes/index.ts` file that contains our Express HTTP handlers. This file can be copied from either the Angular or Aurelia sample, as both are identical.

At this stage, we can compile our React application by typing `webpack` from the command line, and compile our Express application by typing `tsc` from the command line.

Note that both the React compilation steps and the TypeScript compilation steps are generating JavaScript files in the `/dist` directory. In order to run our Express application from the project root directory, therefore, we need to reference the `main.js` module in the `dist` directory, as follows:

```
node dist/main
```

Which seems to serve our application correctly:

```
express listening on port 3000
```

Unfortunately, firing up a browser, and pointing it to `http://localhost:3000` will generate a few nasty errors:

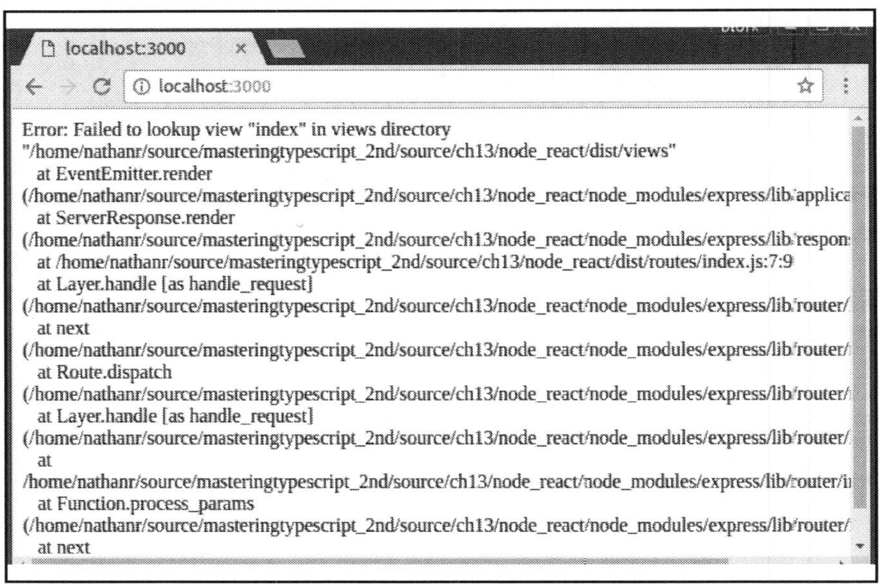


React errors when running Express from the project root directory

Looking closely at these errors, we can see that our Express application is being served up from the /dist directory. As such, the views directory that we specified in our Express application is not the /views directory as we have used before, but is in fact the /dist/views directory.

Let's therefore create a /dist/views directory, and within this, our layout.hbs file and index.hbs files, so that Express can generate our HTML views correctly.

Our layout.hbs view is as follows:

```
<!DOCTYPE html>
<html>
  <head>
    <meta charset="UTF-8" />
    <title>Hello React!</title>
    <link rel="stylesheet" href="/css/bootstrap.min.css" />
      <link rel="stylesheet" href="/css/app.css" />
  </head>
  <body>
    {{{body}}}

    <!-- Dependencies -->
    <script src=
      "node_modules/react/dist/react.js">
    </script>
    <script src=
      "node_modules/react-dom/dist/react-dom.js">
    </script>

    <!-- Main -->
    <script src="/dist/bundle.js"></script>
  </body>
</html>
```

Here, we have created the outline of a standard React web page, and included the react.js file and react-dom.js file as <script> tags within the body of the page. Note that we are also including the bundle.js file from the /dist directory, which serves as the entry point to our React application. Our index.hbs file is as follows:

```
<div id="app_anchor"></div>
```

With these two views in place, we can fire up our Express application and browse to `http://localhost:3000`. While this may seem all well and good, if we open up our **Developer Tools** in the browser, and look at the console log, we will see that we still have a few 404 errors:

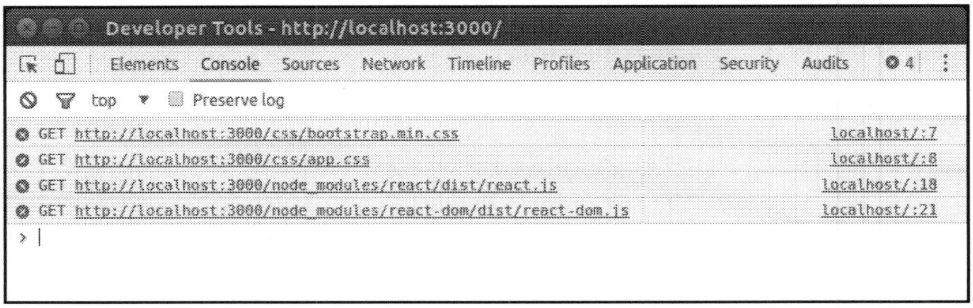


Viewing 404 errors while serving an Express React application

The first two errors indicate that we need to create some `.css` files in the `/dist/css` directory. These files can easily be copied from our earlier samples. The next two errors, however, indicate that we need to have a `/dist/node_modules` directory, which includes the `react` and `react-dom` modules.

# Multiple package.json files

Essentially, the webpack compilation step that React uses means that all of our files used by the browser must be served from the `/dist` directory. Some of our files, however, come from the / (or project root directory). This is the nature of React development environments. Remember that any file that is statically served must be in the `/dist` directory, but any file that is compiled must be in the / or root directory.

To overcome this problem, we can split our `package.json` file into two separate files – one in the / or root directory and one in the `/dist` directory. The `package.json` file in the / or root directory only needs to install packages that are needed by the webpack compilation step, and can therefore be stripped back to the following:

```
{
  "name": "node_react",
  "version": "1.0.0",
  "devDependencies": {
    "source-map-loader": "^0.1.5",
    "ts-loader": "^1.2.2",

},
  "dependencies": {
    "@types/body-parser": "0.0.33",
    "@types/core-js": "^0.9.35",
    "@types/express": "^4.0.35",
    "@types/react-dom": "^0.14.23",
    "@types/whatwg-fetch": "0.0.33"
  }
}
```

Here, the `dependencies` list only contains our `@types` definitions, and the `devDependencies` array has been stripped back to only incude the `source-map-loader` and `ts-loader` Node modules are all that are needed by webpack for the compilation step.

Our `/dist/package.json` file does not need the `devDependencies`, and therefore just contains the following:

```
{
  "name": "node_react_dist",
  "version": "1.0.0",
  "dependencies": {
    "body-parser": "^1.15.2",
    "cookie-parser": "^1.4.3",
    "express": "^4.14.0",
    "express-session": "^1.14.1",
    "hbs": "^4.0.1",
    "promise-polyfill": "^6.0.2",
    "react": "^15.4.0",
    "react-dom": "^15.4.0",
    "whatwg-fetch": "^2.0.1"
  }
}
```

Having two `package.json` files therefore means that if we need new modules used by the Express application, we need to modify the `/dist/package.json` file. Also, remember to issue an `npm install` command in the `/dist` directory to install the required node modules.

# React components

Now that we have React and Node working side-by-side, we can focus on creating the required React components for our navigation bar and login screen. We will start with the `app/NavBar.tsx` class that will render our navigation bar as follows:

```
import * as React from 'react';
import * as ReactDOM from 'react-dom';

export class MenuItem {
  ButtonName: string;
}

export class NavBarProps {
  menuItems ? : MenuItem [] ;
}

export default class NavBar
  extends React.Component<NavBarProps, {}> {
    state: NavBarProps;
    constructor(props?: NavBarProps) {
      super(props);
      this.state = {menuItems : [  ]};
    }
    render() {
      return <div>
      <nav
      className="navbar navbar-default
      navbar-fixed-top navbar-inverse">
      <div className="container-fluid">
        <a className="navbar-brand">Home</a>
        <ul className="nav navbar-nav">
          { this.state.menuItems.map( function (item, i) {
            return(
              <li key={i}
              className="nav-item nav-link active">
              <a href="#"
              >{item.ButtonName}</a></li>
            );
          }, this)}
```

```
            </ul>
          </div>
          </nav>
          </div>;

        }
    }
```

Here, we have the definition of three classes that are all exported. The first is named `MenuItem`, and contains a single property named `ButtonName` of type string. The second is a class named `NavBarProps` that contains an array of `MenuItem` elements. The third is the `NavBar` class itself, which extends `React.Component`, and uses generic syntax to specify that it uses the `NavBarProps` internally. These classes put together mean that we are constructing a `NavBar` React class that has access to an internal array named `menuItems`, each of which has a property called `ButtonName`.

The `NavBar` class has an internal `state` property, also of type `NavBarProps`, and a `constructor` function that accepts an optional class of `NavBarProps`. This optional property will allow any parent React component to create an instance of this class by using either `<NavBar />` or `<NavBar menuItems={...} />` syntax to construct the class.

There are a few points to note about this class. Firstly, we are setting the internal `state` property to be a blank array of `menuItems` in the constructor. Secondly, we are looping through the `menuItems` property of the `state` variable within the `render` function, and rendering an `<li>` element for each item in the array. When the class is constructed, this `state.menuItems` array will have no elements, and as such we will not render any navigation bar buttons.

Thirdly, we are using the `state` property and not the `props` property for our array of navigation bar buttons. Note that React uses the `state` property to allow for automatic re-rendering of HTML elements when the `state` changes. When we need to update the DOM, we simply need to call the `setState` function, and React will regenerate and re-render the DOM.

Note that the HTML that we use within the React component is slightly different to the Brackets designed HTML that we are using. When defining a CSS class for use within a React component, we must specify `className` in the HTML element instead of simply `class`. This means that to render an element with the HTML `<div class="css-class-name">`, we must specify `<div className="css-class-name">` in a React component.

In order to put this navigation bar to the test, let's create the `App` class within the `app/index.tsx` file so that we can render the `NavBar` component to the DOM, as follows:

```
import * as React from 'react';
import * as ReactDOM from 'react-dom';
import NavBar from './NavBar';

export class App
  extends React.Component<{}, {}> {
    render() {
        return <div>
          <NavBar />
        </div>;
    }
  }

ReactDOM.render(
  <App ></App>, document.getElementById('app_anchor')
);
```

Here, we have a very simple `App` class that does not have any settable properties, and is therefore using empty objects for the `ReactComponent` definition. The `App` class has a single function named `render`, which is rendering a child `NavBar` React component. To bootstrap our `App` class, we call `ReactDOM.render`.

With the `App` and `NavBar` React components in place, firing up the application will render a `NavBar` component with no buttons, as follows:

React Application rendering a Navbar

# Consuming REST endpoints

As we did with our Aurelia and Angular applications, let's now update the `NavBar` React component to consume a REST endpoint. In other words, let's issue a `GET` request to the `/menuitems` endpoint, and use the returned JSON to populate our navigation bar. Our updates are to the `NavBar` component constructor, as follows:

```
constructor(props?: NavBarProps) {
  super(props);
  this.state = {menuItems : [  ]};
  fetch('/menuitems')
  .then( (response) => {
    return response.json(); }
  )
  .then( (json) => {
    this.setState({ menuItems : json.menuItems});
  })
  .catch( (err) => {
    console.log(`err : ${err}`);
  });
}
```

Here, we have called the `fetch` function with the name of the REST endpoint just after our existing call to set the `this.state` property. Again, we are using fluent syntax to attach a `then` function that will be called when the call to the REST endpoint returns. Within this first `then` function, we are simply returning a call to `response.json`. This is the syntax that React uses to convert a REST response into JSON format.

Following the first `then` function, we attach a second `then` function that is called with a single `json` parameter. This second `then` function will be called when the first `then` function returns. Within this second `then` function, we are making a call to `setState`, as we mentioned earlier. The call to `setState` will cause React to update the DOM based on the new value of the `menuItems` array, and therefore render our three navigation bar buttons.

While this syntax may seem a little convoluted, with two `then` functions being called in succession, it is the preferred way of working with REST endpoints in React. If you fire up a debugger, and watch the first response object, you will note that the `response` object is not a simple JSON object, but is in fact a first-class React class, that contains the full `GET` request header information, a `body` property, along with callable functions. Conversion of this response property to a simple JSON package is accomplished by calling the `reponse.json` function in this way.

# Login panel component

With our `NavBar` component in place, we can now turn our attention to the login panel. The login panel will need to handle data binding from the HTML form back to our React class, as we have done with Aurelia and Angular. As a start, let's get the basics of a `LoginPanel` in place, and then discuss data binding and form submission a little later.

Our `app/LoginPanel.tsx` file is as follows:

```
import * as React from 'react';
import * as ReactDOM from 'react-dom';

// must export a props class
export class LoginPanelProps {
  userName?: string;
  password?: string;
}


export default class LoginPanel
  extends React.Component<LoginPanelProps, {}> {
    state: LoginPanelProps;
    constructor(props?: LoginPanelProps) {
      super(props);
      this.state = { userName : '', password: ''};
    }
    render() {
      return <div id="sideNav" className="login_sidenav">
      <form onSubmit={this.handleSubmit}>
      <div className="container">
        <a href="#" className="closebtn" >&times;</a>
        <div className="row">Please Login :</div>
        <div className="row">
          <input className="sidenav-input"
            type="text"
            placeholder="Username"
            value={this.props.userName} /></div>
        <div className="row">
          <input className="sidenav-input"
            type="password"
            placeholder="Password"
            value={this.props.password} /></div>
        <div className="row">
          <input type="submit"
            value="Login"
        className="btn btn-primary btn-lg" /></div>
      </div>
```

```
      </form>
    </div>;
    }

    handleSubmit(event) {
    }

}
```

Here, we have defined a class named `LoginPanelProps` that holds our `userName` and `password` properties. Our `LoginPanel` React component again uses the generic syntax in order to derive from the `React.Component` class. The `constructor` function again specifies the `props` argument as optional, and then sets the internal `state` property to an object with a blank `userName` and `password` property.

Note the HTML that we have included in the `render` function. We have specified a `<form>` tag, with an `onSubmit` attribute set to `{this.handleSubmit}`. This is effectively binding the `onSubmit` event to the `handleSubmit` function within our class.

On a similar note, the `input` element for the `Username` has a `value` attribute set to `this.props.userName`. This syntax will set the value of the input element to the value of our `LoginPanel` class property.

To render this `LoginPanel`, then, we can update our `App` class as follows:

```
import LoginPanel from './LoginPanel';

export class App
  extends React.Component<{}, {}> {
    render() {
      return <div>
        <LoginPanel />
        <NavBar />
      </div>;
    }
}
```

Here, we have imported the `LoginPanel` class and included a `<LoginPanel />` element within the render function.

# React data binding

With our `LoginPanel` rendering to the DOM, we can now focus on data binding between the login panel form elements and our `LoginPanel` class. Remember that we are using the `userName` and `password` properties within the `LoginPanel` class to hold the initial values that are displayed on the web page. Currently they are both blank, and waiting for the user to type in values into these input elements.

In order to trap updates to these form elements, we will need to attach to the `onChange` event within our HTML elements. This is accomplished by firstly defining a function to be called when a value on the form is changed, and secondly notifying the HTML element that it needs to call this function when the value of the element changes. Our updates to the `LoginPanel` are two-fold, as follows:

```
constructor(props?: LoginPanelProps) {
  super(props);
  this.state = { userName : '', password: ''};
  this.handleUserNameChange =
    this.handleUserNameChange.bind(this);
  this.handlePasswordChange =
    this.handlePasswordChange.bind(this);
  this.handleSubmit =
    this.handleSubmit.bind(this);
}
handleUserNameChange(event) {
  this.setState({userName: event.target.value});
  console.log(`username change: ${event.target.value}`)
}

handlePasswordChange(event) {
  this.setState({password: event.target.value});
  console.log(`password change: ${event.target.value}`)
}
```

Here, we have introduced two new functions named `handleUserNameChange` and `handlePasswordChange`. Within our `constructor` function, we are also assigning the value of these functions to the result of a call to `bind(this)`. This is necessary in order to correctly bind the value of `this` argument to be the class instance itself, as we have discussed earlier when we used the Underscore `bindAll` function to accomplish the same result, with a call to `_.bindAll(this, 'functionName')`.

Within these handle functions; we are updating the `state` variables with the current value of the `<input>` element with a call to `setState`. This will therefore keep our `state` variable values in sync with the values that the user is entering into the `<input>` elements.

With these functions in place, we now need to update the HTML elements in order to attach to these functions, as follows :

```
<input className="sidenav-input"
  type="text"
  placeholder="Username"
  value={this.props.userName}
  onChange={this.handleUserNameChange}
  /></div>
<input className="sidenav-input"
  type="password"
  placeholder="Password"
  value={this.props.password}
  onChange={this.handlePasswordChange}
  /></div>
```

Here, we have included an `onChange` event handler for our `Username` and `Password<input>` elements, each targeting the correct handle event within our class.

It is worth noting that React will trigger the `onChange` event for every keystroke that the user inputs. If we fire up our website, and open the **Developer Tools** for our browser, we will note the following console logs:

Developer console showing onChange events

Here, we can see that the change event handler is being fired as each key in the keyboard is hit, whether in the `userName` input element or on the `password` input element.

# Posting JSON data

To round out our work with React, let's update our `LoginPanel` class to generate a `POST` call to our Express REST endpoint. The changes we need to make are within the `handleSubmit` event handler that will be called when the form's **Submit** button is clicked, as follows:

```
handleSubmit(event) {
  event.preventDefault();
  fetch('/login',{ method: 'POST',
    headers: {
      'Accept': 'application/json',
      'Content-type' : 'application/json'
    }, body : JSON.stringify({
        userName : this.state.userName,
        password : this.state.password
    })

  }).then( (response) => {
    console.log(`response : ${response.status}`);
  }).catch( (err) => {
    console.log(`err: ${err}`);
  });
}
```

Here, we have updated our `handleSubmit` event handler function to use the React `fetch` function in order to send a `POST` event to our Express endpoint. In React, the `fetch` function can be used to both issue a `GET` request, as we have seen earlier, or to issue a `POST` event as we are doing here. When using a `POST` event, however, we need to send an object that has three properties, namely `method`, `headers`, and `body`. Our `method` property is set to `POST`, and our `headers` property contains the `'Accept'` and `'Content-type'` properties. The `body` property contains the data that we wish to `POST` to our endpoints.

As we saw earlier, the call to `fetch` uses fluent syntax to attach a `then` function that will be invoked once the REST endpoint returns, or a `catch` function that will be invoked if there is an error.

Our work with React is complete. We have shown how to build React components for our Brackets designed HTML, and also how to bind data from the React state property for automated updates to the DOM. We then discussed how to use REST endpoints for both `GET` and `POST` actions, and used data binding syntax to capture user input within our React classes.

# Summary

In this chapter, we have explored some of the fundamental building blocks in application development. We have shown how to combine an Express web server with the Aurelia, Angular 2, and React frameworks. We discussed how to create Handlebar views to serve HTML pages for each of these frameworks, and how to register static content with Express in order to do so. We then discussed data binding, and in particular, how to request data from an Express REST endpoint in order to dynamically update HTML elements based on the JSON returned. With each of the frameworks, we then explored working with and processing HTML input elements in order to read data from a user input form. Once we had obtained user input, we built code to post this data to an Express REST endpoint.

In our next chapter, we will put all of our learnings together and build a complete Angular 2 application that incorporates all of the building blocks that we have been working with throughout this book.

# 14
# Let's Get Our Hands Dirty

In our final chapter, we will use the techniques and principles that we have learnt up until this point to build a sample web application. This application will use the left-to-right panel design that we explored in `Chapter 11`, *Object-Oriented Programming*, and also interact with REST endpoints, as we discussed in `Chapter 13`, *Building Applications*. We will also reuse the **State** and **Mediator** design pattern, and show how to build unit tests for our application, as we discussed in `Chapter 9`, *Testing Typescript Compatible Frameworks*. We already have all of the building blocks and in-depth knowledge that is required to put together a sample application at our fingertips, so this chapter is all about reuse and component integration. For the sake of brevity, we will use Angular 2 as our application framework throughout this chapter.

This chapter will cover the following topics:

- Overview of the application structure
- Unit testing
- Testing the State and Mediator design panel
- Integrating a new Login panel
- Working with complex JSON structures
- Testing HTTP requests
- Testing UI events
- Filtering data
- Application architecture

# Board Sales application

Our application will be a rather simple one, called **Board Sales**, which will list a range of windsurfing boards on the main page, and then allow the user to view details of any one of the boards on sale by clicking on it. Clicking on a particular board will slide the board detail panel in from the right-hand side. We will also use the left-hand side navigation panel to provide the user with options to filter the board list. If a user clicks on a particular filter, then the range of boards shown will be filtered to match this selection. The main page will be as follows:

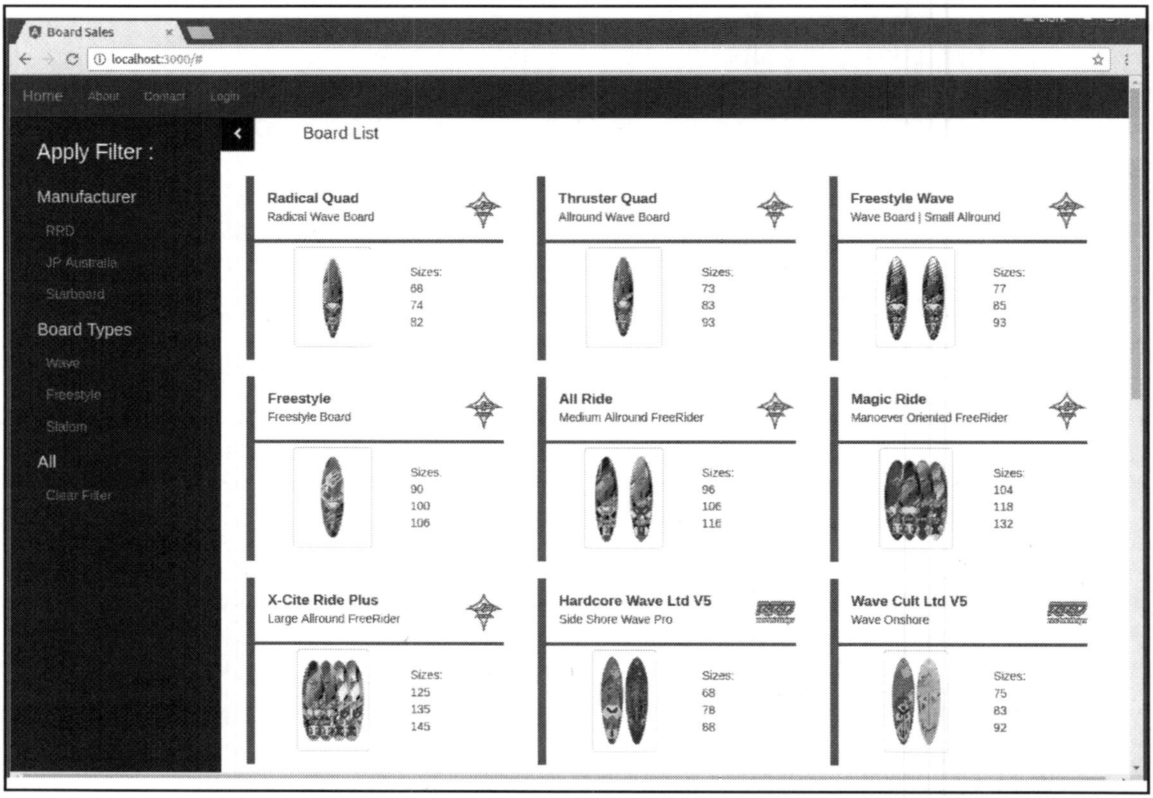


Sample application main board list with filter panel

Here, we can see that we have a top navigation bar, a side-navigation panel on the left-hand side showing filter options, and a main panel with a series of boards displayed.

Modern windsurfing boards come in a range of sizes, and are measured by volume. As we can see in the board list view, each board is shown with a table of available sizes next to it. Smaller volume boards are generally used for wave sailing, and larger volume boards are using for racing, or slalom. Those boards that sit in-between can be categorized as freestyle boards, and are used for performing acrobatic tricks on flat water. Each board has a manufacturer, which corresponds to the logo shown next to each board. Our filter panel on the left-hand side allows the user to select either the manufacturer, or a board type as a filter. So to view only boards made by RRD, the user can click on the **RRD** filter under **Manufacturer**. Likewise, to filter the board list by **Slalom** boards, the user can click on the **Slalom** filter on the left-hand panel.

Clicking on any particular board will show the board detail screen, as follows:

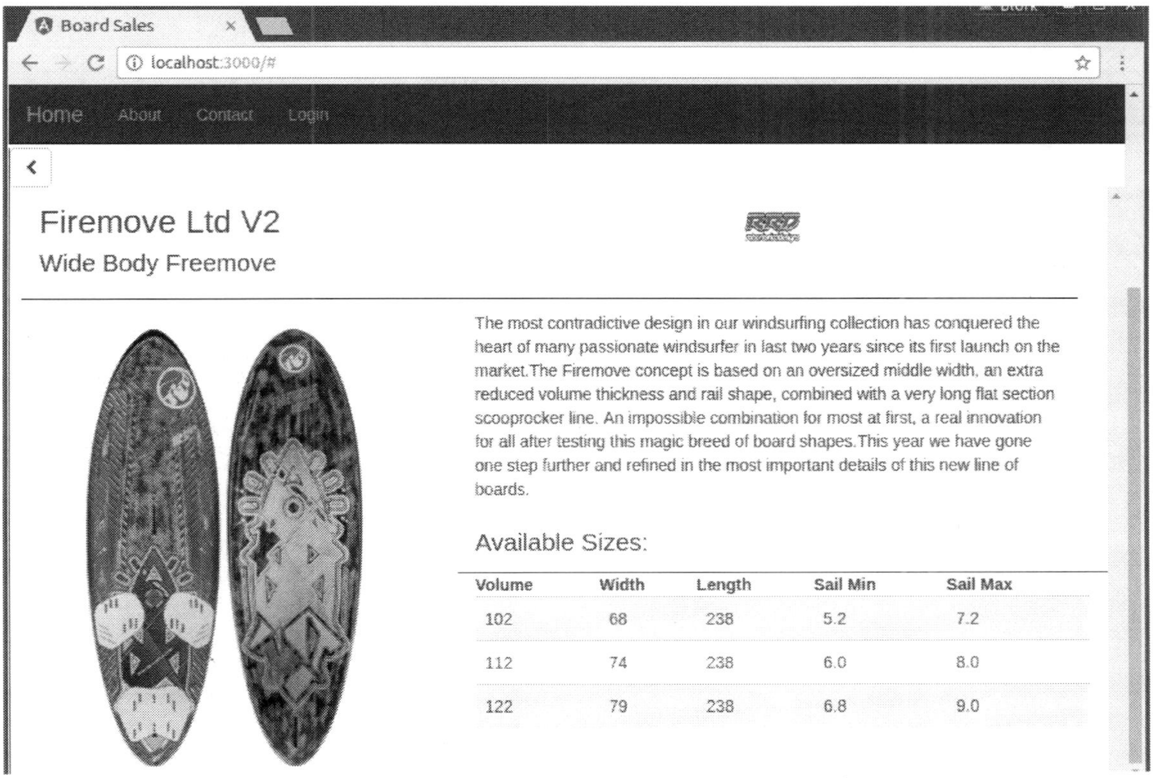


Board detail view

Here, we have a detailed view of a board, with a larger image, a more comprehensive description of the board itself, along with an expanded table of available sizes.

One important aspect of choosing a windsurfing board is the range of sail sizes that it supports. In very strong winds, smaller sails are used to allow the windsurfer to control the power generated by the wind. Likewise, in lighter winds, larger sails are used to generate more power. The combination of board size, board type, and available sail sizes are all used to select the correct board for the sailor and sailing conditions. The detail view therefore lists the minimum and maximum sail sizes that the board can support.

# Angular 2 base application

Back in `Chapter 11`, *Object-Oriented Programming,* we did a fair amount of work to ensure that our application conformed to object-oriented design principles, and implemented the basic left-to-right screen flow that we are looking for. We also explored the State and Mediator design pattern that helped us transition our pages from state to state. In `Chapter 13`, *Building Applications,* we integrated Node and the Express engine into an Angular application so that we can both serve and consume web pages using JavaScript.

We will use the source code from `Chapter 13`, *Building Applications,* as our base application, and then merge some of the files from `Chapter 11`, *Object-Oriented Programming,* to provide the base application. The files that we will need from `Chapter 13`, *Building Applications,* include the following:

- `main.ts`
- `package.json`
- `/src (directory)`
- `/routes (directory)`
- `/views (directory)`
- `/css (directory)`

With these files in place, we can issue an `npm install` from the command line.

We can then compile our application with the following three commands:

```
ng build
tsc main.ts
tsc -p routes
```

Once compiled, we can then run `node main` command from the command line to start our Express application. Browsing to the site at `http://localhost:3000` will show the default login screen from `Chapter 13`, *Building Applications*:

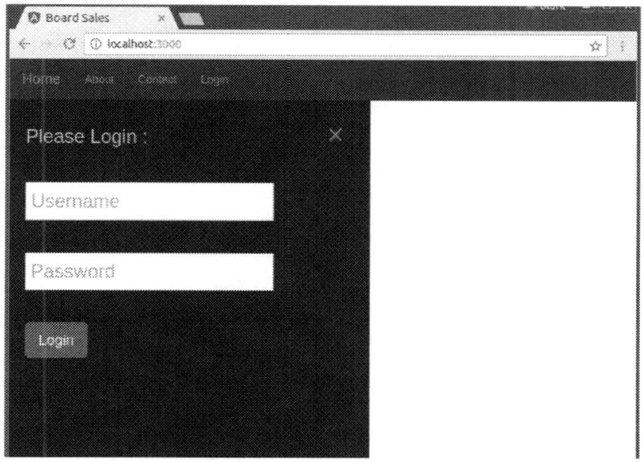


Our base application is now up and running, and ready for a merge of the code to create the left-to-right panel design, and implement the State and Mediator design patterns.

We can combine these command line options into a single step by editing the `package.json` file in the project root directory, and adding an entry into the `scripts` configuration as follows:

```
"scripts": {
  "ng": "ng",
  "start": "ng serve",
  "test": "ng test",
  "pree2e":
    "webdriver-manager update --standalone false --gecko false",
  "e2e": "protractor",
  "build_all": "ng build && tsc main.ts && tsc -p routes"
},
```

Here, we have added a `build_all` script to our configuration which will execute all three of our build steps one after another. In order to run this step, we can use the `run-script` option of `npm` as follows:

```
npm run-script build_all
```

# Unit testing

Any production website, or indeed production source code, should be fully tested before it is shipped. This testing process includes unit, integration, and acceptance tests that give us confidence that the site is behaving as expected. As we did in `Chapter 9`, *Testing Typescript Compatible Frameworks*, let's now set up a test suite for our application, so that we can follow a test-driven development methodology. For unit testing, we will use Karma, which is the standard process of unit testing Angular 2 applications. Our Angular application already has all of the pre-requisites installed in order to use Karma, so we can start Karma by typing the following on the command line:

```
npm test
```

Running `npm test` now will report on the command line that there are currently no tests within our project, as follows:

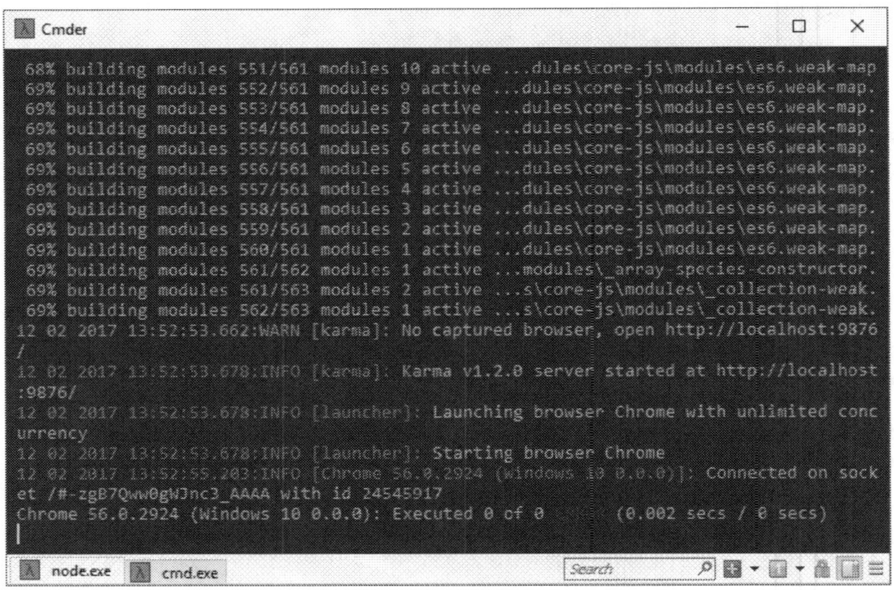


Karma test runner indicating that no tests were found

Remember that if a file has the word `.spec.` in its filename, it will be run as a test, no matter where in the `src` directory the filename exists.

Our test framework is now in place.

# State Mediator tests

The first module that we will merge from `Chapter 11`, *Object-Oriented Programming*, will be the `state.mediator.ts` file that contains our implementation of the State and Mediator design pattern. This file can be copied over without change, as it only contains standard `TypeScript` classes, without any Angular specific code. We can then create a `tests` directory under the `src` directory, and create a test file named `state.mediator.spec.ts`.

> Angular recommends creating `.spec` files in the same directory as the actual component under test. This would mean that the `app` directory would contain both the `state.mediator.ts` file, and the `state.mediator.spec.ts` file. While this may help to indicate which files have tests, the amount of files within an application directory quickly becomes very noisy. It is easier to create a separate `test` directory to house test files, so that they can be located quickly, without having to search through many files in the application directory.

Our first test will be a sanity test to prove that the testing process works, and that Karma is finding our tests, and running them correctly, as follows:

```
describe('app/tests/state.mediator.spec.ts', () => {
  it('should fail', () => {
    expect(true).toBeFalsy();
  });
});
```

Here, we have a simple Jasmine test that should fail. Running `npm test` at this stage will pick up our `state.mediator.spec.ts` file as a test suite, execute the test, and report a failure on the command line, as follows:

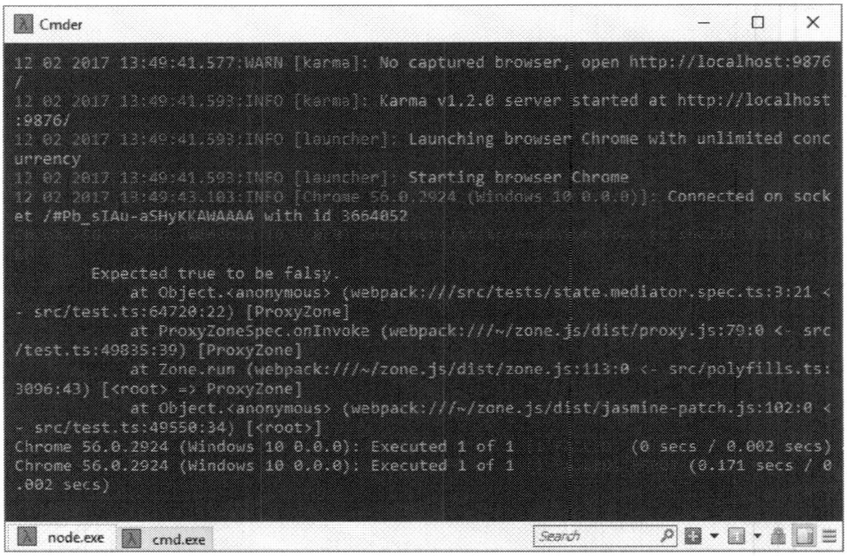


Karma test runner showing one test failure

Note how the test suite has been named–`'src/tests/state.mediator.spec.ts'`. Naming your test suite with the exact filename that contains the test will help to identify which test suite is responsible for the failure in the future. Instead of searching through your source code base for the exact wording on the `describe` function, you will be able to go directly to the file that contains the test. This will also help when debugging tests, as you immediately know which file to look at.

Now that we have our test environment set up, we can focus on the tests that we need for the State and Mediator classes.

The Mediator class contains all of the code for switching between states in our application. It has a few important functions:

- Set the application to an initial state
- Call UI functions on the `IMediatorImpl` interface as a result of moving between states
- Store the current state
- Store the current state of the main panel

Our tests, therefore, will need to cover each of these scenarios. Let's start then, with a test to ensure that the initial state of the application is correctly set, as follows:

```
import { Mediator,
  IMediatorImpl,
  StateType,
  PanelType,
  MainPanelOnly,
  MainPanelWithSideNav } from '../app/state.mediator';
class MockMediatorImpl implements IMediatorImpl {
  showNavPanel() {}
  hideNavPanel() {}
  showDetailPanel() {}
  hideDetailPanel() { }
  changeShowHideSideButton(fromClass: string, toClass: string) {};
}
describe('src/tests/state.mediator.spec.ts', () => {
  let mockMediatorImpl : IMediatorImpl;
  beforeEach(() => {
    mockMediatorImpl = new MockMediatorImpl();
  });
  it('should set initial state', () => {
    let mediator = new Mediator(mockMediatorImpl);
    expect(mediator.getCurrentMainPanelState())
      .toBe(StateType.MainPanelWithSideNav);
  });
});
```

Here, we start with an `import` of the relevant modules from the `state.mediator` file. We then create a class named `MockMediatorImpl` that implements the `IMediatorImpl` interface. Remember that the constructor function of the `Mediator` class requires an implementation of this interface as a parameter. Instead of using the actual `AppComponent` within our test, we can simply mock out the implementation of this interface through a mock class. Also, our tests will not actually be updating any user interface, and are therefore not doing anything when each of these functions are called. This is again an example of good object-oriented code. The `Mediator` class has a single dependency, and we have abstracted that dependency into an interface, to allow us to inject multiple different implementations. In this case, we are injecting a mock object simply for testing purposes.

Our first test simply creates an instance of the `Mediator` class, and then checks that the current main panel state has been set correctly. This test indicates that we are expecting to show the side navigation panel and the main panel, when the application starts up.

Our next unit test will check that the `hideNavPanel` function of our `IMediatorImpl` interface is called correctly, when we move from the initial state of `MainPanelWithSideNav` to the `MainPanelOnly` state, as follows:

```
it('should call hideNavPanel', () => {
  let spy = spyOn(mockMediatorImpl, 'hideNavPanel');
  let mediator = new Mediator(mockMediatorImpl);
  mediator.moveToState(StateType.MainPanelOnly);
  expect(spy).toHaveBeenCalled();
});
```

Here, we start by creating a spy on the `hideNavPanel` function of our `mockMediatorImpl` class. We then create an instance of the `Mediator` class, and call the `moveToState` function with a state type of `MainPanelOnly`. This function call will be used within our application to hide the left-hand side navigation panel, as we saw in `Chapter 11`, *Object-Oriented Programming*. Note that we `expect` that the `spy` should have been called. This test is therefore testing the following code within the `Mediator` class:

```
if (nextState.isSideNavVisible())
  this._mediatorImpl.showNavPanel();
else
  this._mediatorImpl.hideNavPanel();
```

We are moving to a state where the side navigation panel is hidden (`MainPanelOnly`), and therefore should see the `hideNavPanel` function called when this code is executed.

Our next test will check that the state of the main panel is updated, when we move from the `MainPanelWithSideNav` state to the `MainPanelOnly` state. Remember that we are storing the state of the main panel so that when a user navigates to the detail panel and then back again, the state of the main panel is restored correctly. Our test is as follows:

```
it('should store current MainPanelState with SideNav hidden', () => {
  let mediator = new Mediator(mockMediatorImpl);
  mediator.moveToState(StateType.MainPanelOnly);
  expect(mediator.getCurrentMainPanelState())
    .toBe(StateType.MainPanelOnly);
});
```

This test simply moves to the `MainPanelState`, and then calls the `getCurrentMainPanelState` function directly afterwards to ensure that the stored internal state has been updated correctly.

# Login screen state

Our current application does not have the side navigation components or right screen components integrated into it as of yet, and it is simply showing a login panel. What we need to do now is to integrate the login panel into our State and Mediator pattern so that we can control when and where the login panel is displayed. To do this, we need a new `StateType enum` entry, and a new `PanelType enum` entry, as follows:

```
export enum StateType {
  MainPanelOnly,
  MainPanelWithSideNav,
  DetailPanel,
  LoginPanel
}
export enum PanelType {
  Primary,
  Detail,
  OverlayPanel
}
```

Here, we have updated our `StateType` enum to include a `LoginPanel` state, and have also updated the `PanelType` enum to include an `OverlayPanel` entry. Remember that the panels we are displaying are either the `Primary` panel (with or without side navigation), the `Detail` panel, or an `Overlay` panel. This `OverlayPanel` could include other screens, such as a Contact Us panel or a Register panel. It makes sense, therefore, to create a new `PanelType` so that we do not interfere with the current logic of switching between the main and detail panels.

Our `IState` interface will now need to be updated to include an `isLoginVisible` function, as follows:

```
export interface IState {
  getPanelType() : PanelType;
  getStateType() : StateType;
  isSideNavVisible() : boolean;
  getPanelButtonClass() : string;
  isLoginVisible(): boolean;
}
```

Again, this is a simple one-line change to our interface definition, but it will require that all of the current states are updated to implement this function. Their implementation will simply return `false`.

We now need a new `State` class, as follows:

```
export class LoginPanel implements IState {
  getPanelType() : PanelType { return PanelType.OverlayPanel; }
  getStateType() : StateType { return StateType.LoginPanel; }
  getPanelButtonClass() : string { return '';}
  isSideNavVisible() : boolean { return false; }
  isLoginVisible(): boolean { return true; };
}
```

Here, we have created a new class named `LoginPanel` to represent our login panel state. The `PanelType` will be `OverlayPanel`, the `StateType` will be `LoginPanel`, and the `isLoginVisible` function now returns `true`. We can now create a unit test to ensure that these values are set correctly, as follows:

```
it('should create LoginPanel state object with correct
parameters', () => {
  let loginState = new LoginPanel();
  expect(loginState.getPanelType()).toBe(PanelType.OverlayPanel);
  expect(loginState.getStateType()).toBe(StateType.LoginPanel);
  expect(loginState.isLoginVisible()).toBe(true);
});
```

Here, we are creating a `LoginPanel` object, and ensuring that each of the parameters are set correctly. While this may not seem like a particularly useful unit test, remember that it is there to ensure that our objects are behaving correctly. If we need to make modifications to these state classes, our simple tests will guard against inadvertent changes, as the properties of each of these classes drive our application flow.

The showing or hiding of the login panel will need to be implemented by the user interface, and then triggered by the `Mediator` class. In order to trigger the showing and hiding of the login panel, we will need to update our `IMediatorImpl` interface to include these functions, as follows:

```
export interface IMediatorImpl {
  showNavPanel() : void;
  hideNavPanel() : void;
  showDetailPanel() : void;
  hideDetailPanel() : void;
  changeShowHideSideButton
    (fromClass: string, toClass: string) : void;
  showLoginPanel() : void;
  hideLoginPanel() : void;
}
```

Here, we have added two new functions, named `showLoginPanel` and `hideLoginPanel` that will control the display of the login panel. Again, these functions will need to be implemented by the class that implements this interface.

We need to make two more changes to the `Mediator` class to incorporate the new `LoginPanel` state. Firstly, we need to create an instance of this state as a `private` variable of the `Mediator` class, as follows:

```
export class Mediator {
  private _mainPanelState = new MainPanelOnly();
  private _detailPanelState = new DetailPanel();
  private _sideNavState = new MainPanelWithSideNav();
  private _loginState = new LoginPanel();
```

Here, we have created a new private member variable named `_loginState` to house an instance of the `LoginPanel` state class, as we have done with the other states.

Secondly, we also need to return the instance of this class in the `getStateImpl` function, as follows:

```
getStateImpl(stateType: StateType) : IState {
  var stateImpl : IState;
  switch(stateType) {
    case StateType.DetailPanel:
        stateImpl = this._detailPanelState;
        break;
    case StateType.MainPanelOnly:
        stateImpl = this._mainPanelState;
        break;
    case StateType.MainPanelWithSideNav:
        stateImpl = this._sideNavState;
        break;
    case StateType.LoginPanel:
        stateImpl = this._loginState;
        break;
  }
  return stateImpl;
}
```

Here, we have added a new `case` statement to return the instance of the `LoginPanel` state class within the `getStateImpl` function.

Let's now write a unit test to ensure that these functions are called correctly, as follows:

```
it('should call showLoginPanel', () => {
  let spy = spyOn(mockMediatorImpl, 'showLoginPanel');
  let mediator = new Mediator(mockMediatorImpl);
  mediator.moveToState(StateType.LoginPanel);
  expect(spy).toHaveBeenCalled();
});
```

This test is simply spying on the `showLoginPanel` function that we created earlier, and checking whether this function is called when we move to the `LoginPanel` state. Running the test at this state, however, will fail with the following message:

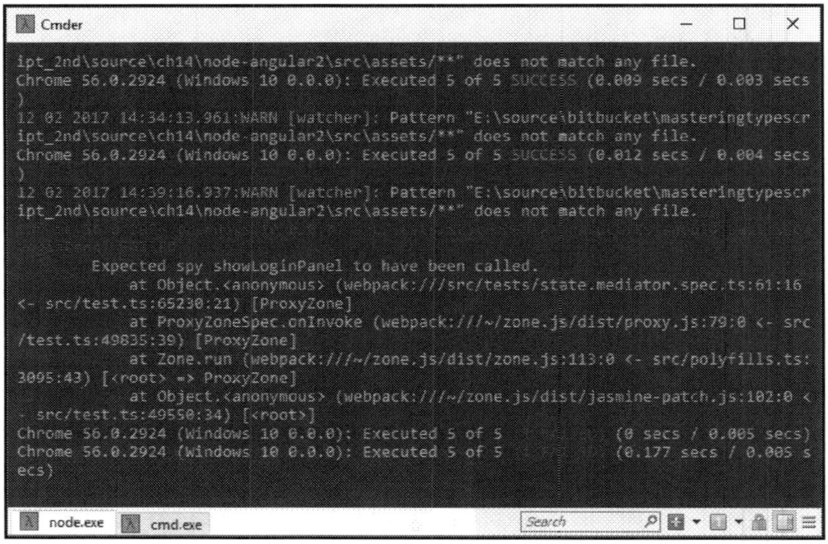


As expected, the new function, named `showLoginPanel`, will not have been called, as we have not made any changes to the `moveToState` function to handle our `LoginPanel` state. Let's do so now:

```
moveToState(stateType: StateType) {
  var previousState = this._currentState;
  var nextState = this.getStateImpl(stateType);
  if (nextState.isLoginVisible())
    this._mediatorImpl.showLoginPanel();
  else
    this._mediatorImpl.hideLoginPanel();
```

Here, we are calling the `isLoginVisible` function to determine if we should show or hide the login panel. Remember that all of the existing states will return `false` when this function is called, and only the new `LoginPanel` state will return `true`, which will trigger the `showLoginPanel` function to be called. With this change in place, our test will now pass.

# Panel integration

We can now turn our attention to integrating the left-to-right panel design that we worked through in `Chapter 11`, *Object-Oriented Programming*, into our current Node and Express application. Remember that this consisted of the following components:

- `sidenav.component`: The left-hand side navigation panel that will be used for our filter mechanism
- `app.component`: The main application controller that coordinates UI elements
- `navbar.component`: The top navigation panel
- `rightscreen.component`: The right-hand side panel that will be used to display board details
- `app.module`: The Angular 2 component registration module

The components that need to be copied into our current application are the `sidenav.component`, the `app.component`, and the `rightscreen.component`. We will leave the `navbar.component` and the `app.module` files as they are for the time being.

Compiling the application at this stage will produce the following error:

```
app/app.component.ts(11,14): error TS2420: Class 'AppComponent'
incorrectly implements interface 'IMediatorImpl'.
Property 'showLoginPanel' is missing in type 'AppComponent'.
```

Remember that we have updated the `IMediatorImpl` interface to include two new functions, named `showLoginPanel` and `hideLoginPanel`, so these functions will need to be implemented in the `app.component.ts` file.

Before we run the application to see if it works, we will need to make a few minor tweaks here and there. Firstly, we need to update the `app.module.ts` file to register our components for use within the HTML, as follows:

```
// existing imports
import { LoginComponent } from './login.component';
import { SideNavComponent } from './sidenav.component';
import { RightScreenComponent } from './rightscreen.component';

@NgModule({
  imports:       [ BrowserModule, HttpModule, FormsModule ],
  declarations: [
    AppComponent,
    NavbarComponent,
    LoginComponent,
    SideNavComponent,
    RightScreenComponent,
  ],
  bootstrap:     [ AppComponent ]
})
export class AppModule { }
```

Here, we have imported the `SideNavComponent` and `RightScreenComponent`, and then included them in the declarations array of the `AppModule` class. Remember that in order to use any of our components within HTML files, we need to declare them first. This allows us to use `<sidenav-component>` and `<rightscreen-component>` tags in our `app.component.html` file.

Lastly, we will need to include `font-awesome` in our `package.json` file, and update our `angular-cli.json` file to include the `font-awesome.min.css` file.

With these changes in place, we can fire up our application, and we will now have the original left-to-right panel implementation working within our Node application, as follows:

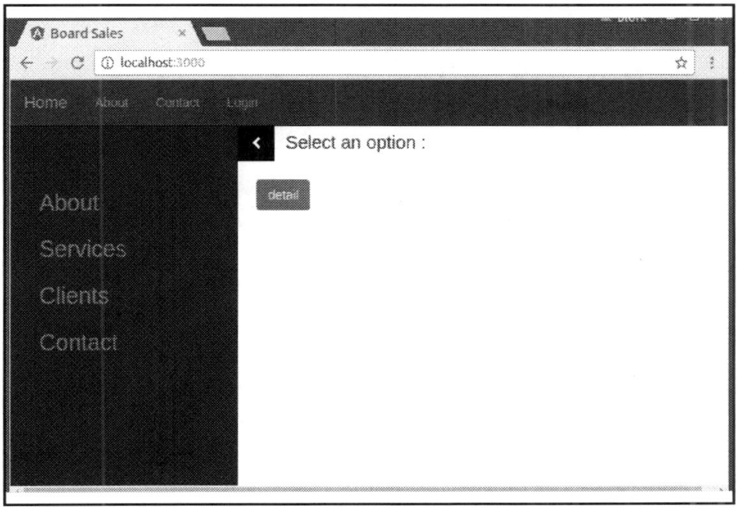


## JSON data structure

With our basic application shell in place, we can now concentrate on the data structure that we will use to show both the board list on the main panel, and the board detail view on the right-hand side detail panel. A class diagram of this relationship is as follows:

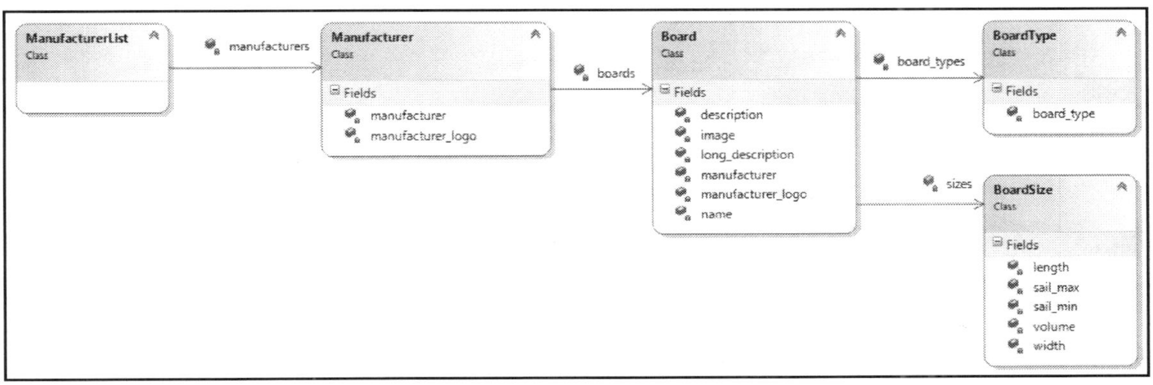


Here we start with the `ManufacturerList` object that contains an array of `Manufacturer` objects. Each `Manufacturer` object has three properties. Firstly, a `manufacturer` property, which contains the name of the manufacturer, and secondly a `manufacturer_logo` property, which will contain the name of the image to render as the manufacturer's logo. The third property is named `boards`, and it contains an array of `Board` items.

Each `Board` item contains a `name`, `description`, `image`, and `long_description` property, as well as the `manufacturer` name and `manfufacturer_logo` properties from its parent. The `Board` item contains two array elements, named `board_types` and `sizes`. The `board_types` array will contain a list of strings that hold the type of board.

Remember that any particular board could be a hybrid between a `Wave` board and a `Freestyle` board, for example, so we need an array to hold this relationship. The `sizes` array contains a list of the `BoardSize` elements, each with a `length`, `volume`, and `width` property, along with a `sail_max` and `sail_min` property to hold minimum and maximum sail sizes for each board.

Note that the names of the classes in this diagram are not relevant at this stage; it is only the structure that is important.

This structure can be represented in JSON format, as follows:

```
"manufacturer": "JP Australia",
"manufacturer_logo": "jp_australia_logo.png",
"boards": [
  {
    "name": "Radical Quad",
    "board_types": [ { "board_type": "Wave" } ],
    "manufacturer": "JP Australia",
    "manufacturer_logo": "jp_australia_logo.png",
    "description": "Radical Wave Board",
    "image": "jp_windsurf_radicalquad_ov.png",
    "long_description": "There is no question ....",
    "sizes": [
      { "volume": 68,
        "length": 227, "width": 53,
        "sail_min": "< 5.0", "sail_max": "< 5.2" }
    ]
  }
```

Here, we have an extract of the JSON structure used to represent a single manufacturer, along with the boards that it produces. This structure matches our preceding class diagram.

> Class diagrams of JSON data structures are a very handy reference material when working within a team-based structure, and to help understand the capabilities of the system. It is far easier for business analysts and even fellow developers to refer to a class diagram than it is to trawl through reams of JSON data to understand data structures. If you are working with complex, nested structures within your application, then try to generate these sorts of diagrams from your code for consumption by the rest of the team.

We can now create an Express JSON endpoint to serve this JSON data to our application within the `/routes/index.ts` file, as follows:

```
router.get('/boards', (req, res, next) => {
  res.json(
[
  {
"manufacturer": "JP Australia",
"manufacturer_logo": "jp_australia_logo.png",
"logo_class" : "",
"boards": [
  {
// the rest of the JSON structure
```

Here, we have created a REST endpoint named `'/boards'` to simply return the JSON data structure.

> Data structures like this would normally be served from a database or object store of some sort. For simplicity, we are currently returning a hard-coded JSON data structure.

Our application will need to consume this JSON data structure, so let's create a TypeScript file that describes this structure as a set of interfaces, in a file named `IBoardList.ts`, as follows:

```
export interface IBoardSizeItem {
  volume: number;
  length: number;
  width: number;
  sail_min: string;
  sail_max: string;
}
export interface IBoardType {
  board_type: string;
}
export interface IBoardListItem {
  name: string;
  description?: string;
  image?: string;
  long_description?: string;
  board_types?: IBoardType [];
  sizes?: IBoardSizeItem [];
}
export interface IManufacturer {
  manufacturer: string;
  manufacturer_logo: string;
```

```
  boards?: IBoardListItem[];
}
```

Here, we have created a set of interfaces to match our JSON data structure, as documented in the class diagram.

## The BoardList component

With our REST endpoint in place to serve the list of manufacturers and boards, we can now start building the Angular component that will render the list of boards on the main panel. This component will be named `boardlist.component`, and it will have a corresponding `.ccs` and `.html` file. The `boardlist.component.ts` file is as follows:

```
import { Component, Injectable, EventEmitter, Output }
  from '@angular/core';
import { Http, Response, Headers, RequestOptions }
  from '@angular/http';
import { Observable } from 'rxjs/Rx';
import {
  IBoardSizeItem,
  IBoardType,
  IBoardListItem,
  IManufacturer
  } from './IBoardList';
@Component( {
  selector: 'boardlist-component',
  templateUrl: './app/boardviews/boardlist.component.html',
  styleUrls: ['app/boardviews/boardlist.component.css']
})
@Injectable()
export class BoardListComponent {
  manufacturerList: IManufacturer [];
  constructor(private http: Http) {
    console.log(`BoardListComponent constructor`);
    this.http.get('/boards')
      .map(res => res.text())
      .subscribe(
      (data) => {
        let jsonResponse = JSON.parse(data);
        this.manufacturerList = jsonResponse;
      },
      err => {
        console.log(`error : ${err}`);
      },
      () => {
        console.log(`success`);
```

```
            }
            );
        }
    }
```

We start by importing the relevant modules that we need from `'@angular/core'`, `'@angular/http'`, `'rxjs/Rx'`, and our newly created interfaces from `'IBoardList'`.

The `BoardListComponent` class is decorated by the `@Component` decorator, and it specifies the `selector`, `templateUrl`, and `styleUrls` properties as per usual. It is also decorated with the `@Injectable()` decorator in order to inject the `Http` component as part of the constructor. This class has a single property named `manufacturerList` that will house the JSON data structure that is fetched from the REST endpoint.

The `constructor` function uses the Angular `Http` module to connect to our REST endpoint named `'/boards'`, and if successful, it will set the `manufacturerList` property to the JSON data structure that is returned.

This class is no different to any REST enabled class that we have seen before, and so the code should be pretty self-explanatory.

# Unit testing HTTP requests

As we are trying to follow a test-driven development methodology for building components for our application, let's take the time to write a set of unit tests for this `BoardListComponent` class.

Our class constructor contains some internal logic that we would like to write a unit test for. Firstly, it issues an HTTP request to a REST endpoint. Secondly, if this request was successful, it will store the returned data structure into a property named `manufacturerList`. Our unit test, therefore, will need to accomplish the following:

- Set up a mock REST endpoint to be called during the unit test
- Allow us to modify the JSON that is returned to the component
- Inject this mock endpoint into the component
- Ensure that the internal properties that house this data are correctly assigned

## Mocking Angular's Http module

Let us therefore create a new test, in the `/src/tests/` directory named `boardlist.component.spec.ts`, as follows:

```
import { DebugElement } from '@angular/core';
import { async,
  ComponentFixture,
  TestBed,
  inject } from '@angular/core/testing';
import { By } from '@angular/platform-browser';
import { Http,
  BaseRequestOptions,
  Response,
  Headers,
  RequestOptions,
  ResponseOptions } from '@angular/http';
import { MockBackend, MockConnection } from '@angular/http/testing';
import { BoardListComponent } from '../app/boardlist.component';
describe('src/tests/boardlist.component.spec.ts', () => {
  it('should connect to a mock http provider', () => {
    expect(true).toBeFalsy();
  });
});
```

Here, we are importing a number of modules from the `'@angular/core'`, `'@angular/core/testing'`, `'@angular/platform-browser'`, `'@angular/http/testing'`, and `'@angular/http'` modules. We will not go through these in detail at this point, but we will use these modules when we construct the complete test itself.

We are also importing the `BoardListComponent` class itself, and have written a simple sanity test to ensure that the test is picked up by our Karma test environment, and is purposely failing.

With a failing test in place, we can now start to flesh out the mock HTTP request handler. Remember that we want to be able to inject the data that is return by the HTTP request handler as part of each test, so that we can build a full suite of tests for our component. Some of these tests will be edge-case tests, and may throw exceptions, or return invalid JSON. Writing edge-case tests like these helps to insulate our application when errors occur. In other words, what happens when the REST endpoint is unavailable? How will the component react?

Building a mock HTTP request handler in an Angular test environment is accomplished in two phases. Firstly, we need to register a mock HTTP handler with the Angular dependency injection framework, and secondly, we need to specify the JSON that this handler will return within our test.

Our mock HTTP registration is written in the `beforeEach` function, as follows:

```
beforeEach( async(() => {
  TestBed.configureTestingModule(
    {
      declarations : [ BoardListComponent],
      providers : [
        MockBackend,
        BaseRequestOptions,
        {
          provide: Http,
          useFactory: (
            instance: MockBackend,
            options: BaseRequestOptions
          ) => {
              return new Http(
                instance,
                options
              );
          },
          deps: [
            MockBackend,
            BaseRequestOptions
          ]
        }
      ]
    }
  )
  .compileComponents();
}));
```

This seems like a fairly confusing block of code, so let's take a look at it inside-out. In other words, let's focus on the deepest block of code in this nested code block, and then work our way outside from this point. If we use this technique, then the code block becomes more understandable.

We are mocking the `Http` object that will be injected into the `BoardListComponent` by the Angular DI framework. However, in order to create an instance of an `Http` object, we need two things–an instance and some base options. This can be seen in the innermost call, as follows:

```
return new Http(
  instance,
  options
);
```

The `instance` and `options` objects that are used here are passed into the enclosing `useFactory` function, as follows:

```
useFactory: (
  instance: MockBackend,
  options: BaseRequestOptions
) => {
// return new Http
}
```

The `instance` and `options` parameters that are used by this function are, in fact, provided by the dependency injection framework, and are therefore named as dependencies by the `deps` property, as follows:

```
deps: [
  MockBackend,
  BaseRequestOptions
]
```

Then, the `useFactory` function is providing an instance of the `Http` interface, and therefore has a provide property, as follows:

```
provide: Http
```

This `useFactory` configuration must be registered as a provider for our tests, and therefore is included in the `providers` property, as follows:

```
providers : [
  MockBackend,
  BaseRequestOptions,
  {
    provide: Http
```

The dependency injection framework must also know which class instance to inject these providers into, and this is specified by the `declarations` property, as follows:

```
declarations : [ BoardListComponent],
providers : [
  MockBackend,
```

Finally, the `declarations` and `providers` properties are used by the call to `TestBed.configureTestingModule`.

This entire code block, therefore, can be described as a series of steps, as follows:

- Call the `TestBed.configureTestingModule` function, passing in a configuration object
- Use the `declarations` property to determine which object needs dependencies injected into it
- Use the `providers` property to declare which objects will be available for dependency injection
- If one of the providers specifies a `provide` property, then use this as the interface for injection
- If one of the `providers` specifies a `useFactory` function, then call this function to create an instance of the interface for injection
- If one of the providers specifies a `deps` property, then use these as dependencies to the `useFactory` method

Simple, right? Well, not really, but this is the nature of Angular's DI framework.

# Using the mock Http module

With our `beforeEach` function in place, we can now focus on the test itself, which is as follows:

```
it('should connect to a mock http provider',
  async(
    inject (
      [MockBackend],
      (mockBackend : MockBackend) => {
        // configure response
        mockBackend.connections
          .subscribe( (conn : any)  =>
         {
          conn.mockRespond(
            new Response(new ResponseOptions(
```

```
                { body: JSON.stringify(
                  [ ]
                )}
              )));
          }
        ); // end of subscribe function
        let fixture =
          TestBed.createComponent(BoardListComponent);
        let boardListInstance = fixture.componentInstance;
        expect(boardListInstance.manufacturerList)
          .toBeDefined();
        } // end of test block
      ) // end of inject function
    ) // end of async function
  ); // end of it function
```

Again, this code block seems rather complicated, so let's take a look at the inner-most code, and work our way outward. The test starts with a call to the `mockBackend.connections.subscribe` function. This function is setting up the JSON response to return through our `MockBackend` instance, and it will return the JSON object within the `JSON.stringify` function, which in this case is an empty array.

Once this JSON response has been constructed, we can create an instance of the `BoardListComponent` class by calling the `TestBed.createComponent` function. The returned value of this function is stored in the `fixture` variable. To access the actual instance of the `BoardListComponent`, we must use the `componentInstance` property of the `fixture` variable. Once we have a handle to the `fixture.componentInstance`, we can interrogate the `manufacturerList` property and ensure that it is not undefined, in other words, that it has been initialized.

Remember that our `BoardListComponent` class will only create the `manufacturerList` property when a valid JSON response is received from the REST endpoint. This means that our test is checking that the HTTP response is valid, by testing whether the `manufacturerList` property is defined.

The `mockBackend` object is created through the Angular dependency injection pipeline, and therefore needs to be wrapped in a call to the `inject` function. This `inject` function has the same syntax as the `require` function that we used for module loading, and it is called with an array of interfaces to inject, and a callback function that receives concrete implementations of these interfaces.

The `inject` function is then wrapped as an `async` function within our Jasmine test.

Now that we have the basics of a mocked `Http` module, let's create a new test that returns the actual JSON that we are expecting from our REST endpoint. In the interests of brevity, the only changes to this test are to return an updated JSON object, as follows:

```
{ body: JSON.stringify(
  [
    {
      manufacturer: 'test',
      boards : [
        { name : 'test1'},
        { name : 'test2'}
      ]
    }
  ]
)}
```

Here, we have modified the JSON response to return a single `Manufacturer` object within it that has two associated `boards`. Our test for this JSON response is as follows:

```
let fixture = TestBed.createComponent(BoardListComponent);
let boardListInstance = fixture.componentInstance;
expect(boardListInstance.manufacturerList.length).toBe(1);
expect(boardListInstance.manufacturerList[0].boards.length).toBe(2);
```

Here, we are interrogating the `manufacturerList` property to ensure that it contains a single element, and are then checking the `boards` property to ensure that it contains two sub elements.

# Rendering the board list

Now that we have a set of unit tests that test the internal logic of the `BoardListComponent`, and ensures that it will load the list of manufacturers from our REST endpoint, we can turn our attention to rendering the HTML within the main panel. This will entail updating our `boardlist.component.html` template, as follows:

```
<div *ngFor="let manufacturer of currentList">
  <div *ngFor="let board of manufacturer.boards" >
    <div class="col-sm-4 board_panel"
        (click)="boardClicked(board)">
      <div class="board_inner_panel">
     <!-- board template  -->
     <!-- refer to sample code -->
     {{board.name}}
```

```
            {{board.description}}
            <table>
              <tr *ngFor="let size of board.sizes">
                <td>{{size.volume}}</td>
              </tr>
            </table>
             </div>
          </div>
        </div>
      </div>
```

This HTML template (which has been truncated for brevity) includes three `divs` that use the Angular `*ngFor` syntax for looping through array elements. The first `*ngFor` is looping through the `currentList` property of the `BoardListComponent` class, and using the variable `manufacturer` to reference each array element. Within this loop is the second `*ngFor` directive that is looping through the `boards` array for each element in the `manufacturer` array. The third `*ngFor` loop is rendering a `<tr>` element to render the `volume` property of the `board.sizes` array.

These `*ngFor` loops in our HTML template correspond to the data structure that is returned from our REST endpoint.

> For the full source code for this HTML template, and the CSS styles that are used in the `boardlist.component.css` file, please refer to the sample code download included with this book purchase.

Applying some CSS styles in the `boardlist.component.css` file renders the board list on the main page, as follows:

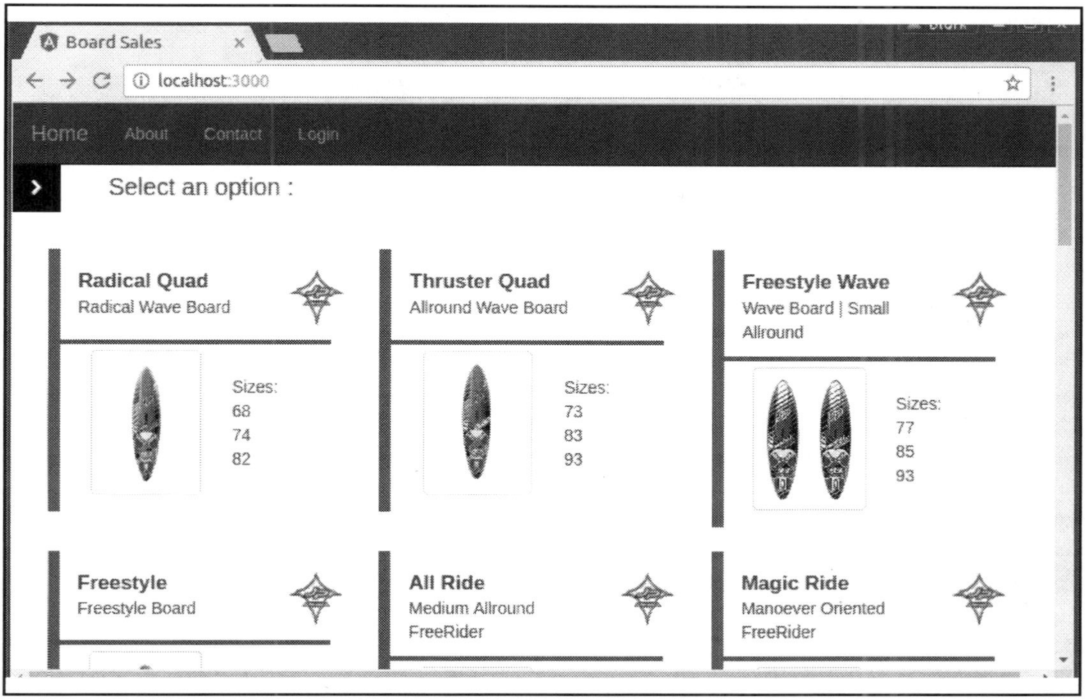


The BoardListComponent class rendering the board list

# Testing UI events

With the basics of the board list done, we can now turn our attention to displaying the detail panel when a user clicks on a board in the board list. As we have done in earlier chapters, we will use Angular's `EventEmitter` class to emit an event from the `boardlist` component that will be picked up by the `app` component. When this event is received, it will trigger a state change via the `Mediator` class to move to the detail panel. We already have a click handler registered in the `boardlist` HTML file, as follows:

```
<div *ngFor="let board of manufacturer.boards" >
  <div class="col-sm-4 board_panel"
    (click)="boardClicked(board)">
```

Here, within the `*ngFor` loop for the `boards` array, we have registered a `boardClicked` event that will raise an event. This event uses the entire `board` object as a parameter to the `boardClicked` event handler. Our event handler is therefore rather simple, as follows:

```
@Output() notify: EventEmitter<IBoardListItem>
  = new EventEmitter<IBoardListItem>();
boardClicked(board: IBoardListItem) {
  console.log(`clicked: ${board.name}`);
  this.notify.emit(board);
}
```

Here, we have registered an Angular `EventEmitter` named `notify` using the `@Output()` property decorator. Note how the `EventEmitter` is using the `IBoardListItem` interface as the model for the event. Our earlier `EventEmitter` implementations have previously used simple strings, but here we are now using a more complex model.

So how do we write a unit test for this event ? The answer is relatively simple. All we need to do is subscribe to this event in our test code, and then simulate a DOM click event on one of the board elements. Our test is therefore as follows:

```
it('should raise an event when a board has been clicked',
  async(
    inject (
      [MockBackend],
      (mockBackend : MockBackend) => {
        // configure response
        mockBackend.connections.subscribe(
          (conn : any)  =>
          {
            conn.mockRespond(
              new Response(new ResponseOptions(
                { body: JSON.stringify(
                  [
                    {
                       manufacturer: 'test',
                       boards : [
                         { name : 'test1'},
                         { name : 'test2'}
                       ]
                    }
                  ]
                )}
              )));
          }
        ); // end of subscribe function
          let fixture =
            TestBed.createComponent(BoardListComponent);
```

```
                fixture.detectChanges();
                let boardItem =
                  fixture.debugElement.query(
                    By.css('.board_panel'));
                expect(boardItem).toBeDefined();
                let eventEmitted : IBoardListItem;
                let component = fixture.componentInstance;
                component.notify.subscribe(
                 (event: IBoardListItem) => {
                   eventEmitted = event;
                 });
                 boardItem.triggerEventHandler('click', null);
                 expect(eventEmitted).toBeDefined();
                 } // end of test block
              ) // end of inject function
          ) // end of async function
    ); // end of it function
```

The first part of this test is setting up the JSON response, with a single manufacturer and two boards, as we have discussed earlier. Our test begins by creating an instance of the `BoardListComponent`. Once this has been done, we then call the `fixture.detectChanges` function. This function call is required in order to update the DOM within our test suite. Once the DOM has been updated, we can then call the `fixture.debugElement.query` function to search through the DOM for a particular HTML element. In this case, we are simply looking for the first `div` that has a class named `board_panel`. This is the element that we will trigger a click event on.

The next part of the test defines a variable named `eventEmitted` to hold the `IBoardListItem` object that will be sent as part of the event handler. We then get a handle to the actual instance of the `BoardListComponent` class through the `fixture.componentInstance` property, as we have done previously.

Our test then calls the `subscribe` function on the `notify` property of the `BoardListComponent` class, which will register an event handler within our test. This event handler simply assigns the event that was raised to our local `eventEmitted` property for interrogation later.

We then call the `triggerEventHandler` function on the DOM element itself. This call is simulating a DOM click event, which will then raise an event through our event handler. Finally, we are checking that the event itself has been raised correctly, and that the name of the board within the event matches the expected JSON value.

We now have a series of tests for our `BoardListComponent` class that covers its entire life cycle, from loading JSON from the backend, to rendering elements in the browser, and handling of DOM events. The techniques used in these tests can easily be extended for all of the other components within the application.

# Board detail view

Now that our application is raising click events on the main panel, we can turn our attention to handling this event in the app component, and calling the `Mediator` class to change application state, and show the board detail page. This is as simple as updating the `app.component.html` file to trap the event itself, as follows:

```
<div class="main-content">
  <boardlist-component
    (notify)='onNotifyBoardList($event)'>
  </boardlist-component>
</div>
```

Here, we have specified that the `onNotifyBoardList` event handler should be called when an event is raised from the `boardlist` component. The function within our app component is as follows:

```
onNotifyBoardList(board: IBoardListItem) {
  this.rightScreen.board = board;
  this.mediator.moveToState(StateType.DetailPanel);
}
```

Here, we are simply setting the `board` property of the `rightScreen` component to the value that was raised in the event. We then call the `Mediator` class to move to the `DetailPanel` state.

Our `rightScreen` component does not have a `board` property as of yet, so let's update this component and the HTML file to render a board detail panel. Our update to the `rightscreen` component is a simple one-liner, as follows:

```
export class RightScreenComponent
{
  board: IBoardListItem = { name: 'no board selected'};
  // existing code
```

Here, we have simply added a public property named `board` of type `IBoardListItem` to hold the currently selected board. Our HTML template can then be updated, as follows:

```
<div id="myRightScreen" class="overlay">
  <button class="btn btn-default" (click)="closeClicked()">
    <span class="fa fa-chevron-left"></span>
  </button>
<div class="overlay-content">
  <!--various styling -->
  {{board.name}}
  <!--various styling-->
  {{board.description}}
  <!--various styling-->
  <tr *ngFor="let size of board.sizes">
    <td>{{size.volume}}</td>
    <td>{{size.width}}</td>
  </tr>
</div>
</div>
```

Here, we have added a few properties within the `overlay-content <div>`, and also have an `*ngFor` loop to render each of the details of the `sizes` array.

> Note again that this is not the full HTML content, so please refer to the sample code.

With a little CSS in place, our detail view now comes to life, as follows:

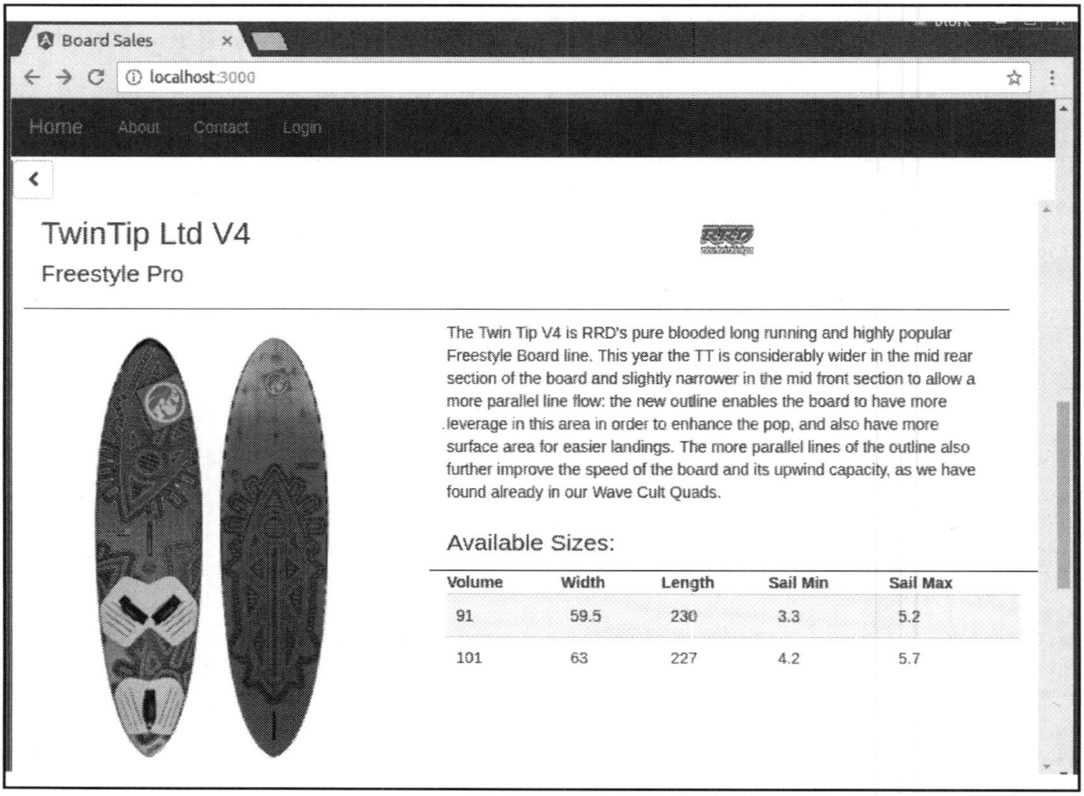


# Applying a filter

With the board list and detail views completed, we can now turn our attention to the `sidenav` component that will show our filter options. Before we filter items, however, we need to define a few interfaces to cover the data structure that we will use for our filter elements, as follows:

```
export enum FilterType {
  Manufacturer,
  BoardType,
  None
}
interface IFilter {
  filterName: string;
  filterType: FilterType;
```

```
  filterValues?: string [];
}

export interface IApplyFilter {
  filterType: FilterType;
  filterValue : string;
}
```

Here, we have defined an `enum` named `FilterType` that represents the type of filter that we are applying. Remember that we want to be able to filter our board list by either `Manufacturer` or `BoardType`, hence the `Manufacturer` and `BoardType` enum values. We will also need an enum value that represents no filters, which will in effect clear any currently applied filter, hence the `enum` value of `None`.

The `IFilter` interface is the data structure that we will use to render the HTML. It has a `filterName` property, which will be the top level header, a `filterType` property, and then a simple array of available `filter values`.

The `IApplyFilter` interface is what will be used when we raise an event from this component. It just has a `filterType` and a `filterValue` property to represent the filter that was selected.

In order to render these filters within our `SideNavComponent` class, we will just need a few minor changes, as follows:

```
export class SideNavComponent {
  @Output() notify: EventEmitter<IApplyFilter>
    = new EventEmitter<IApplyFilter>();
  filterList: IFilter [] = [
  {
    filterName: 'Manufacturer',
    filterType: FilterType.Manufacturer,
    filterValues: ['RRD', 'JP Australia', 'Starboard']
  },
  {
    filterName: 'Board Types',
    filterType: FilterType.BoardType,
    filterValues: ['Wave', 'Freestyle', 'Slalom']
  },
  {
    filterName: 'All',
    filterType: FilterType.None,
    filterValues: ['Clear Filter']
  }
  ]
  closeNav() {
```

```
      document.getElementById('mySidenav')
          .style.width = "0px";
    }
    showNav() {
      document.getElementById('mySidenav')
        .style.width = "250px";
    }
  }
```

Here, we have updated the `SideNavComponent` class to emit an event of type `IApplyFilter`, through the standard Angular event emission syntax. We have then defined a property named `filterList`, of type `IFilter []` that is used to hold the data structure for our filter elements.

> We could have created a JSON endpoint within our Express application to serve this data structure, but for the sake of brevity, we will just include the data structure directly.

We can now update the `sidenav.component.html` file, as follows:

```
<div id="mySidenav" class="sidenav">
  <h1>Apply Filter :</h1>
  <div *ngFor="let filter of filterList;">
    <div class="filterHeader">{{filter.filterName}}</div>
    <div *ngFor="let filterValue of filter.filterValues" >
      <a href="#"
        (click)= "filterClicked(filter, filterValue)">
          {{filterValue}}
      </a>
    </div>
  </div>
</div>
```

Here, we have two `*ngFor` loops within the template to loop through the `filterList` array, and then to loop through the `filterValues` array of each array element.

The interesting piece of this template, however, is the click event handler. Note how it is raising an event that takes two parameters. The first parameter is the parent filter from the outer `*ngFor` loop, and the second parameter is the `filterValue` from the inner `*ngFor` loop.

The implementation of this `filterClicked` function therefore must include both parameters, as follows:

```
filterClicked(filter: IFilter, filterValue: string) {
  this.notify.emit(
    {
      filterType : filter.filterType,
      filterValue: filterValue
    });
}
```

Here, the `filterClicked` event handler does indeed have two parameters–the first of the `IFilter` type, and the second of the `string` type. As the first parameter is the full `IFilter` type, we can therefore interrogate the `filterType` value of this parameter to determine the filter type that was selected.

With this information at hand, we raise a new event that is of type `IApplyFilter`, which includes both the `filterType` and the `filterValue`.

We can now listen for this event in our `app` component HTML, as follows:

```
<sidenav-component (notify)='onNotifyFilter($event)'>
</sidenav-component>
```

And implement the event handler in our `app` component itself, as follows:

```
onNotifyFilter( filter: IApplyFilter) {
  this.boardList.applyFilter(filter);
}
```

Here, we are simply calling the `applyFilter` function on the `boardList` component when we receive the event. Currently, however, we have not registered the `BoardListComponent` class as a view child, so we will need to do this in our `AppComponent` class, as follows:

```
@ViewChild(BoardListComponent)
private boardList: BoardListComponent;
```

And finally, we need the implementation of the `applyFilter` function on the `boardlist` component, as follows:

```
applyFilter( filter: IApplyFilter) {
  this.currentList = new Array();
  if (filter.filterType == FilterType.Manufacturer) {
    for (let manuf of this.manufacturerList) {
      if (manuf.manufacturer == filter.filterValue) {
        this.currentList.push(manuf);
      }
    }
  }
  // code for board type filter
  if (filter.filterType == FilterType.None) {
    this.currentList = this.manufacturerList;
  }
}
```

Here, we have the definition of the `applyFilter` function, which takes a single argument of the `IApplyFilter` type. The first thing that this function does is clear the `currentList` property, which is currently holding the entire (unfiltered) board list. If the `filterType` being passed in is of the `Manufacturer` type, then we loop through the master list (`this.manufacturerList`), and only copy the `manufacturers` into the current list that match the filter value.

If we are clearing the filter, then all we need to do is set the `currentList` property to the original copy of the master list, that is, `this.manufacturerList`.

> We have not shown the code for the filter on `BoardType` in this snippet, as it generally follows the same pattern as the `Manufacturer` filter. Except that it drills down into each board type to filter the board array based on board type. Again, please refer to the sample code for a full listing.

With these changes in place, opening the side navigation bar and selecting a filter will apply this filter to the current board list, as follows:

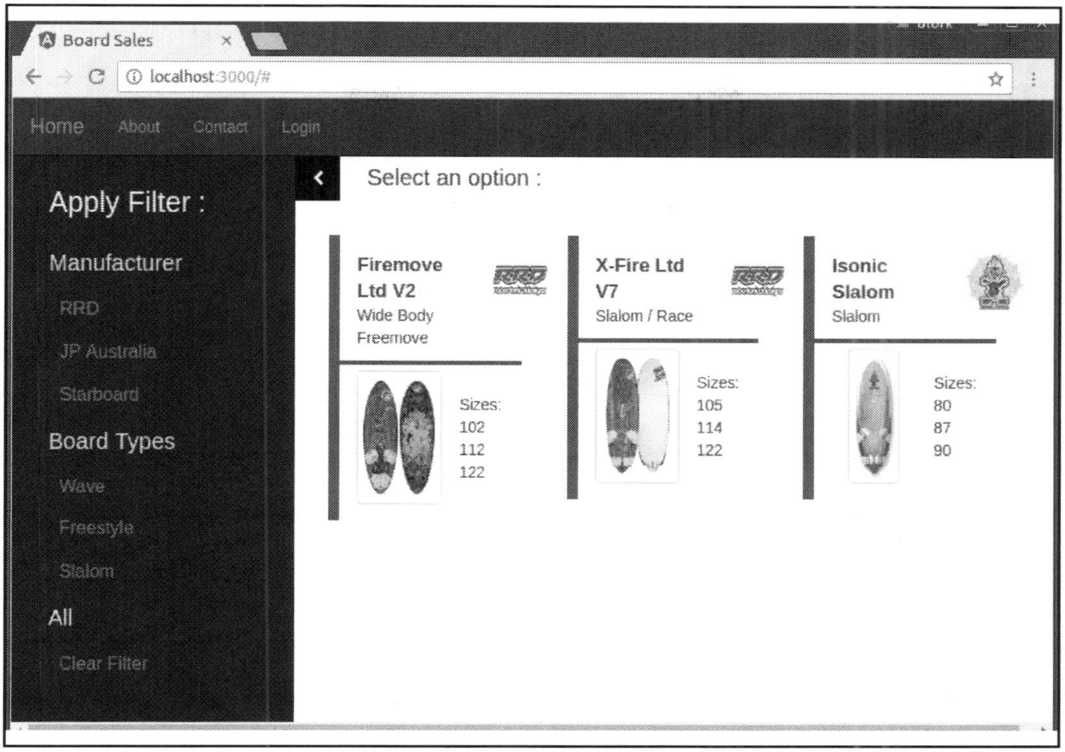


Board list with a filter applied

# The login panel

The final change that we will need to make is to show the login panel when a user clicks on the **Login** button on the navigation bar. To get this working, we already have most of the elements in place, and therefore simply need to wire up a couple of event handlers in the right places.

Firstly, we will need to react to a click event on the navigation bar itself. This means that we need a click handler within the `navbar` component, as follows:

```
navClicked(item : IButtonName) {
  this.notify.emit(`${item.ButtonName}`);
}
```

This event handler simply raises an event to say that one of the navigation bar items has been clicked, and includes the button name.

We will also need to register for this event in the app component, by updating the HTML as follows:

```
<navbar-component (notify)='onNotifyNavbar($event)'>
</navbar-component>
```

Here, we have defined a function named onNotifyNavbar as a handler for a notification event. The implementation of this is fairly simple, as follows:

```
onNotifyNavbar(message:string) {
  if (message == "Login") {
    this.mediator.moveToState(StateType.LoginPanel);
  }
}
```

Here, we are simply checking that the message has come from the "Login" button, and if so, are we calling the Mediator class to move to the LoginPanel state. Remember that this will trigger a call to either the showLoginPanel or the hideLoginPanel function in the app component. The implementation of these functions is as follows:

```
showLoginPanel() {
  document.getElementById('loginPanel')
    .classList.remove('login_sidenav_fade');
  document.getElementById('loginPanel')
    .style.visibility = "visible";
};
hideLoginPanel() {
  document.getElementById('loginPanel')
    .classList.add('login_sidenav_fade');
  setTimeout(() => {
    document.getElementById('loginPanel')
      .style.visibility = "hidden";
  }, 1000);
};
```

The showLoginPanel function is removing the login_sidenav_fade CSS class, and then setting the visibility attribute to "visible". The hideLoginPanel function is doing the exact opposite, but is also setting a one second timeout before setting the visibility attribute. This is done so that we get a nice fade-out animation when the login panel is hidden.

Our event handler is currently only showing the login panel, so we now need to hide it when the user logs in successfully. Again, this is a simple matter of raising an event in the `login` component, as follows:

```
this.http.post('/login', jsonPacket , {
  headers: headers
})
.map(res => res.text())
.subscribe(
  data => data,
  err => {
    console.log(`error : ${err}`);
  },
  () => {
    console.log(`success`);
    this.notify.emit("LOGIN_SUCCESSFUL");
  }
);
```

Here, we have added a `notify.emit` function call when the REST endpoint returns successfully, to raise the event that will trigger the `hideLoginPanel` function call. Again, we will need to register for this event in the `app` component, as follows:

```
onNotifyLogin(message: string) {
  this.mediator.moveToState(
    this.mediator.getCurrentMainWindowState());
}
```

Here, we are simply calling the `Mediator` class to move to the current main window state. This function has not been implemented in our `Mediator` class as of yet, so let's update it to be able to store the current state of the main window before the login overlay was shown, as follows:

```
export class Mediator {
  // exising variables
  private _mediatorImpl: IMediatorImpl;
  private _mainWindowState: Istate;
  getCurrentMainWindowState() : StateType {
    return this._mainWindowState.getStateType();
}
```

Here, we have created a new private variable named _mainWindowState, and defined the getCurrentMainWindowState function to return this value. We will also need to update our moveToState function slightly, in order to store this value at the correct time, as follows:

```
moveToState(stateType: StateType) {
  var previousState = this._currentState;
  var nextState = this.getStateImpl(stateType);
  if (nextState.isLoginVisible()) {
    this._mediatorImpl.showLoginPanel();
    this._mainWindowState = previousState;
  }
  else {
    this._mediatorImpl.hideLoginPanel();
    // existing state logic
  }
  this._currentState = nextState;
  if (this._currentState.getPanelType() == PanelType.Primary ) {
    this._currentMainPanelState = this._currentState;
  }
}
```

Our change to the moveToState function is to check whether the nextState we need has the login panel visible or not. If it does, we must store the current state of the main window in our _mainWindowState variable. If it does not, then we continue processing as per normal. This change will allow us to show the login panel as an overlay no matter what the state of the current main panel is. In other words, we can be on the detail panel and then click on the **Login** button, and the application will respond correctly, as shown in the following screenshot:

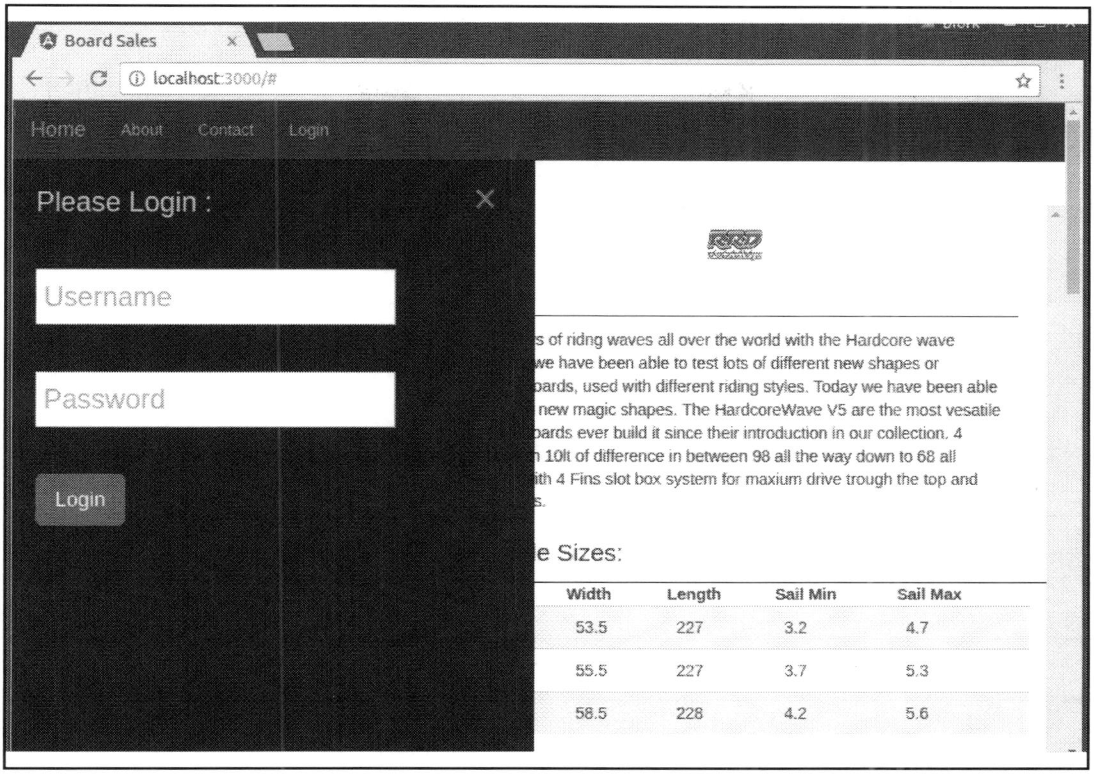

The login overlay panel showing when in detail view

Our work with the sample application is complete.

# Application architecture

If we look back at the work we have done on the sample application, we will notice that the architecture used is of sound quality. Our application is made up of a number of independent components. Each of these components are dedicated to one single area of responsibility. A `navbar` component, for example, is only responsible for rendering and responding to events that occur within the navigation bar itself. This component architecture was also evident when we merged components from previous chapters together into a single, large application. Most of the components only needed a few minor modifications, and were then ready for use.

All of our components communicate through events, and are therefore loosely-coupled. The app component itself is the event aggregator. It is responsible for listening to various component events, and then coordinating the application state accordingly. Our state handling code has also been encapsulated into the `State` and `Mediator` classes, and as we have seen, this design pattern has helped immensely in simplifying our application code.

# Summary

In this chapter, we have built a sample application by piecing together components from earlier chapters. We started with a strong focus on unit testing, and built a test framework that covers the main features of our application. Through this test framework, we can simulate application state, simulate REST endpoint integration, and also simulate UI events such as button clicks.

Most of the work in putting the sample application together was a matter of minor changes to existing components, and wiring up application events correctly.

Hopefully, you have enjoyed the journey of building this sample application, and seeing the various techniques that we have discussed in earlier chapters, put into practice. We have finally arrived at an industrial strength, enterprise ready, TypeScript built single-page Angular and Node application.

# Index

## @

# B



# C

# D



# E

## F



## G



## H



## I

## S



## T

85159947R00307

Made in the USA
Middletown, DE
23 August 2018